SULLIVANESQUE

RONALD E. SCHMITT

SULLIVANESQUE

Urban Architecture and Ornamentation

UNIVERSITY OF ILLINOIS PRESS

URBANA AND CHICAGO

Publication of this book was supported by grants from the Graham
Foundation for Advanced Studies in the Fine Arts and the University of
Illinois at Urbana-Champaign Research Board.

Frontispiece: Guaranty Building, Buffalo, N.Y., Adler and Sullivan; photo by
Ralph Marlowe Line. Illustration, page vi: Midland Terra Cotta Company
Catalog, detail of design for stock Sullivanesque ornament.

All photographs reproduced in this book were taken by the author
unless otherwise noted.

Library of Congress Cataloging-in-Publication Data
Schmitt, Ronald E.
Sullivanesque : urban architecture and ornamentation /
Ronald E. Schmitt.
p.   cm.
Includes bibliographical references and index.
ISBN 0-252-02726-4 (alk. paper)
1. Architecture—Illinois—Chicago—19th century. 2. Architecture—
Illinois—Chicago—20th century. 3. Sullivan, Louis H., 1856–1924—
Influence. 4. Architectural terra-cotta—Illinois—Chicago. 5. Decoration
and ornament, Architectural—United States. I. Title.
NA707.S34   2002
720'.9773'11—dc21   2001005637

CONTENTS

ACKNOWLEDGMENTS   vii

1. Nature Patterns in the Urban Landscape   1

2. Early Sullivanesque: Skyscrapers and Prominence   15

3. Later Sullivanesque: Small Buildings and Anonymity   52

4. Sullivan's Former Employees   92

5. Ornament: Materials, Artisans, and Early Suppliers   141

6. Stock Sullivanesque and the Midland Terra Cotta Company   168

7. Sullivanesque Architects in Chicago   199

8. Chicago Streets: A Sullivanesque Vernacular   230

   Epilogue   261

   APPENDIX: AN INVENTORY OF SULLIVANESQUE BUILDINGS   267
   NOTES   301
   INDEX   333

Color photographs follow pages 70 and 150

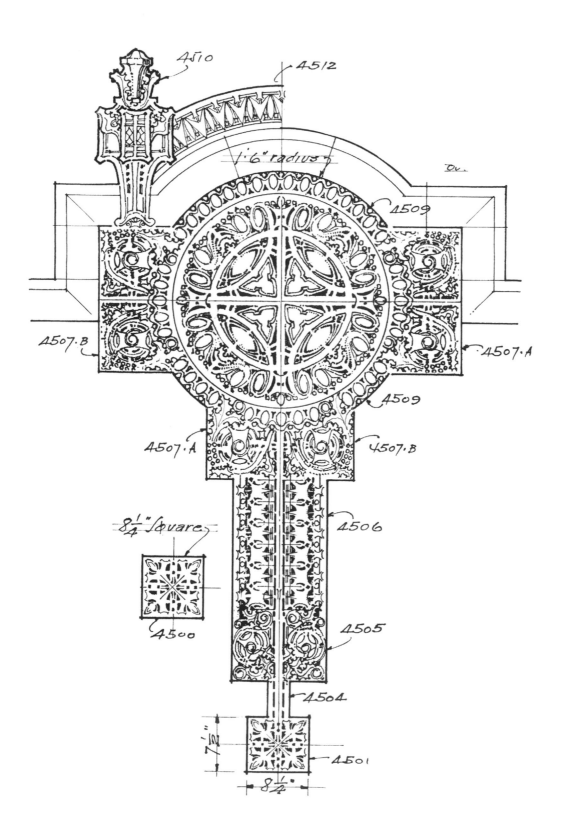

4510

4512

1'6" radius

Ov.

4509

4507·B

4507·A

4509

4507·A

4507·B

4506

8¼" Square

4500

4505

4504

7½"

4501

8¼

ACKNOWLEDGMENTS

MY FIRST EXPOSURE to the work of Louis Sullivan was as a young architecture student in a freshman design studio. One of the exercises was a composition study using ink wash, in the Beaux-Arts tradition. However, the subject was not the classical orders but a composition based on elements and ornament from the architecture of Louis Sullivan. The studio critic, Ralph Marlowe Line, was an expert on Sullivan and an accomplished photographer. He had provided an introduction and some of his own photographs for a new edition of Louis H. Sullivan's *The Autobiography of an Idea* (New York: Dover, 1956). Influenced by my studio experience, I read the book and was immediately hooked. Later, in a course on the history of modern architecture taught by Walter Creese, the context of Sullivan's work became clearer. After years of practicing architecture in Chicago, I returned to my alma mater, the University of Illinois at Urbana-Champaign, to teach design and had the opportunity to discuss Sullivan again with Ralph Line. I'm pleased that some of his beautiful photographs of Sullivan's work appear in this volume. I believe that Ralph Marlowe Line (1904–89) would have been pleased as well.

The archival collection of the Northwest Architectural Archives (NWAA) of the University of Minneapolis Libraries was invaluable to my research. During my many and extended visits to the archives, the staff members were always helpful, accommodating, and generous with their time. My thanks to Alan Lathrop, curator; Barbara Bezat, curatorial assistant; and Vivian Newbold, then with NWAA.

Many people shared information during my study of the Sullivanesque. Among the most accommodating and helpful were David Carnegie, son of the architect William G. Carnegie, and Alan Himelblau, son of A. L. Himelblau, who was also an architect. I appreciate the assistance provided by the staff of the Commission on Chicago Landmarks. Special thanks go to Timothy Samuelson and Charles Pipal.

Research for this study was funded in part by a grant from the Graham Foundation for Advanced Studies in the Fine Arts, Chicago. This publication was made possible by a grant from the Graham Foundation and by a grant from the University of Illinois at Urbana-Champaign (UIUC) Campus Research Board. I appreciate the support and encouragement of members of the School of Architecture at UIUC and extend thanks especially to Jane Cook, whose dedicated work and word-processing skills I value greatly.

My deepest thanks go to my wife, Rosalie Shaul Schmitt, for her stalwart support as I wrote this book. In addition, she was always an excellent traveling companion during our extensive travels through the Midwest and elsewhere as I researched and photographed Sullivanesque architecture.

ACKNOWLEDGMENTS

SULLIVANESQUE

CHAPTER 1

NATURE PATTERNS IN THE URBAN LANDSCAPE

SULLIVANESQUE ARCHITECTURE was based on an aesthetic derived from the designs of Louis H. Sullivan (1856–1924) and adapted to mass production. It successfully integrated "high art" with functional construction. Although it diluted the high art of Sullivan, the Sullivanesque nevertheless retained a surprising vitality. The style was embraced by architects and speculative developers and gained a popular, mostly regional appeal that lingered for decades. The gap between the refined art of the originator and the "low art" of the imitators was relatively narrow. The adoption of the Sullivanesque style generally improved the design caliber of the speculative building and the resulting urban fabric. A kind of commercial vernacular evolved that was unique in American architecture.

The Sullivanesque, predicated on Louis Sullivan's system of design composition and his personal vocabulary of ornamentation, was an integral but distinctive part of the progressive architectural movements centered in Chicago. Sullivan was an inspiration for three movements: the Chicago School, the Prairie School, and the Sullivanesque. He was an acknowledged leader of the Chicago School and an unwilling instigator of the Sullivanesque. His ornament and the way he composed it clarified the functional and/or structural expression for a building. More important, his architecture became an art form that could inspire. It is not surprising that architects who admired and were stimulated by Sullivan's work would adopt his aesthetic expression as their own.

Louis H. Sullivan and his followers William Gray Purcell, George G. Elmslie, and Frank Lloyd Wright wanted to create an American architecture expressive of democracy and the industrial age. They understood the potential of the machine to economically produce building components and ornament. Derived from Sullivan's floral and fluid ornamental designs composed over geometric grids, standardized components of terra cotta enabled distinctive building facades to be assembled economically. Manufactured Sullivanesque terra cotta gave focus and prominence to inexpensive, often commonplace, utilitarian buildings in commercial strips of the period in Chicago, the greater Midwest, and, occasionally, elsewhere in the country. In the broadest sense, Sullivan's dream of a democratic architecture was captured in a number of otherwise anonymous buildings, many of which are rapidly being altered or demolished.

Chicago architects, led by Louis Sullivan, embraced the mammoth scale and functional demands of new building types for the late nineteenth-century industrial city. Members of the Chicago School, as it is now called, pioneered the design of multistory buildings with skeletal steel structural framing. However, the immense scale of the tall building and the aesthetic questions it presented were issues not satisfactorily addressed

People's Savings and Loan Association Bank (1917–18), Sidney, Ohio; Louis Sullivan, Architect. Photo: 1993.

Ornament on lintel at entrance, People's Savings and Loan Association Bank (1917–18), Sidney, Ohio; Louis Sullivan, Architect. Sullivan's name was incised in the terra-cotta piece. Photo: 1993.

Ornamental piece on front facade of store building for Fred Hein (1924), Chicago; B. J. Bruns, Architect. This is stock terra-cotta ornament from the Midland Terra Cotta Company. Photo: 1991.

until Louis Sullivan's design (in partnership with Dankmar Adler) for the Wainwright Building (1891) in St. Louis. "It must be every inch a proud and soaring thing," Sullivan decreed for the skyscraper.[1] Like some other Chicago architects, Sullivan thus rejected the prevailing eclectic practice of cloaking new building types in the garb of historical styles. Sullivan announced "form follows function." However, to Sullivan, function was not limited to utility but included the symbolic and the spiritual. To help achieve these virtues, Sullivan designed ornament for his buildings that was integral to his architecture. This ornament had a botanical theme and was composed with an underlying geometrical order. Inspired by publications of naturalists such as Charles Darwin, Sullivan used sinuous forms of nature for his ornament to complement and enhance the simplicity of his boldly geometric urban forms.

The ornament that Sullivan developed for his building facades was highly original and personal, yet many historians have attempted to establish precedent for it. Some have claimed Viollet-le-Duc was a primary inspiration. A few say it was Sullivan's Celtic ancestry that drew him to early Celtic Christian art.[2] Others have dismissed Sullivan's ornament as merely an American interpretation of the art nouveau style and have lumped his designs with the work of Antoni Gaudí, Victor Horta, and Charles Rennie Mackintosh. Still others, especially contemporaries of Sullivan, said his inspirations were the Arabesque style, Byzantine designs, or Romanesque architecture. Some or all of these may have provided inspiration, but to isolate one as the primary source is simplistic. In fact, Sullivan's ornament was an emotionally individualistic creation that challenges written description, but one has only to see it to appreciate its distinctive beauty. It then becomes easy to recognize its various interpretations and permutations.

Sullivan's ornament seems to have evolved through four phases. Edgar Kaufmann Jr. was among the first historians to recognize these stages. Each progressive stage had less association with other affiliations and became more independent and individualistic. As Kaufmann identified them, these successive stages were: (1) the conventionalized botanical, as expounded in books on ornamentation by the nineteenth-century Scottish industrial designer Christopher Dresser and exemplified by the work of Sullivan's first employer, Frank Furness; (2) the Queen Anne, a reinterpretation of "correct" styles of the past; (3) the poetic expression of structure, as advocated by Viollet-le-Duc and Victor Horta; and (4) the symbolic, an expression of moods and psychological conditions.[3]

Sullivan's earliest decorative designs were patterned after those of Frank Furness, who in turn had been influenced by Gothic revival innovations of English architects of the 1860s and 1870s.[4] Sullivan's first ornamental designs were stiff and angular although his subject, like that of most of his ornament, was plant life. Each element of the composition stood alone and isolated. Around 1883, Sullivan began to interlace various elements of greenery, and the shapes became freer and more flowing. Instead of describing individual "specimens," the designs represented stylized, intertwined foliage. By 1885, Sullivan's ornament was vivacious and fully curvilinear. Within five years, his

Opposite: The verticality of the tall building was emphasized by the rhythm of the piers in Adler and Sullivan's Wainwright Building (1891), St. Louis. Only every other pier contained a structural column. The spandrel panels of ornamental terra cotta were recessed, allowing the verticals to dominate. Photo: 1993.

sumptuous ornament had achieved full life. It was distinctive, with beautiful and grace-ful, verdant compositions. The theme for his ornament remained natural vegetation although he sometimes incorporated images of animal life. Like many nineteenth-cen-tury romantics, Sullivan was enthralled by nature and especially by botany. Through-out his life, he studied plants, attempting to learn as much as he could about nature's rules of composition.[5] Sullivan came to think of ornament as a symbol for structure. In his book *Kindergarten Chats*, Sullivan wrote: "There exists a peculiar sympathy between ornament and structure. Both structure and ornament obviously benefit from this sym-pathy, each enhancing the value of the other."[6]

The maturing of Sullivan's ornament coincided with his breakthrough design of the Wainwright Building and subsequent master works. This maturation was characterized

Terra-cotta ornamental medal-lion, M. A. Meyer Wholesale Store Building (1892–93; demolished 1968), Chicago; Adler and Sulli-van, Architects. This piece was one of the few ornamental ac-cents on this simple but visually powerful building. Photo: Ralph Marlowe Line, 1948.

by his interpretation of luxuriant and free-flowing foliage. However, the forms were not arbitrary; like vines on a trellis, the "natural growth" was guided by the framework of an underlying geometry. Geometry structured his ornament just as structural systems supported his architecture.

Late in his life, in *A System of Architectural Ornament*, Sullivan summarized the philosophy and symbolic content of his ornamentation and revealed various geometrical derivations for his characteristically personal ornament. This project was commissioned by the American Institute of Architects (AIA) and consisted of nineteen portfolio plates with accompanying notes that were prepared in 1922. Sullivan devoted the first seven plates to graphic portrayals and cryptic notes about the process of developing his ornament. When delineating either an organic or inorganic (geometric) shape, Sullivan used a simple outline as an underlying structure to give order to the free forms that evolved. For example, a simple leaf form (organic) could establish an initial shape and provide inspiration for an ornamental design. An alternative choice, an inorganic shape, would involve the "manipulation of forms in plane-geometry." On plate 4, "The Awakening of the Pentagon," Sullivan explained: "Rigid geometry here shown progressing, through man's manipulation of a central idea, into plastic, mobile and fluescent phases of expression tending towards culmination in foliate and efflorescent forms." Sullivan's ornament symbolized, literally, nature and, figuratively, humankind. To Sullivan, the collective power of man comprised "five groups": physical, intellectual, emotional, moral, and spiritual. Like a poet, Sullivan intended his ornament to evoke a certain mood or emotion and to pay homage to "man's powers." Sullivan equated man's powers to the seed germ, "which is to seek and eventually to find its full expression in form."[7] According to Sullivan's philosophy of parallelism, man and nature, man and his works, science and art, organic and inorganic could be fused or "blend into an integral phenomenon—this time by powers of man's imaginative will."[8] To Sullivan, the creative act was a spiritual union of man and nature, and his ornament was a visual realization of this unity.[9] Sullivan's fluid floral motifs idealized nature and symbolized the need for man's harmony with nature. Certainly his stylized naturalistic ornament was welcome in the usually treeless urban settings of his buildings.

A misconception about Sullivan's famous phrase "form follows function" has been that "function" means pure utilitarianism. Following that interpretation, European modernists limited their definition of function and rejected ornamentation. To Sullivan, however, function entailed more than just utility and included the use of ornamentation. An idealist and a romantic, Sullivan intended his ornament to delight the viewer but also to ennoble architecture with a democratic spirit. Undoubtedly, many people could not perceive the symbolic or figurative "function" of his ornament. However, they could enjoy his ornament literally, as it was exquisitely beautiful. Its distinctive beauty was widely admired, and, although the ornament was highly original and complex, it was widely copied, much to Sullivan's chagrin and resentment. A number of Chicago manufacturers of building materials such as plaster molding and terra cotta made similar ornament and marketed these pieces as Sullivanesque. The Sullivanesque style was immediately recognized and identified as such at the time. It was characterized by use of imitative ornament and the composition of building facades in the manner of Louis Sullivan.

Sullivan's ornament was made in cast iron, plaster, stone, wood, and glass. However, it is most often associated with terra cotta. Terra cotta was an ancient material, used by the Greeks, Etruscans, and Romans. The name "terra cotta" comes from the Italian and means "baked clay." After a decline in use, terra cotta was revived in the eleventh century and utilized until the sixteenth century, when it was again neglected. It wasn't until the nineteenth century in Germany and England that terra cotta was once more revived as a building material.[10] Terra cotta use in the United States was pioneered in Chicago after the Great Fire of 1871. It provided necessary fireproofing for cast iron and steel structural members in exterior walls of buildings.[11] It was employed in Chicago skyscrapers not only because of its fireproofing qualities, but also because of its light weight, durability, and weather resistance. However, its potential decorative qualities were also soon realized. In addition, terra-cotta ornament, as a clay product baked and fired from an easily molded plastic state, was discovered to be a relatively inexpensive material.

Sullivan realized the potential of this rediscovered building product. The twisting and whirling movement of foliate relief was well suited to the hand sculpting of the clay models from which molds were made. Rigid and controlled right-angled geometrics were more difficult for the modeler to maintain, given the plastic nature of clay. A practical benefit of Sullivan's swirling lines was their ability to dominate and mask construction joints of the different pieces that formed the terra-cotta ornament.

Several terra-cotta companies manufactured replicas of Sullivan's designs and made them available to other architects. (The various companies are discussed in chapters 5 and 6.) Thus, makers of ready-made terra-cotta pieces, called stock, economically produced Sullivan-like ornament and made the Sullivanesque style possible, practical, and widespread. For example, the Chicago-based Midland Terra Cotta Company created an extensive line of stock architectural terra-cotta pieces in the vein of Sullivan's ornamental designs. This stock terra cotta was not of the same quality as Sullivan's custom designs, but it was a reasonable substitute and made the decorative enhancement of commonplace buildings more widely possible and economically feasible.

Some of Sullivan's early major designs, such as the Guaranty Building in Buffalo (1894–95) and the Schlesinger and Mayer Department Store in Chicago (commissioned in 1898), had facades clad entirely in terra cotta. Such terra-cotta facades were more expensive than those of brick with terra-cotta trim. Additional shop drawings, increased modeling labor, additional molds, and considerably more construction coordination were required for walls faced completely in terra cotta. For reasons of economy, Sullivan undoubtedly turned to the predominant use of brick for his later commissions and restricted use of terra cotta to important, concentrated areas of building facades. After the

Stock terra-cotta ornament on the McCullom Brothers Candy Factory (1917), Galesburg, Illinois. Aldrich and Aldrich, local architects, used a popular rosette with supplemental pieces from the Midland Terra Cotta Company. The disc design was inspired by Sullivan's medallion on the M. A. Meyer Wholesale Store Building. Photo: 1991.

Schlesinger and Mayer addition of 1903, Sullivan employed full terra-cotta facades only for the tiny Home Building Association (1914) in Newark, Ohio, and the William Krause Music Store (1922) in Chicago. Other architects considered these same factors in determining terra-cotta usage in buildings of the Sullivanesque.

The elements of the Sullivanesque style provided a creative but realistic design solution for nonresidential buildings, especially in the tight confines of urban settings such as downtowns and neighborhood commercial strips of large cities. In such areas, the building was usually a part of a continuum, a space-defining frontage, that is, the street. The building lots were typically narrow and deep, with rear alley service, and forced the use of party walls. Maximum site coverage for nonresidential speculative development was common as economics dictated efficient land use. Since setbacks were usually not required, commercial buildings fronted the public right-of-way and stretched the full lot width so the linear space of the street became well defined. The street facade was usually the only segment of these buildings visible to public view, which meant that its composition as a two-dimensional surface or shallow relief became a dominant issue. Interiors of commercial buildings were generally utilitarian and flexible to accommodate changing needs of different tenants, so the emphasis of design became the exterior wall facing the street. The street space remained the focus for movement and civic activity as the building facades formed both a conduit and a backdrop. This importance of the street contrasted with the later twentieth-century practice of setting the building apart from its context as an object in space. The placement of a building as a freestanding object in the urban context today too often results in the fragmentation of the built environment as a scaleless and dehumanizing abyss.

In the urban setting of the Sullivanesque building, the exterior wall facing the street became the "canvas" for artistic expression and building identification. The wall surface needed embellishment and permanency. The use of ornament, and with it texture,

Roseland Safety Deposit Bank (1914), Chicago; William G. Carnegie, Architect. The facade was entirely of white terra-cotta facings and stock ornament although the central eagle and shield had custom glazes. Photo: c. 1915, courtesy of David Carnegie.

Stock terra-cotta ornamental
assembly from the Midland
Terra Cotta Company for the
Jandrey Grove Building (1915),
Neenah, Wisconsin; Sindahl
and Matheson, Architects. This
ornament was based on a
cartouche for the First National
Bank Building (1910–11) in
Rhinelander, Wisconsin; Purcell,
Feick, and Elmslie, Architects.
Photo: 1991.

pattern, and color, became the logical way to beautify and individualize a building (and to distinguish its occupants). Louis Sullivan's designs, especially those for his later, smaller buildings, established a method of composition and a system of ornamentation that were readily adaptable to the design of building facades and to varying functional demands. The alignment and abutment of contiguous building facades gave unity and urban scale to the street; however, the separate buildings could become lost in the total fabric unless given an individual identity. Sullivan's design approach accomplished this objective as well. His compositional methods, especially the use of symmetry without rigid adherence to it, and his unique ornamentation helped identify an individual building within the overall setting. At the same time, Sullivan's buildings—and most Sullivanesque buildings—were respectful of their context without resorting to contextualism. Building scale and materiality were usually compatible to the setting but conformance to the prevalent building style was not a dictate.

An article by F. W. Fitzpatrick in the *Western Architect* in 1913 extolled the merits of the Sullivanesque. In this essay, entitled "American Architecture," Fitzpatrick criticized East Coast architects for bickering about the adaptation of the Gothic revival or Renaissance revival style when both were "fraudulent." He concluded:

> The "Sullivan School" is growing in numbers and in skill, it takes its art more soberly, more seriously and sanely. . . . Its basic principle is to design a building in plan not so that it will fit some portico or facade of some particular bath or temple of

old, but so it will best serve the commercial, religious, or domestic purpose for which the building is intended, and the openings for light and air are placed there where they are needed, and in such size and shapes as best serve those needs. Then the structure is put about those rooms, it is of steel framing or of solid masonry mass, as seems best fitted from an engineering point to that particular kind of building. And, finally, the enveloping surface of that structure is made to express both its purpose and its construction, and is decorated as ornately or little with flat ornament, inlays, enamels, colors, moldings, and materials as the pocket of the owner will permit or the good taste of the architect sees fit.[12]

Louis Sullivan and those following his lead were developing a decorative modern architecture appropriate for its time, culture, and place. Architectural historians have grouped Sullivan's early large-scale, multistory designs with the Chicago School, while they have categorized his later, small projects, such as his bank designs, as expressions of the Prairie School. Since Sullivan was a philosophical leader for both of these broad progressive movements, these inclusions seem reasonable. Ironically, at the time, only Sullivan's work and the designs by others based on Sullivan's principles and individualistic ornament had an immediate identity or label, the Sullivanesque. Both Sullivan's models and other architects' imitative designs were called Sullivanesque, although Sullivan was displeased with this association and resented the "counterfeiting" of his ornament. At that time, what came to be known as the Chicago School was called the commercial style, and the extended domestic structures of Sullivan's former apprentice, Frank Lloyd Wright, and others had not yet been identified as the Prairie School.[13]

The present study concentrates on the Sullivanesque lineage within the broad boundaries of these progressive architectural modes. Sullivanesque designs were produced in substantial numbers by 1922 and were built as late as 1928.[14] George G. Elmslie and William Steele were responsible for some Sullivanesque designs constructed even in the 1930s. In many ways, the Sullivanesque was a precursor of the art deco movement of the late 1920s and early 1930s, especially in the design of smaller buildings. The facades of low-rise art deco buildings often seemed composed on Sullivanesque principles, with similar organization and positioning of ornament. However, the subjects and compositions of ornamental reliefs were different.

The Sullivanesque embodied interwoven but seemingly contradictory relationships, for example, between nature and urbanization or the hand crafted and the machine made. Functionalism was intended and accommodated but was not merely utilitarian. Louis Sullivan intended his buildings to fulfill human needs, including spiritual and emotional requirements. Human scale was conveyed through compositional and proportional relationships of building elements and by the use of materials with certain patterns, colors, textures, and ornamentation. The Sullivanesque building not only engendered "delight" but had visual strength and accommodated scale relationships of several types. That is, it could look good from any distance, allowing a perception of civic or urban

scale from afar, a human scale as one drew closer, and even a warm, intimate scale at touching distance. Intricate ornament, placed at door surrounds and other easily viewed locations, helped create a tactile quality. An integration of architecture with the other visual arts, especially sculptural reliefs, was fundamental.

The reasons for the endurance of the Sullivanesque are numerous and complex. The style seems to have been propagated for promotional and economical reasons as well as for its aesthetic and philosophical appeal. The success of the style can be attributed to six factors. First, certain architectural journals promoted Sullivan's personal design approach and style. Second, Sullivan was a consummate artist and was perceived as a cultural hero, which prompted lesser architects to try to emulate his work. Third, small-scale buildings, including strip commercial structures of the period, were generally compatible with the Sullivanesque. Such buildings shared party walls and usually had only one or two major facades as part of an urban frontage. Sullivan's design approach was facade oriented and offered apt solutions for such a context. Fourth, Sullivan's ap-

Detail of second-story terra-cotta ornament for a commercial building remodeling (1920), 11429–31 S. Michigan Avenue, Chicago; Clarence Hatzfeld, Architect. Photo: 1987.

proach to facade composition allowed flexibility for utilitarian purposes, which was a growing concern in burgeoning urban centers. Fifth, stock terra cotta was, at the time, economical in cost. Speculative strip commercial buildings usually had low construction budgets. Stock Sullivanesque ornament could meet budget demands while giving identity and beauty to a building. Finally, several Chicago terra-cotta companies promoted the Sullivanesque, motivated in part by self-serving commercialism.[15]

The Sullivanesque ranged from "high art," as epitomized by the work of Louis Sullivan and George G. Elmslie, to the "low art" of the commercial vernacular espoused by builder architects. Sophisticated or primitive, collectively it was a rare creative flourish in American architecture during decades of prevailing design eclecticism.

CHAPTER 2

EARLY SULLIVANESQUE

Skyscrapers and Prominence

THE SULLIVANESQUE STYLE went through two stages. In the first, the style enjoyed great prominence, its application fueled by the excitement of Dankmar Adler and Louis Sullivan's skyscraper designs. This phase lasted approximately fifteen years, from about 1895 to 1910, although in some locations, such as Chicago, it was shorter, and in other regions, especially in the southwestern United States, it stretched beyond 1910. This was an optimistic period, as pioneer settlements were rapidly being transformed into regional centers of industry, commerce, and trade. The Sullivanesque style offered solutions to the design problems presented by new types and scales of buildings. The tall building became a familiar building type for the Sullivanesque although designers of smaller buildings also adhered to Sullivanesque principles. The second phase of the Sullivanesque (1911–30) lasted longer than the first but during this period the style became somewhat obscure. A few important architects created just a few small but noteworthy buildings, and many unknown architects incorporated the Sullivanesque for more commonplace buildings.

Prestigious commissions and important buildings characterized the initial phase of the Sullivanesque. At that time, the skyscraper was considered the pinnacle of architectural commissions. Regional metropolises could boast one or more Sullivanesque skyscrapers and were often home to architects of the Sullivanesque. These architecture firms were generally leaders in their respective cities and won important, highly visible commissions.

In 1890, Sullivan synthesized the utilitarian and aesthetic demands of the tall office building in his masterful design for the Wainwright Building in St. Louis. The "skyscraper," a new building type with vertical mass, monumental scale, and awkward proportions, was made possible by the invention of the elevator and new skeletal structural systems utilizing steel beams and columns. How to treat the exterior facades of the multistory building posed a dilemma for architects. Previously, architects had figuratively "stacked" low building atop low building until the desired height was reached, but this technique denied the inherent qualities of these new buildings of the industrial age. Sullivan provided a different solution and his design became a model that other architects adopted. However, this bold step was preceded by a series of evolutionary design advancements from the Adler and Sullivan architectural office.

Louis Sullivan was hired in May 1879 to head Dankmar Adler's office in Chicago and, a year later, the firm's name became Adler and Sullivan, Architects.[1] Dankmar Adler (1844–1900) was an accomplished architect although now he is remembered mostly as Sullivan's partner, the one who got clients, managed the business, directed the engineering, and was an acoustics expert. Adler's decision to take in Louis Sullivan, twelve years his junior and relatively inexperienced, was prescient. Each man complemented the other and the partnership flourished.

Sullivan's evolution as principal designer during his partnership with Adler seems to have gone through three phases. During the first (1879–85), Sullivan was strongly influenced by the Victorian Gothic style and he attempted to recall the designs of his previous employer, Frank Furness of Philadelphia.[2] Sullivan's designs during this early phase were uneven. They were marked by a personal style of ornamentation that was derived from the Gothic but which often had a fussy, sometimes nervous quality. (Exceptions were found in the firm's industrial projects, which were spartan and utilitarian with building facades of simple brickwork and regularly spaced windows.) Sullivan sometimes attempted to use Furness's compositional devices, such as exaggerated, overscaled elements, to provide a center of interest or focus for building facades; but these attempts were usually timid and not very successful. Sullivan's facades for commercial buildings were overwhelmingly symmetrical while his compositions for residential designs were asymmetrically composed. But ornamentation was usually gathered near the top of the facades, which seemed to invert the scale of the buildings and erode the visual strength of the designs. The facades of his commercial buildings usually had dominating vertical piers of masonry while beam spandrels were suppressed; in addition, the spandrels were often a different material and were sometimes ornamented.[3] Still, Sullivan's works were creative and original at that time, especially for Chicago.

Sullivan's design approach abruptly changed direction in 1886, prompted by the construction of H. H. Richardson's Marshall Field Warehouse (1885–87; demolished 1930) in downtown Chicago. Working in his characteristic robust Romanesque style,

Richardson gave the Field building strength through simple but bold geometrical massing, honest expression of the massive stonework, and exacting proportions. In 1886 Adler and Sullivan secured a prestigious commission from Ferdinand Peck and his investors for a large mixed-use project that included a new Chicago opera house, an income-producing hotel, and offices. Sullivan's initial designs for the Auditorium Building were trite. With steeply pitched roofs, multiple dormers, and confusing ornamental patterns on the immense facades, the designs for the exterior lacked cohesion and compositional strength. However, after a series of schematic studies, this was rectified. The program also changed, necessitating constant design revisions. The flux of requirements, including increases in area, changing commercial demands, and budget revisions, may have worked to Sullivan's advantage. He had to keep the design simple to adjust for the client's shifting needs. The final flat-roofed design was a simplified statement influenced by the majestic clarity of Richardson's Field Warehouse.[4] Sullivan deftly handled the exterior massing. The Auditorium Building rose ten stories and there was a seventeen-story tower that contained offices, including those of Adler and Sullivan. The office tower encased a water tower and marked the main entrance to the assembly space.

The large Auditorium Theater (seating 4,237) was Adler's acoustical success. The theater's interior, illuminated by electric lighting—an innovation—was sumptuous in its detailing and ornamentation. A trusted employee of Adler and Sullivan, Frank Lloyd Wright, was responsible for developing some of the interior designs. Sullivan explained in the publication *Industrial Chicago* (1891) about the ornamentation of the Auditorium Building: "The plastic and color decorations are distinctly architectural in conception. They are everywhere kept subordinate to the general effect of the larger structural masses and subdivisions, while lending to them the enchantment of soft tones and of varied light and shade."[5] Sullivan acted upon this premise—that decoration should reinforce and enhance structural shapes and architectural forms—throughout his career.

Sullivan's exploration of the Romanesque, as represented in the Auditorium Building, was of short duration and included another Chicago building, the Walker Warehouse (1888–89; demolished 1953). With its Romanesque influence and exterior bearing walls of stone, the seven-story Walker building has generally been dismissed by architectural historians as unimportant. However, the composition of the facades, organized with a base, shaft, and cap, foreshadowed Sullivan's subsequent designs for tall buildings. The Walker had little ornamentation and revealed Sullivan's concentration on building form and exacting proportions as a springboard to his next design phase. Sullivan offered advice to others that he himself may have tried briefly to heed: "It would be greatly for our aesthetic good if we should refrain entirely from the use of ornament for a period of years, in order that our thought might concentrate acutely upon the production of buildings well formed and comely in the nude."[6] But even the Walker Warehouse had some ornament—most notably on the impost blocks for the paired entry arches on each street facade.[7]

With the design of the Wainwright Building (1890–91) in St. Louis, Sullivan

achieved an expression that was both individual and universal. Much as H. H. Richardson had influenced American architecture and architects earlier, Sullivan provided a new model for many architects, especially those in the Midwest who would design tall buildings. This new aesthetic had an unlikely source: a small tomb in Graceland Cemetery, Chicago. Rejecting the prevailing derivative mausoleum design, which often depended on Greek and Roman temple forms, Sullivan created an original architecture for the Getty Tomb (1890).[8] The form of the tomb is a simple cube resting on a stone platform and capped with a slightly projecting stone roof cornice. On the side elevations, this cornice has three shallow reverse-curved segments, creating a scalloped profile that seems to recall gentle frozen waves. The exterior walls have a high base of smooth dressed limestone, and each stone is overscaled in size. In contrast, the wall surfaces above are delicately ornamented with stone relief carvings of octagonal patterns; each octa-

Auditorium Building (1887–89), Michigan Avenue at Congress Street, Chicago; Adler and Sullivan, Architects. Photo: 1964.

gon contains an eight-pointed star, slender and graceful. Arched openings center on each facade and each arch has prominent stone voussoirs with alternating bandings of ornate carvings and smooth surfaces. Marking the arched entrance to the tomb are two bronze gates, cast with intricate and refined ornamentation. (A plaster cast of the gates was exhibited in 1900 at the Paris Exposition and Sullivan was cited for their design.)[9] Without a utilitarian program, functional responses became transcendental in the Getty Tomb.

Sullivan designed two other mausoleums, one for Martin Ryerson (1889) in Graceland, and the other for Charlotte Dickson Wainwright (1892) in Bellefontaine Cemetery, St. Louis. These tombs were more assertive than the Getty in the use of geometric massings. The Ryerson mausoleum is a dynamic form and devoid of ornament. Its visual interest lies in the truncated obelisk-like form that seems to emerge from the battered walls below and in the materials used—dark granite and polished blue limestone with massive coursing and prominent joint work. The Wainwright Tomb incorporated ornament as bandings that reinforce the tomb's pure cubic shape. This block is further refined by low walls and wide steps that reach out into the landscape, and by a dome that appears to be a sphere rising halfway out of the cube. The Ryerson Tomb, devoid of ornament and composed of dark, bold forms, may represent Sullivan's attempt to symbolize masculinity. In contrast, the two tombs for women were light in color, refined in the use of ornament, and more precise in geometrical clarity.

The Wainwright Building was commissioned by a St. Louis brewery owner, Ellis

Louis Sullivan's Carrie Eliza Getty Tomb (1890), Graceland Cemetery, Chicago, could be considered the precursor of the architect's design philosophy for the modern building. Photo: Ralph Marlowe Line, c. 1950.

Wainwright. Initial perspectives of the building were done by a St. Louis architect, Charles K. Ramsey, and showed a Romanesque design.[10] Ramsey was noted in St. Louis as the architect for the Houser Building, a seven-story office building in the Romanesque style.[11] Ramsey teamed with Adler and Sullivan as associate architects on the Wainwright project. Sullivan's design was a radical departure from his or anyone else's work up to that time. The ten-story building appeared to be a cube in massing, seven structural bays wide by six bays deep. The street facades aligned with the public right-of-way and maintained street-edge definition. However, a light court was carved into the rear of the mass, from the north, to admit natural light and allow for natural ventilation. This produced a U-shaped plan in which no floor area is far from a window.

The Wainwright facades were organized vertically as having a base, shaft, and cap. The base was formed of street-level stores and building entrances plus a second floor containing service and commercial or office space. The shaft was composed of seven office floors, cellular in nature, and was expressed externally by continuous vertical piers or pilasters that alternated with recessed windows and floor spandrels. At the building corners were wide piers that resolved the rhythm of the multiple piers. The cap of the building, a full story high, was formed by two distinct but unified elements, an ornamental frieze of terra cotta and a cantilevered cornice.

The exterior materials were weather-protecting and fire-proofing claddings over an underlying structural grid of iron columns and steel beams. The material for the base was red sandstone, finely jointed and laid in an ashlar pattern, separated from the ground by a two-foot-high water table of red Missouri granite. The massive-looking corner piers and the repeated pilasters were red brick, with ornamental terra-cotta panels bearing floral motifs used at the top and bottom of each pilaster. The spandrel panels, frieze, and projecting cornice were of ornate red terra cotta. Seven pieces of terra cotta combined to form an ornamental design for each spandrel panel and this pattern was repeated for each panel on that same floor. However, a different spandrel design was used for each floor. Swirling floral motifs in terra cotta decorated the frieze, while overlapping circles banded the cornice fascia. Except for the base of the building, vertical elements of the facade were red brick, and horizontal features, such as building cap and secondary elements, were ornamented in red terra cotta.

Some historians have criticized the design of the Wainwright Building for its "dishonesty" since structural columns are behind alternate vertical brick pilasters and the heavy corner piers don't have any major structural significance. In addition, the second floor is contained within the base yet its plan is the same as that of the office floors above that comprise the shaft of the building; it simply has a different external expression. These criticisms seem based on the unilateral "functionalism" and "structural integrity" of 1950s and 1960s Modernism. To Sullivan, functionalism included the need to manipulate or subordinate a part to achieve a composed, unified whole and to evoke symbolic meaning and emotional content.[12]

Adler and Sullivan, again working with Charles K. Ramsey, were responsible for

Opposite: Wainwright Building (1891), St. Louis; Adler and Sullivan with Charles K. Ramsey, Architects. Photo: 1993.

two other high-rise buildings in St. Louis. These were the St. Nicholas Hotel (1892–94; demolished 1974) and the Union Trust Building (1892–93), now known as 705 Olive Street. The St. Nicholas had projecting oriels or bay windows, stacked vertically, and was topped by a steeply pitched roof. A great hall for a restaurant was contained under the massive sloping roof but was removed in a 1901 remodeling by the St. Louis architects Eames and Young that added four stories and a flat roof. Sullivan was not involved in the vertical expansion and office conversion, although Eames and Young's new ornamentation was sympathetic to the existing Sullivanesque designs. Sullivan's original design was undoubtedly influential; many architects visited his hotel when the St. Nicholas hosted the 1895 national convention of the American Institute of Architects (AIA). The fourteen-story Union Trust Building, like the Wainwright, had a U-shaped plan, but the light court faced the street and the resulting narrow void seemed to articulate two parallel slab structures. However, the prominent base, two stories high, maintained the street edge. The base was originally distinguished by cantilevered figures of lions, monumental in scale, but these were removed in a 1924 alteration. Terra cotta for the Wainwright, St. Nicholas, and Union Trust buildings came from the Winkle Terra Cotta Company (founded 1883) of St. Louis.[13] After facing demolition several times, the Wainwright Building was saved when the state of Missouri purchased it and, through a competition, added embracing buildings (1981) designed by Mitchell/Giurgola, Architects, in association with St. Louis architects Hastings and Chivetta.[14]

Concurrently with their St. Louis projects, Adler and Sullivan were the architects for several skyscrapers in Chicago. The Schiller (1891–92; demolished 1960), later known as the Garrick, incorporated a large theater. The thirteen-story Stock Exchange Building (1893–94; demolished 1971) had an unusually high base that contained a large trading room. Since the narrow canyon of LaSalle Street created views of forced perspective, the facade of the Stock Exchange appeared curtain-like, dominated by the rhythmic progression of bay windows. After demolition of the building, the triumphal-arched entrance and trading room were reconstructed at the Art Institute of Chicago.

At the same time as the skyscraper projects, some "low-rise" commissions were produced in Adler and Sullivan's office. The most celebrated was the Transportation Building (1893) for the World's Columbian Exposition in Chicago. Like other buildings for the fair, it was a temporary structure. Exposition buildings were typically of white plaster and in the style of Beaux-Arts classicism; however, Sullivan's design was highly original, with a monumental "Golden Doorway" and luxuriant, colorful ornament. Contemporaneous residential projects by Adler and Sullivan were progressive designs. One of these was a townhouse (1891–92; demolished 1970) intended for Sullivan's mother and located on Lake Park Avenue, Chicago, which incorporated Sullivan's ornamental motifs stamped in copper cladding.[15]

Adler and Sullivan's three-story Victoria Hotel (1892–93; demolished 1961) in Chicago Heights, Illinois, gained little recognition and is now forgotten. However, it was an antecedent of the Prairie School. The exterior featured horizontal banding of ornamented stucco on the top story with brick used for the first two stories. A wide overhanging hip roof, combined with the treatment of wall surfaces, created a strong sense of horizontality. The basic elements of the Prairie School were present but required greater clarity and refinement (a distinction Frank Lloyd Wright achieved the following year with his Winslow House in River Forest, Illinois). Another handsome but largely forgotten Adler and Sullivan design was the seven-story M. A. Meyer Wholesale Store Building (1892–93; demolished 1968). The structural cage was clearly readable through the crisp, taut brick cladding. Ornamentation was minimal, with only decorative medallions positioned on the end piers at the second floor and aligned with the second-floor spandrel. However, this ornament seems to have been the primary inspiration for a stock roundel made by the Midland Terra Cotta Company.

The Guaranty Building (1894–95), or Prudential Building as it was known from 1899 to 1983, in Buffalo, New York, may have been the nineteenth-century design that most clearly prefigured the curtain walls of twentieth-century high-rise architecture. This "skin-and-bones" architecture put emphasis on the encasing membrane; the expression of the skeletal structural system was not obvious but rather subliminal. The overt expression of structural bays, which might quickly have become boring, was controlled as structural members were clearly visible only in select locations, such as the ground-story base. The lightness and delicacy of the outer walls suggest an underlying structural armature and create a sophisticated sense of subtly expressed structure. Sullivan "embossed" the terra-cotta surfaces of the Guaranty Building with an overlay of decorative patterns that create a grid which is subordinate to the modulation of the vertical piers and horizontal recessed floor spandrels and windows. From a distance, the ornamental repetitions appear like series of overscaled rivets, which seems to symbolize the underlying steel structure and helps create an appropriate urban scale for the building. Viewed up close, the ornamental details provide references for human scale as well as delightful intricacies. The surface reliefs also obscure the construction joints and irregularities of materials that are inevitable in any building construction. The task of preparing shop drawings and manufacturing, shipping, and erecting the puzzle pieces of custom terra cotta was a monumental undertaking performed by the Northwestern Terra Cotta Company, Chicago.[16] The Guaranty Building, the last built commission of the Adler and Sullivan partnership, was widely published and admired. It proved to be a catalyst for other architects to try the Sullivanesque approach, and they initially adapted it to tall buildings.

The year 1893 began troubling times for the Adler and Sullivan firm. Frank Lloyd Wright and Sullivan parted in anger as Wright left the firm. The Panic of 1893, a severe economic depression, took its toll on the building industry; construction was curtailed and few architectural commissions were available. Dankmar Adler, worried about providing for his wife and three children, accepted an offer as architect and sales manager for the Crane Elevator Company, and the Adler and Sullivan partnership was dissolved in July 1895. After only six months with Crane, however, Adler returned to

Overleaf:

Victoria Hotel (1892–93; demolished 1961) in Chicago Heights, Illinois; Adler and Sullivan, Architects. This design utilized many stylistic features found in Prairie School buildings. The roof eave to the left of the tower was later altered. Photo: Ralph Marlowe Line, 1951.

Adler and Sullivan's M. A. Meyer Wholesale Store (1893; demolished 1968) was almost devoid of ornamentation. However, the few decorative medallions inspired stock terra-cotta facsimiles. Photo: Ralph Marlowe Line, 1948.

private practice. He wanted to resume partnership with Sullivan, but his overtures were spurned. Both men practiced architecture separately and neither ever again enjoyed the success their partnership had brought.[17]

After the Adler and Sullivan breakup, Sullivan's first built design was the Bayard Building (1897–98) in New York, with Lyndon P. Smith as associate architect. Located at 65–69 Bleecker Street, this twelve-story structure was the only building Sullivan designed for New York City. The steel structural frame on the street facade was clad in a layer of white matte-glazed terra cotta supplied by the Perth Amboy Terra Cotta Company. In 1898, Sullivan designed a front facade for the Gage Building, Chicago, although the principal architects for the building were Holabird and Roche. Since three different millinery firms occupied respective frontages in the building at 18–30 South Michigan Avenue, an identity for each was desired. Three separate facades resulted— two by Holabird and Roche with red brick cladding, and one by Sullivan with off-white decorative terra cotta and, for the street-level storefront, ornate cast iron.[18] The cast iron was removed during a modernization and some pieces were salvaged for display at the Art Institute of Chicago and at the School of Architecture, University of Illinois at Urbana-Champaign.[19]

Sullivan received a significant commission in 1898 for the Schlesinger and Mayer Department Store, and the initial phase of construction on Madison Street was completed in 1900. The second phase of expansion (1902–3) anchored the important southeast corner of State and Madison, in Chicago's Loop. The Schlesinger and Mayer store, later better known as Carson Pirie Scott, was a landmark design. White-glazed terra-cotta sheaths (and fire-proofs) the clearly expressed grid of columns and beams. Terra-cotta ornament covers the jambs and head returns at the deep-set Chicago windows. Cast-iron ornament outlines the ground-floor display windows just as an ornate frame complements a special picture. The horizontality of the superstructure and the building's clarity of structural expression were obvious influences on the work of later European modernists, especially as reinterpreted in the formative periods of the International Style in the 1920s and 1930s.[20] The beauty of Sullivan's design for the Schlesinger and Mayer Department Store building was even more remarkable given the difficult phasing and construction problems Sullivan faced.[21] Unfortunately, this proved to be Sullivan's last large commission.

Another expansion of the store, along State Street, was undertaken in 1906. However, a different architectural firm, D. H. Burnham and Company, designed that phase. Although he was Sullivan's antagonist, Daniel Burnham (1846–1912) recognized good design and reproduced Sullivan's treatment for the addition. Finally, in 1960–61, Holabird and Root adopted Sullivan's aesthetic for a final addition along State Street. Even after the removal of the building's projecting cornice in 1948, Sullivan's design still amazes the observer. A restoration (1980) under John Vinci's direction has helped recapture the building's original appearance and has furthered the appreciation of Sullivan's genius.

Opposite: Guaranty Building (1894–95), Buffalo, New York; Adler and Sullivan, Architects. Although marred by cleaning in 1955, the terra-cotta-clad facades of the building are rich in ornamental reliefs. Photo: Ralph Marlowe Line, c. 1951.

Sullivan's modern design idiom, which developed after the architect's initial design explorations of the Victorian Gothic and the Richardson Romanesque, was initially associated with large-scale tall buildings and was applied mostly to offices, hotels, and mixed-use buildings. This phase developed as Sullivan worked in partnership and in individual practice, both of which involved work with powerful clients and brought prestigious commissions. The second phase of Sullivan's design career comprised just a few commissions for small buildings outside the urban center. Together, both phases of Sullivan's career produced progressive designs that provided models for the Sullivanesque.

Sullivan also wrote articles and presented papers at professional meetings to amplify his views. The most important of his articles first appeared in *Lippincott's Magazine* (March 1896) and was subsequently reprinted, excerpted, paraphrased, and quoted in various other publications, including the *Western Architect*. Entitled "The Tall Office Building Artistically Considered," the essay was one of the most prescriptive of Sullivan's writings; it advocated the "base, shaft, and cap" solution with vertical emphasis for high-rise design.[22] It was an influential essay that had positive benefits at the time. However, many architectural designers have blindly accepted its principles over the years even though building scale has increased tremendously and Sullivan's solutions do not necessarily apply today. But in the late nineteenth century, Louis Sullivan's designs for tall buildings were a revelation; apt solutions for large, multistoried buildings were finally realized. Sullivan's compositional principles were followed and even his distinctive ornamentation was sometimes employed as architects adapted, modified, and eventually developed their own designs for the new high-rise building type. A number of skyscraper designs inspired by Sullivan's example could be found in the burgeoning cities of the Midwest.

Minneapolis was growing rapidly in the late nineteenth century; population increased 350 percent from 1880 to 1890. The resulting construction boom attracted many architects to the twin cities of Minneapolis and St. Paul. One of these practitioners was Frederick Kees (1852–1927). Born in Baltimore, Kees apprenticed with local architects and began his own practice in that city. However, the Panic of 1873 forced him to close his office and relocate to Chicago.[23] In 1878, he moved to Minneapolis and worked for LeRoy Buffington, the self-proclaimed "inventor" of the skyscraper. After dissolution (1898) of a partnership with Frank B. Long and working in several other architectural partnerships, Frederick Kees formed a joint venture with Serenus Milo Colburn in 1900.[24] This partnership resulted in progressive designs and included Sullivanesque examples that, in one case, rivaled Adler and Sullivan's Wainwright Building.

Kees and Colburn's Chamber of Commerce Building (1900–1902) in Minneapolis was indebted to the Wainwright Building but surpassed it in refinement and visual impact. Now known as the Grain Exchange and listed on the National Register of Historic Places, the Chamber of Commerce Building resembled the Wainwright in exterior organization of base, shaft, and cap. However, the Minneapolis building contrasts

Opposite: This photo shows Sullivan's Schlesinger and Mayer/Carson Pirie Scott Department Store (1899–1900 and 1902–3) with the original thin, projecting cornice, before construction of a respectful 1961 addition to the south. Replacement of the cornice in 1948 by a crisp, clean parapet made this progressive design seem even more "modern." Photo: Ralph Marlowe Line, 1948.

with it in its reserved grayish beige color; its more polished ornamentation; its punched windows, which relieve the severity of intact masonry corner-bays; and the use of an upper wall return to unite the building "shaft" before it meets a projecting cornice (since removed). Both buildings are ten stories high and easy to overlook now in the welter of parking lots and newer, taller high-rises. However, both are masterpieces. Each is satisfying in the overview yet beckons the viewer to explore more closely. The Wainwright seems more vibrant, with its red cladding, while Kees and Colburn's building seems more serene. Terra cotta for the Chamber of Commerce Building came from the American Terra Cotta and Ceramic Company of Chicago and was distributed through the company's agents, S. J. Hewson and Company, Minneapolis.[25]

Another Minneapolis office building was on the drawingboards in the Kees and Colburn office at about the same time as the Chamber of Commerce; this was the Advance Thresher Building (1900). In some ways, it even more closely resembled the Wainwright, especially with its cladding of warm russet brick and terra cotta. Its ornament was inspired by Sullivan although it was more static and somewhat stilted. Nevertheless, Kees and Colburn's design was compelling and became a model for others in their exploration of the Sullivanesque. Plates of this building published in the *Western Architect* contributed to similar compositions elsewhere.[26] Kees and Colburn themselves virtually matched the design in what appears to be an addition but is really a separate adjoining building. The Emerson-Newton Implement Company Building was built (1904) to the east of the Advance building and matched cornice height and basic appearance with the earlier building. The two buildings seemed to become one as they abutted and so closely resembled each other; however, the seven stories of the newer building were squeezed into the same height as the six-story Advance Thresher Building.[27] These two buildings are now on the National Register.[28]

Subsequent designs by Kees and Colburn were more restrained and conservative. Ornamentation was reduced and Sullivanesque terra cotta was reserved for highly visible locations such as major entryways. For example, a large, six-story warehouse (1902) for the Deere and Webber Company resembled earlier Romanesque structures. The only ornament of Sullivanesque terra cotta, from the American Terra Cotta and Ceramic Company, was relegated to the main entry portal.[29] Kees and Colburn's Great Northern Implement Building (1910–11) conveyed visual strength through its simplicity and exacting proportions. Sullivan-like ornamentation was used only for large square panels positioned at the springline of the arched openings for the top floor of the seven-story, masonry-clad building. Although a strong sense of structure was imparted through use of piers and unifying arches that emphasized the vertical, the exterior pier spacing was independent of the interior grid of structural bays. Like Sullivan, Kees and Colburn valued a facade that they thought had aesthetic merit more than a consistently exact expression of structure.[30]

The last known Sullivanesque design by Kees and Colburn was for a large garage for the L. S. Donaldson Company (1915), Eighth Street South and Thirteenth Avenue

Chamber of Commerce Building (1900–1902), now the Grain Exchange, Minneapolis; Kees and Colburn, Architects. Except for the cornice replacement, Kees and Colburn's design is intact. The ten-story building was among the tallest and most prestigious structures in Minneapolis when constructed. Photo: 2001.

South, Minneapolis. Now demolished, the building had facades of brick with stock Sullivanesque terra-cotta ornament from the Midland Terra Cotta Company. Kees and Colburn used decorative terra cotta for dozens of buildings, but most designs were based on classical motifs.[31]

Kees and Colburn's designs were published frequently in the *Western Architect*. For example, the Deere and Webber Warehouse appeared in the January 1903 issue and the Great Northern Implement Building in May 1912. Since Kees served as the president of the Minneapolis company that published the professional journal, this coverage of his work was not unexpected. The *Western Architect* was the one professional journal that devoted substantial coverage to progressive architecture, although it focused primarily on eclectic design.[32] It was not surprising that Kees and Colburn completely reverted to the practice of eclectic design, even after their successful experiments with the Sullivanesque.

Another Minneapolis architect who creatively used Sullivan's language of ornamentation was Edwin H. Hewitt (1874–1939). Hewitt's design for the P. R. Brooks Residence (c. 1906) in Minneapolis was influenced by Frank Lloyd Wright's hip-roof Prairie houses but the ornament links Hewitt's design with the Sullivanesque. Ornamental medallions flanking the entrance, the grillwork at the doorway, and a decorative frieze tucked under the roof overhang were clearly inspired by Sullivan's work. Published in the *Western Architect* (December 1906), the P. R. Brooks Residence was a model for other architectural designers. Hewitt, a graduate of the University of Minnesota, opened his office in 1904 and his early designs were promising, but traditionalism soon overtook his work.[33]

Elsewhere in Minnesota, the Duluth architectural firm of Palmer, Hall, and Hunt was responsible for some early Sullivanesque designs. These included a warehouse and an office building in Duluth that were published, respectively, in the October and November 1902 issues of the *Western Architect*. The office building had a fussy appearance but the seven-story Wholesale Building for F. A. Patrick (1902) was a simple, powerful statement. Each of its two street facades was essentially symmetrical. The repeated piers, with recessed floor spandrels and windows, were collectively composed and framed by massive end piers. The verticality of the piers was terminated by a broad horizontal banding, wall return, and cantilevered roof cornice. In addition, the narrow piers were capped by ornate capitals. Inspired by Adler and Sullivan's Wainwright Building and by Kees and Colburn's Advance Thresher Building in Minneapolis, the facades were handsomely managed and proportioned. The only compromise was the introduction of entry doorways carved into each of the wide piers at the street corners, which eroded the building's visual strength and confused its robust symmetry.

Another Duluth building, the Cathedral of the Sacred Heart, by Tenbusch and Hill, Architects, raised the ire of Louis Sullivan. The bronze doors of the cathedral closely resembled ornamental bronze doors designed by Sullivan, and he complained in a letter published in the *Interstate Architect and Builder* (December 8, 1900) that his work was

Opposite: Base of the Chamber of Commerce Building, Minneapolis. The ornate columns create a rhythmic progression along the street. Photo: 1989.

being plagiarized.[34] Of course, many of Sullivan's designs were the basis for the Sullivanesque as admiring designers attempted to match his work.

In Chicago, Harry B. Wheelock used intricate patterns of Sullivanesque ornament in white-glazed terra-cotta spandrel panels for the Western Methodist Book Concern (1899; demolished 1990). Designed to house a printing plant and book storage, the building was used later by the Stop and Shop company as a grocery store on the lower floors and a warehouse above.[35] Unfortunately, this structure, listed on the National Register, was razed by the city for a tax-increment financed urban renewal project. This demolition was part of a 1989–90 clearance of an entire city block (Number 37) in the heart of the Loop, and Block 37 still sits vacant more than a decade later. (Some Sullivanesque ornamental panels from Wheelock's building were salvaged and found their way into the hands of collectors.)[36] Born in Galesburg, Illinois, Harry B. Wheelock (1861–1934) studied engineering for two years at the University of Michigan before assuming his father's architectural practice in Chicago; the younger Wheelock maintained his office in Adler and Sullivan's Schiller/Garrick Theater Building.[37]

An early Sullivanesque apartment building (1901) was built in the Chicago suburb of Evanston. The architect for the handsome three-story complex of brick and ornamental terra cotta was John D. Atchison of Atchison and Edbrooke, a Chicago firm. Perspective drawings of this apartment building appeared in the 1903 exhibition catalog of the Chicago Architectural Club.[38] But the promising architectural partnership dissolved; Harry W. J. Edbrooke left Chicago for Denver, Colorado, around 1908 and Atchison had immigrated earlier to Canada.[39] Atchison formed a partnership with another American, Herbert Rugh, and was involved with at least one other documented Sullivanesque design. The Fairchild Block (1907) was a six-story steel-framed and brick-clad building on Princess Street, Winnipeg, Manitoba, and housed a farm implement company. The major terra-cotta ornamental features were large plaques, comprised of four pieces, that were placed like column capitals on piers between segmented-arched window bays. The letters F, C, and O were incorporated in the swirling foliate patterns as identification for the Fairchild Company.[40]

In Chicago, several Sullivanesque masterpieces originated from the team of Richard E. Schmidt (1865–1959) and Hugh Garden (1873–1961). Garden was a freelance designer employed by Schmidt, an architect, and eventually the two men formed a lifelong association. In 1906, Schmidt made Garden and the structural engineer Edgar Martin (1871–1951) partners and the firm name eventually became Schmidt, Garden, and Martin.[41]

Richard E. Schmidt was born in Ebern, Bavaria, while his parents were visiting in their native Germany.[42] Richard's father was a doctor and wanted Richard to follow him and two older brothers into medicine but Richard was determined to become an architect. After a year in an architect's office, Schmidt entered the Massachusetts Institute of Technology. After two years at MIT, Schmidt returned to Chicago and worked for Adler and Sullivan. In 1887, Schmidt opened his own office.[43]

Although important early designs were done under the firm name of Richard E. Schmidt, Hugh Garden must be noted as a principal contributor. Hugh Mackie Gordon Garden was born in Canada and graduated (1887) from Bishop's College School, Lennoxville, Quebec. In 1893, Hugh Garden relocated to Chicago and freelanced as an architectural illustrator, designer, and short-term draftsman.[44] Garden's renderings included a perspective of the Cheltenham Beach Project (1894) for Frank Lloyd Wright and, for Louis Sullivan, the Guaranty Building (1894–95) in Buffalo, New York. Garden's association with Richard E. Schmidt started in 1897.[45]

Although several progressive designs preceded it, the first truly Sullivanesque design by Richard E. Schmidt was a city house for Albert E. Madlener (1902). Its clarity of organization and expression was highlighted by the proper touches of ornamentation. The three-story house sits close to the street corner at West Burton Place and North State Parkway, Chicago, and is linked to a stable/garage by a small walled-in garden (now used for display of architectural artifacts). The exterior at the first story has limestone bandings that alternate with brick; limestone facings, incised with crisp Sullivan-like ornament, frame the entry doorway. Similarly, limestone outlines the second-floor window openings in the brick facades. The top floor, where a ballroom is located, is reduced in scale by a "panelization" of the wall surface. This is accomplished by horizontal bandings of limestone that align with the window heads and sills and thus frame brick panels of decorative infill between window jambs. Cripple-columns of limestone, with stylized capitals, are positioned adjacent to each window jamb and set in front of recessed decorative windows. This horizontal treatment of the top floor is further emphasized by a cantilevered "cornice," which shelters and shades the top-floor windows. Above this projecting cornice, a parapet continues the cube-like brick massing up to the final horizontal strata of limestone coping. The proportioning of the facades into dissimilar horizontal tiers allowed the architect freedom to position windows asymmetrically. It was a strategy used frequently for Sullivanesque facade compositions. Previously, historical facades appeared regimented by a vertical alignment of windows.[46]

In 1963, the Graham Foundation for Advanced Studies in the Fine Arts purchased the Madlener House and saved it from impending demolition, which was the fate of so many neighboring mansions that were razed to make way for high-rise apartments. The house was restored in 1963 by the architect Daniel Brenner and listed on the National Register of Historic Places in 1970. A collection of architectural artifacts, featuring Sullivanesque ornamental pieces, was installed (1987) in the courtyard under the direction of the architect John Vinci.[47] Thanks to the Graham Foundation, Richard E. Schmidt and Hugh Garden's Madlener House survives as an excellent specimen of Sullivanesque design and Chicago history.

Another important Sullivanesque design by the Richard E. Schmidt firm was the Chapin and Gore Building of 1904. This eight-story building has a street frontage of eighty-one feet with four structural bays; the structural frame consists of cast-iron columns and heavy timber beams.[48] Floor loadings for the lower warehouse levels were

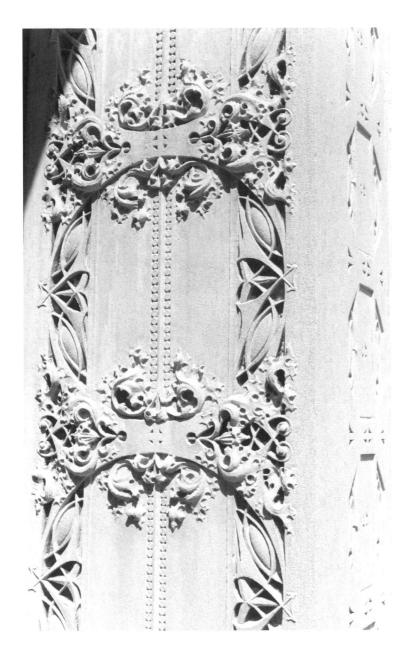

Albert E. Madlener House
(1902), detail of carved limestone ornament surrounding
the entranceway. Photo: 1993.

250-pounds-per-square-foot capacity while the upper five office floors were engineered for loadings of 100 pounds per square foot.[49] The treatment of the street facade expressed these functional and structural differences within the building as the warehouse levels have smaller windows than those on the upper office floors. The professional journal *Architectural Record* featured the building in an article that appeared in February 1908.[50]

A 1959 remodeling of the Chapin and Gore Building resulted in an altered ground-floor storefront and the removal of the projecting cornice, pier capitals, and continuous head ornament.[51] More recently, the building has undergone major renovations (1995–97). It now houses administrative offices for the Chicago Symphony Orchestra and has been connected to Daniel Burnham's Orchestra Hall (1905) by a six-story addition at the rear. Skidmore, Owings, and Merrill was the architectural firm for these alterations and additions.[52]

Opposite: Albert E. Madlener
House (1902), Chicago; Richard
E. Schmidt, Architect, with Hugh
Garden, designer. Photo: 1993.

Richard E. Schmidt had expertise in designing medical facilities, which resulted in many hospital commissions. Among early projects was an advanced design for Michael Reese Hospital, begun in 1905. The plan of the building had two legs, which defined the street edges at Twenty-fourth and Ellis Avenue. The two wings were joined by a diagonal connection and this resulting 45-degree angle opened the street corner for an entry plaza and vehicular drop-off. In addition, this diagonal segment between the two wings was treated as an entry pavilion in a Sullivanesque manner. The entrances were framed by stylized ornament, and upper-story windows and vertical piers were composed with the entry openings.[53] The building design was free of historical vestiges and presented an efficient but progressive image.

One of the important buildings associated with the Sullivanesque was the Schmidt firm's Montgomery Ward Warehouse located on the east bank of the North Branch of the Chicago River at Chicago Avenue. The vast building (1906–8) stretched and bent with the river's edge to the north. Like a cliff, the hard-edged warehouse rose from the water and marked the waterway with a meaningful scale and movement. At the same time, the manipulation of facade elements created human-scaled references within the civic-scaled framework. The underlying structural frame of concrete gave organization to the facade but it was not overt and therefore not dully repetitive like so many obvious and soon trite structural expressions. Although columns were readable, beam spandrels continued across vertical surfaces, creating a horizontal movement that reinforced the inherent horizontality of building massing. The design of the facades gathered floors into three horizontal groupings: a river-related podium rising to a height established by the street datum, a two-story base at street level defined by uninterrupted columns with subordinated but decorated spandrels, and a six-story superstructure. Decorative but simplified Sullivanesque ornament was used sparingly in some important locations, for example, the recessed second-floor spandrel panels and the column capitals of the two-story base, and as an accent to relieve barren surfaces. However, the narrow Chicago Avenue facade, where the main entrance was located, had exuberant Sullivanesque ornamentation. The building was considered radical because of the architects' extensive use of concrete, which was a newly rediscovered material at the time.[54] The design was also aesthetically radical and successful. Hugh Garden took Sullivan's horizontal explorations for the Meyer Building and the Schlesinger and Mayer Store and gave them new meaning and scale.

The warehouse for Montgomery Ward was a swan song of progressive design from Schmidt, Garden, and Martin; thereafter, the firm produced eclectic and uninspired designs. However, three exceptions were a hotel (1915) in Saginaw, Michigan; a design (c. 1919) for a "Factory Building" at St. Paul, Minnesota; and a large candy factory (1921) for Bunte Brothers, Chicago.

Six stories high and a city block long, the hotel for Nelson and Levin in Saginaw recalled earlier aspects of Sullivanesque designs by Schmidt, Garden, and Martin. Supplied by the American company, continuous terra-cotta bandings were aligned with

Opposite: Chapin and Gore Building (1904), Chicago; Richard E. Schmidt, architect, with Hugh Garden, designer. Photo: 1965.

heads and sills of punched window openings for the upper stories.[55] On the major facade, second-floor windows were closely spaced with brick piers between openings. These one-story-high piers were capped by terra-cotta ornament, which featured a triangular shape surrounded by sculpted foliage. The ground-floor storefronts were capped by an ornate banding of terra cotta. The entry bay was emphasized by brick piers with full-height verticality that contrasted with the dominant horizontality. The effect was reminiscent of the entry treatment at Michael Reese Hospital.

The factory design for St. Paul was especially noteworthy as its composition of bold cubistic massings recalled the strength and vitality of the firm's earlier work. This design appeared in the Thirty-second Annual Chicago Architectural Exhibition and was republished in the *Western Architect* (April 1919).

In many ways, the design for Bunte Brothers in Chicago resembled the earlier proposal for St. Paul. The Bunte Brothers Building had cubistic building massings and ornament rendered in Sullivanesque fashion. Resurrected too were some Sullivanesque motifs such as the sculpted eagles for pier caps. (Decorative eagle reliefs were sometimes featured on Sullivanesque buildings; an example is Sullivan's Columbus, Wisconsin, bank of 1919, which is discussed in chapter 3.) However, the Bunte ornament usually was simplified and overscaled while the Sullivanesque massings and mannerisms seemed transitional, like a preview of decorated modernism, the art deco style of the 1920s and 1930s. Richard E. Schmidt and Hugh Garden worked together for a lifetime.[56] However, in an eight-year span at the turn of the twentieth century, they may have produced their most successful and visionary designs.

Several well-known Chicago architects usually associated with the Prairie School designed some buildings with ornamentation based on Sullivan's work. For example, the firm of Spencer and Powers introduced Sullivan-inspired ornament around the entryway of the Edward W. McCready House (1907) in suburban Oak Park. Robert C. Spencer (1864–1953) was interested in the arts and crafts movement and his ornamental designs, featuring broad leaves and static botanical forms, were usually consistent with those of the movement. However, the ornament for the McCready house featured Sullivan-like shapes, repetitions, and underlying geometrics. After the McCready House, the designs of Spencer and Powers became more eclectic, with the Tudor style as a major influence.

Another Chicago architect, George Washington Maher (1864–1926), created his own distinct interpretations of Sullivanesque and Wrightian imagery. Maher's John Farson House (1897) in Oak Park and the James Patten House (1901; demolished) in Evanston were most consistent with Sullivanesque ornamentation. The more modest Frank Schneidenhelm House (1902) in Wilmette had restrained ornament for porch columns and dormer trim. In a small store and office structure called the University Building (1905–6), in Evanston, the influence may have moved in the reverse direction. The building had columns with squared-off capitals and ornament that may have influenced Sullivan's design of the interior of his bank in Cedar Rapids, Iowa. Maher used

moldings and incised lines to complement the restrained ornament of the dressed limestone exterior. He employed similar stonework for the Swift Hall of Engineering (1909)
at Northwestern University, Evanston. There, however, Maher utilized vertical ornamental features to flank the entry portals while smaller ornamental designs adorned two
piers that separated the three distinct openings. Maher used similar design devices at
the J. R. Watkins Medical Products (1911) complex in Winona, Minnesota. Maher's
favorite botanical themes were based on the poppy and the thistle. Maher developed
his own identifiable style from elements of the Sullivanesque, the Prairie School, and
the arts and crafts movement. Although he factored in historical eclecticism later in his
career, he was a creative force in Chicago. Maher has remained understudied and mostly
unappreciated.

A number of architects elsewhere in the Midwest were responsible for some early
and significant Sullivanesque designs. Some of these architects were prominent; however, none was fully committed to the Sullivanesque and most treated it as just another
style in their eclectic approach to design. Nonetheless, several excellent Sullivanesque
designs were constructed in Missouri. Two of these were in St. Louis and were designed
by the local architect Theodore C. Link. Kansas City had a fine example designed by
Root and Siemens of that city.

Theodore C. Link (1850–1923) was a distinguished St. Louis architect who designed
several landmark structures with Sullivanesque associations. The most important was
St. Louis's Union Station, a transitional design, much like Adler and Sullivan's Auditorium Hotel Building in Chicago of five years earlier. The station was constructed after
a national design competition in which the firm of Link and Cameron was selected as
the winner in March 1891. Construction started in 1892 and the building was first used
on September 2, 1894.[57] The exterior was inspired by the work of H. H. Richardson,
but Link employed a French Romanesque variation of the Boston architect's designs.
The interior, especially the Great Hall on the second level, was indebted to Sullivan's
ornament in the Auditorium Hotel. The Great Hall, with its decorative Sullivanesque
qualities and stencil-painted barrel-vaults, is a beautifully grand space. Like many other railroad stations in the United States, the building was eventually neglected and faced
demolition after passenger service was abandoned. However, the station house was
converted in 1985 to a hotel, and the vast train shed, designed by George H. Pegram,
was remodeled into an urban entertainment and shopping center.[58]

Link adapted the Sullivanesque for a St. Louis high-rise constructed (1910) at 1509
Washington Avenue and Fifteenth Street. This ten-story office building for the Roberts, Johnson, and Rand Shoe Company featured Sullivan-inspired ornament and an
ornate projecting cornice with trellis-like perforations.[59] A German immigrant who
arrived in America in 1870, Theodore C. Link had studied in at Heidelberg University
and at the Ecole des Beaux-Arts in Paris. He worked in a number of American cities
before moving to St. Louis.[60]

The Kansas City, Missouri, architectural firm of Root and Siemens was responsible for the handsome Sullivanesque design of the eleven-story Scarritt Building and Arcade (1906–7) in that city. In basic exterior massing, the Scarritt resembled Adler and Sullivan's Union Trust Building (1892) in St. Louis. The bases for both buildings filled their respective sites, while the office superstructures were U-shaped in plan and gave an appearance of paired slabs when viewed from the street. Terminations of the towers were similar; the top two stories of each were defined by projecting horizontal banding, fenestration that differed from the shaft, and a heavy cantilevered cornice. Besides Sullivanesque exterior ornament, the Scarritt had a four-story-high interior galleria with wrought iron railings decorated in Sullivanesque patterns.[61] Walter C. Root (1859–1925) of the Root and Siemens partnership was the younger brother of the Chicago architect John W. Root (1850–91) of the famous Burnham and Root firm. Upon completion of the Scarritt Building and Arcade, Root and Siemens located their offices in the building.[62]

Mason Maury was one of the few architects in Kentucky to experiment with progressive design in the early years of the twentieth century. This initiative may have been sparked by Maury's former partner, William J. Dodd, who worked in Chicago for the so-called "father of the skyscraper," William Le Baron Jenney, before moving to Louisville in 1885. Maury and Dodd designed the first skeletal steel structure in Kentucky, the Louisville Trust Company (1891), although they cloaked the exterior in elements of the Romanesque style. After the Maury and Dodd firm was dissolved in 1896, Maury formed a partnership with Arthur Cobb. Subsequently, Maury designed a store for the Kaufman-Straus Company (c. 1908) and a Woman's Club (c. 1910), the latter resembling Wright's 1893 Winslow House in River Forest, Illinois. Both the store and the club building were in Louisville.

The six-story Kaufman-Straus Building has a front facade influenced by Sullivan's Gage Building; its widely spaced fluted columns culminate in exuberant bursts of ornamental "foliate" that "spread" onto the parapet wall.[63] The street facade is composed of storefront base, end piers, columns, and parapet wall. This framework creates a monumental scale; as counterpoint, human-scaled elements—floor spandrels and sculpted window mullions—establish a recessed, secondary wall plane within each structural bay. The window mullions echo the column shape but are reduced in scale and rise only from the third through fifth floors. The underlying skeletal steel structure is well-defined while claddings of beige terra cotta and brick provide fireproofing, color, and decorative patterns. The ornamental foliate, however, is more stiff and broad-leafed than Sullivan's customary designs; nevertheless, Maury's design resulted in a handsome composition and, despite remodeling, survives as a "jewel" encased in the Galleria, an indoor mall development in downtown Louisville.[64]

Maury displayed the designs for the Woman's Club project and the Kaufman-Straus Building in the First Exhibition of the Louisville Chapter, American Institute of Architects, held April 12–26, 1912. These were radically new designs for the locale. The following year, Maury left Louisville for Los Angeles.[65]

Kaufman-Straus Building (c. 1908), Louisville, Kentucky; Mason Maury, Architect. The building is now altered and surrounded by an indoor mall. Photo: 1993.

The American Southwest and Southeast were fertile locales for Sullivanesque applications, although many of the buildings there were constructed as the first stage of Sullivanesque influence was waning and as the second phase developed, after 1910. It was an era in which the style lost prestige and became almost exclusively a local language for smaller buildings. Representative work of the Sullivanesque in the Southeast centered in Jacksonville, Florida, and primarily was designed by Henry J. Klutho (1873–1964) or his former employees. Klutho acknowledged that both Louis Sullivan and Frank Lloyd Wright influenced his designs.[66] However, Klutho blended these sources, especially in regard to ornamentation, with a personal expression that bordered on eccentricity. He often manipulated architectural scale, creating exaggerated sizes and forms distinct from those found in common practice; in that manner, Klutho was similar to Sullivan's mentor Frank Furness. Klutho's designs usually showed surprising creativity and freshness although some bordered on caricature. Klutho was an important figure whose Sullivanesque adaptations merged with regional vernacular, as advocated by Louis Sullivan and George G. Elmslie.

Henry John Klutho was born in Breese, Illinois, a small town forty miles east of St. Louis, Missouri. He studied business in St. Louis at the time Adler and Sullivan's Wainwright Building was rising, when building construction in the city was at a peak. Klutho decided to become an architect and went to New York, where he worked in various architecture firms. In 1901 he relocated to Jacksonville, Florida, drawn by a building boom after a great fire in that city. Klutho's practice prospered and he was highly regarded for his "traditional" architecture. While honeymooning in Niagara Falls in June 1904, he saw buildings designed by Frank Lloyd Wright and Louis Sullivan in nearby Buffalo. Impressed, he believed he should explore the possibilities of their creative architecture. Klutho met Wright, they became friends, and the Kluthos were guests at the Wright home and studio in Oak Park during visits back to Illinois.[67]

Klutho's own house (1908) resembled Wright's Prairie School houses; however, its patio canopy of glass skylights was supported by a metal structure decorated with Sullivanesque motifs. Klutho's design of the ten-story Seminole Hotel (1908–9; demolished 1974) in Jacksonville embodied some of Sullivan's skyscraper aesthetic, expressed in strongly vertical piers and recessed floor spandrels; however, its heavy geometric ornament was akin to that of Wright's Larkin Building. The seven-story Burbridge Hotel (1911; demolished 1981) had a simple exterior massing with little ornament except for a bracketed projecting cornice. However, decorative plasterwork based on Sullivan designs graced the interior.[68]

The large four-story St. James Building (1910–12) was Klutho's major accomplishment. An innovative and attractive concrete structure, it was built for Cohen Brothers, a department store. The store was on the ground and second levels; rental offices occupied the two upper stories. The offices wrapped around an octagonal central court with a glass roof dome seventy-five feet in diameter, which became the focus of the department store. The block-long front facade defined one edge of a city square, Hemming Park. With its powerful facade treatments, the St. James made an urban statement of the highest quality. The terra-cotta ornamentation was designed by Klutho and made by the Conkling-Armstrong Terra Cotta Company, Philadelphia. Unfortunately, the skylight was removed (1927) and the light court was filled in with floors to provide more space. Although Klutho had his office in the building for many years, he moved out to protest the destruction of the light court.[69] The exterior was also defaced; the most serious alteration was a 1959 "modernization" of the street-level storefront in which changes were made in the sidewalk canopies and display windows.

Klutho's Florida Life Building (1911–12), Jacksonville, was unique. Tall, narrow, and graceful, it was comprised of twenty-eight-foot-wide floor slabs stacked eleven stories in the air. It was the tallest building in Jacksonville upon completion.[70] Claddings include slender terra-cotta trim that rises the height of the building and, at the top, bursts into lavish Sullivanesque ornamental capitals. These visually support an ornate projecting cornice. Large Chicago windows emphasize the tautness of the exterior skin over the concrete structure. The Florida Life Building was featured in the *Western Architect* in August 1914. Three months earlier, that journal had published Klutho's other Jacksonville designs, including the landmark St. James Building (1910–12); the Germania Club (1912), with its exaggerated Viennese-inspired forms; and the Shriner's Morocco Temple (1910–11), which combined Sullivanesque, Wrightian, and Egyptian revival ornament.[71]

After the Florida Life Building, a succession of Klutho designs employed Sullivanesque terra-cotta ornament. These included the three-story Claude Nolan Garage and Showroom (1911–12; facades destroyed) and the Criminal Court Building (1913–15; demolished 1968), both in Jacksonville, and the James Hotel (1916) in Palatka, Florida.[72] Several schools designed by Klutho had touches of Sullivanesque ornament. In the Panama Park Elementary School (1915), the major features were Sullivan-like terra-cotta eagles atop decorative capitals of swirling foliate. The East Jacksonville Elementary School Number Three (1917; demolished 1981) used Sullivanesque cartouches as major accents on the exterior. Decorative plasterwork on the interior included pilaster capitals influenced by George G. Elmslie's stylizations of elongated triangles and engaged ribbings.[73]

By 1917, Klutho began turning away from the Sullivanesque and the Prairie School. Sullivanesque ornamentation lingered in Klutho's designs for the Napier/Wilkie Apartments (1923) and the proposed S. A. Lynch Building (1924), but changing tastes demanded the trappings of romantic historicism. Klutho responded accordingly although he introduced art deco compositions to Jacksonville when that style became acceptable around 1930.[74]

As part of the "form follows function" ideology promulgated by Louis Sullivan and his adherents, regional differences prompted varying design adaptations and evolutions. Cultural, geographical, and climatic variations would result in differing design responses and, therefore, regional identities. The Sullivanesque system of design and imagery was adjusted to regional conditions by Klutho in Florida and, to a great extent, by Henry C. Trost (1860–1933) in the Southwest. Each embraced Sullivan's design philosophy and, to varying degrees, his system of ornamentation, and each suitably adapted these for his own region. Like Klutho, Trost was a transplanted midwesterner. However, unlike Klutho, Trost worked in Chicago (c. 1888–97), and some suggest he may have been employed by Adler and Sullivan, but this has not been proven.[75]

After an early nomadic architectural career, Trost formed a partnership (1904) in El Paso, Texas, with a brother and a nephew. The firm name was Trost and Trost. Henry C. Trost served as architectural designer and was responsible for a number of Sullivanesque and regionally adaptive designs. The firm produced two concurrent and progressive designs for YMCA buildings in 1907. Both were Sullivanesque, although the one in El Paso seemed more consistent with midwestern examples while the one in Phoenix, Arizona, seemed more appropriate to that locale. The Phoenix YMCA had a raised first floor and its window openings were defined by rounded arches. Smaller multiple arched windows were grouped as a horizontal banding at the second story. A banding of Sullivanesque ornamental trim separated the second story from an "attic" frieze with ribbon windows, which were tucked under a wide overhanging tiled hip roof. Additional ornament in the Sullivanesque vein included "pier" treatments between second-story arched windows and medallions, which served as terminating features to the decorative wall banding between the second and "attic" (third) floors. The El Paso YMCA (1907; demolished 1961) was a "classic" Sullivanesque design.[76] Major exterior features of the three-story building included an effusively ornamented arched entryway; recessed spandrels with decorative motifs at the second floor; and a series of small windows at the top floor, which expressed the transient rental rooms within and contrasted with the two-story-high arched windows for the larger spaces of activity and assembly below.

Trost and Trost pioneered reinforced concrete construction in the Southwest. The use of concrete was appropriate in an area remote from steel mills, and concrete approximated the surface appearance of the region's traditional adobe walls. Trost and Trost used concrete for multistory office buildings, which were composed according to Sullivan-defined principles with base, shaft, and cap. Ornament was positioned and utilized in a manner consistent with use by Sullivan. However, definition and movement within the ornamental framework were hampered by the limitations of the concrete material; its coarseness lent itself to forms of greater dimensions and larger scale than terra cotta. Intricate Sullivan-like ornament rendered in terra cotta or cast iron was not possible in raw concrete, and ornamentation was therefore simplified and made "flat," with little relief or complexity. The outline or perimeter shape of "ornamental" pieces became more important than sculpted surfaces of detailed relief. The result was a Trost and Trost reinterpretation of the Sullivanesque within the "nature of the material," as Wright advocated, which was consistent with the plain wall surfaces of the local vernacular architecture.

Among concrete office buildings of simplified Sullivanesque style designed by Trost and Trost for El Paso were the five-story Caples Building (1909), which had exterior wall surfaces of brick as well as concrete; the Rio Grande Valley Bank Building (c. 1909); the Roberts-Banner Building (1910); the Posener Building (1911; demolished 1941); and the Mills Building (1910–11).[77] Of these, the twelve-story Mills Building was the most prominent, which the architects recognized by moving their offices into it. Even to its rounded corner, the form of the Mills Building resembled Sullivan's Schlesinger and Mayer Building in Chicago. However, the facade treatments differed. Sullivan's building had an obvious horizontality while Trost and Trost's facades had a vertical emphasis conveyed by concrete structural piers and massive window mullions dominating suppressed floor spandrels. Ornament was sparse but heavy-handed when used. Despite the Mills Building's vertical expression of the facade, there was an over-riding horizontality to the building; this effect was created not only by the proportion of greater building length to height but by the strongly horizontal base and cap. Each was two stories high, and together they contained the verticality of the eight-story "shaft." The cap was defined by a shallow projection of the tenth-floor balcony and composed with window arches at the top story and a cantilevered roof cornice. The *Western Architect* (October 1913) published a full-page photograph of the building. The same photograph appeared in G. H. Edgell's 1928 book, *The American Architecture of Today*, as Edgell used the building as an example to describe Sullivan's influence.[78]

One of the finest Sullivanesque designs by Trost and Trost was the four-story, hundred-room Hotel Gadsden (1906–7) in Douglas, Arizona. Unfortunately, a fire severely damaged the building in 1928; Trost and Trost designed a reconstruction but transformed the exterior according to the Spanish colonial style. Nonetheless, the lobby, altered in plan, retained most of its original Sullivanesque character. Wall treatments and decorative plaques closely imitated Sullivan's seed pod motifs.[79] Trost and Trost designed other hotels but for these the architects employed mission revival or, later, Spanish colonial styles, as they fully embraced eclectic design after 1912.[80]

Elsewhere in the Southwest, several skyscraper designs closely resemble those of Louis Sullivan but are little known. In Oklahoma City, Oklahoma, the architect William Wells followed Sullivan's rules and aesthetics, and, although few in number, his high-rise designs could easily be mistaken for those of Adler and Sullivan. William Abijah Wells (1878–1938) studied for a year at Kansas University before he moved to Chicago to study at the Chicago School of Architecture, which was jointly operated by the Armour Institute and the Art Institute of Chicago.[81] How long Wells attended the architectural program in Chicago is not known, and he evidently did not graduate.[82] He was a member of the Chicago Architectural Club in 1898 and maintained this membership for years after he left Chicago.[83] Wells relocated in 1904 to Oklahoma City and by 1907 had formed a partnership with an Englishman, Arthur J. Williams (b. 1866).[84] Oklahoma City was a good place for an architect to be, as construction was booming; in three years, from 1907 to 1910, the population almost doubled.[85]

The first known design by Williams and Wells was the Pioneer Building (1907–8), Oklahoma City. The Pioneer Telephone and Telegraph Company occupied the top two floors of the seven-story structure but in 1910 began expanding onto other floors.[86] The top two stories formed a cap for the building, and Sullivanesque ornamentation topped the uppermost columns and banded the roof cornice. The street-corner location, Third and Broadway, allowed two entrances, but the one in the narrow Broadway facade was more important as it was framed by Sullivan-inspired ornament. This ornament closely resembled the terra-cotta entry framework, including fan and pinnacles, of Sullivan's Condict/Bayard Building in New York although the patterns of the fan surface more closely resembled those of the Gage Building in Chicago. This detail and the storefront of Sullivan's Gage Building, as well as a perspective of the Condict Building and a detail drawing of the entrance, were published in *The Chicago Architectural Annual*, the catalog for the Chicago Architectural Club's 1902 annual exhibition at the Art Institute of Chicago. Wells undoubtedly had a copy of the catalog and probably used it as a pattern book.

The *Catalogue of the Fourteenth Annual Exhibition of the Chicago Architectural Club* (1901) featured photographs of Sullivan's Guaranty Building in Buffalo. Close-ups showed Sullivan's decorative terra-cotta surfaces of rotated squares and interlaced foliate. Wells adapted these patterns for some of the ornamental terra cotta on his masterpiece, the Colcord Building (1909–10) in Oklahoma City. However, the plan and massing of the Colcord more closely resembled that of Adler and Sullivan's Union Trust Building (1893) in St. Louis. The Colcord's U-shaped plan extended to grade whereas the Union Trust had a two-story base that filled out the site at street level and the U-shaped configuration began only on the third floor. In Wells's design, the two flanking wings were intended to define a processional space as well as a light court. Access to the main entry, which was located in the connecting arm, was through this courtyard. The major wing is twelve stories high while the entry arm, housing elevators and over-ride, rises fourteen stories. Unfortunately, the design was phased and one wing was never built. The result was an L-shaped plan and entry court ill-defined by an adjacent existing building. Nevertheless, the Colcord Building, especially with its facade treatment of exquisite ornament, is handsome and appealing.[87]

The building was named for its developer, Charles F. Colcord, and became immediately recognized as a prestigious location. For example, the Oklahoma City Chamber of Commerce leased the twelfth floor of the building in 1910.[88] The Pioneer and Colcord Buildings were Wells's two major Sullivanesque designs. Very little is known about other work he may have done, apart from some simple residences.

Texas was receptive to the Sullivanesque. A number of architects attempted designs influenced by Sullivan's work and ornament; however, many of these endeavors were timid, bound by historicism. For example, the Dallas architect James E. Flanders designed several churches that attempted to break from tradition through the use of bolder forms and asymmetrical massings. Sullivan's ornamental motifs were liberally incorporated in one building, and in another case, such usage was restrained. The results were mixed; the overall impression of Flanders's church buildings was of a modified Gothic style that retained too many traditional ecclesiastical elements, such as pointed-arched windows, bell towers, and steeply pitched roofs. Still, these buildings were interesting. Decorative friezes reminiscent of motifs from Sullivan's Transportation Building were incorporated into the chancel of the Trinity Methodist Church (1903; demolished 1985) in Dallas. In his design for the First Methodist Church (1904–5) in Pittsburg, Texas, Flanders framed the louvered openings of the bell tower with luscious bandings of Sullivanesque ornament. St. John's Methodist Church (1910), Stamford, Texas, revealed Flanders's most liberal play of external massings, but use of ornament was minimized. The architect designed a traditional courthouse in the classical style (1905) for Navarro County in Corsicana, Texas; curiously, however, Flanders introduced a Sullivanesque frieze in the major space under the central tower.[89]

The Dallas firm of Lang and Witchell, whose principals were Otto H. Lang and Frank O. Witchell, produced a number of multistory office and commercial buildings that followed Sullivan's principles for the composition of facades. The ornamentation, however, was generally based on historical styles or simple geometric patterns. Sullivanesque exceptions include the sixteen-story Southwestern Life Building (1911–13; demolished); the eight-story Cotton Exchange (c. 1913; demolished); and the Central Fire Station Building (1908; demolished). The grouped windows on the brick front facade of the firehouse were framed by wide contrasting trim; from the collected fenestration, five mullions rose like staffs to the parapet, where decorative Sullivanesque clusters terminated each one.[90]

A large and intriguing project by Lang and Witchell is the Sears Roebuck complex (1913) on Lamar Street in Dallas. The main warehouse, nine stories high and one block long, has facades that are decidedly horizontal in emphasis, with bandings aligned with window heads and sills. The exterior was influenced by Schmidt, Garden, and Martin's Montgomery Ward Warehouse. As in the Chicago model, ornament was used sparingly; however, Sullivan-like ornament was concentrated at the main entrance. Lang and Witchell's most successful Sullivanesque design was the ten-story Raleigh Hotel (1912), in Waco, Texas. The handsome facades are clad in red brick and cream-colored terra cotta. Except for the end bays, the bays across the building facade are joined by terracotta bandings that align at each windowsill. Large and beautiful clusters of terra-cotta Sullivanesque ornament engage the horizontal banding at the second story. These clusters are focal pieces and are united with the facade by projecting brickwork, which encompasses the terra-cotta design.[91]

Several county courthouses designed by Lang and Witchell incorporate Sullivanesque features. The exterior of the Cooke County Courthouse (1910) in Gainesville, Texas, is eclectic, an adaptation of Beaux-Arts classicism. However, the interior has spaces defined by Sullivanesque elements. A major centralized space is sheltered by an art-glass skylight of Sullivan-inspired shapes and patterns. Square in plan but with clipped corners where the structural piers rise to support the upper walls of the "rotunda" tower, this lantern space has perimeter surfaces flowered with Sullivanesque ornament that unites with the designs in the skylight. A courthouse (1912) for Johnson County in Cleburne, Texas, has an interior that shares characteristics with the one at Gainesville. The walls and art-glass skylight of the central space have decorative treatments that replicate Sullivan's ornament. On the exterior of the courthouse, Sullivanesque ornament is combined with vestiges of historicism, such as classical columns located at the second floor of the central pavilion and set atop a rusticated base.[92]

In addition to its Sullivanesque designs, the Lang and Witchell firm was responsible for houses in the style of the Prairie School. Charles Erwin Barglebaugh joined the firm in 1907 after moving to Dallas from Chicago, where he had worked for both Frank Lloyd Wright and Walter Burley Griffin. Barglebaugh was the chief designer for Lang and Witchell until about 1916.[93] The July 1914 issue of the *Western Architect* featured architecture in Dallas; Lang and Witchell's work was prominent. The same issue pictured the Dallas office building of the John Deere Plow Company (1902), J. P. Hubbell and Herbert M. Greene, Architects. The seven-story Deere Building closely resembled Kees and Colburn's Advance Thresher Company Building in Minneapolis, Minnesota. Both had fenestration collected and centered in each facade and framed by solid masonry wall segments at the building corners. In addition, massings, proportions, the projecting cornice, and ornamental details were similar, although the Dallas building had minimal and simplified ornament.[94] The John Deere Building later was known as the Texas Implement Building and then the Texas School Book Depository, an infamous name in American history as it was from a window of this building that Lee Harvey Oswald shot President John F. Kennedy in 1963.

In Fort Worth, Texas, the firm of Sanguinet and Staats designed a lively and colorful street facade for the Flat Iron Building (1907–8). Inspired by Sullivan's work, the seven-story Flat Iron Building was composed with the customary facade arrangement of base, shaft, and cap.[95] Two-story piers topped by capitals of stylized ornament and complementary brick work defined the base while a heavy horizontal band acted as a pier terminus or "cornice" that served as a datum for the shaft. Another banding was aligned at the seventh-floor windowsills and terminated the four-story-high piers of the shaft. Engaging this banding were ornate pier capitals, above which were arched openings for the top-floor windows. Ornamental insets in the facades and a cantilevered cornice completed the exterior treatment. The design demonstrated the expressive variations that could evolve from the Sullivanesque.

The West Coast had many multistoried office buildings. Some recalled Sullivan's organization of facade design and many incorporated ornate terra cotta. There were a number of high-quality terra-cotta companies on the West Coast, including Gladding, McBean, and Company, which is still in existence. However, West Coast buildings had ornament based on historical styles; truly Sullivanesque designs were few. When a Sullivanesque design is found, terra cotta was most likely supplied by a Chicago company.

Such was the case for a six-story office building, the Oriental Block (1903), in Seattle, Washington. The Sullivanesque terra cotta was supplied by the Northwestern Terra Cotta Company, Chicago. Architects for the Oriental Block, later the Corona Hotel, were Bebb and Mendel of Seattle.[96]

The Sullivanesque was a midwestern style although early examples could be found scattered across the continent. Practitioners in diverse locations were likely to have been transplanted midwesterners. For example, Henry J. Klutho of Jacksonville, Florida, was a former St. Louisan. Often, the Sullivanesque advocate was professionally seasoned in Chicago—such was the case with Henry C. Trost of El Paso, Texas, and William Wells of Oklahoma City, Oklahoma. In Canada, the architect John D. Atchison of Winnipeg, Manitoba, designed his first Sullivanesque structure while practicing in Chicago. Like disciples, these architects dispersed to various points and attempted to match Sullivan's designs. As representatives of the early phase of the Sullivanesque, they adopted Sullivan's design principles and used similar ornament for prestigious buildings.

CHAPTER 3

LATER SULLIVANESQUE

Small Buildings and Anonymity

BY THE EARLY twentieth century, the Sullivanesque was no longer fashionable among America's tastemakers; mainstream architects and clients turned away from the style. Yet the Sullivanesque was still a valid aesthetic due to its original design attributes and adaptability to functional needs. It remained for architects such as Sullivan himself, William Gray Purcell and George G. Elmslie (whom I discuss in chapter 4), William L. Steele, and a few others to pursue the Sullivanesque and expand its aesthetic expression. In the second phase of the Sullivanesque (1911–30), these architects produced a small number of works but high-quality designs, in mostly undistinguished settings of minor cities and small towns. The most important aspect of the second phase was that during it, a number of lesser-known architects embraced the Sullivanesque. These little-known and, oftentimes, journeyman architects adapted the Sullivanesque for ordinary commercial and neighborhood buildings, mostly in Chicago but also in scattered midwestern towns and, occasionally, beyond.[1]

This later stage of the Sullivanesque was long lasting, enduring approximately through the second and third decades of the twentieth century. During this time, design eclecticism dominated; some architects experimented with the Sullivanesque, much as they did with historical but less appropriate styles. This second phase of the Sullivanesque is important but has been understudied. It is important not because of its "masterpiece" designs, but because it led to an overall improvement in design quality for commonplace buildings. The quality of design from the architects of speculative projects was elevated as was the quality of the resulting urban fabric. Based on Sullivan's understandable rules of design and the availability of imitative stock terra-cotta components, a shared and unified urban vernacular style became possible.

The second phase of the Sullivanesque is closely associated with the Midland Terra Cotta Company, which began making terra-cotta ornament in 1911. With the exception of a few works by master architects and their preferred suppliers, most terra-cotta ornament for Sullivanesque designs during this period was the product of this company. The broad dissemination of the Sullivanesque was the result of company publications, mostly circulated catalogs of design plates and, to some degree, advertisements. During the first stage of the Sullivanesque, professional architectural journals had covered the Sullivanesque ideology and aesthetic, but after 1915 and except for Louis Sullivan's own designs, there was very little published nationally about the style. Midland's publications and distribution couldn't compensate for this lack of broad coverage.

Although the Sullivanesque was represented in the second stage over widely scattered geographical areas, it appeared infrequently in those places. By 1918, the style had become mostly regional, and by 1922, almost exclusively local. Although obscure nationally, the Sullivanesque actually thrived in the Chicago area. There, however, most applications were low in the hierarchy of importance and scale of building commissions. These later Sullivanesque designs were usually for small commercial buildings in which the street facades were the focus of design attention. It is no coincidence that the eclipse of the Sullivanesque paralleled that of Louis Sullivan's career.

After the Schlesinger and Mayer building, Sullivan's architectural practice declined. Many factors contributed to this, not the least of which was Sullivan's propensity to alienate clients. His personal life fell into disarray. In July 1899 he married Mary Azona Hattabaugh, but it was not a successful marriage. They separated in 1909 and divorced around 1917. Sullivan's economic status plummeted, and in 1910 he lost his Ocean Springs, Mississippi, retreat. He was forced to leave his longtime office in the tower of the Auditorium Building in 1918 and relocate to 431 South Wabash Avenue.[2] Soon he was forced to abandon even that office. William Gates of the American Terra Cotta and Ceramic Company gave Sullivan office space in converted residences used by Gates's company.[3] Broke, alcoholic, and in declining health, Sullivan was supported by generous friends over the last few years of his life. Although Sullivan experienced a decline, it took place over a period of twenty years and during that time he was still creative, although he had diminishing opportunities to exercise his talent. Nonetheless, Sullivan's later, small-scale work was superb and in many ways may even have surpassed the quality of his earlier modern phase.

More often than not, it is difficult to design very small buildings. Such buildings have a scale of minor significance and are seldom regarded as important in the architectural hierarchy. Large buildings inherently provide more opportunities to arrive at good design as there is enough critical mass to manipulate the parts in order to compose interesting forms, create rhythm, and vary scales. Major and minor themes can be developed, and articulation of structure can be expressed sensibly. Just sheer bulk can provide drama and presence. The small building has limited possibilities and poses more restrictions and pitfalls. Creation of a strong or assertive image becomes difficult without resorting to complex shapes and overarticulation, which can result in strange, diminutive scales and caricature-like results. The design of small nonresidential buildings in an urban context is an unappreciated challenge. Sullivan successfully met that challenge and provided models that others adopted, perhaps not in as masterly a fashion but usually with interesting results.

For his small buildings, Sullivan did not resort to overt structural expression but suggested the underlying skeletal steel structure in an almost subliminal manner. He did this through the dematerialization of the exterior wall, which he achieved by subtly manipulating and organizing the components comprising the facade, such as the fenestration, string courses, bandings or beltings, and, most important, ornamentation. His selection of materials, including his choice of colors, patterns, and reliefs, was masterful. Sullivan arranged these elements into new architectural compositions of beauty and dignity. Sullivan reinterpreted the exterior wall as an envelope necessary only for privacy, security, and climate control; the wall no longer had the solidity of a traditional bearing-wall structure. Sullivan's ornament symbolized nature in a manner appropriate for an urban context. His designs were sympathetic to those surroundings while achieving a very personal expression.

The first small-scale commercial building that Sullivan designed after the dissolution of his partnership with Adler was a store for Eli B. Felsenthal (1905; demolished 1982) in Chicago. This low-budget two-story building became a prototype for the later Sullivanesque. It provided a design language adaptable to small commercial buildings. Tapestry brick in a range of rich colors was laid in intricate patterns to create panels in the upper wall surfaces in which decorative terra-cotta insets were integrated. Since the Felsenthal Building contained two separate stores, they were given differing heights for individual identity. The corner store dominated with a projecting cornice. Its second-story windows were grouped as a horizontal banding. Narrow terra-cotta panels, with simple ornamental designs at the top, acted as window mullions while masking the underlying columns and reinforcing the horizontality of the fenestration. The cantilevered terra-cotta cornice was a carry-over from Sullivan's high-rise designs. Sullivan subsequently abandoned the cornice in his small buildings. This may have been for economical reasons, but more likely he felt a cornice wasn't necessary. The protruding cornices of his tall buildings had provided a terminus for the vertical lines that dominated in his skyscrapers. The cantilevered projection was especially effective in terminating the forced perspective viewed from the street; however, this solution was unnecessary in low, flat-roofed buildings.

It was two years before Sullivan had another commission built. In 1907–8, the

National Farmers' Bank was constructed in Owatonna, Minnesota. This may have been Sullivan's masterpiece. It certainly is one of his most spellbinding interior spaces. Like a cathedral, it evokes a hush and sense of awe, but without overpowering volume, as the bank hall is only sixty feet square and forty-nine feet high. The interior combines natural light, filtered through the colored art glass of a skylight and arched windows, with lighting from large decorative terra-cotta "chandeliers." It has colorful surfaces, decorative patterns of stenciled walls, painted and gilded plasterwork, murals, brickwork, and ornate terra cotta. Color and light unite. The overscaled arches on the exterior are not structural but define ocular sources of filtered and tinted natural light and, in what seems to be a contradiction, express the nonbearing condition of the exterior walls. It is a sophisticated yet congenial design. Terra cotta for the Owatonna bank came from the American Terra Cotta and Ceramic Company; Kristian Schneider modeled the ornamental terra cotta on a freelance basis.[4] Despite remodelings, the bank remains one of Sullivan's most compelling designs.[5]

Sullivan's next two built commissions were for houses. The Henry Babson Residence (1907–8; demolished 1960) in Riverside, Illinois, was especially handsome. It combined Prairie School residential organization with Sullivanesque interpretations and ornament. Terra cotta for the house was from the Northwestern Terra Cotta Company.[6] Northwestern had supplied most of Sullivan's terra cotta for years but, after its top modeler, Kristian Schneider, left the company in 1906, it never again provided terra cotta

Eli B. Felsenthal Store (1905; demolished 1982), Chicago; Louis Sullivan, Architect. The store was the model for many smaller commercial buildings, especially in Chicago's neighborhoods, designed in "Sullivan's style." Photo: Ralph Marlowe Line, c. 1952.

55

National Farmers' Bank (1907–8), Owatonna, Minnesota; Louis Sullivan, Architect. Photo: 1994.

for a Sullivan project, except for the Babson House.[7] The Josephine Crane Bradley House (1909), now a fraternity house in Madison, Wisconsin, featured Sullivan's ornamentation, but simplified and interpreted in wood.

Sullivan's next five constructed designs were in Iowa. These were the Peoples Savings Bank (1909–11), Cedar Rapids; St. Paul's Methodist Episcopal Church (1913–14), Cedar Rapids; John D. Van Allen and Son Dry-Goods Store (1913–15), Clinton; Henry C. Adams and Company Land and Loan Office Building (1913), Algona; and Merchants National Bank (1914), Grinnell. All of these designs were published in various professional journals. Despite Sullivan's diminishing practice, his work was still admired. The architectural journals *Western Architect* and *Architectural Record* consistently featured his completed buildings. His work was also published abroad. For example, in Howard Robertson's *The Principles of Architectural Composition*, published in London in 1924, Robertson compared a Sullivan bank, Peoples Savings in Cedar Rapids, with a typical eclectic design patterned after the classical style. Robertson said of Sullivan's bank: "This 'building' breaks away from tradition, and is a straightforward solution of the particular conditions affecting the design. It is by no means completely satisfactory, but it is vital and interesting."[8]

With four stories and substantial mass, the design of the Van Allen Store returned to the principle of structural expression, well defined and meticulously proportioned. In many ways, this retail building was based on Sullivan's earlier Schlesinger and Mayer Department Store although the treatment of "colonnettes," which run vertically over the upper three stories, recalls stylized columns from the Gage Building facade.[9]

Two lending institutions completed Sullivan's design foray in Iowa. The Adams Building (1913) in Algona is a small, one-story structure, now badly altered. This building was designed to accommodate a second-story addition, and Sullivan prepared a design and working drawings (dated March 14, 1920) for such an expansion but it was not built. The larger Merchants National Bank (1914) in Grinnell has often been described as a "jewel box" design, with its simple massing but resplendent materials, patterns, and ornament.

Five additional built commissions concluded Sullivan's architectural practice. Four of these were small banks, in the towns of West Lafayette, Indiana; Newark and Sidney, Ohio; and Columbus, Wisconsin. Sullivan's final constructed building design was a facade for the Krause Music Store in Chicago.

Louis Sullivan championed the idea of creating appropriate forms and spaces in architecture. This goal seems to have been shared by most Sullivanesque architects,

John D. Van Allen and Sons Dry-Goods Store (1913–15), Clinton, Iowa; Louis Sullivan, Architect. The structural columns were highlighted by ornamental terra cotta. Photo: Ralph Marlowe Line, c. 1950.

Merchants National Bank (1914), Grinnell, Iowa; Louis Sullivan, Architect. The bank is representative of Sullivan's small-town bank commissions, which essentially concluded his career. Photo: 1989.

although they succeeded to varying degrees. It was the compositional principles and the ornament used for building facades that identified the Sullivanesque style. Sullivan used terra-cotta bandings to visually lighten the building facade by segmenting the wall surfaces. He employed terra-cotta medallions to soften the brickwork and to provide a focus or element of balance to complete the facade composition. On simple small buildings such as the Purdue State Bank (1914) in West Lafayette, Indiana, Sullivan restricted the use of terra cotta to simple repetitive units for string courses and accents. This technique served as an archetype for many Sullivanesque designers.

The People's Savings and Loan Association Bank (1917–18), Sidney, Ohio, was a rare Sullivan example of almost exact symmetry in a building. Characteristically, Sullivan grouped the openings together and framed the collection in ornamented terra cotta. The front facade was dominated by a "false" arch of terra cotta framing a field of sky-blue ceramic tile, which created an urban-scaled, monumental entrance. Secondary to the major theme of the arch was the actual entry, which was scaled for human proportions and surmounted by a pair of decorative terra-cotta lions. Sullivan masterfully manipulated scale, using grouped and exaggerated elements to establish a presence and civic scale for a small but important building in the midwestern community.

The Farmers' and Merchants' Union Bank (1919) in Columbus, Wisconsin, also projected a strong image of symmetry. However, the front facade was not symmetrical at the ground level since the entry was to one side, toward the street corner, with a large window opposite. This manipulation of facade composition allowed flexibility for locating the required street-level openings. The upper wall surfaces of the facade were treated symmetrically, which is emphasized by a centered ornamental cluster, complete with a terra-cotta eagle, that juts above the parapet. The symmetrical upper wall surfaces of Sullivan's facade designs created a strong sense of balance and repose that gave a building significance and presence beyond its actual physical size. This strategy of facade composition reappeared with consistency in Sullivanesque buildings.

Sullivan again used symmetry, emphasized by a central medallion silhouetted against the sky, to organize the facade of his last built design. The William Krause Music Store (1922), Chicago, was done in association with a former Sullivan employee, William C. Presto. The result was an exuberant facade, richly ornamented in green-glazed terra cotta. The horizontal lines of terra-cotta facings and the central shaft of ornament, which terminates at the sky with an effervescent flourish, seem like a bar of music.

Sullivan wrote about his architectural philosophies and theories; in fact, his last years of creativity concentrated on written compositions. Several of his manuscripts were posthumously published as books: *Democracy: A Man-Search* (written in 1908) and *Kindergarten Chats* (written in 1901–2).[10] Sullivan also wrote *The Autobiography of an Idea*, which, along with *A System of Architectural Ornament*, he saw in print just before his death. He died on April 14, 1924, in a cheap Chicago hotel.

Purdue State Bank (1914), West Lafayette, Indiana; Louis Sullivan, Architect. Photo: Rosalie Shaul Schmitt, 1987.

William Krause Music Store (1922), Chicago; William C. Presto, Architect; facade design by Louis Sullivan. Photo: 1990.

Sullivan left a rich legacy to American architecture. He provided philosophical impetus, formulated compositional principles, and established ornamental models that inspired the Sullivanesque. However, he was not happy to see others profit from designs based on his work or make compromises when he would not. Nevertheless, imitation was an extension of Sullivan's efforts and much of this work was delightful and creative, even in the smallest, simplest buildings. The Sullivanesque style evolved from Sullivan's own creations and combined influences from former Sullivan employees, especially Purcell and Elmslie and, to a lesser extent, Frank Lloyd Wright. The impact of several Chicago terra-cotta companies and a host of other, mostly anonymous, architects has been overlooked. Through their efforts, the Sullivanesque proliferated, and Sullivanesque designs, usually incorporating stock terra-cotta ornament, could be found in scattered locales across the United States and even in Puerto Rico.

The Sullivanesque appeared in Puerto Rico through the adaptive efforts of Antonín Nechodoma (1877–1928). Born in Prague, Bohemia, Nechodoma grew up in Chicago, became a contractor, and built small stores and flats in a Bohemian neighborhood on Chicago's West Side. After a failed marriage, Nechodoma left Chicago in early 1905 for Jacksonville, Florida, where the city was rebuilding after the great fire of 1901. By 1907, Nechodoma had become a partner in the Jacksonville architectural firm of McClure, Holmes, and Nechodoma. However, virtually all of Nechodoma's clients and commissions were in Puerto Rico and, after a stay (1907–12) in the Dominican Republic, he relocated to Puerto Rico.[11]

Inspired by the Wasmuth portfolio of Frank Lloyd Wright's works, Nechodoma designed houses in the Prairie School style, but some of his nonresidential designs were Sullivanesque. He made liberal use of colorful decorative tiles for accents and pier capitals on many building facades, and these tilework patterns resembled flat Sullivanesque ornamental designs. When Nechodoma had a bank commission, he turned to Sullivan's work for inspiration. For the Bank of Nova Scotia (c. 1920) in San Juan, Nechodoma used decorative reliefs to flank the entrance, and these appeared as if they were from Sullivan's People's Savings and Loan Association Bank in Sidney, Ohio. The interior closely resembled that in Sidney, complete with ornamental designs and the same stylized urn atop a freestanding pier.[12]

Atlantic City, New Jersey, was the site of a 1924 apartment building designed in the Sullivanesque style by Seward G. Dobbins, Architect. The front facade was handsomely composed by the Atlantic City architect, who specified stock terra cotta (order no. 24307) from the Midland company.[13] The use of Midland terra cotta in the East was rare, given the shipping distance from Chicago and the numerous competing terra-cotta companies located on the East Coast. Only occasionally could buildings with Midland's Sullivanesque pieces be found there. Two such cases were a three-story commercial building (1923) designed by H. C. Davis for Honaker, Virginia, and the Mason County Bank in New Haven, West Virginia, a 1920 design by Baty and Halloran, Architects. However, these were not pure examples of the Sullivanesque, as other stylistic elements were mingled with Sullivanesque ornamentation.[14]

People in the southwestern United States maintained a strong interest in the Sullivanesque. Texas, especially, continued to be receptive to the style well into its second phase. Charles Erwin Barglebaugh, who had been a designer with the Dallas architecture firm of Lang and Witchell, formed his own architecture partnership around 1915. The firm of Griffith and Barglebaugh was responsible for the six-story First National Bank Building (1916) in Paris, Texas. This was a "classic" Sullivanesque design with exterior massing delineated by base, shaft, and cap. The structural bays were well defined and verticality was stressed by brick-clad piers that dominated the recessed spandrel panels and windows. The two street facades were clad in red brick and contrasting decorative terra cotta with a cream-colored glaze. However, the ornamentation was subdued; Sullivanesque terra cotta was most pronounced at the overhanging cornice.

Barglebaugh changed partners in 1916 and his last Sullivanesque design was in 1919, while in partnership with Lloyd R. Whitson. This was the seven-story Armor Building, now known as the Hogg Building, in Houston, Texas.[15] Upper stories of the building were for office use while the ground floor originally housed auto sales, although the building now has been converted to residential lofts. The facades are clad in brick and the piers are emphasized by decorative terra-cotta panels that align with the second-floor spandrel.

The San Antonio architecture firm of Atlee B. Ayres was responsible for a number of county courthouses in Texas with a range of Sullivanesque applications. These designs were actually by George Willis, a designer with the Ayres firm. Willis, who was with Frank Lloyd Wright for four years before moving to Dallas in 1902 and subsequently to San Antonio, was the designer for Atlee B. Ayres from 1910 to 1917. The Jim Wells County Courthouse (1912) in Alice, Texas, is perhaps the most faithful and attractive Sullivanesque realization of the group. Closely set piers, each capped with a stylized capital, define the main facade. All of the ornamentation is in cast concrete but is surprisingly effective considering the limitations of modeling in this material. Compromises detract from the Ayres firm's design for the Cameron County Courthouse (1912) at Brownsville. A Beaux-Arts exterior masks the interior grand rotunda with its art-glass skylight and Sullivanesque terra-cotta ornament. The Kleberg County Courthouse (1914) in Kingsville is a conservative but pleasant statement that features a Sullivanesque cartouche and stylized columns in terra cotta on an entry porch. In Refugio, the 1917 courthouse for the county of that same name may be the most successful exterior among these courthouses.[16] A centralized entry pavilion, capped by a large Sullivanesque cartouche, punctuates the facade and is the backdrop for an entry porch. The dominating ornament is the focus for the entire composition. Atop the building, exaggerated foliate patterns—subject to the limitations of the crude concrete material—create the interest and scale necessary to catch one's eye and finalize the composition.

The impact of the Midland Terra Cotta Company's own Sullivanesque designs and stock ornament reached Texas. Several buildings there are known to have been based on Midland design plates and used stock terra cotta with Sullivan-inspired motifs. Among these were the C. E. White Seed Company Building (1917) in Plainview, by L. A. Kevy, Architect; and the New Palace Theater (1925) in McAllen, by Fred D. Jacobs, Architect. The facade of the New Palace Theater featured a medallion assembly centered at the parapet with ancillary banding and ornament.[17] In addition, Waco, Texas, had a one-story automobile sales and garage building (1925) that utilized three Midland medallions.[18] Each Sullivanesque disc was centered above an arched entrance and capped the parapet. These entrances included a central pedestrian portal flanked by an entrance and an exit for automobiles. The architect for this building was Milton W. Scott.[19]

Some of the most eccentric architecture in America was designed by Bruce Goff (1904–82), who, early in his career, greatly admired Wright and Sullivan, with whom

Armor/Hogg Building (1919), Houston, Texas; Barglebaugh and Whitson, Architects. Photo: 1999.

he corresponded. Born in Alton, Kansas, Bruce Alonzo Goff began an architectural apprenticeship at age ten with the Tulsa, Oklahoma, firm of Rush, Endacott, and Rush.[20] In 1920, two years before he graduated from high school, Goff designed a mausoleum for Grant McCullough that was inspired by Sullivan's Getty Tomb. Goff's design of the tomb gates closely resembled Sullivan's famous bronze gates of the Getty. Goff's design for the Rush, Endacott, and Rush project (1922) for the Tulsa Chamber of Commerce Building was magnificent. The block-long Fifth Street elevation was masterfully composed and appointed with rich Sullivanesque ornament.[21]

Harry W. J. Edbrooke (1873–1946), an architect in Denver, Colorado, designed at least one major Sullivanesque building. His department store for A. T. Lewis and Son (1917) had a handsome facade fronting on Denver's Stout Street. Large expanses of window glass and decorative patterns of gleaming white Sullivanesque terra cotta provided a curtain-like wall cladding over the structural frame. The six-story building was renamed in 1933 after the Denver and Rio Grande Railroad acquired it to house its main office; the building has now been converted to residential lofts. Edbrooke had moved to Denver (c. 1908) after practicing alone in Chicago following the 1903 dissolution of the Atchison and Edbrooke architectural partnership.[22]

Small commercial buildings in the Sullivanesque style can be found in the Great Plains states. In Topeka, Kansas, there was the two-story McClintock Building, which housed C. M. Knowlton Drugs. This building had ornamental terra-cotta trim and distinctive columns set in the large window opening at the second story. This transitional design (c. 1911) was by N. P. Nielsen, a Topeka architect, and was published in the *Western Architect* (December 1911). The Lincoln School (1915–17), designed by William T. Schmitt, in Salina, Kansas, is a noteworthy design.[23] Terra-cotta ornament is well employed—especially as caps for the many pilasters. Distinctive Sullivanesque ornament from the Midland Terra Cotta Company can also be found in the Graham Building (1920), Muskogee, Oklahoma, by Dickman and Nieman, Architects, and in an addition to a hotel for T. F. Powers (1919), Fargo, North Dakota, by the architect William F. Kurke.[24] A 1919 apartment complex in Omaha, Nebraska, was a project of interest. This development had eight apartment buildings, each four stories high. Building entrances were flanked by brick pylons capped with decorative terra-cotta reliefs. Terra-cotta trim and accents for the brick facades completed Sullivanesque decorative elements. The complex was developed, designed, and constructed by the Drake Realty Company.[25]

The influence of the Midland company reached Kentucky as several architects used stock terra-cotta Sullivanesque ornament to complement their original designs. One example of this was a 1924 store with a second-floor flat, in Louisville, designed by local architects Weakley and Hawes.[26] Another Sullivanesque design in Louisville is the Olympic Building (1926), an apartment hotel designed by E. P. Lynch.[27] With projecting canopies and a well-composed array of terra-cotta features, this three-story yellow brick building is an attractive design. Although poorly maintained, the building is still

A. T. Lewis and Son Department
Store (1917), Denver, Colorado;
Harry W. J. Edbrooke, Architect.
Photo: 1999.

an important example of its genre. Several schools in Louisville were influenced by the Sullivanesque. Perhaps the most successful was the William R. Belknap School (c. 1916). The main elevations were well conceived while other portions of the building, such as the windowless end walls, were overworked with terra-cotta trim composed in abstract patterns intended to relieve otherwise blank walls. Much of the terra-cotta ornament, especially the large vertical ornamental reliefs, successfully replicated Sullivan's work, but some pieces were clumsy and heavy-handed.[28] The school was designed by J. Earl Henry (c. 1884–1919), a native of Urbana, Illinois, and a 1906 graduate of the University of Illinois. Henry moved to Louisville and worked for Brinton B. Davis before becoming the city architect for schools in 1912.[29]

Ernest Olaf Brostrom (1888–1968), a Kansas City architect, was an avid admirer of both Louis Sullivan and Frank Lloyd Wright. Born in Sweden, Brostrom immigrated to this country and worked in Sioux City, Iowa, for the firm of Eisentraut-Colby-Pottenger. Brostrom left Sioux City in 1907 to manage the firm's interests in Kansas City and stayed to open his own office.[30] Around 1921, Phillip T. Drotts joined Brostrom in partnership.[31] Brostrom, who had sought employment with Frank Lloyd Wright in 1910 and occasionally visited Louis Sullivan, tried to emulate their work.

Store and Flat (1924), Louisville, Kentucky; Weakley and Hawes, Architects. Photo: 1992.

Olympic Building (1926),
Louisville, Kentucky; E. P. Lynch,
Architect. Photo: 1993.

Brostrom's Rushton/Holsum Bakery (1919–20) in Kansas City, Kansas, and the Jensen-Salsbery Laboratories (1918–19), Kansas City, Missouri, were especially indebted to Frank Lloyd Wright's Larkin Building (1904). The Brostrom design most strongly influenced by Sullivan was the Peacock Apartments (1921) in Kansas City, Missouri. The complex consisted of two slab-like buildings, each nine stories high and connected only at the basement level. The two buildings were separated by an open courtyard at grade, approximately thirty-eight feet wide. A landscaped garden was developed in the front two-thirds of the court and a service yard with vehicular ramp down to underground parking occupied the rear third. One building was designed with square corners, the other with a rounded corner in response to its location at a street intersection, in a manner similar to Louis Sullivan's Schlesinger and Mayer Department Store in Chicago. Each apartment building was capped by a projecting band of ornate terra cotta, above which were brick parapet walls terminated by a coping of richly ornamented Sullivanesque terra cotta. The building with the rounded corner had a main entrance of paired doors carved into the curving stone base. The entry was surmounted by a terra-cotta relief of a peacock with spreading tail feathers. Another entrance, also capped with a peacock in terra cotta, was centrally located in the base of the square-cornered building. The complex was published in several professional journals at the time, including the *Western Architect*[32] and *American Builder*.[33] In a 1925 remodeling, Brostrom created a one-story link that joined the two buildings at ground level, and separate building entrances were abandoned as one entrance was constructed in the new connecting lobby. The arched entryway in the new barrel-vaulted lobby was circumscribed with Sullivanesque terra cotta.[34] The complex was renamed the Newbern Hotel, and the November 1927 issue of the *Western Architect* devoted several pages to the remodeled complex.[35]

Like their Chicago counterparts, terra-cotta companies in St. Louis made stock ornamental terra cotta. Some of this was in the Sullivanesque style and resembled decorative components from Chicago's Midland Terra Cotta Company. A number of small commercial buildings along St. Louis shopping streets had Sullivanesque terra cotta; however, the number was small compared to that in Chicago. The company that made the Sullivanesque stock terra cotta in St. Louis remains unidentified with any certainty, but it was likely the St. Louis Terra Cotta Company. Stock Sullivanesque terra cotta was used on three small commercial buildings along Cherokee Street in south St. Louis. A commercial building on nearby Gravois Avenue resembled a Sullivanesque design from a Midland catalog (Design No. 1, plate 47); however, the terra cotta was of local manufacture.[36] The small buildings on Cherokee Street are easy to overlook, but each has merit as an example of the use of the Sullivanesque to enhance simple commercial buildings. Terra-cotta accents with flecked gray glaze, which substituted for expensive granite, enliven the brick facade at 2744 Cherokee. Across the street, a very narrow Sullivanesque facade was an anomaly as a tiny addition to the white-glazed terra-cotta facade of Beaux-Arts classicism for the Cinderella Theater. A block away to the east, the 2646 Cherokee building has rich Sullivanesque ornament in various glazes of muted hues and deserves inspection.

In Cleveland, Ohio, the St. Clair Market epitomized the second-phase Sullivanesque. This 1917 structure, designed by the architect H. T. Jeffery, incorporated stock terra cotta and was based on design plates from the Midland Terra Cotta Company. Eight ornate medallions (no. 4508) were featured on the facade and were supplemented by terra-cotta accents.[37] Two other Ohio buildings constructed in 1917 featured Midland's stock Sullivanesque terra cotta. Both structures had narrow front facades. The Queen City Livery in Cincinnati had a terra-cotta name panel centered on the street facade. The architect Ben De Camp used decorative accents and two finials (no. 6501 B), one above each party-wall pier, to complete the composition of the upper facade. In Bucyrus, Ohio, the architect William Unger mixed Sullivanesque ornament with Gothic pieces for a three-story, twenty-four-foot-wide building for L. D. Pickering.[38]

Some Michigan architects used components of stock Sullivanesque ornament from the Midland Terra Cotta Company to create handsome variations on Midland's own facade studies. Several local architects apparently were so proud of their Sullivanesque designs that they moved their offices into the completed buildings. For example, the Kalamazoo architect M. C. J. Billingham located his office in the building he designed for the Kalamazoo Gazette-Telegraph (1916; demolished), and the architect George F. Bachman established offices in his F. P. Smith Building (1915) on Saginaw Street in Flint.[39] Other Sullivanesque designs in Michigan with Midland terra cotta included a one-story commercial building for Ben Harris (1921) in Stambaugh, by David E. Anderson, Architect; a five-story retail store (c. 1928) in Holland; and a two-story retail building (1923) in Niles, designed by the Kawneer Company, manufacturers of storefronts and glazing systems.[40] The Holland building has a colorful street facade decorated with cream-colored glazed tiles and ornamental terra cotta with a golden-beige glaze. Ornament includes a Midland medallion and a complement of accents. The large expanses of window glass had a pattern of mullions and smaller window lights, like transoms, which have since been replaced by scale-less fixed sheets of tinted glass.

Other buildings in Michigan were more individualistic and vivid examples of the Sullivanesque. These included the Wagner Baking Company plant (c. 1919) in Detroit, designed by the Chicago architectural firm of John Ahlschlager and Son; the First State Savings Bank/Farmers State Bank (1913) in Breckenridge; and a ground-floor storefront remodeling (c. 1916; architect unknown) of a nineteenth-century Italianate hotel at the southwest corner of Pearl and Campau Streets in Grand Rapids. The one-story Breckenridge bank building was designed by Joseph Rosatti of the Saginaw, Michigan, firm of Cowles and Mutscheller. Although remodeled, the building still displays some Elmslie-inspired terra cotta and leaded glass windows.[41] The terra-cotta column capitals of the storefront remodeling in Grand Rapids closely resembled those designed by Purcell and Elmslie, especially in the Edison Shop in Chicago.[42]

Minnesota was another state where the Sullivanesque had some acceptance and support, which can be primarily attributed to the efforts of two Minneapolis architectural firms and the admiration held for Louis Sullivan's Owatonna bank. The Minneapolis architects Kees and Colburn were among the first to embrace the Sullivanesque in its early phase. They soon turned away from it but were succeeded as leaders in progressive decorated design by Purcell and Elmslie. (See chapter 4 for discussion of the latter firm's work.) Minneapolis was the home of the *Western Architect*. For a time, this

Hotel remodeling (c. 1916), Grand Rapids, Michigan; architect unknown. This first-floor column capital resembles detail designs by Purcell and Elmslie. Photo: 1992.

publication frequently covered "contemporary" progressive design, including the Sullivanesque, and provided a forum for creative architects. Purcell and Elmslie frequently had articles published in the *Western Architect*, and entire issues were devoted to their work.

William L. Alban, a St. Paul, Minnesota, architect, was involved with the Prairie School movement and produced at least one important Sullivanesque design. A little-known but important Sullivanesque building (1924) was designed by Alban for the Skinner and Chamberlain Company in Albert Lea, Minnesota. This was a large department store, four stories in height, with a street facade five bays wide. Expression of the skeleton frame was the principal design statement for the exterior. However, Sullivanesque terra cotta was interwoven with the brick envelope, providing both counterpoint to and reinforcement of the structure.

The terra cotta that Alban employed was sculpted with Sullivanesque ornament and given colorful glazes in two colors, a warm ivory and a matte green. The terra cotta appears to have been stock from the American Terra Cotta and Ceramic Company; shop drawings were dated March 15, 1924.[43] The American company was noted for its green glaze, which had a silver-gray luster. This finish appears on the green terra-cotta pieces for Alban's building. Essentially, the terra cotta outlines the vertically dominant piers. Brick-clad spandrel panels were recessed and subordinate to the brick piers. Each spandrel carries three terra-cotta accents in a dot-dash-dot pattern. Ivory-colored terra-cotta

Skinner and Chamberlain Department Store (1924), Albert Lea, Minnesota; William L. Alban, Architect. Photo: 1994.

Schlesinger and Mayer/Carson Pirie Scott Department Store (1902–3), Chicago; Louis Sullivan, Architect.

Schlesinger and Mayer/Carson Pirie Scott Department Store (1902–3), Chicago; Louis Sullivan, Architect.

Union Trust Building (1892–93), St. Louis; Adler and Sullivan, Architects.

Advance Thresher Building (left, 1900) and Emerson-Newton Implement Company Building (right, 1904), Minneapolis; Kees and Colburn, Architects. Two buildings appear as one.

Opposite: Chamber of Commerce Building (1900–1902), now the Grain Exchange, Minneapolis; Kees and Colburn, Architects.

Auditorium Building (1894),
Portland, Oregon; F. Manson
White, Architect.

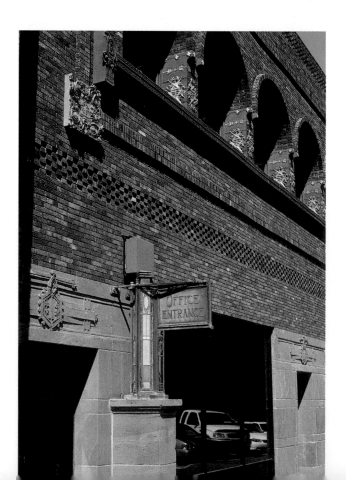

Oriental Block (1903), Seattle,
Washington; Bebb and Mendel,
Architects.

Detail, National Farmers' Bank
(1907–8), Owatonna, Minnesota;
Louis Sullivan, Architect.

Interior, National Farmers' Bank
(1907–8), Owatonna, Minnesota;
Louis Sullivan, Architect.

Detail, William Krause Music
Store (1922), Chicago;
William C. Presto, Architect;
facade design by Louis Sullivan.

Detail, People's Savings
and Loan Association Bank
(1917–18), Sidney, Ohio;
Louis Sullivan, Architect.

Lions over the entrance to
the People's Savings and
Loan Association Bank
(1917–18), Sidney, Ohio;
Louis Sullivan, Architect.

Detail, Skinner and Chamberlain Department Store (1924), Albert Lea, Minnesota; William L. Alban, Architect.

Detail, Independent Order of Odd Fellows Lodge Hall and Commercial Building (c. 1917), Rochester, Minnesota; architect unknown.

Detail, First National Bank (1913), Mankato, Minnesota; Ellerbe and Round, Architects.

Detail of upper facade, Iowa State
Bank (1913–14), Clinton, Iowa;
Jervis (Harry) R. Harbeck, Architect.

Terra-cotta ornament above entrance to Schall's Candy Company
Building (1917), Clinton, Iowa;
architect unknown.

accents alternate with brick and create a "dotted line" that traces the verticality of the piers. The end piers are circumscribed with continuous lines of terra cotta; however, the pieces alternate in color, creating another variation of the dotted line. The staccato rhythm of terra-cotta repetitions seemed to dominate the structure; however, from a distance, these stitch-like edgings of terra cotta strengthen the structural expression. Larger pieces of terra-cotta ornament, such as stylized capitals for the piers and Sullivanesque shields on the uppermost wall surface, join with the terra-cotta tracings to create a unified whole. Finally, an ornamental terra-cotta coping caps the uppermost wall segment, which aligns with the face of the piers.

The street facade of the Skinner and Chamberlain building had a base, shaft, and cap in the mode of Sullivan compositions. The building's strong structural expression created a framework of urban scale; at the same time, human scale and interest was created by the use of terra-cotta ornamental work. Although seemingly a dichotomy, the department store was both a contextual and a "foreground" building. It retains a stately image despite a remodeling of its ground-floor storefront and the addition of an aluminum sidewalk canopy. It still works well within the traditional frontages of South Broadway in downtown Albert Lea.

The use of ornamental terra-cotta trim in various colors of glaze to trace dotted lines on brick building facades, as in Alban's Albert Lea example, appeared earlier, in Rochester, Minnesota. The three-story Independent Order of Odd Fellows lodge hall and commercial building (c. 1917), at the northeast corner of First Avenue Southeast and Second Street Southeast, has exterior claddings of brick adorned by terra-cotta ornament and trim in green and cream. It was the work of an unknown architect (perhaps Alban?).

The First National Bank (1913) in Mankato was given a Sullivanesque design by Ellerbe and Round, Architects (a firm that successfully competed with Purcell and Elmslie for the commission).[44] Green-glazed terra cotta molded in Sullivan motifs was expertly utilized to cap the brick piers and provide human-scaled references for the building. Listed on the National Register of Historic Places, the building now has replacement windows and infill panels on the two-story commercial wing. Leaded glass windows in Sullivan-like patterns grace the bank wing. Another Sullivanesque building in Mankato has been demolished. The Zimmerman and Bangerter Building (1916) was designed by a Mankato architect, H. C. Gerlach, who had practiced architecture in Milwaukee before moving to Mankato (1913).[45] The narrow facade was entirely clad in white-glazed terra cotta. A segmented-arched window at the second story stretched across the facade and was capped by a Midland stock medallion.[46]

As in other midwestern states, the Midland Terra Cotta Company influenced designs for various commercial buildings in Minnesota. Among buildings based on Midland design plates and incorporating stock Sullivanesque terra cotta were a 1916 store for F. Werwerka in Blooming Prairie, which was the commission of the St. Paul architects Buechner and Orth; a 1922 garage, now demolished, for W. A. Tilden, St. Paul,

Shops and IOOF Lodge (c. 1917), Rochester, Minnesota; architect unknown. Detail of parapet ornament and decorative coping. Photo: 1994.

by John M. Alden, Architect; and the First National Bank (1917) in Luverne, by W. E. E. Green, Architect.[47] A photograph of the Luverne bank appeared in an advertisement for Midland in the *American Builder* (December 1918, p. 68); however, the building, town, and architect were not identified. The bank building now serves as the Luverene city hall.

Duluth, Minnesota, architects Bray and Nystrom seemed motivated by the examples of both Wright and Sullivan. But the work of Purcell and Elmslie, who reinterpreted Sullivan and Wright, was their major inspiration. For example, in the Manual Training School (1914) in Eveleth and the Horace Mann School (1914) in Virginia, Minnesota,

First National Bank (1913),
Mankato, Minnesota; Ellerbe and
Round, Architects. Photo: 1990.

Bray and Nystrom merged Wrightian geometric masonry ornament with Sullivanesque terra-cotta motifs, while the building forms seemed freer, like those of Purcell and Elmslie. The works of W. T. Bray and C. E. Nystrom were found in widely scattered small towns of northern Minnesota. Another northern Minnesota town, Aitkin, was the site of another Sullivanesque building (c. 1914) by an undocumented designer.[48]

The Telephone Exchange Building (1915) in Minneapolis, now converted to stores and offices, has two-story brick piers capped by terra-cotta ornament. It was designed by two Minneapolis architects, Downes and Eads.[49] A large seven-story warehouse (1917) for M. Burg and Sons, manufacturers and distributors of furniture, stoves, rugs, and draperies, was a prominent example of the Sullivanesque in St. Paul. Although massive and monumental, the front facade was inspired by Purcell and Elmslie's design of the Edison Shop in Chicago (see chapter 4). However, proportions were greatly altered. Whereas the Edison was narrow and emphasized the vertical, the Burg Building was wider than it was high. Spandrel panels and double-hung windows, which created bands of horizontal glazing, were repeated across the three central structural bays of the Burg Building to form an apparent long clear-span between the two massive piers. These two brick piers, capped with distinctive terra-cotta capitals, dominated the expansive glazing. A photograph of the building appeared in the *Western Architect* (September 1918, plate 6) and identified the architect as W. R. Wilson.[50]

One of the more significant Sullivanesque buildings in Minnesota is located diagonally opposite Louis Sullivan's National Farmers' Bank in Owatonna; the Minnesota Mutual Fire Insurance Company Building sits southeast of the bank. Built in 1922–23, the insurance office was designed by Jacobson and Jacobson. David and Nels Jacobson were brothers and their office was in Minneapolis. Their original Mankato insurance building was two stories high, with a hip roof and a raised basement.[51] Terra-cotta ornament was supplied by the American Terra Cotta and Ceramic Company (order no. 3232), while terra cotta for alterations and a rear addition (1929) came from the Indianapolis Terra Cotta Company, a subsidiary of American.[52] The building became the home office of a successor company, Federated Insurance Companies, and a 1949 remodeling, the first of many, by Magney and Tusler, Architects, removed the roof and

M. Burg and Sons Warehouse Building (1917), St. Paul, Minnesota; W. R. Wilson, Architect. Photo: 1989.

added a third floor.[53] Although Jacobson and Jacobson's original building has been altered, it is still a responsive companion to Louis Sullivan's nearby bank building.

Many of the late examples of the Sullivanesque style were built in Iowa, and half of Sullivan's final ten commissions were constructed within the state. At one time, Sioux City had a large inventory of Sullivanesque designs. Many of these buildings were designed by the Sioux City architect William L. Steele (see chapter 4). In addition, there were Sullivanesque structures in Sioux City for which identification of the architect has been lost, although some of these may have been designed by Steele as well. Among this number is a three-story commercial building at 512 Fourth Street, still extant, clad entirely in white-glazed terra cotta and richly ornamented in Sullivanesque patterns.[54] A similar three-story building (c. 1918; demolished c. 1972) housed Raymond's Clothing on the ground level and the Hill Hotel above. The street facade was composed of white terra cotta and glass with a parapet panel and projecting cornice with repeating patterns of foliate ornament. Next door was another three-story building which housed Morey's and People's Hotel (c. 1920; demolished), but it had a brick facade with contrasting ornament and trim in terra cotta. Banding of terra cotta was aligned with the

Minnesota Mutual Fire Insurance Building (1922–23), now Federated Insurance Company, Mankato, Minnesota; Jacobson and Jacobson, Architects. Entrance of original building. Photo: 1990.

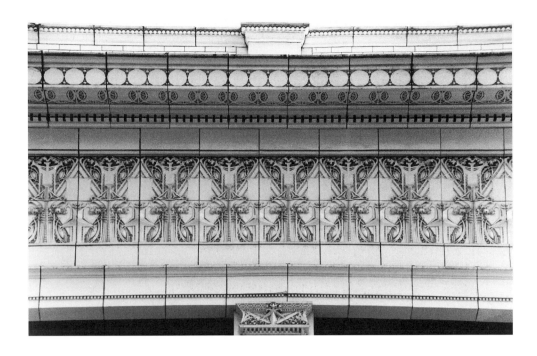

512 Fourth Street (c. 1920), Sioux City, Iowa; architect unknown. Detail of terra-cotta ornament. Photo: 1994.

third-floor window head and was punctuated by an ornate medallion centered on each of four brick-clad structural piers. Although the medallion design resembled that from the Midland company's standard stock, it was from a different manufacturer.[55]

Louis Sullivan's Van Allen Building in Clinton, Iowa, had an impact on one local architect, John H. Ladehoff. Ladehoff established his practice in 1907, but until 1915 his work was uninspired, although he had secured some prestigious commissions in Clinton.[56] With the completion of Sullivan's Van Allen Building in 1915, Ladehoff embraced Sullivan's style. The Henry Pahl Building (1915) in Clinton was the first of Ladehoff's Sullivanesque designs. In addition to Sullivan's in-town model, inspiration came from the Midland Terra Cotta Company. The company supplied the terra cotta for the Pahl Building, and in its order records, under the column where the architect's name should have been, there is the notation "our sketch."[57] However, the Midland shop drawing, dated April 16, 1915, clearly identified the architects as Ladehoff and Sohn.[58] Just as Sullivan had designed facades for other architects' buildings (examples include the Gage, for Holabird and Roche, and the Krause Music Store, for William C. Presto) Midland probably designed the street facade for Ladehoff and Sohn's building. But there is little question about the basis for the front elevation, as it resembled plate 36, design number 1, from a Midland catalog.[59] This Midland design illustrated a facade clad entirely in terra cotta with alternating wide and narrow bandings. The Pahl Building has similar terra-cotta facings but the facade is wider in overall dimension (47' 11") than that shown in the catalog plate. This increase in width required different fenestration, and the terra-cotta bandings and string courses were simply extended accordingly. The cartouche that jutted above the parapet varied slightly from that illustrated but was still based on a Midland stock unit, which in turn was based on an interior ornamental lintel from Louis Sullivan's Owatonna bank. The Midland piece was custom-

Morey's and People's Hotel (c. 1920; demolished c. 1972), Sioux City, Iowa; architect unknown. Photo: 1968.

ized by the addition of the name of the building, "Pahl," inscribed with a blue glaze over stock white.

Ladehoff and Sohn's next built Sullivanesque structure resembled the two-story design in Midland advertisements, which appeared in the *American Contractor and Builder* for February and March 1915. The advertisement included elevation drawings of Midland's design number 2 from catalog plate 36. This adaptation was for the F. G. Sullivan Building in the Illinois town of Savanna, on the Mississippi River, fifteen miles upstream from Clinton, Iowa. Again, the building constructed was wider than that shown on the drawing plate; otherwise the terra-cotta ornament, set in a field of brick, was exactly the same as advertised. Obviously, Ladehoff chose to forgo an original facade design in favor of Midland's advertised special offer: "To Introduce Your Locality— Midland Stock White Terra Cotta."[60] The building, deteriorated but still standing, has survived as few examples have, without major facade alterations. The storefront is intact and includes prism glass (Luxfer?) above the plate glass display windows.

A third Sullivanesque example by Ladehoff and Sohn exhibited more originality. The design of the front facade for the two-story Snow White Drug Store (1917) was not a direct adaptation of a Midland plate although stock terra cotta from the Midland company was utilized.[61] Ladehoff combined white-glazed Sullivanesque ornament with exterior walls of white-glazed brick. The pristine effect of the white-enameled glazing must have been a powerful advertisement as well as functional environment for the Snow White Drug Store. The gleaming surfaces and self-cleaning qualities of glazed ornament and brick must have been a welcome contrast to the usual conditions at that time, wherein already grimy surroundings were darkened with coal soot. The interior was a pristine white as well.[62] Although Ladehoff contributed to an inventory of Sullivanesque buildings, the partnership of Ladehoff and Sohn struggled. With few commissions, the firm was dissolved in 1917.[63]

In addition to Sullivan's Van Allen Building and Ladehoff's known designs, Clinton has several other Sullivanesque buildings. The Iowa State Bank (1913–14) was designed by the architect Jervis (Harry) R. Harbeck with custom terra cotta supplied by the Midland Terra Cotta Company.[64] Harbeck was an obscure figure. Until 1903, he was with the Chicago architect Henry W. Tomlinson, whose office was in Steinway Hall and who formerly was a partner with Frank Lloyd Wright.[65] Harbeck left Chicago for Detroit in 1903. He had relatives in Lyons, Iowa, now part of Clinton, and that connection must have helped to secure the 1913 bank commission.[66] The structural bays

Henry Pahl Building (1915), Clinton, Iowa; Ladehoff and Sohn, Architects. Detail of terra-cotta facings and ornament. Photo: 1980.

of the two-story Iowa State Bank were defined by brick piers, each capped with terra-cotta ornament. Each bay was further identified by terra-cotta trim that angled upward from each pier cap and suggested a stylized pediment; an ornate terra-cotta medallion was positioned at the high point of each superimposed pediment. A rear addition was constructed in 1931 and a 1961 expansion resulted in a remodeling with the entrance relocated to the adjacent new construction.

The two-story building for Schall's Candy Company, Clinton, was distinguished by large and intricate Sullivanesque ornament above the central entrance bay. The architect's name is not known although the contractor for the 1917 building was Haring Brothers.[67] The decorative terra-cotta assembly was comprised of pieces with polychrome glazes and was expertly modeled. The quality and delicacy of this exterior terra-cotta work was rare and seemingly matched the admired quality of interior faience from such noted arts and crafts pottery companies as Rookwood or Grueby. Unfortunately, the building appearance has been marred by the replacement of the original large windows.

Iowa State Bank (1913–14), Clinton, Iowa; Harry R. Harbeck, Architect. The original entrance has been removed. Photo: 1980.

Sullivanesque interpretations based on designs of the Midland Terra Cotta Company were scattered throughout Iowa. George W. Washburn, a Burlington architect, closely replicated the storefront design from the Midland catalog plate 83 when he designed Bock's Florist (1924) in his home city. He duplicated second-story terra-cotta bandings, to reinforce the horizontality of a continuous window, and ornamental features set in the predominantly brick facade. A stock medallion, with supplemental features to create a horizontal elongation, was the culminating focus positioned on the upper wall surface. The Midland company served as the architect for the D. Milligan Company Building (1915; now demolished) in Jefferson, Iowa.[68] The Bagley and Beck Building (1927–28) in Mason City, Iowa, was also inspired by Midland's plate 83. Designed by Karl M. Waggoner of the Mason City architectural firm of Hansen and Waggoner, the building was less than a block away from Frank Lloyd Wright's City National Bank and Park Inn (1910).[69] The Bagley and Beck Building was better known as the local J. C. Penney store, as that retailer occupied the premises upon the building's completion and until the structure was engulfed by construction of an indoor shopping mall that replaced the street.[70]

Other Sullivanesque designs in Iowa, with Midland's stock ornament, included the Farmers Store (1919) in Charter Oak, designed by Edgar L. Barber, an architect from Denison, Iowa; the Smith Brothers Building (1915) in Burt, H. R. Cowan, Architect; and the Joseph Fuhrman Building (1922; demolished) in Dubuque, by J. F. Leitha, Architect.[71] There were many other utilitarian buildings that made token use of terra-cotta ornament, mostly as small accents in brick facades and, often, seemingly scattered without apparent order. Occasionally, there was a Sullivanesque design that was individualistic rather than merely the result of a Midland prescription. Such was the case for the Laurel Building (c. 1916), Muscatine. The six-story building was inspired by Chicago School and Sullivanesque imagery. Despite its originality, the design was not entirely satisfactory because the Sullivan-like ornament was intermixed with severe geometric decorative elements and the facade was awkwardly proportioned. With a high base (the sloping site contributes to this excessively tall base), narrow corner piers, and varying upper-story window heights, the building's proportions needed better resolution.[72] In summary, the Sullivanesque, like its domestic-scale counterpart, the Prairie School, was well represented in Iowa. The most important designs were by Chicago architects brought in by local developers. A greater number of representative but less adventuresome designs were the work of local architects who attempted to apply the message from Chicago.

In addition to Iowa and Minnesota, Wisconsin had an active Sullivanesque movement. The Wisconsin buildings designed by Louis Sullivan were the Grand Opera House remodeling (1890; demolished 1895 after fire; Adler and Sullivan, Architects) in Milwaukee; the Josephine Crane Bradley Residence (1908–9), Madison; and the Farmers' and Merchants' Union Bank (1919), Columbus.[73] Purcell and Elmslie designed a number of structures in Wisconsin. However, most of these commissions were for houses. The nonresidential structures, except for one, were simple and included a church community house in Eau Claire, the Jump River Town Hall, and a land office in Stanley. The exception was the important First National Bank in Rhinelander.[74] Claude and Starck, who lived and practiced in Madison, were the most prolific Sullivanesque designers in Wisconsin. Of course, Frank Lloyd Wright returned to his family's land near Spring Green after twenty-three years in Chicago and Oak Park. By the time Wright returned to Wisconsin, he had emerged from Sullivan's shadow and his architecture was identified as his own. The Wisconsin building designed by Wright that most resembled the Sullivanesque was the A. D. German Warehouse (1917–21) in Richland Center. The brick massing and use of ornamentation seemed consistent with the intent of the Sullivanesque but Wright's ornament was rectilinear, derived from Mayan forms and cast in concrete.[75]

Purcell and Elmslie's Edison Shop in Chicago was an inspiration to many architectural designers. The Masonic Temple (c. 1916) in Prairie du Sac, Wisconsin, is a two-story version of it, built on a limited budget and with crude "homemade" ornament. A sophisticated imitation is located in Racine, Wisconsin, the four-story Badger Building (1915) designed by Edmund B. Funston for M. Tidyman. In this building, as in Purcell and Elmslie's design, brick surfaces framed a large opening, which had two brick piers set within it and spaced near opposite wall segments. In addition, terra-cotta ornament was used in similar fashion, for capitals atop the brick piers and for an ornate cluster, with complementary accents, centered on the parapet wall. The terra cotta was custom-made by the Midland Terra Cotta Company (order no. 5222).[76] There were major differences between the Edison Shop and the Badger Building. The latter was wider and had five small, equal-spaced brick piers that subdivided the horizontal window opening into individual sash openings. These windows have been replaced and the ground-floor front altered; otherwise the building retains its original handsome appearance. Although Edmund Bailey Funston, an alumnus (1892) of the University of Illinois, was credited as the architect of the Badger Building, some local residents say the building was designed by Frank Hoffmann, a 1914 graduate in architecture from the University of Illinois and a Racine native.[77]

The building for the A. L. Gebhardt and Company (c. 1918), Milwaukee, was another Wisconsin structure inspired by Purcell and Elmslie. It was designed by architect Clare C. Hosmer. Three stories high and narrow, the building had a street facade with two piers that acted as large mullions and divided the window glazing into three openings, a large central sash and flanking narrow sashes—like a gigantic Chicago window. Terra-cotta ornament included pier capitals and an ornate cluster centered on the parapet. Unlike in the Edison Shop, the piers for Hosmer's design didn't rise from the ground but started at the second-floor windowsill. Thus, the storefront was wide and unobstructed, but modulation of the facade by the piers was compromised. Hosmer's architectural rendering for the Gebhardt Building was displayed at the Thirty-first Annual Chicago Architectural Exhibition (1918) at the Art Institute of Chicago and

Badger Building (1915), Racine, Wisconsin; E. B. Funston, Architect. Photo: 1993.

appeared in the exhibition catalog.[78] Furthermore, it was published in the *Western Architect* (May 1918).

In November 1913, the *Western Architect* published a Sullivanesque design for a three-story store and office building designed by Percy Dwight Bentley (1885–1968). Bentley's design of the street facade for the Odin J. Oyen Building (1913), 507 Main Street, La Crosse, Wisconsin, featured terra cotta that framed the ground-floor storefront, the brick superstructure, and the pent roof at the parapet. Second- and third-floor windows were grouped into one horizontal opening per floor; the second-story opening dominated as two slender columns, similar to Sullivan's column designs for his Cedar Rapids, Iowa, bank, were positioned to divide the window into a 1:2:1 proportion. A small but important decorative cartouche was centered at the third-floor windowsill and provided a focus to balance the composition. The pent roof, with tile roofing and supporting brackets, was a strong horizontal element that helped cap the building and gave a domestic air, perhaps Bentley's attempt to relate the commercial building to his noted Prairie School residential designs.[79]

Architects were encouraged to try the Sullivanesque by various publications, terra-cotta company promotions, and built examples. Not all attempts were entirely successful. Some designers, not fully understanding the style or too involved in eclecticism, mixed styles of ornament. Occasionally, colorful glazes were substituted for standard white on stock terra-cotta pieces. Then the color seemed sometimes to overwhelm the shallow reliefs of the embellishments. Such was the case for a three-story commercial building and theater in Fond du Lac, which had colorful glazes for mixed styles of ornament, including Sullivanesque motifs. The composition of the facade for this building generally followed Sullivanesque principles and the terra-cotta hues sparkled, but the mixed styles of terra-cotta ornament were a distraction as unity became confused and clarity was lost. A similar effect occurred in the treatment of Zahn's Department Store (1914) in Racine, although the terra cotta was of stock white glaze. The composition of the building's three exposed facades followed Sullivanesque principles, but the stylistic origins of the decorative terra cotta varied. William F. Burfiend was the architect for the retailing structure, which has subsequently suffered from unsympathetic alterations.[80]

Promotional efforts of Chicago's Midland Terra Cotta Company had success in Wisconsin. A number of buildings had stock terra cotta supplied by Midland. In addition, Midland acted as the architect for some Sullivanesque designs, including the O. A. Hilgerman Building (1917) in Rhinelander and the Graham Building (1926) in Kenosha. Midland terra cotta appeared on Sullivanesque buildings such as a Green Bay community building (1921) by F. C. Klawiter, Architect; the two-story Butter Building, Milwaukee; and a building for the Jandrey Grove Company (1915), 124 West Wisconsin in Neenah. Designed by Sindahl-Matheson, Architects, the Jandrey Grove Building has a street facade clad in white-glazed brick and integrated terra-cotta ornamental motifs. The ground-floor exterior has been remodeled, but for once, changes did not substantially detract from the original design.[81] E. A. Juul, a Sheboygan, Wisconsin, architect, designed some Sullivanesque buildings with Midland's stock terra cotta. These included a store (1919) in Sheboygan; a two-story commercial structure for William F. Christen (1921; slated for demolition) in Valders; and the Curtis Hotel (1922; demolished) in Plymouth. William J. Raeuber was a Manitowoc architect who designed several Sullivanesque buildings in that Wisconsin city and employed Midland stock terra cotta. Unfortunately, his exceptional Commerce Building (1925) has been demolished and only a simple store building (c. 1926) remains.[82]

In Indiana, Clifford Shopbell and Company was one of the first architectural firms to experiment with the early twentieth-century progressive design movements emanating from Chicago. Clifford Shopbell (1871–1939) was born in Princeton, Indiana, and first worked for the Evansville and Terre Haute Railroad before associating with several architectural firms in Indianapolis.[83] Shopbell relocated to Evansville, Indiana, and formed a partnership with Will J. Harris in 1897.[84] Shopbell strove to create progressive designs, and five of his houses were published in various 1907 issues of *Keith's Magazine*. The journal was based in Minneapolis, supported the arts and crafts movement, and was similar to Gustav Stickley's magazine, *The Craftsman*.[85] When Harris died (October 9, 1909), the firm became Clifford Shopbell and Company. The Sullivanesque and Prairie School appeared more frequently and with greater success in subsequent Shopbell designs.[86] For example, Shopbell used Sullivanesque terra cotta from the Midland Terra Cotta Company for alterations and additions to the Fellwock Automobile Company (1922) of Evansville. The design for the building facade featured paired Midland lunettes positioned at the parapet and centered on the seventy-five-foot-wide frontage to the street.[87]

Shopbell's Sullivanesque designs culminated in 1924 with the Bozeman-Waters National Bank in Poseyville, Indiana. The terra-cotta ornamental pieces came from the Indianapolis Terra Cotta Company. As noted earlier, the Indianapolis firm was a subsidiary of the American Terra Cotta and Ceramic Company, which had supplied terra cotta for Louis Sullivan's People's Savings and Loan Association Bank (1917–18) in Sidney, Ohio.[88] The Poseyville bank was in fact modeled on Sullivan's design, and some terra-cotta pieces may have been duplicates of those on the Sidney building. The side (Locust Street) elevation of the Poseyville bank was virtually a mirror image of Sullivan's bank. For the front (West Main Street) facade, the architect used a simple adaptation of the side of the building. Over the years and despite changes in the building's occupants, the exterior has retained its integrity; major exterior alterations have involved only changes in signage. The interior has not fared as well, however. A suspended ceiling has destroyed the original high banking space, and large stained glass windows in the west exterior wall have been covered. The Shopbell designer for the Poseyville bank was Edward J. Thole, a native of Evansville, Indiana. Thole's collegiate studies were at the Massachusetts Institute of Technology. Thole admired Sullivan and this admiration resulted in the design at Poseyville.[89] Thole became a principal in the Clifford Shopbell firm in 1924 and the firm name was changed to Shopbell, Fowler, and Thole; but by 1931, the partnership had been dissolved and each architect had his own practice.[90]

Other Sullivanesque examples in Indiana include the Toner Store (1915) in Martinsville, designed by the Midland Terra Cotta Company (and discussed further in chapter 6). Midland's influence on the Sullivanesque in Indiana was strong. Most of the remaining Sullivanesque representations in the state incorporated that company's stock components as architects followed the company's design recommendations. The four-story Williams Building (1916) in Indianapolis, by J. Edwin Kopf, Architect, is a handsome structure using stock terra cotta. One of the most successful Midland-influenced designs was a store building (1922) for G. Rizos in Fort Wayne, designed by John M. E. Riedel of that city. Another example in Fort Wayne was the Joseph Kaplan Building (1925), A. M. Strauss, Architect. South Bend, Indiana, had several good examples of stock Sullivanesque but only a two-story commercial building at 224 Colfax survives. A three-story Sullivanesque building, 122 South Michigan, has been drastically remodeled; only a few terra-cotta ornamental pieces remain visible. The South Bend Tribune Building (c. 1920) has Gothic forms and decorative effects merged with Sullivanesque-like ornament. The architects were Austin, Shambleau, and Wiser. Similarly, ornament in

Bozeman-Waters National Bank (1924), Poseyville, Indiana; Clifford Shopbell and Company, Architects. Shopbell's Sullivanesque design, at the left, contrasts with the classical facade of a competing bank on the right, along Main Street. Photo: 1992.

mixed styles, but with colorful glazes, embellished a theater (1923) for Roy Robleder in nearby Mishawaka. Designed by Myrle E. Smith, the theater is threatened with demolition.[91]

As one could expect, the Sullivanesque had representation in Illinois beyond Chicago and the suburbs. However, the caliber of design and the number of buildings were not exceptional. The talents of Sullivanesque designers from Chicago, such as Sullivan or Elmslie, were not utilized in the state beyond the metropolitan region. Similarly, with the possible exception of Frank Lloyd Wright, who had commissions in Decatur, Dwight, Peoria, and Springfield, and Walter Burley Griffin, with projects in Anna and Edwardsville, Chicago architects espousing "modern" design had difficulty in securing commissions in Illinois communities beyond suburban Chicago. Why did progressive Chicago architects have such little statewide influence? Perhaps it was due to the conservative nature of "downstate" business people as well as the friction that historically existed between metropolitan Chicago and the rest of the state of Illinois. The impetus for building in the Sullivanesque style in Illinois stemmed primarily from the Midland Terra Cotta Company. The company served as architect for some commissions in downstate cities, including Galesburg, Peoria, and Rockford. More important, design models and stock terra cotta from the Midland company provided inspiration and the means for local architects to adapt the Sullivanesque. Therefore, the style appeared in various communities statewide during the later stages of the Sullivanesque movement. The designers for these Sullivanesque buildings were almost always local architects who were well known in their respective communities.[92]

The Galesburg, Illinois, architectural firm of Aldrich and Aldrich was responsible for many buildings in that city. The firm sometimes employed terra cotta in its work and experimented with the Sullivanesque. Norman Kellogg Aldrich had maintained a practice in Galesburg for years and was responsible for many of the elaborate area homes in the Queen Anne style.[93] His son, Harry Glen Aldrich (1889–1973), graduated in 1913 from the University of Illinois, apprenticed in St. Louis, and returned to Galesburg to join his father in partnership as Aldrich and Aldrich, Architects.[94] Harry infused some new thinking into the firm's design approach. Conservatively at first, the Aldriches introduced ornamental accents in the Sullivan vein into straightforward but well-proportioned building facades. These small reliefs brightened what would otherwise have been bland buildings. The small Tate Hardware store in Knoxville and the large Princeton Hotel in Princeton, Illinois, were the first designs (1915) in which the firm utilized this approach. Similar expressions were repeated in the next two years for four buildings in Galesburg.

In 1917, Aldrich and Aldrich designed their most attractive Sullivanesque building. Completed in 1918, the three-story structure was built for the McCollum Brothers Candy Company, Galesburg. The street facade has brick exterior walls, steel factory-sash windows, and Sullivanesque terra-cotta ornamentation. Symmetrically composed, the street facade comprises three bays stretched between massive piers that anchor each end of the facade. A medallion of Sullivanesque ornament from the Midland Terra Cotta Company terminates the upper reaches of each end pier. The central bay differs from the flanking ones by accommodating an entry and stairway landings that forced the spandrel panels out of alignment with those of the adjacent bays. A gable-like parapet with a decorative disc and supplemental terra-cotta pieces caps the center bay while terra-cotta trim circumscribes the upper wall panels for each bay. All of the terra cotta has a special cream-colored glaze that was "warmer" than Midland's standard stock white. The front elevation of the candy factory was handled with a deft touch and, within the framework of the Sullivanesque and its appointed ornament, the integrity of the structure was reinforced and enriched.

Aldrich and Aldrich integrated Sullivanesque terra cotta with brick for the street facade of a three-story building (1920) for the Moose Lodge in Farmington, Illinois; the building now houses a theater featuring live performances. The Folley Mortuary (1925) in Galesburg looks like a typical two-story store building with terra-cotta ornament inset in the brickwork. Aldrich and Aldrich worked with designs incorporating terra cotta until 1925, but none captured the vitality of the firm's 1917 candy factory.[95] The architects then returned to the eclectic design approach so prevalent at the time.

The architect John Hanifen's Sullivanesque work was localized mostly in the Illinois River towns of LaSalle and Ottawa, Illinois. John Walker Hanifen (1886–1938) attended the University of Illinois from 1905 to 1907.[96] After three years of partnership, Hanifen opened his own practice in Ottawa, Illinois, in 1916.[97] Over the next ten years, Hanifen occasionally employed Sullivanesque design principles and terra-cotta ornament for some small commercial structures. Most of these were interspersed along First Street, the retail spine of downtown LaSalle, Illinois. Hanifen's design (1921; demolished) of the front facade for a small building at 636 First Street utilized intricate brickwork and terra-cotta insets that had a deceptively simple but elegant presence. Built for Max Erlenborn, a mortician, the building had a functional arrangement that was consistent with the period's typical ground-floor shop and second-floor dwelling unit.[98] Hanifen's design for a one-story store and gas station (1924; demolished 1989) for Mrs. Jane E. Skelly was highlighted by an ornamental assembly of Sullivanesque terra cotta based on catalog plate 83 from the Midland Terra Cotta Company.[99]

Unlike the Skelly building, which featured a dominant Sullivanesque focal piece, three shops designed by Hanifen had facades laced with linear terra-cotta trim of Sullivanesque reliefs. Two of these buildings were in LaSalle and one in Ottawa. For the John Cummings store (1924) in LaSalle and the Jordan Hardware (1919) in Ottawa, Hanifen utilized Midland stock terra cotta. For the McLellan Company Store (1926) at 735 First Street, LaSalle, Hanifen employed ornamental linear elements as repeated verticals spaced approximately five feet apart.[100] These verticals strips were formed by terra-cotta trim pieces that served as mullions at the second-story windows and defined separate panels of brick on the upper wall. As with all of Hanifen's buildings in LaSalle, the original design has been compromised through "modernizations."

Two additional buildings on First Street in LaSalle are attributed to Hanifen. One is a two-story grocery market distinguished by upper-story brick pilasters supported on haunches of ornamental Sullivanesque terra cotta. The Fitch Laundry (c. 1924) is considerably more attractive. The street facade of this two-story building is a satisfying design. Midland terra cotta is employed with a judicious use of only two Sullivanesque ornament assemblies. These terra-cotta pieces form stylized capitals for two brick piers that frame the central bay. The capitals have a rare, warm mottled-gray glaze that simulates granite. Additional terra cotta, with the same "granite" finish, forms a base or watertable for the building while linear pieces frame the field of fenestration and outline the exterior edges of the facade. Small round windows are positioned at opposite ends of the facade to accentuate the entry doors to second-floor offices. A warm cream-colored face brick is employed for the spandrel cladding, dominant wall surfaces, and piers. Well proportioned and orderly, the facade demonstrates that the Sullivanesque

McCullom Brothers Candy Company (1917), Galesburg, Illinois; Aldrich and Aldrich, Architects. Photo: 1991.

could be a point of departure for an individualized aesthetic statement; at the same time, the facade treatment suggests the art deco style. Despite fenestration changes and other alterations, the building shows that the Sullivanesque may have provided a language for ready translation to the later art deco or art moderne styles.

In addition to Sullivanesque buildings in downstate Illinois by Aldrich and Aldrich, John Hanifen, and the Midland Terra Cotta Company, other Sullivanesque designs appeared in cities and towns such as Albany, Champaign, Eldorado, Freeport, Hoopeston, Kankakee, Paris, Peoria, Rochelle, Rockford, Savanna, and Springfield.

A tiny structure for the First Trust and Savings Bank (1921) in Albany, a small town on the Illinois side of the Mississippi River, was strongly influenced by Louis Sullivan's bank designs. The use of tapestry brick and terra-cotta accents, in Sullivanesque patterns and with green and ochre glazes, was an attempt to echo Sullivan's designs and make the small building more meaningful. Here, the colorful glazes add luster to the "stock" Midland pieces. Designed by J. G. Legel and Company, Architects, the one-story bank building has been converted to house the town's public library.[101]

Kankakee had several Sullivanesque buildings. The Lawrence Babst Building (1918) was designed by Leonard F. W. Stuebe. Stuebe was a 1903 graduate of the University of Illinois and a Danville, Illinois, architect who was noted for his designs of Prairie School houses.[102] Other Sullivanesque buildings in Kankakee were by anonymous designers. A store with second-floor apartments at 256 Merchant Street had decorative terra-cotta accents positioned within the brick facade. A 1923 garage structure, now demolished, had Midland stock ornament (order no. 23114). Another garage (1923) also featured Midland stock terra cotta. Although this garage has been remodeled, the decorative terra cotta still sparkles and enhances the street frontage opposite the county courthouse.[103]

Another Sullivanesque building opposite a county courthouse can be seen on the south side of the square in Paris, Illinois. The facade of the two-story commercial structure for M. Pearman (1924) was like a curtain wall. Large expanses of glazing (display windows, a prism-glass [Luxfer?] clerestory, and paired Chicago windows at the second floor) were combined with minimal solid surfaces of masonry. The masonry work was, in turn, reduced in apparent weight and solidity by terra-cotta ornamental patterns composed within the field of brick. A Midland medallion (no. 4508) combined with a vertical "stem" (no. 4507) became the primary ornamental feature. Similarly, a variation of the basic Midland medallion was the primary ornamental motif on a now demolished commercial building at 707–11 Adams Street Southwest in Peoria.[104]

In addition to the public library by Claude and Starck (see chapter 4), the town of Rochelle, Illinois, has another Sullivanesque example. This is the two-story Bert Comstock Building (1915), designed by the Rockford architects Peterson and Johnson.[105] Edward A. Peterson and Gilbert A. Johnson formed their partnership in 1914 and it endured until 1931.[106] Another Sullivanesque design by Peterson and Johnson is a two-story building for Martin W. Floberg (1923), Rockford. There, red brick was complemented by the white glaze of Midland's stock terra cotta. A cartouche of floral reliefs (no. 5286), based on Sullivan's Owatonna bank model, was centrally located at the roof parapet. Sculpted lion's heads similar to those by Sullivan flanked the large cartouche, and other accents were spotted in a rhythmic pattern about the upper walls.[107]

Virtually all of the Sullivanesque examples in downstate Illinois depend on use of the Midland Terra Cotta Company's stock ornament. However, several buildings display stock Sullivanesque terra cotta made by others, and more may be discovered. This ornament is similar to that of Chicago's Midland company but has decided variations. A commercial building (1928) on Broadway in Alton, Illinois, a suburban St. Louis community, exhibits this terra cotta on a small scale. The town of Wordon, seventeen miles east of Alton, has a school building (c. 1923) with similar decorative terra cotta. The Wordon Elementary School, designed by the Edwardsville architect Michael B. Kane, is a two-story brick mass relieved by terra-cotta decorative bandings and accents. Given the proximity of the examples, it is likely that the supplier of the terra cotta was the St. Louis Terra-Cotta Company.[108]

The availability of stock terra cotta and the examples of catalog plates encouraged anonymous architects to create their own Sullivanesque designs. A large number of designers tried this in various locations across the country, although by World War I continued application occurred in just a few midwestern states. Concurrently, a small number of talented architects—almost exclusively former employees of Louis Sullivan—struggled on with their practices and their own interpretations of the Sullivanesque.

CHAPTER 4

SULLIVAN'S FORMER EMPLOYEES

TWO EMPLOYEES of Louis Sullivan emerged from his office to lead the way to a modern American architecture. Both had enormous talents. One was self-confident and tended toward arrogance while the other was quiet and retiring. The first acknowledged a debt to Sullivan but evolved another expression that, in turn, provoked imitation. The second continued his homage to Sullivan and eventually drifted into virtual obscurity. The two were Frank Lloyd Wright and George Grant Elmslie.

Frank Lloyd Wright, a former principal assistant for Adler and Sullivan, claimed he was never Sullivan's disciple or pupil but "a capable workman who understood the man he served."[1] Wright's assertion may have been overstated as he did learn from Sullivan; in that sense, he was a pupil. Ultimately, the pupil may have surpassed the master. However, after Wright left Adler and Sullivan in a disagreement, Wright's first independent commissions were indebted to Sullivan's aesthetic. Wright initiated his architectural designs in the Sullivanesque vocabulary but soon developed his own distinct style. Generally recognized and self-proclaimed as America's greatest architect, Frank Lloyd Wright (1869–1959) has been the subject of dozens of books and hundreds of articles. Therefore, a review of his life and work is not needed here. However, an examination of Wright's Sullivanesque roots and evolutionary beginnings is appropriate.

A native of Wisconsin, Wright studied engineering at the University of Wisconsin but left school and relocated to Chicago.[2] He soon found employment in the architectural office of Joseph Lyman Silsbee.[3] Silsbee's commissions were primarily residential and his buildings were usually in a geometrical but picturesque Queen Anne style with wood shingle claddings. In late fall 1887, Wright joined the firm of Adler and Sullivan.[4] Wright soon became Sullivan's trusted assistant and designed some of the interior components for the Auditorium Building, including the decorative panels on the side wings flanking the proscenium and the Auditorium bar.[5] Wright drew the plans for the firm's new offices in the tower of the Auditorium Building, and for many years this tower suite served as the offices for Louis Sullivan's architectural firm. Wright had one of four private offices; his was the only one connected directly to Sullivan's.[6]

Since Sullivan was preoccupied with many major commissions, the firm's few residential designs became the responsibility of Frank Lloyd Wright. Wright's experience in residential work with Silsbee and his willingness to perform these services at night in his home probably determined this decision. Even Sullivan's winter home, built in 1890 in Ocean Springs, near Biloxi, Mississippi, was evidently designed by Wright, as was an adjacent cottage for Sullivan's friends, the James Charnleys. A city house for Charnley at 1365 Astor Street, Chicago, was designed by Wright and constructed in 1891.[7] Built on a tight corner site, the house was revolutionary although its quiet dignity is easily overlooked today in surroundings jumbled by high-rises. The facade of the Charnley House was symmetrically composed and reflected the building's interior organization. The floor plan was spacious and "flowed" about a skylighted central stair, a design that anticipated the "open" interiors of Wright's later "Prairie" houses. Stonework framed the front door and flanking windows of the stair hall alcoves. Above this well-defined entry, at the second story, was a projecting balcony that resembled an elongated bay window. The solid surfaces of the balcony have characteristic Sullivan ornamentation, but in an understated shallow relief. At first glance, the balcony seems to be an interjection and suggests the direct hand of Louis Sullivan; however, the balcony and its ornament provide a necessary focus to unite the exterior composition. The exterior massing of the house was capped by an overhanging roof with decorative reliefs stamped into the copper fascia of the roof eaves. The overhanging roof, with its horizontal lines, anticipated similar expressions for capping Sullivan's high-rise designs and, with some exaggeration, Wright's later Prairie houses.[8]

The Charnley House represented a reappraisal of domestic architecture in America. It was a breakthrough design. Wright's own house, built two years earlier in Oak Park, Illinois, owed more to Silsbee's shingled designs than to Sullivan's ideas. However, Wright's association with Adler and Sullivan radically liberated his fertile imagination and creativity. As in a large modern architectural office, where team-generated design is necessary, Wright must have contributed considerably to the partnership of Adler and Sullivan, although this is not fully documented.

Another city house was designed for Sullivan's mother, Andrienne, and has been attributed by some architectural historians to Wright.[9] Sullivan's mother died before the house was completed so Louis Sullivan resided in it for four years until his brother, Albert, who funded construction, took possession for his growing family. (With relations between the Sullivan brothers already strained, this ejection of Louis completely alienated the two for the rest of their lives.)[10] Historically, the house was known as the Albert Sullivan Residence (1891–92; demolished 1970).

Another, more substantial Adler and Sullivan commission displayed characteristics that marked Wright's later designs. The Victoria Hotel (1892; demolished 1961) in Chicago Heights, Illinois, had a pronounced horizontality, which was balanced by a five-story clock tower. The upper wall surfaces of the three-story hotel building were banded by cream-colored ornamented plaster, which, in turn, articulated the wide overhanging hip roof from lower-story brick walls.[11]

Always extravagant with his expenditures—a tendency compounded by the demands of a new home and an expanding family—Wright took on additional work for residential designs. He called these commissions his "Bootlegged Houses" and kept them secret. Most of these houses were based on the picturesque qualities of Silsbee's shingled designs. The most radical and Sullivanesque was the Allison Harlan House (1892;

James Charnley House (1891), Chicago; designed by Frank Lloyd Wright for Adler and Sullivan, Architects. Photo: Ralph Marlowe Line, 1956.

demolished 1963), which was built on Chicago's South Side.[12] The Harlan residence had compact massing punctuated by porch-like wooden balconies and capped by a wide overhanging hip roof. The balconies were festooned with Sullivanesque ornament based on an oak leaf pattern and created by fret-saw cuts in the solid panels of the railing.[13]

The Adler and Sullivan firm had financed Wright's house in Oak Park. When Wright had fulfilled his obligation and requested the deed to his house, a confrontation ensued. Sullivan angrily refused to surrender the deed, accusing Wright of breaking their contract by accepting "outside" commissions. Wright rationalized his position by pointing out that he did work at home for the firm after office hours.[14] Adler later gave Wright the deed but Sullivan was still infuriated; thereafter, in 1893, Wright left to start his own architectural firm. With Cecil S. Corwin as a partner, Wright leased space in the Schiller Building (1891; demolished 1961) in Chicago's Loop. Adler and Sullivan had designed the Schiller Building but Wright had major responsibilities in the project, which may be why he chose this building to house his first office.

Wright's first independent commission, the William Winslow House (1893), River Forest, was a simple but progressive building that signaled a new direction in residential design.[15] Wright organized the plan in layers, from the formal front to the more casual family activity areas facing the rear yard. A central axis symmetrically aligned the reception hall, fireplace, dining room, and conservatory, and this axis became a spine about which more open, asymmetrical spaces were organized. As in the Charnley House, the front entry and flanking small windows were encased by dressed stonework that contrasted with the walls of Roman brick. Second-floor windows united with a banding of ornament that wrapped around the house and seemingly made the walls dematerialize; the broad, overhanging hip roof seemed to hover above the tied-to-the-ground masonry walls. The ornamental banding appeared to be terra cotta but was actually tinted plasterwork of Sullivanesque ornament, an effect first tried in the Victoria Hotel. The basis of the Prairie School was established in the Winslow House although its design was rooted in the Sullivanesque.[16]

In 1894, Wright designed four townhouses for Robert W. Roloson that were squeezed onto a seventy-five-foot frontage on Chicago's South Side. Each of the adjoining townhouses is identified by a gable roof of steep slope and suggests the Gothic style. But second- and third-floor windows were grouped to form a cluster for each townhouse, collected into a single large unit by a framework of stone trim and mullions. Wright's creative fenestration treatment united the frontage and established an urban scale. At the same time, references of human scale were maintained by ornamental spandrel panels of Sullivanesque floriated ornament.

The Francisco Terrace Apartments (1895; demolished 1974) on Chicago's West Side were an innovative investigation into the issues of low-income residential architecture in the city. Wright adapted a European model, a housing block with central courtyard, and humanized it. Dwelling units were reached from a contained courtyard or "garden,"

as Wright called it. Circulation paths to second-story dwelling units were via stairs and a continuous balcony around the courtyard. From the street, the courtyard was accessible through portals that penetrated the building; the major archway was a scaled-down version of the entry arch for Adler and Sullivan's Chicago Stock Exchange (1893). Wright's arch was salvaged and reconstructed in a new building (1978; Harry Weese and Associates, Architects) in Oak Park, Illinois.

Another multifamily building, the Francis Apartments (1895; demolished 1971), was more conventional in plan but more exciting in its aesthetic embellishments. It was designed by Wright for Chicago's South Side. As in many Chicago apartment buildings, a U-shaped plan was adopted, with the open end toward the street for pedestrian access to various entry lobbies. Wrought-iron gates controlled the open end of the court passage but were more important as a decorative feature. A horizontal band of decorative interlocking circles capped the gates and aligned with a horizontal band of terra cotta in the brick base of the building. The terra-cotta banding repeated the motif of interlocking circles although sculpted foliage filled the voids between rings.

An early house design by Wright, the Chauncey L. Williams Residence (1895), River Forest, Illinois, had a steeply pitched roof with picturesque dormers and recalled Silsbee imagery. However, the arched entryway was highlighted by Sullivanesque ornament. More progressive was the Isidore Heller House (1897) in Chicago's Hyde Park; the design marked a transition from Sullivan's influence to Wright's own individualism. The elongated house was sited perpendicular to the street on a narrow city lot. The exterior incorporated many of the architectural features that later characterized Wright's Prairie style: a sense of horizontality, despite the three-story height of the house; a hip roof with wide overhangs; horizontal banding of windows; and a strong relationship to ground and nature, despite the constricted site. As in the Winslow House, a Sullivan-like decorative frieze articulated the roof from the exterior wall, helped "dematerialize" the wall, and emphasized horizontality. The incorporation of human figures into the ornamental frieze coincided with Sullivan's adaptation of human likenesses in his ornamentation; for example, winged females were integrated with foliate designs on Sullivan's Bayard Building (1897–98) in New York. Figures for both buildings were sculpted by Richard Bock. Bock was also employed by Wright for sculpted reliefs for the Helen Husser House (1899; demolished 1925), Chicago.[17]

The Husser House was the last Wright design that carried vestiges of Sullivan's ornament; thereafter, Wright's ornament was his own.[18] However, the purpose and application of ornament by Wright was consistent with Sullivan's principles. But while Wright still embraced Sullivan's philosophy, his architectural realizations became separate and identifiable. Wright's work put more emphasis on form and space and less on facade and ornament. Differences in types of commissions helped force these differentiations. Whereas Sullivan concentrated mostly on commercial projects in tight urban contexts, Wright, early in his independent career, focused on small-scale domestic build-

Opposite: Four townhouses for Robert W. Roloson (1894), Chicago; Frank Lloyd Wright, Architect. Photo: 1964.

ings, usually as freestanding objects in open suburban settings. Wright's work and Wright-inspired designs by others became classified as the Prairie School.

The personal ornament that Wright developed was geometric, often with repeated elements that developed rhythmic sequences and changes in scale. Seemingly abstract, his ornamental designs delight the eye while enhancing overall architectural compositions. How did Wright develop this ornament? Sullivan devised geometric grids to undergird and organize his luscious foliate ornaments. Like a trellis, not readily visible but necessary for supporting tendrils and directing plant growth, skeletal geometric shapes give structure to Sullivan's plant-like designs. Wright's ornament seems to exist in the winter season, the plant life stripped and the structural grids of geometric shapes clearly obvious. However, Wright's literal use of a framework evolved into sophisticated abstractions of natural growth. Wright's childhood play with Froebel blocks, which were comprised of colorful geometric shapes, is often cited as the reason for his ingrained ability to manipulate geometric forms and shapes.

The design process for creating building ornament differed between Sullivan and Wright and this difference most accurately explains the difference in their ornament. In his book dedicated to Sullivan, *Genius and the Mobocracy*, Wright uncharacteristically confided that he always felt somewhat uneasy designing Sullivan's ornament in the Adler and Sullivan office. Wright was not comfortable with freehand drawing, and the design of Sullivan's ornament, with its leafy shapes and swirling tendrils, required loose freehand strokes. Wright preferred drafting with T-square and triangle. Wright admitted that, while he was with Adler and Sullivan and developing their characteristic ornament, Sullivan would sometimes admonish him, "Make it live!" Wright continued: "He would sit down at my board for a moment, take the 'HB' pencil from my hand and, sure enough, there it would be. Alive!"[19] Wright concluded that Sullivan's ornament was "a complete beautiful language of self-expression" and to learn about Sullivan, one "read" that language rather than his buildings or writings.[20]

Out of respect for Sullivan and/or recognition of his own shortcomings, Wright developed a language of ornament based on the controlled manipulation of geometries. Yet the themes and uses of Wright's ornament repeated those of Sullivan. Nature themes prevailed as Wright based his designs on plant structure, but these were abstracted, not representational, because of the straight lines or mechanical shapes Wright employed. It is no coincidence that Wright's interpretations of nature may have been best realized in leaded art-glass windows rather than through the plastic medium of clay or terra cotta. Certainly, Wright's use of straight lines for his glass designs allowed production to be faster and cheaper as less-skilled artists could do the work and less material was wasted than in the production of complex, curvilinear glasswork. Wright's use of proportion, repetition, rhythm, balance, and dominance were masterful as his ornament was of the proper scale and theme to enliven and enhance the architecture. The ornament contributed to his "organic" architecture, which meant the parts created a whole. Remove a part and the whole—the total composition—would be compromised. The positioning

Isidore Heller House (1897), Chicago; Frank Lloyd Wright, Architect. Photo: 1987.

or integration of ornament followed the rules Wright learned from Sullivan. Visual reinforcement of structure, dematerialization of nonbearing walls, references for scale, identification of important functional aspects, and introduction of symbols were the purposes for which Wright, like Sullivan, introduced ornament in his architecture.

The restrictions of Wright's mechanical drawing pushed his ornament toward the abstract. These stylizations both anticipated and influenced modern art and sculpture. In many ways, Wright's geometric designs for ornament were perhaps even more visionary and appropriate for the twentieth century than was his architecture, which was often still weighted toward nineteenth-century agrarian ideals. Wright's ornament of abstracted natural forms was more adaptable to common building materials, such as brick, with projecting or corbelled bats and various patterns, or concrete, with its formwork of wood construction. Unlike Sullivan's ornament, which required a skilled artisan to translate the architect's two-dimensional designs into shallow three-dimensional reliefs, Wright's ornament often could be made directly by construction workers. Wright's ornament was inherently architectonic and urban with its pure geometries. It seemed to glorify the modern industrial age with its machine-like precision and repetitive motifs that recalled urban patterns. Yet, ironically, Wright rejected the urban settlement and advocated a bucolic life style, which he ultimately chose for himself and promulgated through suburban models he later designed, such as his theoretical Broadacre City. A dichotomy also existed in Sullivan and his work. Sullivan's ornament was thoroughly rooted in nineteenth-century romanticism and Darwin's naturalism; and, although Sullivan escaped to nature for holiday and retreat, he seems to have loved the city, even the industrial city of his time, with its grime, congestion, and social disparities. Sullivan anticipated the twentieth-century city of towers. His theoretical studies included set-back needs for high-rise buildings. Sullivan's Schiller Building (1891–92) and unbuilt Odd Fellows Temple project (1891) were demonstrations of tall-building designs that allowed light and air to reach the street.[21]

Interested in the arts and crafts movement in England, Frank Lloyd Wright recognized its importance and was instrumental in forming the Chicago Arts and Crafts Society in 1897.[22] However, he questioned the rejection of the machine as advocated by William Morris. Instead, Wright advocated its mastery and proper use to produce beautiful materials for a democratic architecture.[23] These principles were manifested especially in the design of ornament by Sullivan, Wright, and their followers, three-dimensionally represented by skilled craftsmen or sculptors and reproduced by factories of the building material industries. In summary, Wright was among progressives who led the American arts and crafts movement. But he advocated creatively designed goods and accessories made affordable and more widely available through machine production, thus reaching a broader segment of the public than otherwise possible.

After Wright left Adler and Sullivan, Sullivan's anger simmered for many years and the two men did not communicate. Finally, in 1914 Wright was able to renew his friendship with Sullivan.[24] Wright and Sullivan corresponded and Wright visited with

Sullivan periodically. Sullivan followed Wright's career and praised Wright's designs. Wright, among others, gave money to Sullivan during his later years of hardship. Wright visited the day before Sullivan died (April 14, 1924); during that visit, Sullivan gave some of his best drawings to Wright with the request Wright have them published. In 1949, with the gift drawings as illustrations, Wright's book on Sullivan was finally published. Wright's *Genius and the Mobocracy* was a tribute to Sullivan but more so to himself.

For the period 1910–18, George G. Elmslie, Wright's successor at Adler and Sullivan, carried the burden of leading a new architecture. After Elmslie left Sullivan's firm and formed a partnership with another former Sullivan employee, William Gray Purcell, the firm of Purcell and Elmslie became influential, eclipsing Sullivan and supplanting Wright as leaders of progressive architectural design. Architectural historians have recognized the importance of Purcell and Elmslie but have generally dismissed the later efforts of both architects. However, Elmslie continued to design creatively and espoused Sullivan's cause, although at times his work may have been uneven as his designs evolved and he struggled to maintain his practice. Like Sullivan, who needed Dankmar Adler, Elmslie was most successful in partnership. Therefore, it is not surprising that Elmslie's most successful later works were designed while he was associated with other architects.

George Grant Elmslie was born February 20, 1871, in Aberdeenshire, Scotland. He came to the United States at age fourteen with his family to join his father, John, who had emigrated a year earlier and had settled in Chicago.[25] Elmslie attended Chicago public schools until 1888 when he began working for the architect Joseph Lyman Silsbee.[26] Frank Lloyd Wright was also employed with Silsbee at the time. After Wright left Silsbee to join Adler and Sullivan, Wright suggested the firm hire Elmslie. In 1889, Elmslie became employed by Adler and Sullivan and worked closely with Wright.[27] After Wright left the firm, Elmslie became chief draftsman and remained in that capacity with Sullivan after Adler's departure. While with Sullivan, Elmslie developed much of Sullivan's ornament. According to David Gebhard: "It is one of the ironies of history that this ornament, so closely associated with Louis Sullivan, was, in fact, not developed by him but by George Grant Elmslie. . . . It was Elmslie who brought to fulfillment the ornamental patterns which had earlier been established by Sullivan."[28] Because of Sullivan's deteriorating condition and declining practice, Elmslie became discouraged and despondent. On December 4, 1909, Elmslie finally left his longtime employer and began anew.[29] He relocated to Minneapolis, Minnesota, and joined in partnership with William Gray Purcell and George Feick Jr.

William Gray Purcell (1880–1965) was raised in Oak Park, Illinois, and attended Cornell University, graduating in 1903. When Purcell returned to Chicago, he met George G. Elmslie, who helped him gain a position with Louis Sullivan. However, after just five months of employment with Sullivan, Purcell left for the West Coast to continue apprenticeship and travels. After touring Europe with a former Cornell classmate, George Feick Jr., Purcell formed an architectural partnership with Feick and the two opened an office in February 1907 in Minneapolis, Minnesota.[30]

Purcell and Elmslie had continued their friendship and corresponded regularly. Purcell constantly encouraged Elmslie to leave Sullivan and join the Purcell and Feick firm in Minneapolis. Finally, Elmslie did so. The firm was renamed Purcell, Feick, and Elmslie, Architects. Soon thereafter, on October 12, 1910, the thirty-nine-year-old Elmslie married Bonnie Marie Hunter, a Wellesley College graduate.[31] Elmslie, whose personality was often called reserved and somewhat reticent, even melancholic at times, enjoyed personal happiness for the next two years. However, his wife died in early September 1912 of complications following surgery in Chicago. She was only thirty-one. Elmslie was devastated. He moved back to Chicago that year and opened a branch of the Minneapolis firm. Elmslie argued that the firm needed a Chicago presence to secure important contracts; however, his desire to live with his sisters after the loss of his wife prompted the decision. Thereafter, Purcell and Elmslie worked in separate cities and communicated primarily by exchange of letters and periodic visits.[32] George Feick Jr. (1881–1945), who was mainly responsible for specification writing and some engineering, left the firm in 1913. The renamed firm of Purcell and Elmslie continued to create exceptional designs. Many of these were residential commissions, including Purcell's own house (1913) in Minneapolis, and the Harold C. Bradley House (1915) in Madison, Wisconsin.

Although residences were the most common commissions in the office, Purcell and Elmslie secured other projects as well, most notably banks in small towns. These included the Exchange State Bank (1910) in Grand Meadow, Minnesota; the Madison State Bank (1913; demolished c. 1974), Madison, Minnesota; the First State Bank (1914), LeRoy, Minnesota; G. L. Branson and Company, Bankers (1915), Mitchell, South Dakota; and the Farmers and Merchants State Bank (1916), Hector, Minnesota.[33] Except for the LeRoy bank, all of these banking structures incorporated Sullivanesque terra-cotta ornament designed by Elmslie.

Several additional bank buildings were landmark designs. The First National Bank (1910–11), Rhinelander, Wisconsin, was a mixed-use project with retail space and bank at street level and offices on the second floor. The arched entrance and central axis were emphasized by a large cartouche positioned above the portal at the parapet. As described by Purcell, Feick, and Elmslie, the cartouche was "an enrichment of the field of brickwork by an insertion of an organic and highly decorative area of terra cotta partaking of the very nature of the brick in its substance, color, outline, and texture."[34] This cartouche was widely imitated by other architects in creating their own Sullivanesque designs. The Merchants Bank of Winona (1912) in Winona, Minnesota, is a powerful and eloquent building. Located at a street corner, the bank had two street facades that featured large expanses of art glass to express and illuminate the large, open banking space within. Long-span structural-steel members are clad with Roman brick and terra-cotta ornament and carry the roof above the window walls. Every component is arranged so that the deviation of any part would erode the composition. From the heavy parapet coping, which protrudes beyond the building corners, to the street-level brick "screen" comprised of rhythmic window openings and entryway, each element is refined and contributes to the whole. The building scale was expertly manipulated. There is both human scale, for reference and warmth, and monumental scale, for civic presence and importance.

The most significant structure in Chicago by Purcell, Feick, and Elmslie was the Edison Shop, which stood at 229 South Wabash Avenue. The interiors of the Edison Shop (1912; demolished 1967), done in conjunction with George M. Niedecken of Milwaukee, were exceptional, with close attention given to specially designed furnishings, lighting fixtures, and wooden screens. However, the front facade was the most remarkable achievement. For the narrow four-story building, Purcell, Feick, and Elmslie blended glass with masonry claddings of brick and terra cotta to create a profound image of transparency and reflectivity. The Chicago window, with large fixed sash flanked by narrow operable windows, was stylized by the substitution of brick piers for the usual mullions of wood or cast iron; flanking double-hung windows were replaced by leaded glass in pivoting sashes. At the first floor, a loggia was formed by setting an entry wall of glazing back 8' 4" from the face of the building. The front facade, measuring approximately 78' × 26 ½' wide, combined expansive fenestration and masonry claddings over composite beams of steel and concrete (floor joists were wood, 2" × 12" at one foot on center). Ornamental terra cotta was used for windowsills, pier capitals, and a central focal piece at the parapet. Roman brick was laid with ⅝" horizontal joints, raked square ⅝" deep, and flush vertical joints, which emphasized the horizontal masonry coursing.[35] The

First National Bank Building (1910–11), Rhinelander, Wisconsin; Purcell, Feick, and Elmslie, Architects. Detail of main cartouche. Photo: 1991.

use of Roman brick and the method of coursing were characteristics of Sullivan's brick-work and were also employed by Wright in his Prairie School brick-masonry houses. As in most of Purcell, Feick, and Elmslie's nonresidential buildings, Elmslie-designed Sullivanesque terra cotta was manufactured by the American Terra Cotta and Ceramic Company.[36]

As previously mentioned, in 1912 Elmslie opened a branch of the firm in Chicago. Purcell gained architectural registration (B 391) in Illinois and had first appeared on the roster of Illinois architects in 1911. Elmslie (B 388) was listed for the first time in 1913.[37] Elmslie's move to Chicago did not result in many commissions there. However, these did include an apartment building (1913) for Newman, Baskerville, and Marsh at 5712 Madison Avenue, which was just down the street from where Elmslie resided (5759 Madison Avenue); service buildings in Riverside for Henry Babson (1916); and suburban houses in Flossmoor, Hinsdale, River Forest, and Waukegan.

Purcell and Elmslie became the leading advocates of "modern" or progressive architectural design. Purcell and Elmslie expressed their views about progressive design in various essays and articles. In addition, they wrote about other avant-garde designers,

Opposite: Edison Shop (1912), Chicago; Purcell, Feick, and Elmslie, Architects. The elegant facade shows scars before demolition (1967). Photo: c. 1965.

Below: Merchants Bank of Winona (1912), Winona, Minnesota; Purcell, Feick, and Elmslie, Architects. Photo: Ralph Marlowe Line, 1951.

such as the Chicago architects Spencer and Powers, and Walter Burley Griffin.[38] Gustav Stickley's journal *The Craftsman*, the leading publication about the arts and crafts movement in America, published several Purcell and Elmslie essays. One of these was about the "modern" Dutch architect H. P. Berlage, whom Purcell and Elmslie admired.[39] Purcell and Elmslie hosted Berlage during his 1911 tour of the United States and arranged for him to lecture in Minneapolis.[40] But Purcell and Elmslie's most influential writings were about their own designs. These were published in the *Western Architect* and even entire issues were devoted to their work. These special issues appeared in January 1913, January 1915, and July 1915.

The firm's most important constructed design was the result of a collaboration. In January 1915, William L. Steele won the commission for a new Woodbury County Courthouse in Sioux City, Iowa. Steele, who had worked under Elmslie in Sullivan's office, immediately contacted Elmslie and solicited a collaboration of services for the building.[41] Elmslie and several staff members moved to Sioux City, as much of the design work and contract documents were prepared in Steele's office there. Elmslie designed the courthouse as a base element and tower. The base housed county offices on the first floor and courtrooms and judicial ancillary spaces on the second level. The base, which occupied the quarter-block site, had a central rotunda. The dome was a skylight with colorful patterns of art glass and was straddled by the office tower. The tower of administrative offices was raised above the glass rotunda in order to create large clerestory openings that would allow natural light to penetrate the domed skylight. Only the elevator shafts, fire stair, and four major piers, flanked by minor, brick-encased steel columns, penetrated the base and suggested the tower above. Roman brick, manufactured locally, and ornamental or sculptural terra cotta, from the American Terra Cotta and Ceramic Company, were used in both the interior and exterior of the building.[42] The terra cotta and the interior plaster ornamentation were prepared from models sculpted by Kristian Schneider. Schneider also modeled Elmslie's ornamental designs in iron and bronze for the courthouse. Alfonso Iannelli sculpted the figures at the entrances and John W. Norton was the artist for the interior murals.[43] The collaborative efforts of the various artists were highly successful, and the building remains a work of art.

Although the office tower of the courthouse rests a little uneasily on the base and seems to need a direct or visible connection to the ground, the Woodbury County Courthouse is one of the more satisfying works in American architecture. However, it was not achieved without controversy. For its time, the Purcell and Elmslie design was very radical and did not conform to the classical courthouse archetype. After the acceptance in March 1915 of Purcell and Elmslie's preliminary sketches, the local press and many citizens saw the unconventionality of the design and objected. In an unusual stand for a bureaucratic body, the county supervisors supported the design despite public barbs. The architects, probably guided by the politically astute William Steele, provided leadership. In the February 1921 issue of the *Western Architect*, Purcell and Elmslie

Woodbury County Courthouse (1916–18), Sioux City, Iowa; Purcell and Elmslie, Architects, in collaboration with William L. Steele. Photo: 1994.

wrote about the design and construction of the courthouse. The architects described how their design was efficient and cost effective.[44] Perhaps the supervisors' support for the design had more to do with budget considerations than aesthetics and symbolism. Like Sullivan and unlike Wright, Purcell and Elmslie respected the clients' construction budgets and adherence to them was one of their strengths. Finally, on March 4, 1918, county operations began in the new building. Criticism was replaced by pride and acclaim. It was the last major design by Purcell and Elmslie that was constructed.

Although Purcell and Elmslie were identified as associate architects for the Woodbury County Courthouse, in reality only Elmslie was involved. Purcell was preoccupied with other matters as he became advertising manager for the International Leather and Belting Corporation in 1916 and he relocated to Philadelphia. Three years later, he moved to the West Coast.[45] The Purcell and Elmslie firm had become a partnership in name only and in 1922 the two architects' professional relationship was officially dissolved.

Elmslie subsequently secured commissions for five buildings constructed in Aurora, Illinois. The first of these was the American National Bank. This 1922 project utilized an existing building but major exterior work obliterated the original. The result was a crisp Elmslie design. The main entrance was flanked by brick pylons that projected from the facade. The pylons (since removed) were capped by sculpted figures that emerged from an ornamental background of foliage, regulated by a geometrical order and realized in terra cotta. Human figures sculpted in relief had been important focal pieces on the Woodbury County Courthouse. Similarly, human likenesses were integrated with the architecture of the American National Bank, but the figures were less literal and more a part of the overall ornamental motifs.

The four additional Elmslie buildings in Aurora are listed on the National Register of Historic Places.[46] Originally called the Joseph George and Newhall Building, after the developers, the Keystone Building (1922–23) was constructed on the east side of North Stolp Avenue. (Stolp, previously called Island Avenue, is a narrow street in downtown Aurora centered on an island in the Fox River.) The building has ground-floor shops and three floors of offices. The facade stretches along Stolp while one bay of the building angles with a jog in the street. Tightly spaced brick piers and recessed brick spandrel panels create a rhythmic progression of verticals along the confined urban frontage. Recent demolitions have altered the character of the street but the Keystone Building remains remarkably intact. Free of major alterations, the storefronts retain clerestories of prism glass and ornamental soffits at recessed shop entrances. Sullivanesque terra-cotta ornament included an arched panel above the office entrance, continuous beltings located at the top and bottom of the brick piers, and a terminating "cornice."

Across the street, sandwiched against the river, is the Graham Building. Designed by Elmslie in 1924, built in 1925, and occupied in 1926, the building is eight stories high. Originally an office building, it has been converted to housing for the elderly.[47] The floor plan is roughly the shape of the letter "H" on its side, as light wells were introduced at the party wall locations and the "rear" facade abutted the river. Sullivanesque ornament with a tight foliate weave was used in bandings at windowsills and cornice. It was supplied by the American Terra Cotta and Ceramic Company.[48] The client for the building was William Grant, a general contractor who built Elmslie's Aurora buildings.[49]

Another Elmslie design in Aurora is the Old Second National Bank (1924), with two floors of offices stacked above the main banking floor. A steeply pitched gable roof capped the design; however, end walls were raised above the roof, creating a stepped transitional segment at the eave. Exterior materials included pink granite from New Hampshire for the base, Roman brick for the walls, and red roofing tiles. In addition, terra-cotta ornament by Kristian Schneider and sculpture by Emil R. Zettler were used.[50] Records indicate that the terra cotta came from the Advance Terra Cotta Company, a Chicago concern, which later was acquired by the Northwestern Terra Cotta Company.[51] In the 1960s, the banking hall was marred by remodelings, including the removal of the brick-and-glass teller "cages" and the insertion of a new dropped ceiling to

American National Bank (1922), Aurora, Illinois; George G. Elmslie, Architect. Photo: 1992.

accommodate a tight pattern of square fluorescent lights. In the 1980s, the bank was expanded by construction of an addition with drive-up windows and parking lots. Therefore, the original context of buildings that adjoined the bank and fronted the street has been lost.

The last of Elmslie's Aurora buildings was the Healy Chapel (1927–28). This undertaker's establishment, more than any other Elmslie building, closely resembles Wright's Prairie style houses because of the hip roofs and freestanding horizontal emphasis. However, it even more closely resembles the Everist House (1916–17) in Sioux City, Iowa, designed by Elmslie's friend William Steele. Roman brick, Sullivanesque terra-cotta bandings, and retaining walls were incorporated in a similar way in both buildings.

Elmslie admired contemporary Dutch architecture influenced by romantic nationalism—its intricate masonry, integrated sculpture, and assertive, often exaggerated forms shaped by steeply pitched roofs. Furthermore, Elmslie advocated regionalism as inherent with his and Sullivan's credo, "form follows function." Given the climate of Minnesota, steeply pitched roofs were desirable to shed snow, and many of Purcell and Elmslie's houses had steep gable roofs. However, with but few exceptions, such as an unbuilt bank design (1911) in Mankato, Minnesota, and a municipal building (1917) in the village of Kasson, Minnesota, Purcell and Elmslie's banks and public buildings prior to the early 1920s were flat-roofed and parapeted like Sullivan's nonresidential buildings. However, in the 1920s, Elmslie used sloping roofs for most of his designs. Pitched roofs were not as susceptible to roof leaks and heavy snow loads as flat ones; however, Elmslie probably chose steeply sloping roofs for other reasons. The Dutch influence was undoubtedly a factor. In addition, it may have been a concession to romantic design eclecticism, which swept the United States following World War I and overwhelmed lingering progressive architecture. But, most likely, the major motivation was Elmslie's fixation on bank building design and his desire to transform the bank from "jewel box" to "home."[52] As every child knows, the archetype for home is a box with a gable roof. Elmslie advocated sloping roofs for most of his later work. At the same time, there was a transformation of his dominant ornamental themes from fluid botanical forms to angular, abstracted human figures, with more restrained use of bas-relief ornamental features.

For the Capitol Building and Loan Association (1922–23; demolished) in Topeka, Kansas, Elmslie capped the six-story building with a steeply pitched gable roof. The two-story base housed the building and loan company while the four floors above contained rental offices. The "home" image was completed by the gable roof although front and rear parapet walls rose above and embraced the roof planes. The silhouette of these parapet walls stepped up near the eave and then followed the roof slope. At the ridge, another stepped shape terminated the parapet. The profile of the raised parapets was reminiscent of that in traditional narrow Dutch buildings. The roof slope helped accommodate some of the elevator override but a stylized dormer accommodated the

Opposite: Keystone Building (1922–23), Aurora, Illinois; George G. Elmslie, Architect. Photo: 1992.

balance. As many architectural historians have noted, Elmslie's design resembled the steep roof forms of Adler and Sullivan's St. Nicholas Hotel (1892) in St. Louis.[53] At Topeka, Elmslie's Sullivanesque ornament was less florid and more dominated by geometric order, with repeated motifs in the terra-cotta bandings. Composed with this ornament were sculpted human figures representing Kansas agriculture, industry, and housing. On the side elevation, an abstracted shallow relief in an elongated panel depicted historic scenes of Kansas. The architectural art at Topeka was carried out by a team of artists that Elmslie assembled: Emil Zettler was the sculptor for the figures; John Norton painted the murals in the high-ceilinged banking hall; and Kristian Schneider modeled the terra-cotta ornament, which was supplied by the American Terra Cotta and Ceramic Company.[54] The building was featured in an article by William Steele and published in the *Western Architect* (September 1924).[55]

After 1922, Elmslie's ornamental foliate designs became increasingly rigid as leaf forms became less pronounced and stalks or shafts became more dominant in a geometrically rhythmic manner. Increased emphasis was given to animal life, especially human figures, over plant life as the principal theme on much of Elmslie's later work. The figures usually personified virtuous professions or activities associated with the intended use of the building. This was especially true on larger, important buildings. Eventually, animal life—in even more stylized geometric shapes—became the focus of Elmslie's ornament. In addition, his traditional ornament was reduced in scale and importance, if any ornament was used at all. For example, for two buildings at Yankton College in Yankton, South Dakota, Elmslie reduced ornament to a minimum. The only substantive ornament consisted of terra-cotta capitals bearing bas-relief stylized figures, which capped the brick piers. In addition, both buildings, a science building (Forbes Hall, 1929) and a dormitory (1931), had steeply gabled roofs and other treatments, such as the fenestration, that approached the eclectic style of the collegiate Gothic. Steele and Hilgers of Sioux City, Iowa, were associate architects for Elmslie's Yankton College buildings.[56]

Why Elmslie's design of ornament changed is unclear. Perhaps it represented a natural progression of his personal style; or an attempt, conscious or not, to distance his work from Sullivan's and thus emerge from Sullivan's shadow; or an influence from Wright's purely geometric and abstract nature patterns, which Elmslie would never admit. More likely, Elmslie was responding to published work of the so-called Amsterdam school in Holland. Dutch architects had earlier been influenced by Sullivan, Wright, and Purcell and Elmslie, adopting and incorporating basic forms and simplifying or abstracting ornamentation of leading Chicago architects in their own architecture. However, Dutch ornamentation was less profuse and was concentrated at selected locations, such as entrances. Sculptural figures usually were substituted for foliate themes. In the 1920s, two progressive architectural vocabularies emerged in Holland: that of the Amsterdam school, a romantic nationalistic style, visibly influenced by the Chicago movements; and that of De Stijl, which was philosophically akin to the Chicago movements but aesthetically more closely connected to the Internationalism of the Bauhaus. Given Elmslie's and Purcell's earlier admiration of Berlage and progressive Dutch architecture, Elmslie was undoubtedly influenced by developments in Holland. However, Elmslie, like Wright, despised the International style and attacked it in print.[57] He particularly criticized the Internationalists' limited definition of "functionalism": "The concept, what Functionalism really means . . . must be broadened, widened and integrated with our every activity. It is an inspiration—fluent, plastic, and clothed in garments of romance."[58] Here Elmslie continued to embrace Sullivan's definition of functionalism, which went beyond the utilitarian and addressed emotional and spiritual requirements as well.[59] According to that definition, ornamentation was an integral part of architecture and was needed in order to achieve these purposes.

George G. Elmslie often associated with other architects on projects; they had the commissions and Elmslie had the design talent. On at least four occasions, Elmslie was associated with the German-born Chicago architect Hermann V. von Holst (1874–1955).[60] Von Holst, remembered today as the architect with whom Frank Lloyd Wright entrusted his practice when he left for Europe in 1909, was commissioned by the People's Gas Light and Coke Company (now People's Gas Company) to design a series of "storefront" branch offices on neighborhood shopping streets in Chicago; and for a group of three such offices in the mid-1920s, von Holst used George G. Elmslie as design architect. Although of varying sizes and expressions, each street facade was handled in a similar way. Heavy piers were located at the party walls and symmetrically framed the front facade. The most pronounced Sullivanesque ornamentation was located on each pier, near the cap, and had a vertical emphasis. The first and smallest that was designed by Elmslie was constructed in 1925 on South Commercial Avenue in south Chicago, near the old United States Steel South Works. The one-story building had a wide expanse of glass for its storefront, framed by tapestry brick piers, wall return, and parapet. The ornament was of terra cotta but it came from the Northwestern Terra Cotta Company, a less usual source.[61] The second, a two-story building constructed in 1926 on Irving Park Road, Chicago, is still occupied by the People's Gas Company.[62]

A similar building, but with a facade of more powerful appearance, was constructed on North Larrabee Street in Chicago (c. 1926; demolished c. 1968). Spandrels at the second floor and roof bridged the long voids between massive piers. Small "cripple columns" proportioned the vast second-floor glazing into distinct openings suggestive of one greatly elongated Chicago window. Leaded glass, with art-glass insets in a "V" shape—a characteristic motif of Elmslie—filled the second-story window openings. Art-glass lenses on vertically attenuated lighting fixtures were mounted below Sullivanesque ornament on each end pier. One of Elmslie's more masterful facade compositions, it united Sullivanesque vocabulary with the bold simplicity of art deco imagery.

The fourth Elmslie project with von Holst was less successful as progressive design. The Maxwelton Braes Resort and Golf Club (1930–31) in Baileys Harbor, Wisconsin, reveals a historicist approach to design. Elmslie's struggles to maintain a liveli-

People's Gas Light and Coke Company (1925), South Commercial Avenue, Chicago; George G. Elmslie was design architect with Hermann V. von Holst, Architect. Detail of terra-cotta ornament that capped the heavy piers at the property lines. Photo: 1991.

hood must have forced some compromises. Similarly, eclecticism permeated his built designs for a Congregational church (1928–29) in Western Springs and the Redfield-Peterson House (1920) in Glenview, Illinois.[63] (The Yankton College designs had also suffered from unconvincing historical references.) It required a teaming with another talented architect for Elmslie to regain his direction and create his final significant designs.

Elmslie's last buildings were done while associated with William S. Hutton (1890–1975) of Hammond, Indiana. Elmslie and Hutton created four schools in the Hammond area between 1934 and 1936. In many ways, they are among Elmslie's best work. Unfortunately, their number has been depleted through demolition, and only two remain.

People's Gas Light and Coke Company (c. 1926; demolished c. 1968), North Larrabee Street, Chicago. This was the largest of three office annexes designed by George G. Elmslie with Hermann V. von Holst, Architect. Photo: c. 1967.

The first and largest building was Thornton Township High School (1934–35; now Thornton Fractional North High School), which still stands in Calumet City, Illinois. The central entrance pavilion of the principal elevation has marble-clad piers, human figures sculpted in terra cotta, and decorative metallic screens, which are based on hexagonal motifs and set outside large expanses of glass. Walls and repeated piers of tapestry brick, along with terra-cotta pier capitals and occasional accents, complete the major exterior composition. Elmslie used these thematic elements, but with varying compositional arrangements, for the Thomas A. Edison, Oliver P. Morton, and Washington Irving schools, all built in Hammond in 1936. Of these three, only the Irving school survives.

The Edison and Morton Schools were similar in design. Both had a three-story classroom block with a central entry pavilion. Each educational block was flanked by separate gymnasium and auditorium wings. The terra-cotta applications were similar as well, although Elmslie used different ornamental motifs, and the clay finishes differed in color as well. A slip with reddish hue for the terra cotta at Thomas A. Edison contrasted with the yellowish beige color of the natural clay at Morton.

The terra cotta for all four schools was made by the Midland Terra Cotta Company in Chicago, where Kristian Schneider was then employed. Ironically, the Midland company, which made stock terra-cotta ornament based on designs by Sullivan and Elmslie, manufactured Elmslie originals for Hutton's buildings, while the American company, so long associated with Elmslie's ornament, made the bland glazed terra-cotta blocks used for interior wainscoting in the three Hammond schools. Midland's contract for producing terra-cotta ornament for Hutton and Elmslie's Thornton High School was signed in March 1935.[64] But within five months, Schneider was dead. Although Elmslie fretted about who would complete the work, Schneider was replaced by Fritz Albert, who expertly modeled Elmslie's ornament for the three Hammond schools.[65]

For the Edison and Morton schools, decorative architectural terra cotta included pier capitals and horizontal bandings of repeated ornamental pieces that formed a frieze and mitigated the separation between building and sky. In addition, terra-cotta trim was carefully composed with sculpted figures and helped unite the statuary and the architecture. The statues were focal pieces that helped give identity to the main entrances. The figures for the Thornton Township High School and the Edison School were sculpted by Emil Zettler.[66] The sculpted figures for the Morton School were by Alfonso Iannelli.[67] The schools in Hammond, Indiana, were among the last Sullivanesque buildings constructed, and they concluded the evolution of ornamental designs by Elmslie.

As first suggested in Elmslie's designs for von Holst's People's Gas Company office annexes, Elmslie's projects formed an evolutionary link between the Sullivanesque and the style of decorated modern architecture now termed art deco. In regard to pure design, Elmslie's and Hutton's schools were contemporary Sullivanesque works. But they demonstrated that the compositional themes and underlying order used by Sullivan and

Thornton Township High School (1934–35), Calumet City, Illinois; George G. Elmslie, design architect; William S. Hutton, architect of record. Detail of ornament and sculpture at main entry pavilion. Photo: 1991.

Elmslie could develop into a design strategy for low-rise buildings that reflected the art deco. Architects working in the two styles used similar symmetrical facade compositions and interjected ornamentation in a similar manner. By transforming his dominant ornamental themes and using bas-relief ornament with masonry masses and rhythmic fenestration, Elmslie adeptly adjusted the Sullivanesque to the art deco mode of the late 1920s to 1940s.

Elmslie's designs for the Hammond schools fully demonstrated his firm support for integration of the arts and the collaboration of artists as integral to architecture and its practice. He wrote about this conviction: "Architecture is a broad and inclusive art, embracing in its fold sculpture and mural painting. Easel painting is a secondary phase of the fundamental mural painting and sculpture apart from architecture is also secondary and, in most cases, meaningless. Some monuments are really fine pieces of architecture, but the real home of sculpture is on a building and the real home of painting is on our walls. In many cases I have combined the three elements in one, with the aid of very capable and imaginative men."[68]

Unfortunately, the Thomas A. Edison and Oliver P. Morton Schools were demolished in 1991. One-story schools bearing the same historical names were constructed on the same tracts. The City of Hammond school system had some ornamental terra cotta salvaged for reuse. Fanning and Howey of Michigan City, Indiana, the architects for the new schools, incorporated some decorative pieces into the facades. However, the most successful reuse of the saved pieces was the installation of the sculpted figures, which were positioned at eye level in the interior lobby of the new Oliver P. Morton School. The Washington Irving School survives although it is threatened.[69] However, it was the smallest of the Hutton and Elmslie schools and is devoid of any sculpted figures, although a sympathetic one-story addition (1953) by Hutton and Hutton, which included terra-cotta ornament that duplicated Elmslie's originals, makes it of interest.

The terra-cotta figures and ornament reused on replacement schools, some pieces that are in private collections, and a collection of pieces donated by the Hammond Schools to the School of Architecture of the University of Illinois at Urbana-Champaign all serve as reminders of the handicraft of a team of architects and artisans motivated by the leadership and vision of George G. Elmslie.[70]

The last known buildings erected to Elmslie's designs were four dormitory buildings (1939) at the State of Indiana Boy's School, Plainfield, commissions on which he worked with William S. Hutton.[71] Elmslie remained active, however, creating projects on paper and writing about architecture.[72] Many of his essays, which appeared often in the *Illinois Society of Architects Monthly Bulletin,* were reiterations of Sullivan's ideas for an American and democratic architecture. Elmslie always praised Sullivan's ideals despite his deep-seated feeling of being in virtual servitude and never receiving proper recognition during and after long years of employment with Sullivan. Elmslie had been an integral part of much of Sullivan's architectural practice and then had enjoyed a suc-

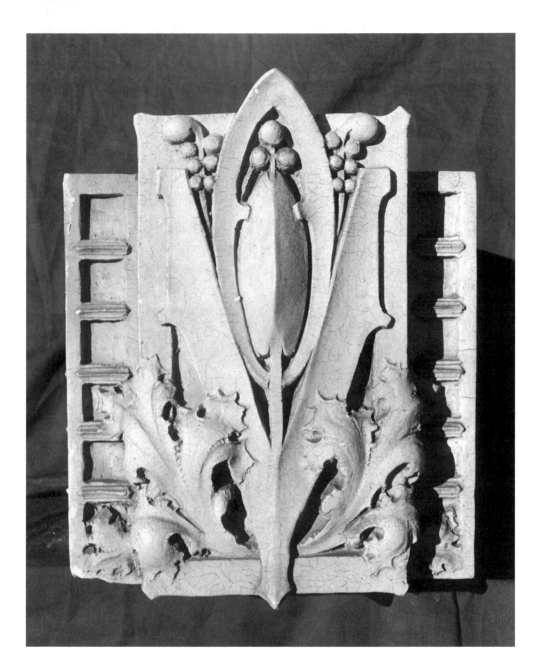

Oliver P. Morton School (1936–37), Hammond, Indiana; George G. Elmslie, Architect. Salvaged pier capital, a gift of the Schools, City of Hammond, Indiana, to the School of Architecture, University of Illinois at Urbana-Champaign. Photo: Paul Kruty, 1997.

cessful partnership with Purcell. The third phase of his career, during which he practiced both alone and as a design associate, remains understudied, yet it resulted in many remarkable designs. The Edison and Morton schools were among Elmslie's most successful works. In 1947 Elmslie was made a Fellow of the American Institute of Architects (AIA).[73] He died on April 23, 1952, in Woodlawn Hospital, Chicago.[74]

In addition to Frank Lloyd Wright and Purcell and Elmslie, a number of architects were once employed by Louis Sullivan, and the group was especially large during the prosperous years of the Adler and Sullivan partnership. The most famous, of course, was Wright, followed by George G. Elmslie and William Purcell. Others, such as Irving Gill, Richard E. Schmidt, and William L. Steele, also gained recognition. Less well known were Ferdinand Boberg, Louis W. Claude, Cecil S. Corwin, Simeon B. Eisendrath, W. F. Kleinpell, John T. Lang, Henry L. Ottenheimer, James B. Rezny, Henry J. Schlacks, Emil Henry Seeman, and Charles F. Whittlesey.[75]

The number of employees during the tempestuous years of Louis Sullivan's independent firm were few in comparison. This number included Parker N. Berry, Adolph O. Budina, William C. Presto, and Homer Sailor. Many of these former employees went on to have successful architectural careers; however, most rejected Sullivan's call for a new architecture, one appropriate for the building types of city industrialization and American culture. Instead, they embraced eclectic design, and this conformance to the prevailing taste may explain their success.

Sullivan's disdain for imitators may have provided architects with further incentive to deviate from his established direction. Nevertheless, a handful of former employees followed the philosophy and personal expression of Sullivan. These included Berry, Steele, Claude and, to a lesser extent, Presto. In a way, these architects were bearers of Sullivan's message, which they transmitted through their work as they dispersed across the country. Most of these individuals were associated with the second phase of the Sullivanesque (after 1910) although a few, such as Schmidt, did their most creative work during the initial phase of the Sullivanesque era.

One of the rising stars of the Sullivanesque was Parker Noble Berry. He had his own architectural practice for just a year and a half before he contracted influenza during the epidemic that raged throughout the country in 1918; tragically, he died on December 16, 1918, at age thirty. For eight years, from 1909 to 1917, Berry had been employed by Louis Sullivan as his chief assistant.[76] Born on September 2, 1888, in Hastings, Nebraska, Parker N. Berry spent his youth in Princeton, Illinois, after his family moved there in 1891.[77] After working for his father, who was a contractor, Berry studied architecture at the University of Illinois but stayed only for the 1907–8 school year.[78] He then moved to Chicago and, hired in late 1909, became Sullivan's chief draftsman after George Elmslie left to join Purcell and Feick in Minneapolis. In 1912, Berry became a registered architect (Illinois B 549). During Berry's tenure with Sullivan, a number of Sullivan's notable small bank commissions passed through the office. One of these, the Henry C. Adams Land and Loan Office Building (1913) in Algona, Iowa, may have been largely the work of Berry.[79]

Just as Frank Lloyd Wright had done while he was employed with Adler and Sullivan, Parker Berry secured independent commissions and secretly worked on his own, outside Sullivan's office. One of the earliest of these was the First State Bank of Manlius, Illinois. A preliminary front elevation drawing, dated January 14, 1914, exhibited the strong influence of Sullivan's Adams Building in Algona.[80] The major difference was the addition of second-floor offices at Manlius whereas Sullivan's Algona building was one story in height. A second-story addition had been proposed for the Algona building several times, and there is a Berry design for an addition with working drawings dated January 6, 1917. However, Berry's design and a subsequent proposal (working drawings dated March 14, 1920) by Louis Sullivan for the Algona building were never realized.[81] As in the Algona building, the front facade of the Manlius bank has a recessed entryway flanked by brick piers capped by planters. A banding of terra cotta aligns with the second-floor windowsills and separates the upper story from the lower portion of the facade. Although the proportions of the facade could have been improved, the terra-cotta ornamentation—produced and manufactured by the American Terra Cotta and Ceramic Company in 1914—was comparable to that of Sullivan.[82] The small building is still inviting and gracious in the bypassed hamlet of Manlius, even though the ground floor is vacant and the second floor is now used as a residence.

Berry's next commissions were in his hometown of Princeton, Illinois. One was a remodeling (1915–16) of an existing building, the Princeton Dry Goods Store, with a

First State Bank (1914), Manlius, Illinois; Parker N. Berry, Architect. Photo: 1991.

new front facade and interior alterations. Shop drawings (dated January 14, 1916) for the Sullivanesque terra cotta were prepared by the Midland Terra Cotta Company, which produced the special order to Berry's design.[83] The red hue of the natural clay integrates with the tapestry brick and complements the warm cream-colored stucco of the upper wall. On the front facade at the second story, narrow brick piers separate large fixed windows from flanking operable-sash windows; wider piers, which separate window groupings, are stucco-faced and punctuated with brick string courses. Terra-cotta ornament caps each narrow pier and marks the intersection with the window lintel of brick headers.

Another remodeling project by Berry in Princeton was the Farmers National Bank (1917) on North Main Street, now unfortunately demolished. Berry's third project in

Henry C. Adams Land and Loan Office Building (1913), Algona, Iowa; although credited to Louis Sullivan, Parker N. Berry worked on the building while employed with Sullivan. The front facade, shown here, has now been badly modernized and the piers, urns, and art glass removed. Photo: Ralph Marlowe Line, 1951.

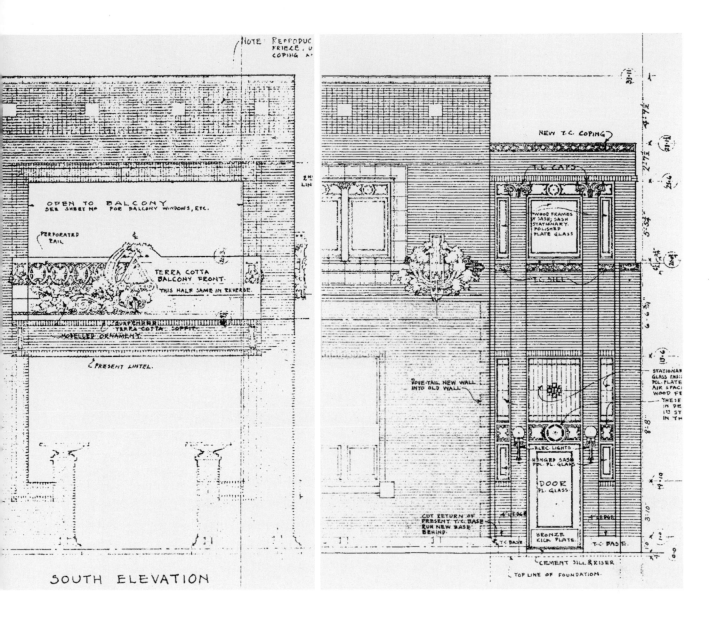

SOUTH ELEVATION

Princeton was the Adeline Prouty Old Ladies Home (1917), designed before Berry established his own practice in May 1917.[84] The building is devoid of ornamentation. Terra cotta from the Midland company was relegated to simple but specially made trim pieces for the roof eave, windows, and porch coping.[85]

Berry's most successful built design was the Interstate National Bank (1917–18; demolished) in the Hegewisch community in far southeast Chicago. Some of Berry's luxuriant ornament, from the American company, survives on site; the upper wall assembly was reused in an otherwise unexceptional two-story brick replacement structure.[86] Berry's Interstate National Bank was published in the November 1918 issue of the *Western Architect* and the plate illustrating the front facade presents a haunting image.[87] If one views the black-and-white plate and recalls the fragments of colorful terra cotta that still exist, one can imagine the sumptuous appearance of the original building. It must have been a surprising but rejuvenating experience to encounter such a work of art, with its vivid textures, colors, and patterns, in the melancholy isolation

Parker Berry's proposal for the remodeling of Sullivan's Adams Building, Algona, Iowa. The front facade is shown at the left and the rear addition is to the right in the partial side elevation. Original blueprints (dated January 6, 1917), collection of the author.

of the Hegewisch community, surrounded by factories, railroads, and other industrial installations.

Other projects further suggest Berry's potential as a Sullivanesque architect. The proposed Lincoln State Bank in Chicago (1912) was a forerunner to Berry's built banks. Although it was to be larger than those banks, it too had a recessed entranceway and dominating ornamental cluster at the parapet. The preliminary design drawing carried a notation that further described Berry's intent: "Front to be of Roman brick with terra cotta trimmings; the general color scheme to be a creamy buff monotone."[88] A large apartment building (1915) for Dr. Frank C. Titzell in Iowa City, Iowa, was another promising design; however, the constructed building did not achieve the potential suggested in the preliminary design drawings. This situation had a parallel to Berry's life; little of Berry's design potential was realized as his career was terminated just as it was beginning.

William L. Steele established an architectural practice in Sioux City, Iowa, in 1904. For the next twenty-four years, Steele practiced in Sioux City, where he was responsible for some attractive designs and was associated with the most important governmental buildings of the Sullivanesque to be built. William La Barthe Steele (1875–1947) was born in Springfield, Illinois.[89] Upon graduation from Springfield High School (1892), Steele entered the state university to study architecture. After graduation in 1896, Steele moved to Chicago and was employed as an architectural draftsman. Following his marriage, and with the help of Dean Nathan C. Ricker (1843–1924) of the University of Illinois, Steele secured a position with Louis Sullivan in 1902.[90] While with the firm, Steele acquired an admiration for Sullivan and developed a warm friendship with Sullivan's chief assistant, George Elmslie.[91]

The major project in Sullivan's office at the time Steele was employed was a twelve-story addition to the original nine-story Schlesinger and Mayer Department Store (now Carson Pirie Scott).[92] This was Sullivan's last major commission and it had a profound impact on Steele. Sullivan's use of wide expansive windows and white enamel terra-cotta claddings for the facades were recalled later by Steele in retailing structures in Sioux City. Early in 1904, Steele left Sullivan's firm and moved to Pittsburgh, Pennsylvania, but he remained there only for a short time.

In September 1904, Steele again relocated, this time to Sioux City, Iowa.[93] After a brief partnership (1905–7) with Wilfred W. Beach, Steele practiced architecture on his own and produced a number of Prairie School and Sullivanesque designs. At the same time, he was an active leader in the community and the profession.[94] He lectured frequently and occasionally had papers and articles published. He addressed the Illinois Society of Architects in Chicago in 1915, and on May 8, 1928, he gave a commemorative address about Louis Sullivan to the Chicago chapter of the AIA.[95] Among Steele's writings, a critique of Elmslie's Capitol Building and Loan Association (1918–22) in Topeka, Kansas, was published (September 1924) in the *Western Architect;* in it, Steele lavished praise on Elmslie's design.[96] Steele became a Fellow of the American Institute of Architects in 1918 and a member of the AIA national board of directors.[97] During the same period in which he was establishing his office and becoming a civic and professional leader, his family was growing; six children were born in Sioux City, joining a daughter who had been born in Chicago.[98]

Like many architects, Steele had clients with conservative tastes and his early work was eclectic. After winning a limited competition (1914) for a new courthouse for Woodbury County in Sioux City, Steele decided that his submission of a vaguely Gothic revival design could be supplanted by a progressive design in the Sullivanesque mode. He contacted George G. Elmslie, his old mentor and friend from Sullivan's office, for a joint venture in the design of the courthouse.[99] Steele was hired as architect for the courthouse on January 5, 1915, and immediately arranged for Elmslie to collaborate as associate architect.[100]

The Woodbury County Courthouse, despite some early objections to its "radical" design, was widely heralded upon its completion. It is one of the outstanding examples of the Sullivanesque style in the country. Because of this success, Steele found greater acceptance of progressive design idioms. He was finally able to secure commissions that enabled him to apply his interpretation of the Sullivanesque. One of the first of these was the Charles Mix County Courthouse (1917) in Lake Andes, South Dakota.[101] The Charles Mix building resembled the base structure at Sioux City, but smaller and without the tower rising above.

The first of Steele's Sullivanesque commercial structures was the three-story S. S. Kresge Building (1917; demolished c. 1980) in Sioux City.[102] Steele recalled the Schlesinger and Mayer store with his use of white-glazed claddings and the expression of the skeletal steel frame. Other shared features were Chicago windows and a thin projecting cornice (Sullivan's building cornice was removed, and most published photographs show the store with the top as a parapet). However, Sullivan had kept the terra-cotta cladding over the structural beams and columns aligned in the same plane. He created deeply recessed Chicago windows with ornament reserved for window returns and horizontal string courses. This, along with window proportions and repetitions, gave the building a horizontal emphasis. Conversely, Steele recessed the spandrel beams and emphasized the verticality of the piers on the Kresge Building. The Chicago windows on Steele's building were not deeply set, and terra-cotta ornament was integrated with the white-glazed brick surfaces. Steele capped the piers with capitals of stylized Sullivanesque ornament, although this ornament seemed somewhat rigid because the swirling movement was tight and the foliate was broad, as if influenced by arts and crafts decoration.[103] Steele may have wanted to create his own "original" ornament and consciously avoided copying Sullivan's designs too literally, given his knowledge of Sullivan's disdain for imitators.

William Steele took in a partner, George Hilgers, and the firm name became Steele and Hilgers in 1920.[104] In the early 1920s, Steele designed his most individualistic and successful interpretations of the Sullivanesque. These include the Sioux City Journal Building, a newspaper plant and office, and the Exchange Building at the Sioux City stockyards. Both were functional and forthright buildings with a simplicity of massing

S. S. Kresge Building (1917; demolished c. 1980), Sioux City, Iowa; William L. Steele, Architect. Photo: 1972.

that expressed power. They were ennobled with restrained but masterful touches of terra-cotta ornament. Both exteriors were of dark-hued brick that presented a somber but dignified appearance. If gender could be assigned to these buildings, they would be masculine.

The fenestration of the three-story Journal building revealed the functional organization of the interior. The majestically tall windows of the high-ceilinged first-floor space not only expressed the press room but helped establish a strong civic scale for the exterior. The placement of rhythmically spaced double-hung windows at the second floor represented the business offices; and the large expanses of steel industrial sash at the top floor clearly defined the newsroom and the type-setting room. Terra-cotta ornament matched the hue of the brickwork and framed important upper-story window openings and the street-level entryway. Although understated, the terra cotta outlined important areas and enriched and elevated the facades beyond well-proportioned utilitarian exteriors. The interior was of similar quality, with wall and ceiling finishes of plaster and selective use of plaster Sullivanesque ornament. The Journal building was demolished as part of an urban renewal project for downtown Sioux City.

Sioux City Journal Building (c. 1921; demolished c. 1980), Sioux City, Iowa; William L. Steele, Architect. Photo: c. 1971.

The dark brick of the three-story Exchange Building is enlivened by Sullivanesque ornament of highly contrasting white-glazed terra cotta. A terra-cotta string course aligns with the upper-story window heads, and the parapet has a terra-cotta coping. These two horizontal bands of terra cotta are connected by vertically elongated ornament laced over brick exterior surfaces; this defines a "frieze" that frames terra-cotta panels containing the name "Exchange Building." At a first-floor entrance, an ornate terra-cotta "lintel" panel creates a decorative surface with relief letters that spell out "The Live Stock National Bank." Although in later years the original windows and doorways were replaced with glass block, the building retains a dignified appearance and remains a refuge from the turmoil of the surrounding stockyards.

Steele again teamed with George Elmslie, when, in the late 1920s, the two were involved in the design of several buildings for Yankton College, Yankton, South Dakota. George Elmslie was listed as architect and the firm of Steele and Hilgers as associate architects for a science building, Forbes Hall (1929), and a men's dormitory (1931). Little is known about these commissions and their architectural connections. It is likely that the college contacted Steele, who served as a conduit to Elmslie. For these important commissions, Steele may have needed Elmslie's design expertise; at the same time, he may have wanted to assist Elmslie, who was struggling in his own practice. It's possible that Steele sought to rekindle his own design fervor by again associating with his old friend and mentor.[105] This may have been the case as Steele returned with rigor to the Sullivanesque for another retailing building in Sioux City.

The Williges Building recalled Steele's earlier use of white terra-cotta cladding for a retailing facade. Although it is conservative when compared to Sullivan's Schlesinger and Mayer Department Store and Steele's earlier S. S. Kresge Building, Steele's design for Williges presented a handsome front facade. Its construction date of 1930–31 places it among the final Sullivanesque designs constructed. On January 1, 1928, William L. Steele entered into a partnership with Thomas R. Kimball and J. Dow Sandham to form the architectural firm of Kimball, Steele, and Sandham, with offices in Omaha, Nebraska, and Sioux City, Iowa.[106] By October 1929, Steele and his family had left Sioux City for Omaha.[107] After 1931, it seems, Steele never designed another Sullivanesque building.

Louis W. Claude (1868–1951) was with the architectural firm of Adler and Sullivan for about two years (January 1890 to the latter part of 1891). His contact with other employees in the Adler and Sullivan firm, especially Frank Lloyd Wright and George G. Elmslie, had a strong influence on his life and work. Claude seems to have been personally closer to Wright, with whom he maintained a long friendship.[108] This affinity between Claude and Wright was probably grounded in their shared roots though it may have been because Claude acknowledged Wright's genius. Both men were born in small Wisconsin towns approximately equidistant from the capital city, Madison. In a scenario similar to that of Wright, Claude graduated from high school in Baraboo, Wisconsin, and then moved in 1887 to Madison, where he attended the University of Wisconsin. Like Wright, while a student Claude was employed part-time with engineers, Conover

Williges Building (1930–31), Sioux City, Iowa; William L. Steele, Architect. Photo: 1994.

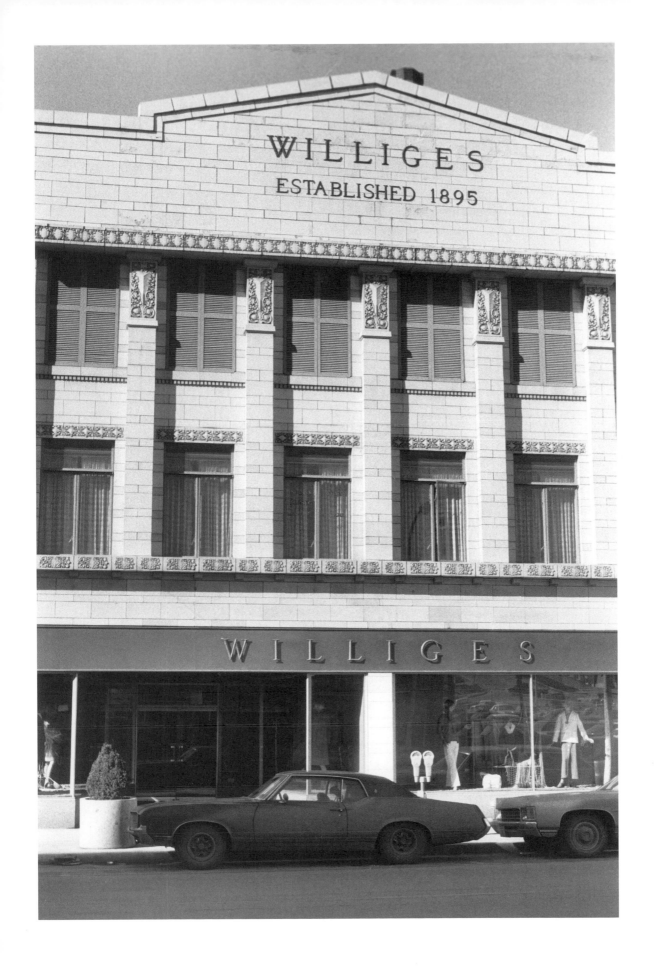

and Porter.[109] In December 1889 Claude moved to Chicago, where he secured a position with Adler and Sullivan and met Wright. After Claude left the Adler and Sullivan firm, he was employed by two other Chicago architects before he returned in 1893 to Madison. After teaching engineering for a brief time at the University of Wisconsin, Claude initiated his own independent architectural practice; and in 1896, he joined in partnership with Edward F. Starck (1868–1947).[110]

As a result of promotional activities and Claude's writings in such publications as the *Wisconsin Library Bulletin*, the firm gained commissions for library buildings; after having constructed some libraries, they became noted as experts in library design. The two partners designed some forty libraries in Illinois, Minnesota, and Wisconsin; in addition, Michigan and Washington each had a Claude and Starck library building. Although the firm was committed to Chicago-inspired "modern" architecture and created designs the architects themselves called "Sullivanesque," Claude and Starck, like many other designers—but unlike the unbending Louis Sullivan—would compromise and adopt eclectic styles favored by their clients.[111] For residential work, these included the Tudor style and Prairie School designs that showed either an arts and crafts influence or an alternative Wrightian flavor. Nonresidential work embraced a range of styles, including classical, Mediterranean, and Prairie with either an arts and crafts or Sullivanesque emphasis. It appears that the Sullivanesque was favored, for it appeared frequently; as early as 1904 it was used for a library in Wilmette, Illinois, and as late as 1927, for a high school in Baraboo, Wisconsin.

The Free Library in Wilmette, Illinois, initiated a series of libraries Claude and Starck designed in the Sullivanesque style. All shared an exterior design organization based on Frank Lloyd Wright's Winslow House (1893) in River Forest, Illinois, and Adler and Sullivan's Charnley House (1891) in Chicago. Symmetry was the keynote for each front facade; similarly for each building, the main entrance was framed by a material, such as stone, that would contrast with the building mass, which was usually of brick. A wide overhanging roof, with dominating horizontal fascia, seemed to hover above the ground. The banding of windows and Sullivanesque ornamentation recalled Sullivan's treatment for the upper wall surfaces of the Victoria Hotel in Chicago Heights, Illinois. This banding dematerialized the upper wall and seemed to disengage the roof from the exterior walls. However, the fenestration in the decorative banding was scaled down to clerestory size while windows were raised in height. Therefore, window and clerestory merged into large unified openings of glazing that clearly expressed the high-ceilinged space of the main floor. Exterior walls were divided into two segments of dissimilar heights, for example, a narrow decorative frieze atop a brick wall. This division seemed at first glance to ignore the high interior space of the main floor; however, the line of demarcation between frieze and brick generally expressed the height of interior wood casework, doors, and bookcases. Interior upper wall surfaces were plaster, to match the ceiling, and were interrupted only by the transom-like clerestory windows. Thus, there was logical integration of exterior and interior vertical relationships.

The Wilmette Library (1904; demolished) had a basic plan and organization similar to that of many small Carnegie libraries of the period; the main level was elevated and there was an English basement below. The lower level, partially below grade, contained support spaces and a meeting room while the raised first floor was given over to primary library functions. The repeated use of the basic concept for these library designs was feasible because the clients' building programs, the buildings' interior organization, and resulting floor plans were similar for libraries in the small towns where Claude and Starck secured commissions. The overall dimensions were the primary variables. Sometimes the rectangular plan was modified to a T-shape by a projecting rear wing to gain more area without excessively increasing the spans of structural members. Again, the basic parti was well established but variations were made to accommodate programmatic differences and create individual identities.

The first of a series of mature library designs in the handsome Sullivanesque style was the Eager Free Library in Evansville, Wisconsin, twenty miles south of Madison. Now listed on the National Register, the building was built in 1908 and was the gift of Almeron Eager, a prominent businessman and industrialist in the small town.[112] Sullivanesque ornament, in carved limestone, served as capitals for the two brick piers at the corners of a projecting entry vestibule. A limestone belting was aligned with the limestone of the vestibule fascia; it wrapped around the building and divided clerestory windows of art glass from larger window sash. In addition, the limestone belting separated an ornate frieze from the brick walls. The belting and frieze, in turn, articulated the building mass from a wide overhanging hip roof clad with red tiles. The frieze of Sullivanesque ornament appeared to be terra cotta but it was actually plaster, which was feasible on an exterior when protected by a wide roof overhang. Like Frank Lloyd Wright, who used ornamental plaster panels on the exterior of several of his Prairie houses, Claude used repeated plaster panels for the frieze of his Sullivanesque design at Evansville. This ornament has the tactile patterns and intimate scale of the best Sullivanesque work, but it was a catalog stock design. Perhaps the only distraction now is the cream color that has been painted over the ornamental plaster, which was originally a green-bronze color.[113]

The next in the succession of Sullivanesque libraries designed by Claude and Starck was constructed in Merrill, Wisconsin. The T. B. Scott Free Library (1911) was the largest of the firm's Wisconsin libraries. Its frieze was similar to the one at Evansville but the Sullivanesque ornament was different; in Merrill it was stock plaster panels (number 3024A). Each panel, 27 inches wide by 36 inches high, was supplied by the Architectural Decorating Company of Chicago.[114] The building was converted to a children's library after a major addition to the rear was constructed in 1969.[115]

Claude and Starck's design for the Flagg Township Library (1912) in Rochelle, Illinois, was very similar to the Evansville, Wisconsin, model. The symmetrical front facade had oriel windows flanking the projecting small entry vestibule. A red-tiled hip roof, ornamental Sullivanesque frieze (a stock panel, number 3024A, which differed somewhat from that at Evansville), and lower walls of brick completed the exterior ensemble. As in many of the original Claude and Starck libraries, a major addition to accommodate growth has been built at the rear.[116] The Public Library (1913) for Detroit Lakes, Minnesota, also had a decorative frieze (3024A panels), oriel windows on the front facade, and brick walls. Listed on the National Register of Historic Places, the original building has a 1990 addition.[117]

The two largest of Claude and Starck's original Sullivanesque-style libraries are in Merrill, Wisconsin, and Hoquiam, Washington, and the smallest was the Carnegie Library (1913) at Barron, Wisconsin. The building at Barron was 26 feet wide and 51 feet long, with a total floor area of 2,652 square feet. The established design concept was followed although the building's proportions were considerably different. The projecting entry vestibule was about the same size as the others, but the main building mass was much smaller. Yet the design formula worked. The number of windows was reduced, but the decorative frieze (3024A panels), brick walls, wide overhanging hip roof, and tile roofing were repeated. The last library of Sullivanesque lineage (1916) by Claude and Starck was at Tomah, Wisconsin, and it too has a major addition.[118]

Surprisingly, all of the architects for the new additions to Claude and Starck's Sullivanesque libraries were responsive to the original architecture. The latter-day designers realized the beauty and harmony of the original designs and respected the unique and irreplaceable details, such as plaster ornament and art-glass windows. In most cases, the

T. B. Scott Free Library (1911), Merrill, Wisconsin; Claude and Starck, Architects. Photo: 1991.

Flagg Township Library (1912), Rochelle, Illinois; Claude and Starck, Architects. Detail of stock fibrous panel supplied by the Architectural Decorating Company, Chicago. Photo: 1993.

historical integrity of the interiors did not fare as well. But the exteriors of Claude and Starck's designs were generally respected and served as guides that helped direct the new designs and suppress the contemporary designer's urge to make an individual and competing statement. The late twentieth-century additions, with their replicated ornamentation, suggest that Sullivanesque design principles and ornament may still have viability.

Claude and Starck used the Sullivanesque for buildings other than libraries. One of these was the Municipal Building in Lancaster, Wisconsin. Designed in 1919 but not built until 1922, the structure served the various uses of fire house, city offices, and civic theater.[119] Each department's space was like a separate building with shared walls. The facades responded clearly to these interior functions and a variety of facade treatments resulted. A unified whole was achieved through the exterior materials: golden-yellow brick and white-glazed terra cotta with Sullivanesque motifs. The office block had closely spaced brick pilasters capped by Sullivanesque terra-cotta capitals. The theater facade was composed with major and minor terra-cotta borders, ribbons of ornament that turned and framed the centrally positioned entry and marquee before continuing to trace a path near the facade perimeter.

The most handsome of Claude and Starck's Sullivanesque designs may have been their school buildings. Two Lincoln Schools built in 1915—one in Monroe, Wisconsin, and the other in Madison—were progressive and attractive designs. Both were similar in plan, with stair towers located at the ends of each building. Both designs were influenced by Frank Lloyd Wright's Larkin Building (1904), especially the side elevation with recessed spandrels and tall, closely spaced piers. In addition, both schools had ornamentation influenced by Purcell and Elmslie's ornamental designs, especially those of the bank at Winona.

The school in Madison, on a hill overlooking Lake Mendota, was organized as a two-and-a-half-story block of classrooms with vertical circulation and entrances articulated on the two opposite ends. This relegation of service elements to the perimeter to allow

Lincoln School (1915), Madison, Wisconsin; Claude and Starck, Architects. Detail of terra-cotta ornament above entrance. Photo: 1994.

consolidated program spaces was an innovation that Wright had introduced in the Larkin Building. Louis I. Kahn later expressed this concept as "served and service spaces." In the Madison school, two floors of classrooms rest on a base and have repeated narrow piers of brick superimposed on horizontal bands of fenestration. A stylized capital of terra-cotta ornament tops each pier. A decorative medallion terminates each end of the wall. These medallions, in glazed white enamel, were copies of the cruciform medallions that were used in a similar fashion on the upper wall segments at the Merchants Bank of Winona (1911–12) by Purcell, Feick, and Elmslie. In addition, pier capitals in the Madison building closely resemble the ornamental designs for those at Winona. The terra-cotta entrance motif for the Merchants Bank seems to have been reproduced over the entries at Madison, with only a school name panel added. However, the terra cotta for the school has a cheaper white glaze than the vivid colors used by Purcell, Feick, and Elmslie.[120] The Madison ornament was probably reproduced by the American Terra Cotta and Ceramic Company.[121] After the school was closed in 1963, it became an art center and then around 1985 was converted to its current use as an apartment building.

The Lincoln School in Monroe, Wisconsin, was similar in concept, but with some differences. It had a much longer facade than that of the Madison building, and the stairs and entrances were integrated into the main building massing rather than treated as appendages. In addition, the brickwork was in a range of deep reds, which clearly contrasted with the white-glazed terra-cotta ornamentation and trim. The raised basement, with punched window openings, formed a base and was accentuated by a terra-cotta belting that served as an integral sill for the first-floor windows. A series of closely spaced piers separated the first- and second-floor horizontal window bandings into separate openings, and these piers had terra-cotta capitals, measuring 32" × 29" × 29", that replicated the ornamental designs of those used by Purcell, Feick, and Elmslie at Winona.[122] Similarly, the ornamental entry used at Winona, with a closed arch and eagle motif, was copied at Monroe as it had been at Madison. Three terra-cotta cruciform medallions, also copied from Winona, were important accents on the uppermost brick wall; one was placed directly above each entrance and one centered on the facade. Strong horizontal building relationships were established at grade and at the sky and these were "stitched" together on the vertical by the rhythmic ribs of the brick piers. The building was enhanced by an almost subliminal but vital link to the ground via an earthen plinth and, at the ends, low retaining walls and broad, gentle steps. Unfortunately, the building suffered a fire in 1973 and was demolished in 1975. Only a few fragments of ornament survive in the hands of collectors.

A third school building of Sullivanesque design and late vintage (1927–28) by Claude and Starck was built in Baraboo, Wisconsin. The three-story high-school building at Baraboo has some of the design features the architects employed earlier. Repeated brick piers, of narrow dimension and with ornate terra-cotta capitals, rise from a base. Arched entrances are framed by an ornate portal and flanking winged lions of terra cotta. The stylized lions, each holding a shield, closely resemble the lion figures that Louis Sulli-

van used on his Ohio projects, the Home Building Association in Newark and the People's Savings and Loan Association in Sidney. All of the Baraboo terra cotta was supplied by the American Terra Cotta and Ceramic Company (order no. 4034), which also produced the terra cotta for Sullivan's buildings in Ohio.[123] The terra-cotta finish used at Baraboo was a mottled tan, matte glaze and resembled granite. A new high school opened in 1962 and Claude and Starck's building is now used as a civic center. Over the span of their partnership, Claude and Starck designed hundreds of buildings.[124] They used a variety of styles in their work but returned, when they could, to the Sullivanesque.

Born on October 16, 1892, in St. Louis, William Charles Presto eventually had a warm friendship with Louis Sullivan that stemmed from his employment with Sullivan for a short time.[125] Presto was responsible for Louis Sullivan's last built architectural design. In 1921, Presto secured the job from a neighbor, William P. Krause, and on

Krause's behalf asked Sullivan to design the front facade for the Krause Music Store at 4611 North Lincoln Avenue in Chicago. The small building consisted of a basement and first-floor shop with an apartment above for the Krause family.[126] The street facade, twenty-five feet wide by twenty-eight feet high, was richly ornamented with muted-green-glazed terra cotta supplied by the American Terra Cotta and Ceramic Company.[127] Within the symmetrically composed facade, Sullivan centered a large, recessed display window that had splayed soffit and jamb returns. Two entry doors flank the window—one on the left for access to the apartment and the other on the right as the shop entrance—and were positioned within the splayed wall segments. The entire recess, almost as wide as the facade, became a proscenium, and the theatrical effect was completed by rows of small incandescent light bulbs integrated into the sloping soffit of ornate terra cotta. The upper story was punctuated by a large and dominating cartouche that extended above the facade. With completion of the building in 1922, business was good for William Krause. But later his fortunes declined and he committed suicide in his upstairs apartment. After 1929 and for succeeding decades, the building housed a mortuary. Now the building houses the Kelmscott Gallery, dealers in arts and crafts, antiques, and architectural artifacts.

Presto's own architectural commissions were relegated to residential work, small apartment buildings, and commercial buildings in Chicago's neighborhoods.[128] Most of his work was competent but uninspiring. His designs for store buildings, for which he employed terra cotta, were generally facades composed according to Sullivanesque principles but were mostly devoid of Sullivanesque ornament.[129] His best and most apparently Sullivanesque designs owe more to the Midland Terra Cotta Company than directly to Louis Sullivan. For a two-story building at West Montrose Avenue and North Christiana Avenue, Chicago, Presto adapted stock terra-cotta ornament from the Midland company. Built in 1924–25, the building was developed by A. D. Schuller for a bowling alley.[130] Presto's design was characterized by expansive banding of horizontal glazing at the second-story street facades. However, the design has been desecrated by the removal of the original glazing and its replacement with an infill of vinyl siding and small in-set windows. Three sets of Sullivanesque ornamental clusters remain at the parapet and distinguish the building. For another building on Montrose Avenue, at the northwest corner with North Artesian Avenue, Presto again utilized Midland's stock Sullivanesque terra cotta. Both of Presto's Sullivanesque designs on Montrose Avenue were constructed at the same time; however, the one at Artesian has been demolished.[131] Although Presto's Sullivanesque designs were successful for inexpensive structures, his major contribution to the art of architecture in Chicago was his role in retaining Louis Sullivan to design the front facade of the Krause Music Store.

Henry J. Schlacks and Henry A. Ottenheimer were both alumni of the Adler and Sullivan office and were together in partnership (c. 1901–6) as the firm of Schlacks and Ottenheimer. After dissolution of their partnership, neither seemed to embrace the Sullivanesque, although Ottenheimer's successor firm, Ottenheimer, Stern, and Reichert, was responsible for some progressive architectural designs.[132] Many of these projects had Prairie School or Sullivanesque origins but were also influenced by Viennese design.[133] One of the more notable achievements of the firm was inducing R. M. Schindler to come to Chicago from Austria in 1914. Rudolph M. Schindler (1887–1953) admired Sullivan and became a friend. Schindler was a designer with the Ottenheimer's firm for three years before he left to join Frank Lloyd Wright at Taliesin and eventually he found his way to California.[134]

Simeon B. Eisendrath was born in Chicago, studied architecture at MIT, and was with the office of Adler and Sullivan for a time before practicing architecture independently in Chicago. In 1899, Eisendrath's Plymouth Building was built on a through lot between South Dearborn Street and Plymouth Court, sandwiched between two famous Chicago School landmarks, William Le Baron Jenney's Manhattan Building (1891) and the Old Colony (1894) by Holabird and Roche. Eisendrath's design was in sympathy with Chicago School principles and incorporated first-floor storefronts of ornamented Sullivanesque cast iron. A 1945 remodeling drastically altered the building, but cast-iron ornament around the Plymouth Court storefront survives, although recently garishly painted. The cast-iron designs resemble those on Sullivan's Schlesinger and Mayer Building and the decorative iron fronts for both structures were cast by the same foundry, Winslow Brothers Iron Works. On the interior of the Plymouth Building, a Winslow newel post survives. It matches those the company made for Sullivan's Schlesinger and Mayer.[135]

By 1900, Eisendrath had relocated to the East. Still, he designed at least one other Sullivanesque building for Chicago. It was a simple walk-up apartment building, U-shaped in plan, and featured ornate entrances of Sullivanesque ornament in red terra cotta. Built in 1910, the building survives despite redevelopment pressures for its prime site overlooking Lincoln Park.[136] Eisendrath became an instructor in the Department of Architecture at the Carnegie Institute of Technology, Pittsburgh, Pennsylvania, and later moved to New York City, where he died on November 26, 1935.[137]

Irving Gill (1870–1936) was with Adler and Sullivan for two years (1890–92) after moving to Chicago from his native Syracuse, New York. He then left for San Diego, California, where he became a leader of progressive architecture. Although some of his earlier work in San Diego, such as the Pickwick Theatre (1904), was grounded in the Sullivanesque, Gill developed a personal style.[138] He blended Sullivanesque design principles, but not the ornament, with regional vernacular and influences from the Viennese movement. In addition, he drew upon the philosophy of the arts and crafts movement as expounded by Gustav Stickley's publication *The Craftsman*, ingeniously incorporating it into highly original work that inherently expressed its place, spirit, and time.

After working as a draftsman for Adler and Sullivan, James B. Rezny (1871–1945) became head draftsman for another well-known Chicago architect, Jarvis Hunt (1861–1941). Rezny held this position for many years before forming a partnership (c. 1913) with an engineer; the firm name was Rezny and Krippner.[139] Rezny designed several small commercial buildings in 1921–22 that had terra-cotta ornament and were in the Sullivanesque style. However, none was exceptional.[140]

The struggle to adhere to, let alone advance, the teachings of Sullivan, must have been difficult for Sullivan's former employees, given the pervasive design climate of eclecticism at the time.[141] Only a handful were successful. The application of the Sullivanesque was mostly left to others, architects who had only indirect knowledge of Sullivan's aesthetic language and therefore perhaps more freedom to adapt it.

CHAPTER 5

ORNAMENT

Materials, Artisans, and Early Suppliers

SULLIVANESQUE ORNAMENT was realized through the efforts of companies and artisans who executed the architects' original designs. Collaboration was necessary to produce the decorative designs and integrate them with the architecture. Generally, Sullivan and Elmslie, unlike Wright, acknowledged the contributions of these companies and individuals. An examination of the contributions of these skilled workers and suppliers is necessary to understand fully the scope of the Sullivanesque style; in some cases, the artisans and suppliers even furthered and promoted the Sullivanesque.

Louis Sullivan's ornamental designs were made in many different materials, including cast iron, bronze, wrought iron, stone, wood, plaster, ceramic tile, painted stencilwork, and glass. However, his ornament is most often associated with terra cotta. Similarly, Purcell and Elmslie utilized the same array of materials for their decorative designs. Like Frank Lloyd Wright, they expanded decorative design through extensive application of ornament to interior appointments such as furniture, carpets, window treatments, and linens. The ornamental designs of Purcell and Elmslie, like those of Sullivan, are mostly remembered as the exquisite terra-cotta work that became an integral and essential part of their architecture.

Although Frank Lloyd Wright used terra cotta, it was not a material he favored. In fact, Wright is not associated with one particular material for ornament. Over the various phases of his lengthy career, he experimented with a greater range of materials for both ornamentation and construction than did Sullivan or Purcell and Elmslie. These materials included concrete, precast concrete, and copper. The exterior ornament for some of Wright's early buildings appeared to be terra cotta but was actually plaster. Wright's designs extended to interior finishes and built-ins, such as wallpapers and furniture, and general accessories including china, glassware, and silverware. Perhaps Wright's decorative designs that are most prized now are the leaded glass windows, lamps, and furniture of his Prairie School period. Exterior ornament on Wright's earliest buildings was inspired by Sullivan, but Wright soon developed his own stylized ornament by defoliating the "trellis" and emphasizing its geometric framework.

Some Sullivanesque architects, including Louis Sullivan and especially Purcell and Elmslie, attempted to achieve the design control that Wright frequently exercised. As in the Prairie School and the arts and crafts movements, design of the total environment was a goal of the Sullivanesque architect. A harmonious integration of interior and exterior was desired but difficult to achieve. With residential work and enlightened clients, this objective was accomplished within the Prairie School more often at the domestic scale. In the predominantly nonresidential buildings of the Sullivanesque, significant emphasis on the interior design was difficult to achieve. Because of constantly changing tenants and differing functional needs in commercial and office buildings, interior spaces and finishes were often altered and remodeled. This meant that utility and flexibility became important design criteria, and interior embellishments, such as ornamentation, were minimal or nonexistent. Therefore, exterior design was usually emphasized and facades became the subject of design concentration. Nonresidential projects and especially speculative developments frequently had tight construction budgets, thus application of inexpensive materials was often necessary. This usually meant that in the Sullivanesque, terra cotta was used for exteriors and plaster for interiors.

Several companies in Chicago made stock ornamental pieces from varieties of plasters called "fibrous plastic," for interiors, and "composition," for exterior use. As described in the book *Industrial Chicago* (1891), fibrous plastic is "composed of paper pulp and canvas with sufficient plastic gypsum and other materials mixed therewith to make a substantial and ornamental covering for walls and ceilings that will not crack and is fireproof"; composition is "manufactured of cement and fibrous materials, molded into flexible molds, thereby securing the greatest relief for the work, which is equally as good for the purpose intended as if carved in solid stone."[1] Catalogs from manufacturers illustrated a wide variety of shapes and design styles. Most of the available ornamental designs were based on historical styles, but some Sullivanesque pieces were manufactured and clearly labeled "Sullivanesque" by two major Chicago companies, the Architectural Decorating Company and the Decorator's Supply Company.

William Steele used a Sullivanesque "Cornice" (no. 3434) from the Decorator's Supply Company to serve as capitals for the plaster-encased square column piers in the office spaces for the Sioux City Journal Building.[2] Claude and Starck used Sullivanesque decorative panels (no. 3024A) from the Architectural Decorating Company for the exterior frieze on several libraries, including those at Merrill, Wisconsin; Rochelle, Illinois; and Detroit Lakes, Minnesota.[3] Plaster panels custom made on the job site were used for the exterior decorative frieze on Wright's Dana House (1903–4) in Springfield, Illinois. However, the deterioration of the exterior plaster for the Dana House required its removal and replication in a 1989–90 restoration.[4] Like Wright, Claude and Starck used plaster or composition for exterior friezes since those were protected by wide roof overhangs. Both plaster and composition required protective coats of paint.

Located in Chicago at 2547 Archer Avenue, at the intersection with Leo Street, the Decorator's Supply Company offered a number of Sullivanesque ornamental designs in different cast materials. A company catalog indicated these choices of materials as "Portland Cement, Exterior Composition, Fibrous Plaster Casts and Compo Casts."[5] As identified also in company catalogs, Sullivanesque components included: "Leaves and Bands (Nos. 2711 & 2758), soffits for Beams (No. 4441), Cornices (Nos. 3434 & 3492), Coves and Cornices (No. 1006), Cornices and Architraves (No. 1160), Friezes (Nos. 2618, 2620, 2667, 4767 & 4775), and Panels (Nos. 1658 & 1660)."[6] The chief designer for the Decorator's Supply Company was a German immigrant, Oscar Spindler (1861–c. 1930).[7] Spindler rose to become vice president (1896) and president (1917) of the company.[8] The Decorator's Supply Company is still in existence and makes products similar to those of a hundred years ago.

Cast Sullivanesque ornament was also available from the Architectural Decorating Company.[9] Situated at 1600–14 South Jefferson Street, Chicago, the company made a wide range of ornament from various materials. As described in company catalogs, these materials included fibrous plaster, which was "cast with moulding plaster reinforced with hemp fiber in connection with interior plaster finish"; exterior composition, which was painted like wood and in which joints between casts were filled with painter's oil putty; and cast stone.[10] Among pieces identified by the company as Sullivanesque were: "Frieze Ornaments (Nos. 6412, 6414, 6419 & 6420), Coves and Cornices (Nos. 2745A & 2746A), Panel Ornaments (Nos. 3024A & 3241), Grotesque Heads (No. 3232A), and Brackets (No. 1926B)."[11] Of these pieces, the two ornamental panels were the most handsome and effective. Both of these cast panels resembled an ornate terra-cotta panel designed by Louis Sullivan for the Home Building Association (1914), Newark, Ohio; however, the panels even more closely approximated a terra-cotta piece from the First National Bank Building (1910), Rhinelander, Wisconsin, by Purcell, Feick, and Elmslie.

The construction boom that followed the Chicago fire of 1871 brought many architects and building artisans to Chicago. Among these was James Legge (1835–90). Born in England, Legge worked in New York before moving to Chicago in the mid-1870s to work as a modeler at the Chicago Terra Cotta Company. Legge later worked independently as an architectural sculptor and modeler. He had a decorating firm that did interior ornament for such Adler and Sullivan projects as the McVicker's Theater

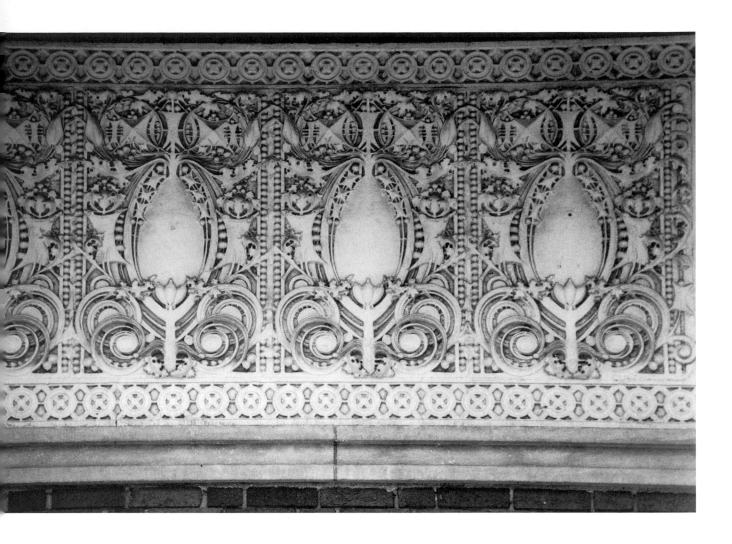

T. B. Scott Free Library (1911), Merrill, Wisconsin; Claude and Starck, Architects. Detail of exterior frieze using stock plaster ornament supplied by the Architectural Decorating Company, Chicago. Photo: 1991.

Remodeling (1885; demolished 1922) and was a subcontractor for the plaster ornamentation at the Auditorium Building.[12]

The interiors of Louis Sullivan's Owatonna Bank have been attributed to the decorating firm of Spierling and Linden. However, there is some debate about this.[13] But the company was involved with progressive architectural designs of the period, including works of Wright as well as Sullivan. Established 1882, the Spierling and Linden Company was headed by Ernest John Spierling (1856–1931) and Frank Louis Linden (1859–1934).[14] The Linden Company was the successor to the Linden Glass Company and the Spierling and Linden decorating concern. It went out of business after Linden died in 1934.[15]

Another prominent Chicago decorating firm, Healy and Millet, was often associated with the work of Adler and Sullivan. For example, the firm was responsible for the interior work at the Auditorium Building and the Chicago Stock Exchange.[16] In addition, Louis J. Millet (1856–1923) later consulted with Sullivan for the bank interiors at Owatonna, Minnesota, and Sidney, Ohio. Although Healy and Millet provided a full range of interior wares and services, the firm became most noted for its stained glass. The company perfected the technique of creating windows by assembling fragments

Opposite: Sioux City Journal (c. 1921; demolished), Sioux City, Iowa; William L. Steele, Architect. Detail of interior plaster encasement of column and beam. Photo: c. 1971.

of various glasses in mosaic fashion rather than using traditional methods of painting. After George Louis Healy and Louis J. Millet dissolved their partnership, Millet continued to practice and to teach at the School of the Art Institute of Chicago (1886–1918).[17] Millet's primary responsibility for the National Farmers' Bank in Owatonna was the production of the art-glass windows and he served as a color consultant and coordinator, although the ornamental plasterwork may have been by Spierling and Linden.[18] The bank has a glowing interior with large arched windows of stained glass, stenciled walls, painted and gilded plasterwork, terra cotta, and roman brick. Despite remodeling, it remains one of the most beautiful interiors in American architecture as well as the Sullivanesque style.

During the Sullivanesque era, some interior decorators in Chicago were not only contractors but made custom architectural materials and accessories, including plaster moldings, ornament, sculpture, and decorative specialties that often included art glass and lamps. However, only the firms previously discussed are known for certain to have been responsible for Sullivanesque designs.[19] In addition, a number of independent or freelance artists and sculptors were involved with designs of the Sullivanesque. Among these artists were Arthur Feudel, Albert Fleury, Oskar Gross, John W. Norton, and Allen Philbrick; independent sculptors included Richard W. Bock, Alfonso Iannelli, and Emil Zettler.

The murals in the theater of Adler and Sullivan's Auditorium Building (1887–89) were painted by Albert Fleury. In addition, Fleury, along with a German immigrant named Arthur Feudel, painted the interior murals for the Schiller/Garrick Theater Building.[20] Fleury also did architectural renderings; one of his most famous was the beautiful watercolor of Sullivan's Schlesinger and Mayer Department Store, now in the collection of the Chicago Historical Society.

The murals for the interior of Louis Sullivan's Owatonna bank were painted by Oskar Gross. The exterior walls that faced intersecting streets each contained a great arched window, and similar arched "openings" were created in the solid interior walls opposite. Within these blind arches were painted pastoral scenes dominated by blue sky and puffy clouds. Although not of the same superb quality as the rest of the interior finishes, Gross's murals were effective in creating a sense of openness. This effect made the blind arches appear important and logical, especially as they balanced the two great arched openings of art glass, which admitted tinted natural light. This project was the only one on which the Viennese-born Gross worked for Sullivan,[21] although Gross worked in Chicago as a muralist and artist for decades.[22] Gross did paint a portrait of Sullivan's former partner, Dankmar Adler, for the Chicago chapter of the American Institute of Architects.[23]

Louis Sullivan's Peoples Savings Bank in Cedar Rapids, Iowa, had interior murals painted by Allen Philbrick.[24] Philbrick painted scenes of Iowa farmscapes and farmhands on the plaster surfaces of the spandrel panels for the clerestory above the main banking space.

Like his mentor, Louis Sullivan, George G. Elmslie made extensive use of interior murals. He usually employed John Warner Norton (1876–1934) as the artist for these murals. This was true for the Woodbury County Courthouse, Sioux City, Iowa; the Capitol Building and Loan Association, Topeka, Kansas; and the Old Second National Bank, Aurora, Illinois. Elmslie may have used Norton because of Norton's association with Frank Lloyd Wright. A noted progressive artist, Norton created murals for Wright's Midway Gardens (1914) on Chicago's South Side. However, Wright was unhappy that these murals were so bold and not subservient to his architecture.[25] Given the petty competitiveness between Elmslie and Wright, it would have been like Elmslie to employ Norton and succeed when Wright could not. The Woodbury County Courthouse murals curiously show representational human figures clad in classical attire. But the scale and color in these murals, especially the use of gold-leaf, related to the architecture and dematerialized the floor spandrels and solid railings that overlook the rotunda space. Norton also painted a mural called *Westward* (1923) in the president's office of Sullivan's Owatonna bank.

Although Richard W. Bock (1865–1949) worked for the Northwestern Terra Cotta Company in the mid-1880s, he is best known for his independent work as a sculptor. Bock performed work for Louis Sullivan and Purcell and Elmslie, as well as for other Prairie School architects; however, he is most noted for the architectural sculptures executed for Frank Lloyd Wright. These include *The Boulder*, for Wright's own home in Oak Park, and sculptural pieces for the Dana House, the Larkin Building, the Martin House, and a bank in Mason City, Iowa.[26] Bock first met Wright in Adler and Sullivan's office while Bock was sculpting relief panels for the interior of the Schiller Theater. These panels were large lunettes that flanked the stage on the side walls above box seats. The decorative frieze for Wright's Heller Residence (1897) was sculpted by Bock and was a Sullivanesque element that combined Sullivan's foliate themes with female figures and geometric elements. Bock's work with Purcell and Elmslie included a small sculptural piece, *Nils on His Goose*, for Purcell's own house in Minneapolis and a fountain for Purcell's father's house in River Forest, Illinois.[27] Although trained in the classical style at the Berlin Academy and the Ecole des Beaux-Arts, Paris, Bock adapted to progressive design and was particularly receptive to Wright's ideas and directions.[28]

Another sculptor, Alfonso Iannelli (1888–1965), came from California specifically to work on Frank Lloyd Wright's Midway Gardens. This collaboration, though filled with tension and debate, resulted in a creative integration of architecture and sculpture; moreover, the geometric human figures cast in concrete anticipated radical explorations in art. Iannelli was a native of Andretta, Italy, and, after stops in New York and California, became a resident of Chicago. For Purcell and Elmslie, Iannelli sculpted the heroic figures that were realized in terra cotta for the exterior of the Woodbury County Courthouse.[29] About twenty years later, Iannelli again sculpted human forms in terra cotta, this time for Elmslie's Oliver P. Morton School (1935–37) in Hammond, Indiana. Influences of progressive design from Wright, the Sullivanesque, cubism, and art deco were synthesized by Iannelli for a public art masterpiece, the Fountain of the Pioneers (1937) for Bronson Square in downtown Kalamazoo, Michigan. The piece has an American theme, inspiration, and spirit. It is a civic statement with forms in concrete, embossed with decorative patterns, and complemented by the vibrant motion and sound of water.

George G. Elmslie incorporated sculptures of human figures in terra cotta in many of his larger buildings. Emil Robert Zettler sculpted figures for the Capitol Building and Loan (1923) in Topeka, Kansas; the Thornton Township High School (1934–35), Calumet City; and the Thomas A. Edison School (1935–37) in Hammond, Indiana. Born March 30, 1878, in Karlsruhe, Germany, Zettler was brought to the United States at age four. He was educated in Chicago public schools and pursued advanced studies at the Royal Academy, Berlin; the Julian Academy, Paris; and the Art Institute of Chicago.[30]

Some of the most wonderful interiors of American architecture were designed by Sullivanesque architects. These interiors dazzle, not by sheer size, but by the quality of the spatial composition and the treatment of surfaces. Lighting effects, use of sumptuous color, rich patterns, the integration of ornament, and the manipulation of scale contribute to vivid but harmonious interiors. Certainly the interiors of Louis Sullivan's Owatonna Bank; the Winona Bank by Purcell, Feick, and Elmslie; and the Woodbury County Courthouse by Purcell and Elmslie are among the most beautiful and distinctive architectural spaces to be found anywhere. However, these lush interiors were rare in the Sullivanesque. Grand spaces were in the realm of governmental and institutional buildings with conservative clients who usually opted for historical eclectic designs. As noted earlier, the Sullivanesque was first adopted for high-rise office buildings, which generally had small, repetitive interior spaces. Later, the style was appropriated for small-scale commercial and auto-related building types because of its adaptability to accommodate functional needs. Generally, these building types didn't have large-scale dramatic interiors. Instead, interiors were spartan and flexible for utilitarian and economical reasons. Ornament for the interior, if any was used, was usually executed in plaster. These buildings were usually an integral part of an urban street frontage and not freestanding objects. Therefore, the exterior facade(s) became the object of design concentration, and ornamentation was incorporated. The usual material of choice for ornament was terra cotta. Although sometimes used on interiors, terra cotta was principally an exterior material and, with its plastic properties, was excellent for molded ornamentation. Terra cotta has been so closely associated with Louis Sullivan that it and the Sullivanesque style have become almost synonymous.[31]

The manufacturing of terra cotta incorporated machine production but it was still labor-intensive. As summarized in the *Dodge Construction News:* "an individual architectural drawing was required for every piece; each piece had to be hand-pressed and finished; joints had to be hand-ground, then fitted together in what was an enormous puzzle."[32] In order to appreciate fully the intricacies of terra cotta as the principal material for Sullivanesque ornament, an understanding of its production is helpful.

Each terra-cotta manufacturer had a drafting department where draftsmen transferred the architect's designs to shop drawings. These shop drawings were used by the manufacturer for production purposes and by the contractor during building construction. For each new piece of terra cotta, a full-size drawing was made and had to take into account the shrinkage of the clay. Shrinkage could be from 9 to 11 percent depending on the properties of the clay and mostly occurred during drying and firing.[33] A three-dimensional model, usually in clay, was sculpted by a craftsman called a modeler. The modeler would refer to the full-size drawings while preparing the model. Upon completion, the model or photographs of the model were reviewed by the architect and approved before the process continued. After approval, a mold was made from the model. Moldmakers generally used plaster of paris to form the mold, which was comprised of various take-apart sections to allow removal of the casting. Complicated shapes required the mold to be comprised of many parts.[34] The completed mold was a negative of the model and was ready to receive the clay for the finished wares.

Preparation of clay for terra cotta was begun by crushing and pulverizing the clay in huge machines until it could pass through 16 to 18 mesh. Once it was pulverized, grog was added. Grog was previously fired terra cotta, which usually came from broken or defective wares, and was ground into small particles. The grog additive helped reduce shrinkage and constituted 30 to 40 percent of the clay body. Crushed, cleaned, and dried, the prepared clay was then placed in a pug mill. A proper proportion of water and other additives, such as a solution of barium carbonate, were mixed and blended with the clay until thoroughly amalgamated. Barium carbonate neutralized soluble salts in the clay.[35] The processed clay was then covered and "aged" for a day or more until excessive moisture evaporated but the clay was still pliable. The clay body was cut into smaller chunks, called slugs or balls, for easier handling during placement and compaction in the molds.

Tubs or carts of clay slugs were moved to the pressing area with its various work stations. The clay then was pressed into molds by hand (attempts to use machines for pressing were always unsuccessful). The pressman kneaded the clay on a board until the slug had a smooth surface and the smooth side was thrown against the mold face.[36] The process was repeated until the mold was lined with clay, thoroughly pressed into place and built up to an even thickness of one to one-and-a-half inches. The pressing process had to eliminate any air pockets or bubbles in the clay assemblage; otherwise, during the firing, steam would form in the trapped air pockets and crack or break the piece. The thickness of the clay was dependent upon the overall size of the piece. Pieces had to be kept small to prevent "warping" or twisting that could occur during the firing process. Also the pieces had to be manageable for a workman to handle on the construction job. Therefore, a large ornamental design would be composed of numerous pieces.

The pressing process was completed with the addition of clay strips, called stiffeners or webbing, across the back of the piece. These acted as reinforcement, especially during drying and firing. The completed piece was boxlike, with a hollow back. The primary reason for an open-back shape was to assure even firing and shrinkage. The hollow space also reduced the weight of the piece and made it easier to handle.[37] For terra-cotta claddings, which required metal anchors for attachment to a building, slots or holes were formed in the back of the clay pieces to receive anchoring devices. Reference numbers or identifications were incised in the back of each piece.

After all press work, the clay was allowed to dry, usually six to twelve hours, and the mold was removed. During the elapsed time, the clay had shrunk some, which made the mold easier to pull away. However, if the clay sat too long, the mold could absorb too much moisture from the clay and adhere to it. If this happened, the mold might be damaged during its removal. Exposed clay surfaces were seldom perfect; therefore, some touch-up by hand was required. A skilled molder worked the clay as necessary to smooth out blemishes.[38] Finally, the ware was taken to a drying room where it was dried by recirculating air heated by steam coils to a temperature of 120 to 140 degrees Fahrenheit. Depending on the plant and equipment, this drying process could take fifteen to forty hours.[39] The ware had to be perfectly dry before it could be fired.

Before the ware was fired, a finish was usually applied. During the early period of the Sullivanesque, slips of natural colors were often used as the finish for terra-cotta ornament. Slips were liquid clays applied to the surface of the ware, and the resulting color was dependent on the kind of clay used for the slip. This technique was often used to simulate stone. Later, ceramic glazes were popular. These enamels were sprayed over the exposed surfaces of the piece. If required, different effects could be achieved, such as mottling or speckling, and these could simulate other materials, such as granite. Ceramic engineers developed many glazing-enamel formulas that produced different colors and sheens after firing.[40] The major obstacle in the glazing process was regulating the constituents so that the contraction of the glaze would match the contraction of the clay during firing.[41] If contraction was uneven, some failures occurred. "Crazing" was the most common problem but this was usually not considered to be too serious. Crazing was when the glaze formed a multitude of tiny cracks in a weblike pattern. It appeared similar to the small cracks on a fractured but intact egg shell. Glaze blisters and spalling were more objectionable problems.

From the spraying room, the wares were moved to the kiln area, where they were placed in a kiln to be fired. The kiln was usually the muffle type, which had a beehive shape. The kiln was gradually heated to a temperature in excess of 2000 degrees Fahrenheit. The exact temperature depended upon the type of kiln and clays to be fired. Firing was a long process during which heat slowly built to the required temperature, and then the kiln was slowly cooled.[42] The total elapsed time varied from a week to ten days, again dependent upon the kiln specifications and types of clay. Tunnel kilns were

Detail, Bozeman-Waters National Bank (1924), Poseyville, Indiana; Clifford Shopbell and Company, Architects.

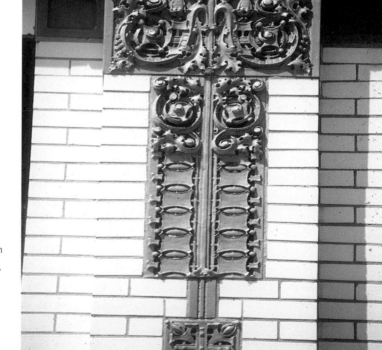

Terra-cotta ornament, Fitch Laundry (c. 1924), LaSalle, Illinois; attributed to John Hanifen, Architect.

Detail of upper facade, commercial building for Martin W. Floberg (1923), 120–34 Church St., Rockford, Illinois; Peterson and Johnson, Architects.

Detail, Merchants Bank of Winona (1912), Winona, Minnesota; Purcell, Feick, and Elmslie, Architects.

Opposite: Art-glass dome, Woodbury County Courthouse (1916–18), Sioux City, Iowa; Purcell and Elmslie, with William L. Steele, Architects.

Terra-cotta ornament, First
National Bank (1924), Adams,
Minnesota; George G. Elmslie,
Architect.

Pier capital, Oliver P. Morton
School (1936–37), Hammond,
Indiana; George G. Elmslie
with William S. Hutton,
Architects.

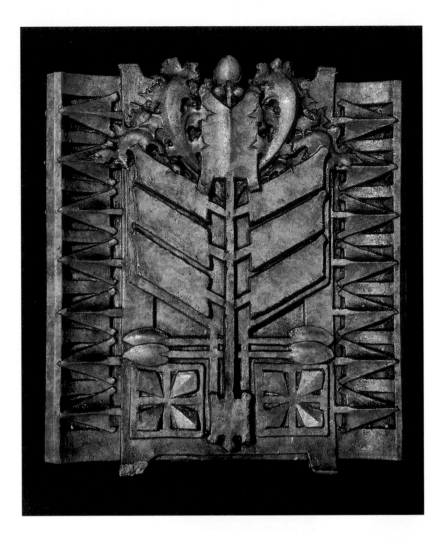

Pier capital, Thomas A. Edison School (1936–37), Hammond, Indiana; George G. Elmslie with William S. Hutton, Architects.

Terra-cotta capitals, Lincoln School (1915), Madison, Wisconsin; Claude and Starck, Architects.

Terra-cotta facade, Toner Store
(1915), Martinsville, Indiana;
building and ornament designed by
Midland Terra Cotta Company.

Masonic Temple (1914), St.
Joseph, Illinois; building and orna-
ment designed by Midland Terra
Cotta Company.

Store building (1921–22),
7638–48 N. Paulina, Chicago;
Carl M. Almquist was the architect
but Midland Terra Cotta Company
records indicate the company
designed the street facade.

Detail, Bosert and Cohlgraff Store
(1922), 7639–45 N. Paulina, Chicago;
building and ornament designed by
Midland Terra Cotta Company.

Store for Fred Hein (1924),
Chicago; Benedict J. Bruns,
Architect.

Detail of second-story terra-cotta ornament for a commercial building remodeling (1920), 11429–31 S. Michigan Avenue, Chicago; Clarence Hatzfeld, Architect.

Entrance, William E. Nesbit Building (1914), Chicago; Louis C. Bouchard, Architect.

an improvement and replaced the beehive type in some terra-cotta plants. With a tunnel kiln, the firing process could be reduced to three to five days.[43]

From the kiln, the wares were taken to the fitting or polishing department. The pieces were inspected for fit and size. Any rough edges were smoothed by a grinder. The number and kind of pieces for an order were checked to make sure the fabrication corresponded to shop drawing requirements. Oftentimes, for clarification, the identification number was painted on the back of a piece in addition to the incised markings, since these were often faint. These references, keyed to the shop drawings, informed the contractor of the exact location of specific pieces during building construction. After approval, the terra cotta was taken to the shipping department, where it was carefully packed with straw in wooden crates. Terra cotta was durable but until it was set in place, it could be chipped or broken by a hard blow. Breakages could delay the construction while replacement pieces were fabricated. Sometimes extra pieces were included in an order to compensate for possible breakages. This was fine for redundant pieces like ashlar block or repeated ornament, but special pieces were a problem. After the crates were packaged and secure, the order was shipped to the construction site.

The optimum production time after shop drawing approval was typically eight to twelve weeks. Much of this time went into preparing the model, approvals, and mold-making. Terra-cotta manufacturing was a time-consuming and labor-intensive process. But compared to carving stone into ornament, manufacturing terra cotta was fast and cheap.[44] In addition, terra cotta was approximately half the weight of stone for a piece of comparable size. This savings in weight transferred to cost savings for structural members and foundations. Substantial economical savings with terra-cotta usage occurred when a mold could be reused for duplicate pieces. The advantages of mass production were then maximized and labor tasks were considerably reduced.

Terra cotta was manufactured to replicate many different styles; however, it took Louis Sullivan and George G. Elmslie to exploit its inherent properties and give it an expression that emerged from the material itself. More so than any other architectural aesthetic, the Sullivanesque was a manifestation of its primary medium, terra cotta.

Several terra-cotta companies in Chicago were at various times the primary manufacturer of Sullivanesque ornament. The first of these was the Northwestern Terra Cotta Company, which was essentially the second terra-cotta manufacturer to be located in Chicago. Several former employees of the first terra-cotta company, the Chicago Terra Cotta Company (founded 1868), formed a competing enterprise named True, Brunkhorst, and Company. This terra-cotta partnership evolved into the Northwestern Terra Cotta Company.[45] Early in 1910, the Northwestern company acquired the Chicago Terra Cotta Company and promptly shut down the Chicago company's plant at Blodgett Station, near Highland Park, Illinois. Soon after, on September 14, 1910, William O. Tegtmeyer (b. 1862), the president of the Chicago Terra Cotta Company, died.[46] Prior to these events, a third terra-cotta company had been established (1887) in Chicago. This was the American Terra Cotta and Ceramic Company.

For years, both the Northwestern and American companies were national leaders in the terra-cotta industry and dominated the Chicago market. Both companies made ornamental designs for Louis Sullivan and some Sullivanesque ornament for other architects as well. Another Chicago concern, the Midland Terra Cotta Company, was founded in 1910 and attempted to challenge the two major Chicago companies. Midland manufactured Sullivanesque designs in addition to other ornament. It pioneered the concept of "stock" terra cotta and carried "catalog-order" Sullivanesque designs. Northwestern, American, and Midland were the three major Chicago-based terra-cotta companies that manufactured Sullivanesque ornament. The Winkle Terra Cotta Company in St. Louis, Missouri, made terra-cotta ornament for the Adler and Sullivan designs built in that city.[47] Sullivan's Bayard Building in New York City had terra cotta supplied by the Perth Amboy Terra Cotta Company of Perth Amboy, New Jersey. The Conkling-Armstrong Terra Cotta Company of Philadelphia made Sullivanesque ornament for some of Henry J. Klutho's designs in Florida.

Two additional terra-cotta companies competed for a while in the Chicago market.[48] Only one of these is known to have made ornament for a Sullivanesque design. Organized in the summer of 1912, the Advance Terra Cotta Company became the fourth Chicago company simultaneously competing for terra-cotta contracts.[49] Initially, Advance's offices were at Clearing, Illinois, but they were soon moved to Chicago Heights, where the company's factory was constructed.[50] The only known Sullivanesque terra-cotta ornament made by the Advance company was for George G. Elmslie's Old Second National Bank (1924) in Aurora, Illinois. The Advance company and its factory were acquired in 1928 by the Northwestern Terra Cotta Company. The Federal Terra Cotta Company was a New York concern, which for about five years (c. 1911–16) maintained an office in Chicago and tried to compete in the highly competitive market there.[51]

At one time, the Northwestern Terra Cotta Company was the largest manufacturer of terra cotta in the country and was closely associated with the beginnings of the Sullivanesque movement. The company supplied most of the terra cotta for Adler and Sullivan's buildings and for Louis Sullivan until 1907. For example, Northwestern made the intricate ornamental claddings for Adler and Sullivan's Guaranty Building (1894–95) in Buffalo, New York.[52] At Sullivan's Schlesinger and Mayer store, the windows of the lower two stories were framed with decorative cast iron by Winslow Brothers, and the upper superstructure was clad with terra cotta made by Northwestern.[53]

The Northwestern Terra Cotta Company was incorporated in 1887 after a reorganization of True, Hottinger, and Company, successor to the original (1877) firm of True, Brunkhorst, and Company.[54] The main plant was located on the city's northwest side at Clybourn and Wrightwood Avenues. Among the succession of company officers, probably the two most important were Gustav Hottinger and Fritz Wagner, especially in relationship to Louis Sullivan and the Sullivanesque. One of the original founders of the company, Gustav Hottinger (1848–1929), was born in Vienna. He studied art, became an accomplished sculptor, and moved to Chicago in 1869.[55] In an attempt to help Louis Sullivan through financial difficulties in 1905, Hottinger lent him money. With Sullivan's continuing financial decline, it was Hottinger who acquired Sullivan's Ocean Springs, Mississippi, retreat in 1910.[56]

Trained as an architectural draftsman, Fritz Wagner (1853–1919) was vice president and general manager of the Northwestern company. Born in Bavaria and a graduate of Nuremberg University, Germany, Wagner was well educated and a gifted speaker.[57] He was the first president of the National Terra Cotta Society, which established standards and promoted the industry, and he was an ardent supporter of the Chicago Architectural Club.[58]

The person who interpreted and sculpted the architect's two-dimensional design into a three-dimensional clay model was important. Molds for terra-cotta ornament were made from the (approved) models. The modeler at Northwestern who made the Sullivan-designed ornament for the exterior of the Schiller/Garrick Building was German-born Frederick Almenraeder (1832–1900).[59] However, the modeler for most of Louis Sullivan's ornament was Kristian Schneider. During the construction of Adler and Sullivan's Auditorium Building, Schneider was employed by James Legge and crafted decorative plasterwork. Schneider's abilities to interpret and execute ornamental designs were appreciated by Sullivan, and when Schneider established his own business around 1890, he was chosen to model Adler and Sullivan's decorative designs in plaster for the Kehilath Anshe Ma'ariv Synagogue, the second alteration of the McVicker's Theater, and the famous "Golden Doorway" of the Transportation Building for the 1893 fair.[60] In 1893 Schneider became a modeler with the Northwestern Terra Cotta Company and translated Sullivan's drawings and instructions into clay for that company. In addition, Schneider worked "on loan" and even sculpted the ornament cast in iron by Winslow Brothers for the Schlesinger and Mayer building.[61]

Schneider became an expert on Sullivan's ornament and modeled Sullivanesque ornament for other architects. He not only modeled the Sullivanesque ornament made by the Northwestern company for architect Harry B. Wheelock's Western Methodist Book Concern (1899; demolished 1990), Chicago, but he designed this ornament as well.[62] Schneider left Northwestern in 1906 and subsequently became chief modeler for a competitor, the American Terra Cotta and Ceramic Company. The ornament for the Babson House (1907) in Riverside, Illinois, was the last Sullivan-designed terra cotta made by Northwestern. Because of his association with Louis Sullivan, Schneider is probably the best remembered of the Chicago terra-cotta modelers. There were many others but only a few gained recognition.

Robert Zeunert was a sculptor and designer with Northwestern for twenty-eight years until his death in 1910.[63] Fritz Albert, a modeler previously with the American company, replaced Schneider at Northwestern. Born in Berlin, Germany, Albert (1865–1940) was educated at the Royal Academy of Berlin and came to the United States in 1893 to work at the World's Columbian Exposition in Chicago. After study in Rome, he returned to Chicago. He became a modeler with the American company but left in

1906 for a position with Northwestern. There he headed the modeling department and stayed until the late 1920s. After that time, Albert was self-employed as a sculptor and did some freelance modeling for the Midland Terra Cotta Company as well as for Northwestern. Albert modeled the ornament designed by George G. Elmslie for three schools in Hammond, Indiana. This was among the last Sullivanesque ornament made (1935–36). Kristian Schneider was scheduled to do this work for the Midland Terra Cotta Company but his death in August 1935 prompted Albert's substitution. However, with the Depression, Albert had little work and he died on April 17, 1940, the day the mortgage on his home was foreclosed.[64]

Fernand Moreau (1853–1920), a French immigrant, worked as a modeler for the American Terra Cotta and Ceramic Company during most of his years in Chicago; however, after World War I and until his death in 1920, he was with the Northwestern company.[65] John Sand, a native of Luxembourg, became a modeler for Northwestern in May 1920, at the age of seventeen. In 1927, at the time the Sullivanesque seemed to be evolving into art deco, Northwestern brought six French sculptors to Chicago. According to Sharon Darling, Northwestern did this to gain leadership of the emerging modern French decorative style and to avoid strengthening the predominately German union of modelers. Edouard Chassaing was considered the most talented of this group of French artisans.[66]

The Northwestern Terra Cotta Company, although the largest terra-cotta company in the Chicago market, felt the competition of the American Terra Cotta and Ceramic Company. In addition to terra cotta, American produced a line of art pottery called Teco (pronounced "tea-ko"). This ware had architectonic forms with an exceptional green glaze. After Teco won awards and attracted attention at the 1904 St. Louis World's Fair, Northwestern officials felt it should have a competing line of pottery. The company began pottery production and the new ware was called Norweta, a forced contraction of "Northwestern." A favorite finish on the pottery seems to have been a light blue crystalline glaze over creamy white ground.[67] Around 1920, the company acquired the Chicago Crucible Company and then marked its pottery with that name.[68]

The Northwestern Terra Cotta Company was established during a frenzied period of construction activity in Chicago; however, Northwestern's success could be attributed to excellent management, a good product, decent service, and massive advertising. The company advertised extensively and was keenly aware of its image—especially in the early decades of the twentieth century. More so than other terra-cotta companies, it ran major advertisements in leading architectural journals such as *Architectural Record* and the *Western Architect*. Its advertisements frequently featured high-rise buildings that utilized company wares. These buildings were designed by prominent architects, who were always identified by name in the ads. Unlike other Chicago terra-cotta companies, Northwestern consistently had a major listing in *Sweets Catalogue of Building Construction*.[69] In addition, the company saturated local Chicago building-trade publications with its advertisements. It always had a prominent ad in the annual Illinois Society of Architects *Handbook for Architects and Builders*. Among terra-cotta companies, only Northwestern regularly had a notice in *The Economist*, a weekly Chicago real estate and investment newspaper.[70] Interestingly, Northwestern avoided advertising in journals such as the *American Contractor* or *American Carpenter and Builder* (later titled *American Builder*), which featured small-scale speculative developments. The company must have bypassed these journals because their readerships represented a small market, or because close association with the publications devalued Northwestern's touted quality, or both. Northwestern especially avoided identification with the *American Builder*, which had a special arrangement with a Chicago competitor.[71]

The Northwestern Terra Cotta Company was highly aware of public relations and promotions in addition to magazine advertising. For example, Northwestern created several successful promotional items for the Clay Products Exposition of 1912 held at the Chicago Coliseum. These included a 940-pound chain made of terra cotta. Publicity photographs featured a chain segment draped around a female model. The exposition's central feature was Northwestern's pavilion, which the *Brick and Clay Record* described: "The star feature of the entire show, that being the magnificent pavilion forming the central hub for all the other displays on the Coliseum floor. . . . [It was] 35 ft. in height from the floor and was composed of about 250 individual pieces of terra cotta. The columns and entablature were on the Doric order, with a copy of an old Roman vase, in Pompeiian colors, made for the Del Gardo Museum at New Orleans, surmounting the pavilion."[72]

When the opportunity arose to promote an architectural expression as well as the company, Northwestern chose eclectic design rather than a progressive Chicago-inspired approach such as the Sullivanesque. This was no oversight. By 1912, the architectural establishment had embraced historicism and Sullivan's career was in eclipse. At that time, Sullivan's work and the Sullivanesque were more closely associated with competing terra-cotta companies. In opposition to this, Northwestern ballyhooed the pompous Pompeian pavilion at a national trade show in Chicago. The company, which first produced Adler and Sullivan's ornamental designs in terra cotta, abdicated the cause of an indigenous modern architecture and advocated eclectic historicism.

Even though Northwestern usually produced historically inspired ornament and ridiculed "stock" terra cotta, the company occasionally produced Sullivanesque ornament, which was repeated for various buildings as "stock." Company publications sometimes alluded to pieces that could be duplicated, including those in the Sullivanesque style. For example, a 1908 Northwestern Terra Cotta Company catalog carried three pages of photographs of clay models of ornament keyed with identification numbers. The illustrated examples included designs from Adler and Sullivan. Of the fourteen ornamental pieces illustrated on one page (47), nine were by Sullivan. The catalog preface explained: "Pages 47, 49 and 51 show photographs of modeling. The designs will not be duplicated, except by permission of the respective architects."[73] However, the inclusion of the photographed pieces and accompanying catalog numbers suggests that the ornamental designs were indeed available for duplication. Furthermore, the catalog preface acknowledged Northwestern's stock terra cotta.[74] However, subsequent company publications and advertisements usually ignored stock pieces. If mentioned at all, stock terra cotta had negative connotations.[75]

Stock terra cotta was analogous to production pieces of art pottery. Art pottery was a favorite medium of the arts and crafts movement. Louis Sullivan, Frank Lloyd Wright, and other Chicago architects were sympathetic to this movement, but they saw the machine as a tool to be mastered and not an enemy to be rejected. The arts and crafts movement originated in England as a rebellion against industrialization and resulting dehumanization. English practice precluded everything but the use of simple tools since the crafting process and the self-satisfaction of the craftsperson were paramount. Obviously, with the English process, only a limited number of craft pieces could be produced by hand in a given time; therefore, volume was low and prices became high. Another intent of the arts and crafts movement was to make quality craft objects readily available to all people; thereby the level of appreciation for the arts would be elevated and society as a whole would be improved. However, the wares of craftspeople in the English movement, with limited quantities and high prices, were affordable only to the upper class. American followers of the arts and crafts movement emphasized aesthetically pleasing wares made available (that is, affordable) to the masses. They realized that only by embracing, not rejecting, machine production would such availability be possible.

Stock terra cotta, like art pottery production pieces, became a celebration of "the machine," or mass production. With stock terra cotta and arts and crafts pottery, some production pieces may have equal value or even greater significance than "original" pieces, such as hand-decorated art pottery, because they are, as Frank Lloyd Wright advocated, "in the nature of the material" and "sprang from the machine." The artisan somehow captured the essence of both the liberating forces and the limiting qualities of the machine and fused this with his or her own creativity. For example, Teco art pottery, made from molds as production pieces by the American Terra Cotta and Ceramic Company, is in high demand today by collectors because of its architectonic character, strong forms, and fine proportions as well as its lustrous but single-color glazes—especially "Teco green." In regard to the wares of the Rookwood Company of Cincinnati, some collectors crave only pieces with vellum glazes and handpainted portraits or scenes and dismiss Rookwood's production pieces. Yet many of the production wares captured the intended spirit of the arts and crafts movement more faithfully since design and form emerged honestly from the inherent qualities of the clay material and functional considerations of mold duplication. Conversely, the handpainted scenes often denied the material and form and simply used the surface as a convoluted canvas.

With use of the same clay material, glazes, and production methods, art pottery and architectural terra cotta shared much in common, so much so that often both were produced by the same factory and company. In Chicago, the Northwestern Terra Cotta

Company and the American Terra Cotta and Ceramic Company made pottery as well as architectural terra cotta.

Early in the Sullivanesque movement, and in addition to the commissions of Adler and Sullivan, the Northwestern Terra Cotta Company made custom ornament for Sullivanesque architectural designs in Chicago. These included such buildings as the Western Methodist Book Concern, designed by Harry B. Wheelock, Architect; and the Chapin and Gore Building (1904), Richard E. Schmidt, Architect, with Hugh Garden as designer.[76] After 1907, however, the few orders of Sullivanesque ornament from Northwestern were virtually all for stock terra cotta only. For example, in 1922, Levy and Klein, Architects, designed a series of two-story brick buildings for M. Astrahan that utilized Sullivanesque terra-cotta ornamentation for string courses, trim, and accents. The terra-cotta pieces were small and the ornament understated; but upon close inspection, the designs reveal an intricate Sullivanesque richness. A slim isosceles triangle, short side up, formed the field for the most prominent ornamental accents. As stock terra cotta, the pieces were duplicated for at least three known Chicago locations. These were 3854–64 N. Lincoln Avenue, 4253–57 Milwaukee Avenue, and 2647 W. Lawrence Avenue.[77]

A more flamboyant use of stock Sullivanesque ornament appeared on several Rissman and Hirschfield designs (1922–23) in Chicago. These included a store and office building for M. Shooman at 3015–25 Milwaukee Avenue and a store and apartment building for Nathan Schoenberg at 2452–56 N. Lincoln Avenue. Both featured the same terra-cotta medallions. One cartouche framed opposing circles in relief and encased flowing foliate within a rectangular field. The other was more prominent and was a replication of the focal piece for Purcell, Feick, and Elmslie's First National Bank, Rhinelander, Wisconsin. This imitative design, comprising several pieces fitted together, appeared too on the terra-cotta facade of a small one-story building (1923; architect unknown) for an automobile salesroom at 2522 S. Michigan Avenue.[78] Thus, Northwestern produced stock Sullivanesque terra cotta even though the company frequently repudiated the use of stock.

The Sullivanesque connection to the Northwestern company was recalled in a company publication, *Northwestern Terra Cotta*. The December 1937 issue featured "A Christmas Tribute," which was an original drawing (1923) by Louis Sullivan that featured a composition of his luscious ornament. An accompanying caption recalled: "For many years most of the bewitching ornament created by Louis Sullivan for exterior use was modeled at Northwestern Studios and was produced in NORTHWESTERN TERRA COTTA."[79]

The Depression was especially difficult for terra-cotta companies and Northwestern was no exception. With changing trends in architecture, such as the advent of the International style, which rejected ornament, terra cotta use diminished. Northwestern closed its Chicago yard in 1956 and maintained the facility it acquired in Denver in 1923 until 1960, when the company went out of business.[80]

The terra-cotta company most often associated with the Sullivanesque is the American Terra Cotta and Ceramic Company. This connection is obvious given that almost all of the terra-cotta ornament designed after 1907 by leaders of the Sullivanesque movement were products of the company. With few exceptions, the ornate terra cotta of Sullivan's designs while he worked alone, including those for all but one of his famous small banks, were from the American company. Similarly, the same company produced nearly all of the terra cotta for Purcell and Elmslie. Parker Berry and William Steele also utilized Sullivanesque ornamental designs manufactured by the American Terra Cotta and Ceramic Company.[81] The major reason leading architects of the Sullivanesque turned to this company was to secure the services of the company's chief modeler, Kristian Schneider.

Kristian Schneider (1864–1935) was the principal modeler of Louis Sullivan's ornamental designs. It was Schneider who interpreted Sullivan's drawings in three dimensions. Schneider was born December 27, 1864, in Bergen, Norway, and came to Chicago in March 1885. As noted earlier, he worked for James Legge, who had the plastering

Opposite: Automobile sales building (1923) at 2522 S. Michigan Ave., Chicago; architect unknown. Detail of stock Sullivanesque terra cotta from Northwestern. Photo: 1990.

Commercial building for M. Astrahan (1922), Chicago; Levy and Klein, Architects. Detail of stock Sullivanesque terra cotta from Northwestern (order 22122). Photo: 1992.

contract for Adler and Sullivan's Auditorium Building. While carving clay models for plaster molds on the Auditorium Building, Schneider met Sullivan and thereafter crafted the clay models of Sullivan's ornamental designs.[82] In 1893, Schneider joined the Northwestern Terra Cotta Company as a modeler and stayed until 1906, when he opened a studio with another former Northwestern employee, Henry F. Erby. Schneider modeled Sullivan's Owatonna, Minnesota, bank ornament in 1907 on a freelance basis for the American Terra Cotta and Ceramic Company. In 1909, Schneider joined the American company as chief modeler, a position he held until 1930.[83] Schneider's position at American teamed him with another extraordinary man, William Day Gates.

William D. Gates was the founder of the American Terra Cotta and Ceramic Company. Gates was born on July 29, 1852, in Ashland, Ohio, and at an early age relocated with his family to McHenry County, Illinois.[84] Gates graduated in 1875 from Wheaton College in Illinois and studied law at the Chicago College of Law. With an inheritance from his father, Gates purchased some farmland near Crystal Lake, Illinois. Using clay from his land, Gates experimented with making pottery. An old mill on the property was outfitted to grind clay and kilns were erected. Soon his plant, Spring Valley Tile Works, was producing drain tile. After production expanded to include garden ornaments and some building components such as chimney tops, Gates renamed his company the Terra Cotta Tile Works. Finally, in 1887, after a fire and rebuilding, reorganization of the company, and expansion of the product line to include a full range of architectural terra cotta, the operation was again renamed and became the American Terra Cotta and Ceramic Company.[85]

Gates's early experiences in pottery making were not forgotten. He continued to experiment with pottery and, from the first two letters of "terra cotta," derived the name Teco for his pottery. "Gates Potteries" became a synonym for his American Terra Cotta and Ceramic Company. Teco was registered in 1895 as a trademark, and in 1901 Teco pottery was made available to the general public.[86] Pottery production was a perfect complement to the manufacture of architectural terra cotta. When the construction business was low, workers could concentrate on pottery. Pottery could be fired with pieces ordered for architectural jobs and could occupy nooks and crannies in the kilns. Gates's production of pottery was good business, but it also deepened his affection for the arts and crafts movement.

Immersed in the philosophy of the arts and crafts, Gates tried to establish a model factory. The mill pond location for his terra-cotta works was an idyllic setting and a refuge from the sooty city.[87] He was proud of the virtues of working in clay and believed that the inclusion of pottery with architectural terra-cotta work furthered arts and crafts principles. In addition, creating pottery was an outlet for Gates's own creativity and helped satisfy his desire to make functional objects beautiful and available to the public at large. Gates used machine production methods whenever possible. This efficiency helped improve the time a worker could devote to more creative work rather than the drudgery of production. More important, mass production of useful and beautiful wares reduced costs and made the items more affordable to a larger segment of society. This principle was the basis for Teco pottery and extended to terra cotta and Sullivanesque architecture.

In addition to pottery making, Gates's artistic endeavors included sketching and painting in watercolor, and he was keenly interested in architecture.[88] Gates was an associate member of the Chicago Architectural Club and was active in the organization. He was undoubtedly a sincere participant although his visibility and connections there served his business interests as well.[89] The Chicago Architectural Club held an annual juried exhibit of work by club members, nonmember architects, and others, and Gates exhibited his Teco pottery in 1894, 1895, and 1900.[90] Gates invited a number of Chicago architects to design pottery pieces. This resulted in an "Exhibit of Vases Designed by Members of Chicago Architectural Club" in the sixteenth annual exhibition of the Chicago Architectural Club, held at the Art Institute of Chicago from March 26 to April 17, 1903.[91] Eventually, at least thirty production pieces of Teco were designed by Chicago architects, including W. B. Mundie, Hugh M. G. Garden, R. A. Hirschfeld, W. J. Dodd, W. K. Fellows, William Le Baron Jenney, Melville P. White, and Max Dunning.[92] Furthermore, rare pieces of Teco were designed by Louis Sullivan and Frank Lloyd Wright as a special order or part of terra-cotta orders. As Gates envisioned, the form and color of Teco wares have made them enduring works of art despite being production pieces. The same craftsmanship and glazes used for Teco ware were carried over into terra cotta manufactured by Gates's company.

The principal activity of the American Terra Cotta and Ceramic Company was manufacturing custom terra cotta as designed by architects for specific building commissions. Nonetheless, an issue of a company publication, *Common Clay*, carried a text that stated: "But our albums are full of delightful designs of small buildings, many of which will repay reproduction."[93] This implied that the American company, like its Chicago competitors, made stock terra cotta and could do architectural design work. Stock Sullivanesque ornament from the American company was utilized for the Skinner and Chamberlain Department Store (1924) in Albert Lea, Minnesota; the commissioned architect was William L. Alban of St. Paul.[94] However, other obvious references to stock terra cotta in shop drawings and catalogs are rare, which suggests that stock terra cotta was a minor segment of production at American, as contrasted to its Chicago competitors.

One of the most significant architectural designs by Gates's American company appeared in the March 1921 issue of *Common Clay*, the monthly magazine the company had begun publishing the previous July. The plate, "Design for a Small Bank Front," subtitled "Sullivanesque Trim," illustrated a one-story, twenty-five-foot-wide facade handsomely ornamented in Sullivanesque terra cotta. The upper wall surface had a name panel reading "First State Bank," with the date 1919 above. Well composed and nicely proportioned, it was an intriguing storefront design. The name of the company draftsman was not identified. However, the designer was apparently familiar with Sullivan's

work. The American company made terra-cotta ornament for Louis Sullivan's buildings and many draftsmen prepared shop drawings for Sullivan's approval.[95]

William Gates and Louis Sullivan became friends through their business associations. Gates promoted Sullivan and his work whenever possible. Since the American Terra Cotta and Ceramic Company produced virtually all of Sullivan's terra cotta after 1907, it was natural that the company would feature Sullivan's designs in company advertisements and promotions. An advertisement for the company, published in the December 1914 issue of *The Brickbuilder*, featured a photograph of an ornamental panel from Sullivan's Home Building Association in Newark, Ohio. According to the accompanying text: "Plastic Ornament, which is the decorative keynote of modern tendencies in architectural design, can be expressed most effectively in architectural terra cotta. The great ingenuity of the designer in working out graceful scrolls and intricate foliage can be imparted to the modeled clay and then glazed to insure durable and lasting qualities. The facilities of the American Terra Cotta and Ceramic Company for executing work of this character are unexcelled because of their wide experience in working with the leading exponents and advocates of this style of architecture from the time of its inception."[96]

Common Clay also directly publicized Sullivan and the Sullivanesque. For example, the first issue had a one-page photographic spread entitled "Lions in Architecture," which featured sculptured lions in terra cotta from representative Sullivan banks. The

Skinner and Chamberlain Department Store (1924), Albert Lea, Minnesota; William L. Alban, Architect. Detail of stock Sullivanesque terra cotta. Photo: 1994.

"Design for a Small Bank Front," *Common Clay* (Mar. 1921): xvii. Sullivanesque design (1919) by unknown designer, American Terra Cotta and Ceramic Company.

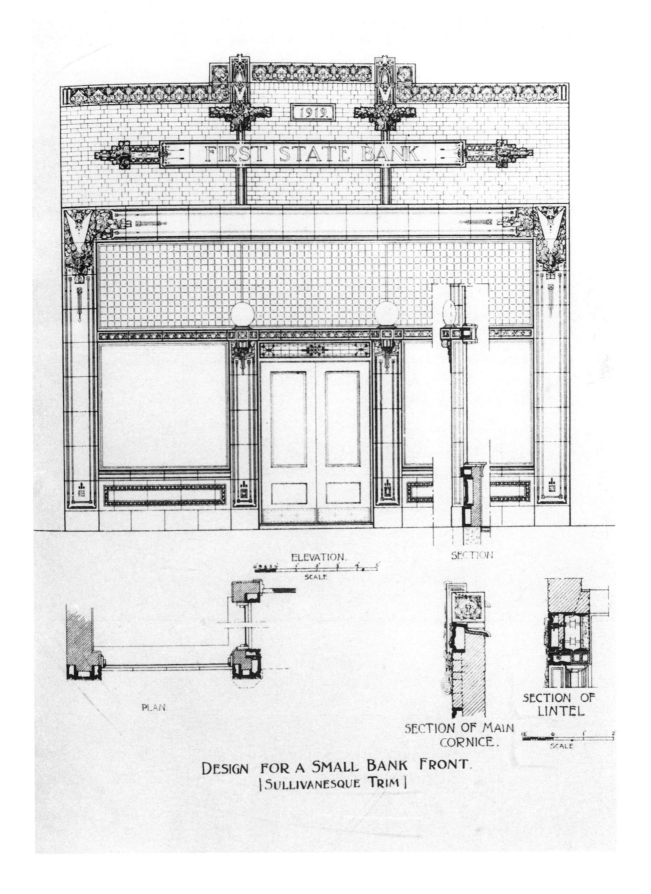

1919.

FIRST STATE BANK.

ELEVATION.
SCALE

SECTION

PLAN

SECTION OF MAIN
CORNICE.

SECTION OF
LINTEL

SCALE

DESIGN FOR A SMALL BANK FRONT.
[SULLIVANESQUE TRIM]

163

text told readers, "Every once-in-a-while, we shall show you cuts from the king of beasts, conventional and unconventional. For the first issue we turned to Mr. Louis H. Sullivan, the mighty man of American architecture."[97] The September 1920 issue featured Sullivan's Farmers' and Merchants' Union Bank in Columbus, Wisconsin. The next month's issue referred to Sullivan in a feature on Kristian Schneider and described Schneider as "equally at home in any style of ornament or decoration, but particularly so in what is known as 'Sullivanesque.' His deft fingers modeled all of the ornament shown last month in our illustrations of the Columbus Bank, and we are showing here a picture of the clock installed in the bank at Owatonna. Although we know that Mr. Sullivan does not think very well of the design of this clock, yet it is a splendid example of what Mr. Schneider is capable of, and we show it for that reason."[98]

As Sullivan's economic woes increased, Gates was among the many friends who lent or gave him money. Sullivan's last office was rent free, in a back room of an American company building on South Prairie Avenue in Chicago.[99]

Although the plant of the American Terra Cotta and Ceramic Company was located in Terra Cotta, a post office and railroad stop named for the plant and located near Crystal Lake, Illinois, in McHenry County, main offices were always in downtown Chicago, forty-two miles to the southeast.[100] The terra-cotta works was constantly being upgraded although its picturesque setting remained intact. The American Terra

Opposite: Sullivanesque plaque illustrated in *Common Clay* 1, no. 2 (July 1920): 13.

Advertisement for the American Terra Cotta and Ceramic Company, *The Brickbuilder* 23 (Dec. 1914): 9.

PLASTIC ORNAMENT, which is the decorative keynote of modern tendencies in architectural design, can be expressed most effectively in architectural terra cotta. The great ingenuity of the designer in working out graceful scrolls and intricate foliage can be imparted to the modeled clay and then glazed to insure durable and lasting qualities. The facilities of the American Terra Cotta and Ceramic Company for executing work of this character are unexcelled because of their wide experience in working with the leading exponents and advocates of this style of architecture from the time of its inception.

Ornamental Terra Cotta Panel on the Home Building Association Bank Building, Newark, Ohio   Louis H. Sullivan, Architect

AMERICAN TERRA COTTA AND CERAMIC COMPANY

PEOPLE'S GAS BUILDING, CHICAGO, ILLINOIS   Works at Terra Cotta, Illinois

IN MEMORIAM

WILLIAM CHANDLER PETERSON

SECOND LIEUTENANT CO. B 5TH REGT. U.S.M

BORN IN | KILLED AT
CRYSTAL LAKE | CHATEAU-THIERRY
DECEMBER 24TH | JUNE 6TH
1894 | 1918

THIS TABLET WAS A LABOR OF LOVE,
VOLUNTARILY DESIGNED AND EXECUTED
BY HIS FELLOW WORKMEN. IT SPEAKS
FOR ITSELF. THE BARE FACTS BURNED
IN IMPERISHABLE CLAY, MADE IMMORTAL
BY LOVING HANDS, TELL THE WHOLE
STORY WHEN WORDS FAIL US.

"LIGHT LIE THE EARTH UPON THEE,
SOFT BE THE SOIL THAT COVERS THEE."

Cotta and Ceramic Company expanded rapidly from 1911 to 1913.[101] By 1913, the company employed 225 people.[102] That same year William D. Gates stepped aside as managing president and assumed the position of chairman of the board. Gates was the driving force behind the company, but many people were instrumental in its success. Unlike many architectural firms and building material companies, which usually preferred their workers remain anonymous, American frequently revealed the names and contributions of its employees. Human-interest stories about workers were a regular feature in "Who's Who," a column in *Common Clay*.[103] A special tribute to William C. Peterson, a former employee who was killed in World War I, appeared in the second issue of *Common Clay*. A photograph of a terra-cotta tablet, bordered in rich Sullivanesque motifs, served as a memorial to him and "was a labor of love, voluntarily designed and executed by his fellow workmen."[104]

The American Terra Cotta and Ceramic Company attracted talented sculptors or modelers. The best known, as noted earlier, was Kristian Schneider. He was preceded at American by Fritz Albert and Fernand Moreau. Albert left in 1906 to assume a similar position at Northwestern. Attracted to Chicago for the 1893 Columbian Exposition, Moreau taught at the Art Institute of Chicago before assuming a position as a modeler at American in 1904. Moreau left the company during World War I. Other modelers at the American company included B. Nelson and W. C. Heidel. Some projects were the work of "free-lance" sculptors. For instance, Richard W. Bock modeled a fountain and a small sculpture for Frank Lloyd Wright's Dana House (1903–4).[105] Although many people contributed to the success of the American Terra Cotta and Ceramic Company, in essence it was a family business. In September 1877, William Day Gates married Ida M. Babcock in La Grange, Illinois. They had four sons and two daughters.[106] The sons studied ceramic engineering at Ohio State University and became active in the American company.[107]

In addition to his demanding responsibilities at the American Terra Cotta and Ceramic Company, William D. Gates was actively involved in a host of professional and artistic organizations. As mentioned previously, Gates was a member of the Chicago Architectural Club and served as president of the Chicago Arts and Crafts Society. His longstanding memberships in the Chicago Athletic Association and the Cliffdwellers allowed social and philosophical exchanges with Chicago architects.[108] Within the terra-cotta industry, William D. Gates was a national leader. He was instrumental in forming the American Terra Cotta Manufacturers Association, from which developed the National Terra Cotta Society. Established in 1912, the society served the interests of the entire terra-cotta industry.[109]

In 1909, Gates married for a second time, after his first marriage ended in divorce. His new wife was the former Katherine Fallon of Chicago.[110] The American Terra Cotta and Ceramic Company still needed Gates's direct control as a construction strike in 1915 severely hurt the company and income fell. John Crowe resigned as company president and Gates stepped in and righted the company.[111] World War I created a decline in construction orders, which was experienced by other terra-cotta companies as well. However, after the war, construction orders for terra cotta boomed.

It was in April 1918 that the American Terra Cotta and Ceramic Company acquired the Indianapolis Terra Cotta Company and made it a subsidiary.[112] After the American takeover, the Indianapolis plant produced some ornamental terra cotta in the Sullivanesque style. These included the pieces for Clifford Shopbell's 1924 bank in Poseyville, Indiana (order no. 2415), for which some of the molds from Louis Sullivan's Sidney, Ohio, bank seem to have been adapted. Another Sullivanesque order from the Indianapolis company was for an office alteration (c. 1929) in Owatonna, Minnesota (order no. 3036). The architects were Jacobson and Jacobson.[113]

When the Great Depression was triggered in October 1929, the American Terra Cotta and Ceramic Company was quickly decimated. The Indianapolis plant was closed in early 1930. Soon after, the main works at Terra Cotta, Illinois, suspended production for a time. Gates lost control of the company and ownership was transferred to George A. Berry Jr., Gates's attorney. In 1932, Fritz Wagner Jr. became president of the reorganized company, which was renamed the American Terra Cotta Corporation, but production was on a limited scale.[114] From more than 115 orders in 1929, orders dropped to about 50 annually for the next seven years except for 1933, when fewer than two dozen orders for terra cotta were processed.[115] In 1930, American's star modeler, Kristian Schneider, left to take a position as chief modeler for the Midland Terra Cotta Company. William D. Gates went into forced retirement and lived at his house in Terra Cotta, Illinois. He painted and wrote articles, mostly on local history, for a Crystal Lake newspaper. He died January 28, 1935, at the age of eighty-two.

For more than eighty years, the American Terra Cotta and Ceramic Company was a force in the construction industry. It is now best known for production of Teco pottery and as the premiere manufacturer of Sullivanesque terra cotta. However, American's production concentrated on terra cotta for eclectic historical designs even though Louis Sullivan and Purcell and Elmslie were explicitly linked to the company. In fact, the company that was even more closely linked to the Sullivanesque and supplied most Sullivanesque terra cotta was a different and little known Chicago manufacturer.

CHAPTER 6

STOCK SULLIVANESQUE AND
THE MIDLAND TERRA COTTA COMPANY

IN THE SECOND STAGE of the Sullivanesque (after 1910), the style was disseminated by a number of builder-architects of smaller, lower-echelon commissions. Their
work was mostly confined to the Midwest and centered on Chicago. At the same time,
acceptance of the style in other regions was dwindling, and important mainstream architects everywhere were turning to design eclecticism.

The regional proliferation of the Sullivanesque in these years was aided greatly by
the efforts of the Midland Terra Cotta Company. Midland, which didn't start making
terra cotta until 1911, produced Sullivanesque ornament as one of its important lines.
The company mass-produced Sullivan facsimiles and made them readily available and
affordable as "stock" terra cotta for use in more commonplace architecture. For a time,
Midland promoted the Sullivanesque in its advertising. Perhaps more important, the
company codified the Sullivanesque and disseminated the compositional principles of
the style by means of design plates in free portfolio catalogs. In addition, it provided
architectural services for developers and contractors as well as design services for journeyman architects. Thus, Midland's Sullivanesque designs appeared often in Chicago
and throughout the Midwest.

One of the founders of the Midland Terra Cotta Company and its first president
was the Chicago architect William G. Krieg. Krieg was born January 20, 1874, in Chicago. Educated in public schools and by private study, Krieg began working at age four-

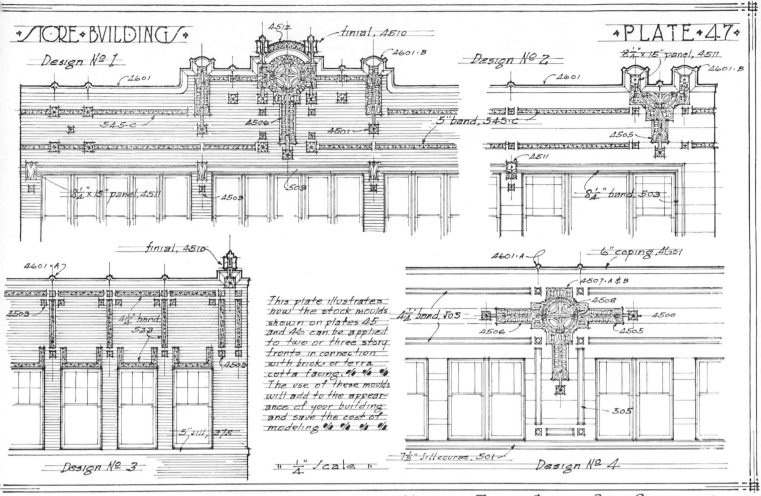

Midland Terra Cotta Company catalog (c. 1922), plate 47, store buildings, designs 1–4.

teen as an assistant and apprentice for his father, Frederick Gustav Krieg, a building contractor. In 1892, William Krieg became a foreman for his father's company and two years later assumed the duties of estimator and bookkeeper. Krieg became a partner in his father's contracting firm in 1895. However, just a year later he left and started an architectural partnership with Frederick E. Gatterdam (1865–1944).[1]

After two years, the Gatterdam and Krieg partnership was dissolved and Krieg practiced alone until September 1908,[2] when he was appointed city architect for Chicago. He held this position for two years until he resigned on September 1, 1910, to concentrate on the formation of a new terra-cotta company and on the design of the company's factory in Cicero, Illinois.[3]

Alfred Brunkhorst was the co-founder of the Midland Terra Cotta Company. Brunkhorst was the son of John Brunkhorst, one of the founders of the Northwestern Terra Cotta Company.[4] Krieg and the younger Brunkhorst raised capital in the fall of 1910 and began planning construction of a factory for the new company. The company was officially incorporated on December 10, 1910.[5] The first officers of the company were

William G. Krieg, president; Alfred Brunkhorst, vice president; and Walter S. Primley, secretary and treasurer.[6]

Midland purchased twenty acres of the old Grant Locomotive Company land on the northeast corner of West Sixteenth Street and South Fifty-fourth Avenue in Cicero.[7] The factory site was served by the Baltimore and Ohio Chicago Terminal Railroad, and shipments of shale from Indiana for the terra cotta came by rail to the company's siding. William Krieg designed the new factory buildings; the total gross floor area exceeded fifty thousand square feet. In January 1911, Cox Brothers was awarded the general contract with a construction cost around $100,000.[8] Construction was rushed and the project was completed in May 1911.[9] Krieg's design for the Midland plant consisted of three principal buildings plus secondary structures and storage sheds. Each major building had brick exterior walls reinforced by brick pilasters spaced along the inside wall faces. The Midland plant was equipped with machinery designed and built by A. L. Schultz and Son especially for the manufacture of terra cotta.[10] Terra-cotta production in the Midland plant was underway by June 1911.

At the factory site, a two-story office building replaced the Midland company's original one-story factory office, and the new building was profusely ornamented in terra cotta. However, Midland's main offices were located in downtown Chicago. Initially, the company had its corporate offices in the Teutonic Building, at Washington and Wells Street, Chicago. However, the company moved in April 1911 to the Chamber of Commerce Building (Baumann and Huehl, Architects, 1888–89; demolished 1926), located at the southeast corner of LaSalle and Washington Streets.[11]

By the end of 1911, Midland expanded its factory site by an additional ten acres.[12] The Midland factory grounds are now part of the Cicero plant of the Hotpoint Corporation and only the office structure remains.

Unlike the American Terra Cotta and Ceramic Company, which was open about its workers and publicized some of them in promotional pieces, especially in the journal *Common Clay*, Midland was not prone to divulging the names of its employees. The identities of the designers for Midland's Sullivanesque terra cotta are unknown. It must be assumed that William Krieg had a prominent role. However, some architectural salvage salespeople in Chicago today say that Louis Sullivan designed a particular ornament but didn't get credit for it. Some years ago, one dealer actually had this printed on sales tags attached to fragments of Midland's Sullivanesque stock ornament. A few Chicago historians believe this attribution is possible, since, after 1910, Sullivan was especially desperate for money and the caliber of some of Midland's ornament seems close to that of Sullivan's. Such speculation has no basis in fact, however, as Sullivan's vanity would not allow him to work without acknowledgment and no evidence has been uncovered to support the conjecture.

Similarly, a few knowledgeable people suggest that perhaps George G. Elmslie designed some of Midland's Sullivanesque ornament and portfolio studies for facades. Since Elmslie was also often short of money, this may seem plausible. However, Elmslie lived in Minneapolis from 1910 to 1912 and was occupied with his architectural partnership until World War I. He was again immersed in his own practice in the early 1920s. Only a lull between 1918 and 1920 would seem to have given Elmslie time and cause to "freelance" the Midland designs. But almost all of Midland's Sullivanesque ornament and most of its design plates were done before 1918. Furthermore, Elmslie was almost obsessed with receiving recognition for his designs since he believed Sullivan didn't give him his just due. It is unlikely Elmslie wouldn't have told someone about "his designs" (for Midland), and no conclusive evidence has surfaced to support the theory either. However, one Elmslie authority, who is familiar with his designs and drawing style, believes that a few of Midland's design plates, especially plate 52, "Entrances," were drawn by Elmslie. Most modelers of Midland's terra-cotta ornament remain anonymous. Only a few of the prominent personalities of the Midland company are known.

Hans M. Mendius was important in the history of the Midland Terra Cotta Company. Born on December 31, 1879, in Germany, Mendius came to the United States at age eleven and studied to become an architect but never became registered.[13] Mendius

Midland Terra Cotta Company catalog (c. 1924), plate 52, entrances, designs 1–4.

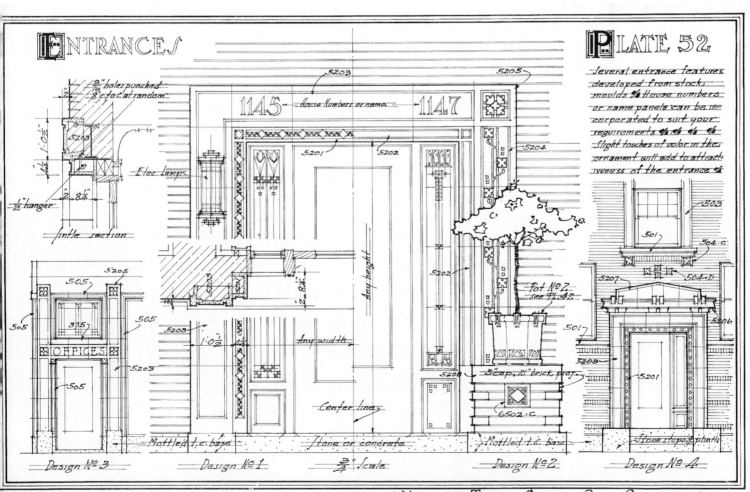

was employed in various architects' offices as draftsman, superintendent of construction, and specification writer from 1896 until 1911, when he joined Midland with the dual positions of cost estimator and salesman. He advanced rapidly and became sales manager and second vice president in 1913. He was named vice president in 1915 and succeeded William G. Krieg as president of the company in 1918.[14] Mendius headed Midland until the Depression, when he relocated to the West Coast.[15]

Walter Simonton Primley was with Midland for the entire life of the company. He was secretary and treasurer from Midland's inception and held that position until he became its third and final president. Primley succeeded Hans Mendius and served until the company's demise in 1939, after which Primley relocated to New York City.[16] Very little is known of other members of the Midland Terra Cotta Company. Alfred Brunkhorst was soon succeeded by F. S. Ryan as vice president of the company, and when Ryan died in July 1918, he was replaced by Hans Mendius. When Mendius succeeded Krieg as the company's president in 1918, August W. Miller was named vice president.[17]

Among the Midland company's plant management and technicians, only a few names have surfaced. Henry F. Krieg and Barney S. Radcliffe were high in the operating management of the plant.[18] Radcliffe seems to have been active in professional organizations; for example, he presented a paper, "Burning with Forced Draft," on May 18, 1918, at a meeting of the Chicago section of the American Ceramic Society. Interestingly, Louis Sullivan, whose ornamental designs were unashamedly copied by the Midland company, was the guest of honor and principal speaker at that same meeting.[19]

The manufacture of architectural terra cotta was a labor-intensive operation, and a major activity was drawing, which was done for documentation and other purposes. The drafting department was a vital area and required a large pool of trained people. Full-size drawings or tracings were made of every new piece of terra cotta. The drawings allowed for shrinkage that occurred during the firing process. Midland's "stock" terra cotta saved on drafting requirements and eliminated modeling. However, for each building project, shop drawings were still required. Shop drawings recorded each terra-cotta piece for the job and where it was to be placed in the building. If conditions warranted special installation, the construction assembly was also drawn, usually as detail wall sections. Each set of shop drawings included a partial detail elevation of the terra-cotta pieces that combined into assemblies for the building facade. Each piece of terra cotta was identified on the drawing and each manufactured ware had reference marks painted on an unfinished surface that were keyed to the drawing. A diagrammatic plan of the partial exterior wall was sometimes included, especially for exterior walls that had "depth" with deep-set openings, projections, wall returns, and/or splayed segments. Storefronts, with terra-cotta bulkheads and trim, were almost always shown in plan as well as elevation. Except for the most simple of facades, an entire elevation was shown for each building face that had terra-cotta components. Showing the building facade intact and to scale, these drawings were referred to as "key elevations." At Midland, the "key" drawings were often small-size sheets and were separate from the detail elevations and other shop drawings, which were usually drawn on large, same-size sheets. The drawings were usually made with ink on linen except for the smallest of simple jobs, for which the draftsman used pencil on tracing paper.[20]

Shop drawings were checked and approved by the architect for the building before the terra cotta was made. The shop drawings were used by Midland workers to manufacture and complete each order and by the building contractor during construction although Midland crews sometimes installed the terra-cotta work, especially on larger and more complex jobs. Most of Midland's draftsmen were engaged in the production of shop drawings although a few did architectural design drawings for builders and architects as well as Midland's own design plates.

The full names or last names of some Midland draftsmen are known. Although only the initials of draftsmen usually appeared on the company's shop drawings, occasionally a name was spelled out; however, this was often a nickname or last name only. Three men—George Johnson, A. Measom, and George J. Nejdl—were in Midland's drafting department before 1913 and were with the company for more than ten years. Two others were longtime employees and seem to have joined the company in 1915. These were Risch (first name unknown) and C. H. Koedel. A. H. Freise was another long-term employee who must have joined the staff in 1916. Of these men, Risch may have been the most important as he rose to head the drafting area and was responsible for checking shop drawings and sending them to the shop.[21] However, Johnson and Nejdl also had important duties, which will be discussed later.

The war years 1917 and 1918 were slow for Midland and the number of employees dropped. In addition, the change in the company's presidency, as William Krieg left the position, had a major impact. After 1918, personnel seemed to be constantly changing; there were many "short-term" draftsmen of one or two years' employment. None of the Midland draftsmen were registered architects while employed with the company.[22]

Architectural terra cotta had traditionally been custom designed and custom made. Midland's initial contracts and some subsequent orders followed this procedure. For example, Midland produced the elaborate and colorful Moorish terra-cotta ornament for the Medinah Temple (1912–13; Huehl and Schmid, architects) at Ontario, Wabash, and Ohio Streets in Chicago.[23] Midland's custom-made Sullivanesque ornament included the architect George Kingsley's Hebard Warehouse at Sheridan and Sheffield in Chicago (this July 1911 order was Midland's thirty-fourth job).[24] However, Midland was the latecomer and smallest of the three major terra-cotta companies in Chicago; it was competing with the well-established companies of Northwestern and American. Midland needed an edge. It needed to cater to another market. For these reasons, Midland developed "stock" terra cotta.

Stock terra cotta was produced by reusing existing molds. Midland did not keep a large inventory of terra cotta on hand; instead, standard units were produced from molds used over and over. This recycling eliminated the need to model a clay original from which a mold would be made. Therefore, workers such as designers, draftsmen, modelers, and moldmakers were eliminated from the production process. Time and money were saved; the production costs were reduced and the sale price could be cheaper.

Stock terra cotta could be used to enhance low-budget projects for such speculative developments as apartment buildings, "strip" commercial structures, garages, and even industrial buildings. Midland put much emphasis on this aspect of their business. Within a year after beginning their operation in 1911, Midland was taking orders for stock terra cotta. From 118 total orders for the year 1911, business increased to 354 orders for 1915, the majority of them for stock terra cotta. This number contrasts with the American Terra Cotta and Ceramic Company's order total for 1915, which was approximately 158.[25] However, it is safe to conclude that Midland's average order was smaller in number of pieces and weight than those of the Northwestern and American companies, both of which concentrated on custom work for larger buildings.

An integral part of Midland's stock terra cotta was the finish, which was available only in a white enamel of uniform glaze except on a few standard pieces used for base courses and water tables. These latter components were also available in a mottled gray, which simulated granite, and were popular for bulkheads under store windows.[26] The white enamel glaze was cheaper than other colors and was a neutral hue compatible with any color or material. Sculpted reliefs, modeling, and incising, often subtle, were most "readable" with white finishes. Shadows played over the white surfaces and shapes were clearly defined. Dark finishes would have mitigated the shallow reliefs and minimized the shading. The standardization of white enamel simplified the glazing operation and helped reduce any variations between orders. These factors helped contribute to the time- and cost-saving benefits of stock terra cotta. In addition, the white enamel glazes were advertised as "self-cleaning" although some promotional materials acknowledged that the terra cotta was "easily hand-cleaned with soap and water." For the coal-fired industrial eras, this was a major consideration. Limestones and common brick soon turned dark and dingy-looking with the accumulation of soot from coal smoke in Chicago and other American cities. The gleaming white terra-cotta ornament was a welcome change and its pristine enamel glaze became one of its biggest attractions and sales advantages.

As noted earlier, Midland's chief competitors, the American and Northwestern companies, both produced pottery as well as architectural terra cotta. No substantial evidence has surfaced to indicate Midland did the same, although Midland did have stock white terra-cotta lines of garden urns and planters. Some of these pieces were inspired by classical forms. In addition, Midland offered a handsome Sullivanesque planter (no. 1614) with a rounded bowl entwined with ornamentation and banded by a decorative rim. Drawings of art pottery appeared as accessories in a few catalog plates, number 15 for example, which suggested that pottery production may have been considered.

Stock terra cotta made ornamental designs and decorative trim available and affordable for use on buildings that otherwise would not have had such content because of budget constraints. The decorative enhancement of more buildings became feasible, which meant that more people could enjoy this art form. The problem was the choice of ornament or decorative design. The Midland company was founded after the demise of the Chicago School and at the beginning of the decline of the Prairie School. Historical precedent prevailed over progressive approaches and design eclecticism was rampant. Therefore, most of Midland's custom work followed historical styles. For economic survival, this demand also mandated the production of stock terra cotta in the eclectic ornamental motifs of past styles. However, Midland developed several contemporary lines. These included arts and crafts motifs and a simple geometric system of ornamentation influenced by Frank Lloyd Wright's stylized rectilinear designs. Neither was very successful and each was used infrequently. Most important, Midland developed an extensive line of stock terra cotta based on Louis Sullivan's ornamental designs.[27]

Krieg and his colleagues at Midland must have admired Sullivan and his ornament. They attempted to duplicate Sullivan's system of ornamentation in their own terra cotta, which was based on Sullivan's decorative motifs entwined on geometric armatures. The company had examples of facade designs prepared with illustrative plates to show the "proper" ways to use this ornament. Since Midland was the smallest of the three major companies producing terra cotta in the Chicago area, perhaps Krieg and Mendius hoped that their company's emphasis on and promotion of a "new, progressive architecture," as espoused by Sullivan and his followers, would put Midland at the forefront of a renewed interest and thus capitalize on its revival. (To some degree, this happened locally but not nationally.) For whatever reasons, Midland developed Sullivanesque stock terra cotta, featured it in company catalogs, and, for a time, promoted it in their advertising.

Sullivan's original ornamental designs were replicated by the Midland Terra Cotta Company. For example, the terra-cotta lintel-piece over the interior opening of the entryway at Sullivan's Owatonna Bank was the prototype or inspiration for several Midland imitations. These were Midland stock pieces, catalog numbers 7701 and 7702, which were often used as decorative lintels over entrances or as focal pieces on upper walls or parapets. These terra-cotta assemblies were slightly smaller than Sullivan's original and were simplified for manufacture and for ease of placement during construction. The assembled pieces had right-angled perimeter configurations with dimensions modulated for brick coursing. The floral interlaces were simplified from Sullivan's design, although in many ways the Midland pieces had a visual strength that captured the essence of Sullivan's work, much as a sketch sometimes produces a stronger, more vibrant image than a finished drawing. On the other hand, a few of the Midland stock components, especially the smaller trim pieces, were oversimplifications of Sullivan designs and approached caricature.[28]

The Midland Terra Cotta Company developed many stock designs formed by various modular component pieces. One of the most popular was a circular terra-cotta medallion two feet six inches in diameter, made from two half-circle pieces (no. 4508) put together. A common expansion of this design was the addition of an outer ring to enlarge the completed medallion to three feet in diameter. "Tabs" could also be added to form an ornate, symmetrical cruciform shape upon which the medallion design appeared to be superimposed. The inspiration for the circle and tab assembly may have come from Purcell, Feick, and Elmslie's Merchants Bank (1911) in Winona, Minnesota, which had similar pieces flanking the lettering for the bank's name on the upper wall surfaces. However, the circle was subjugated to the cruciform shape at Winona, whereas in the Midland piece the circle dominated. In fact, the circle often appeared alone, in isolation. Used in this way, it became clear that this disc was based on an ornament medallion on the M. A. Meyer Wholesale Building by Adler and Sullivan. Another frequent variation was to employ only one half-circle (no. 4508) piece. The semicircular motif, used in conjunction with supplemental pieces and with the straight edge adjacent to the parapet cap, appeared often on many Sullivanesque buildings. The lunette and variations of it were featured on plate 45 in the Midland catalog portfolios and had the following descriptions: "The ornamental features on this plate and on Plate 46 can be used in many ways to make your building ornate—they have been specially designed by our artists with this idea in view."[29]

Differing designs of nearly infinite variety could be derived by interchanging, adding, or subtracting standardized stock terra-cotta pieces. For example, the basic 7701 or 7702 Midland pieces described previously could be enlarged and transformed with the addition of supplemental but complementary "arms" and extensions to approximate the appearance of the dominating cluster atop the main facade of the First National Bank (1910–11), Rhinelander, Wisconsin, by Purcell, Feick, and Elmslie. The Midland facsimile was illustrated and described, without reference to its origins, in an article in the February 1915 issue of the *American Carpenter and Builder*: "Some of the handsomest terra cotta pieces we have ever seen are specified in these storefronts. . . . The cost of modeling alone of this one piece exceeded the introductory price quoted on the entire storefront. It is designed in the Sullivanesque Style, a beautiful showy piece, that will have an advertising value on any business street."[30]

The advertising practices of the Midland Terra Cotta Company contrasted with those of its Chicago competitors. Midland rarely was listed in Sweet's catalogs. Midland's officers must have felt it was not worth the cost of inclusion even though Northwestern always had a major listing and the American Terra Cotta and Ceramic Company usually was included. An exception was the 1914 edition of Sweet's, in which Midland had a two-page spread. This entry had most of a page devoted to four plates illustrating stock terra cotta and a brief text of explanation. Two plates, "D: Store Front Treatment" and "G: Porch Treatment," had notations identifying "Sullivanesque Ornament" for the terra cotta shown on the detail elevation drawings (the other plates were "A" and "16"). However, the photographs on the other page were of clay models with eclectic ornament. The only building photographed was a pseudo-Gothic structure, the

Midland Terra Cotta Company catalog (c. 1922), plate 45, stock Sullivanesque terra cotta.

Midland Terra Cotta Company catalog (c. 1922), plate 46, stock Sullivanesque terra cotta.

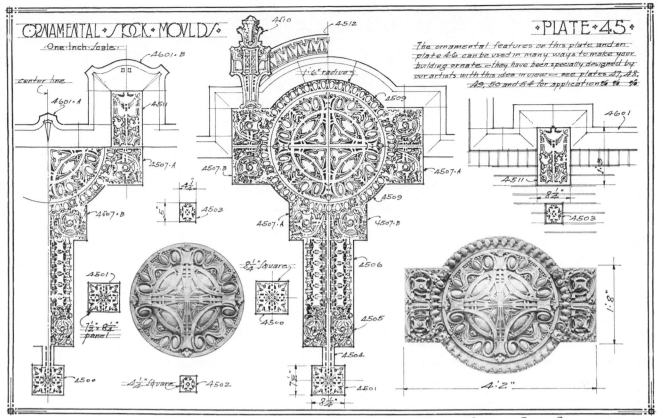

ORNAMENTAL·STOCK·MOVLDS·

·One·Inch·Scale·

·PLATE·45·

The ornamental features on this plate and on plate 46 can be used in many ways to make your building ornate — they have been specially designed by our artists with this idea in view — see plates 47, 48, 49, 50 and 54 for applications

‖ Midland Terra-Cotta Co ∘ Chicago ‖

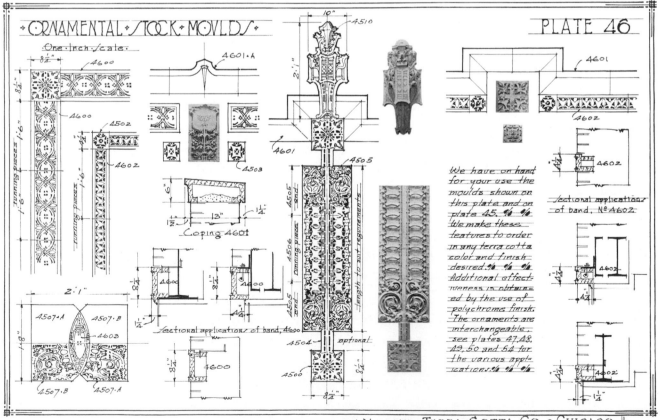

ORNAMENTAL·STOCK·MOVLDS·

·One·Inch·Scale·

PLATE 46

Coping 4601

sectional application of band, 4600

We have on hand for your use the moulds shown on this plate and on plate 45. We make these features to order in any terra cotta color and finish desired. Additional effectiveness is obtained by the use of polychrome finish. The ornaments are interchangeable. see plates 47, 48, 49, 50 and 54 for the various applications.

sectional applications of band, No 4602

‖ Midland Terra-Cotta Co ∘ Chicago ‖

177

ten-story Barnheisel Building on Michigan Avenue in Chicago, designed by W. Carbys Zimmerman.[31]

During the first decade of its existence, Midland rarely advertised in national mainstream architectural journals such as *Architectural Record* even though Northwestern often did and American sometimes ran an advertisement. Midland was represented in the *Western Architect*, although less frequently than the other two major Chicago terra-cotta companies.[32] It was a different situation with the annual publication of the Illinois Society of Architects, *Handbook for Architects and Builders*, in which all Chicago terra-cotta companies were represented for the period 1911–20. In 1915, Midland's advertisement in the handbook featured an elevation drawing of a small store in brick with ornate Sullivanesque terra cotta as Midland unleashed a campaign that featured the Sullivanesque. This started an "ad war" between the Chicago terra-cotta companies in the pages of the handbook. In subsequent editions, Northwestern had larger full-page spreads, while Midland, American, and the Advance companies had smaller but still prominent advertisements. By 1919, Midland's paid appearance in the handbook featured eclectic design; facade alternatives (plate 69) for a bank in classical revival style were illustrated.[33] Except for local or regional publications and as mentioned previously, Midland usually didn't advertise in upper-echelon professional journals; instead, the company advertised in trade journals directed to speculative builders and their architects. These included the *National Builder, American Contractor,* and the *American Carpenter and Builder.*[34] Of these journals, Midland's association with the *American Carpenter and Builder* was the most important.

The *American Carpenter and Builder* was published in Chicago. William A. Radford was editor-in-chief, president, and treasurer, and E. L. Hatfield was vice president and general manager. G. W. Ashby, a Berwyn architect, was a stockholder, and his designs were published often.[35] This journal featured articles on small commercial buildings, houses, two-flats, farm buildings, and small apartment buildings. The content was directed toward small-scale builders and developers and their architects. In February 1914, a strong connection was established between the magazine and the Midland company. That issue was the first time Midland advertised in the journal, and a full-page advertisement ran with a photograph of a four-story apartment building of eclectic design. More important, a feature story also appeared, the first of a series that helped promote terra-cotta usage. The concurrent appearance of articles about Midland's terra cotta and Midland advertisements seems more than coincidence. It appears that this series of articles may have been published because of Midland's advertising contract with the journal. Called "Terra Cotta Talks," the series was illustrated with drawing plates from the Midland company and, although unattributed, could easily have been written by a Midland sales representative. Subsequent articles followed and stressed Midland stock terra cotta. All were illustrated with drawing plates prepared by Midland and used in company catalogs. In addition, Midland advertisements, often full-page, ran monthly in the journal for seven years, until January 1921. Inexplicably, none seems to have appeared after that issue.[36] This was curious since a letter from "M. Mendius, President of the Midland Terra Cotta Co." had been printed in the April 1920 issue of *American Builder* and extolled the virtues of the journal in its handling of Midland's advertising.[37]

In February 1915, an article in the *American Carpenter and Builder* referred to a Midland promotion that ran as a two-page advertising spread in the same issue. The advertisement featured drawings of two Sullivanesque facades for small stores and heralded: "To Introduce Your Locality: Midland Stock White Enameled Terra Cotta." The facade designs were handsome and faithfully extrapolated some of the best Sullivanesque features for application to tiny, inexpensive buildings. At the same time, the text copy may have helped tarnish the reputation of the Sullivanesque. It blared, "Special Offer, $300 and $250, as specified—This Offer Good for 30 days only," a sales pitch that was nonetheless repeated the following month.[38] This vulgar commercialism and exploitation of Sullivan's ornamental design approach must have angered Sullivan and troubled his friends. It may have demeaned the entire Sullivanesque movement. This hard sell was not repeated. Subsequent advertisements in the journal were in better taste.

Design plates were featured for many of the advertisements that appeared in 1915. Photographs of constructed buildings that employed the company's stock terra cotta were published later that year. Architects were identified with their respective buildings. As time went on, however, Midland infrequently identified the architects' names for the buildings that appeared in company advertisements. It might seem that this omission would have been offensive to the uncredited architects and potentially could have reduced the company's clientele. However, this didn't seem to be a serious problem. Perhaps assistance provided by Midland during fabrication or even the design stage precluded such recognition of the architect. Midland evidently usurped some designs of a few architects and published them as part of their own design plates, but this may have been done with the approval of the architect. Obviously, Midland replicated Sullivan's ornament, so it is possible the company didn't always have an architect's permission to use his design. How much of the design of the main facade for a building was Midland's and how much could be attributed to the creativity of the journeyman architect was often difficult to distinguish. In summary, Midland's advertising in the *American Carpenter and Builder* in 1915 had a major impact on the acceptance of stock terra cotta and especially of the Sullivanesque. By 1919, however, Midland's advertisements were almost exclusively illustrated by eclectic designs.

Midland advertisements often invited architects to "Write for a Portfolio." An ad on page 90 of the July 1914 issue of the *American Carpenter and Builder* cajoled: "How Many Times must we tell you to Write for that 'Portfolio'?" The Midland "portfolio" was a catalog comprised of loose-leaf drawing plates. The unbound format allowed an architect to trace plates easily in preparing architectural drawings and for Midland to quickly edit the catalog contents for free distribution. Plates were undated so drawings weren't perceived as outmoded over time. Beautifully drawn to scale, plates were a

Overleaf:

Left-hand page from two-page advertisement, *American Carpenter and Builder* (Mar. 1915): 104–5. This promotion ran in the February and March 1915 issues of the journal.

Right-hand page from two-page advertisement, *American Carpenter and Builder* (Mar. 1915): 104–5.

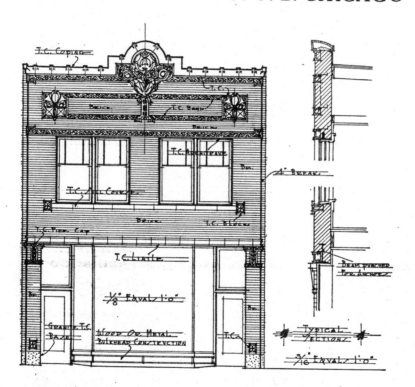

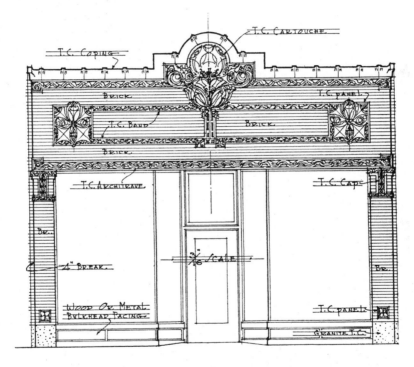

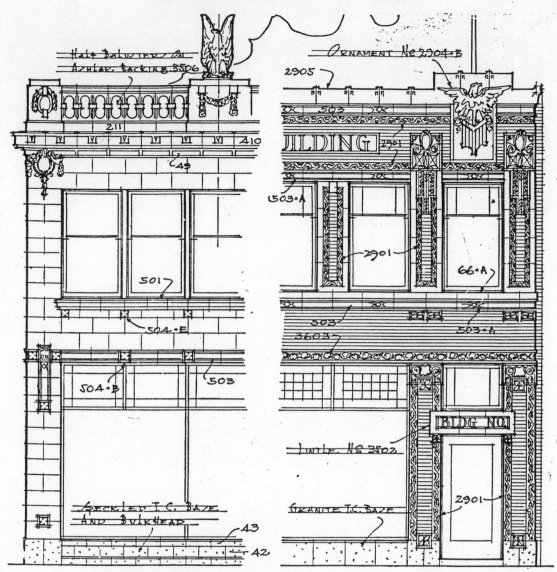

Clipping of Plate 35 (1915 Portfolio) showing application of stock terra cotta to two story buildings

AN UNUSUAL SITUATION

¶ It is not unusual for people to expect delivery of terra cotta within three weeks or even three days after placing an order—it's extremely unusual to get it as quickly as this— yet, users of Midland stock white enamel find such deliveries the USUAL thing—let us prove it to you on your next building.

MIDLAND TERRA COTTA CO.
1515 LUMBER EXCHANGE BLDG., CHICAGO, ILLINOIS

generous size, 9 ½" × 14 ½", and were identified by a number or letter. Plates numbered 1 through 44 and lettered A through G were prepared before 1915. Plates 45 through 60 were added during 1915–16 while plates 61 through 86 were prepared around 1917–20.[39]

Some portfolio plates illustrated an inventory of stock terra-cotta components and gave physical dimensions and properties. Plates 45 and 46, for example, recorded many Sullivanesque pieces. However, most of the plates showed designs that suggested how stock terra cotta could be utilized. Wall sections and details complemented the elevation drawings and some perspectives. Section and detail drawings conveyed technical information. Design plates were easily understood drawings that served as important models for the Sullivanesque style.

Midland's advertising and free portfolios must have reached thousands of builders, developers, and architects. Many of them may have been unfamiliar with Louis Sullivan and his work, but Midland made them very aware of the Sullivanesque. The majority of the first fifty-four plates featured Sullivanesque ornamentation and facade designs for typical small buildings. Plates 55 through 76 stressed eclectic designs influenced by various historical styles; however, plates prepared at a later date returned to the Sullivanesque. Plates 81 through 86 were examples of exuberant Sullivanesque designs that contrasted to the more conservative proposals of earlier design plates.[40] Design plates not only illustrated how stock terra cotta could be employed but served as prototype designs to copy or adapt. Midland catalog portfolios became, for some architects and builders, "pattern books" in the vein of the nineteenth-century publications that builders and architects used as design sources and instruction.

The predominant nonresidential building type of the early twentieth century was the speculative commercial building. Commercial strips of the period were usually defined streets of urban scale and image. Most often, buildings fronted tightly on the street right-of-way and backed onto a service alley; adjacent buildings abutted through use of party walls. Therefore, the design of the exterior of a building was usually an issue of street facade. Louis Sullivan solved the problem beautifully with an original approach that was in equal parts personal, American, and modern. Midland embraced Sullivan's design solutions, reinterpreted them, infused its own vitality, and made the resulting buildings more obtainable by making them more affordable. Without written treatise or philosophy, Midland holistically conveyed the Sullivanesque possibilities through simple but effective graphics. The multiple examples of facade designs made clear, even to the journeyman architect, the range of expressions and individualism possible while sharing the language of the Sullivanesque. These Sullivanesque examples and the resulting built interpretations became a form of commercial vernacular. With a uniformity of materials, aesthetics, scale, technology, building types, and regional geography, "Midland's Sullivanesque" fit the definition of vernacular architecture. However, the buildings were not sufficiently concentrated in a specific location to make this commonality obvious. Instead, they were diffused over a large geographic area,

Opposite: Advertisement,
American Carpenter and Builder
(July 1915): 105.

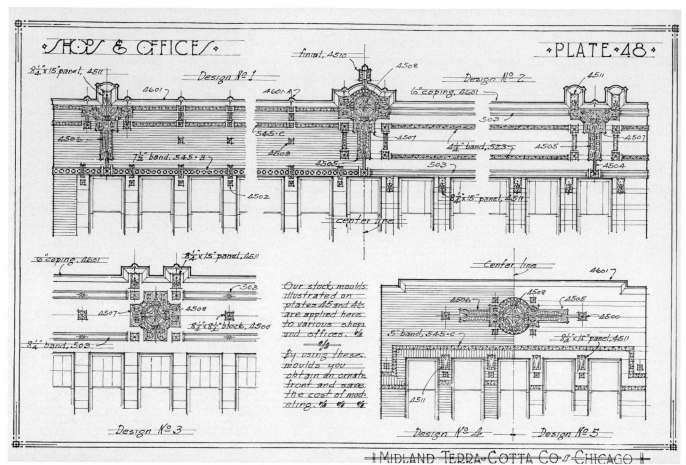

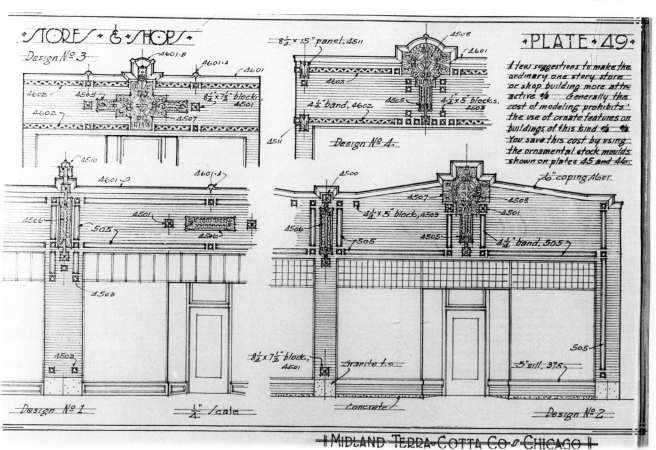

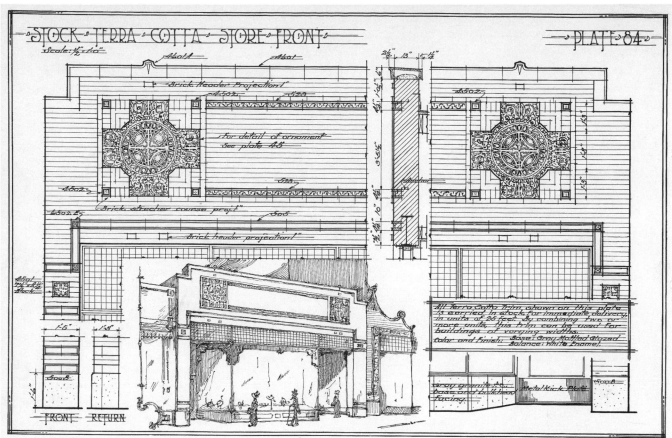

Midland Terra Cotta Company catalog (c. 1924), plate 84, stock terra-cotta storefront.

overwhelmed and overshadowed by an excessive number of dissimilar historical styles. The Sullivanesque was a minority style.

The Sullivanesque architectural designs portrayed in Midland plates were of high quality. Although they owed a debt to Sullivan, most of the facades illustrated were not direct copies of his work but exhibited an independent creativity and originality. They respected the directions established by Sullivan: ornament was positioned to help define the juncture of column and beam spandrel; ornament helped define important elements, such as entrances; ornament was a compositional device; and the use of ornament helped dematerialize the exterior wall to suggest the underlying structural frame. The representation of a skeletal structural system and the expression of the facade envelope as non-loadbearing were achieved through the introduction of ornamental belts, carefully composed accents, and selective but dominating clusters of ornament. In addition, and consistent with Sullivan's work, Midland's facade designs were usually well composed and skillfully proportioned. The most constant similarities lay, of course, in the styles of ornament, although Midland's stock pieces and glazes could not approach the exquisite quality of Sullivan's terra-cotta ornament.

It is not known who was directly responsible for the designs of ornament and building facades shown on Midland plates; however, William G. Krieg must receive much

Opposite:

Midland Terra Cotta Company catalog (c. 1922), plate 48, shops and offices, designs 1–4, Midland catalog.

Midland Terra Cotta Company catalog (c. 1922), plate 49, stores and shops, designs 1–4.

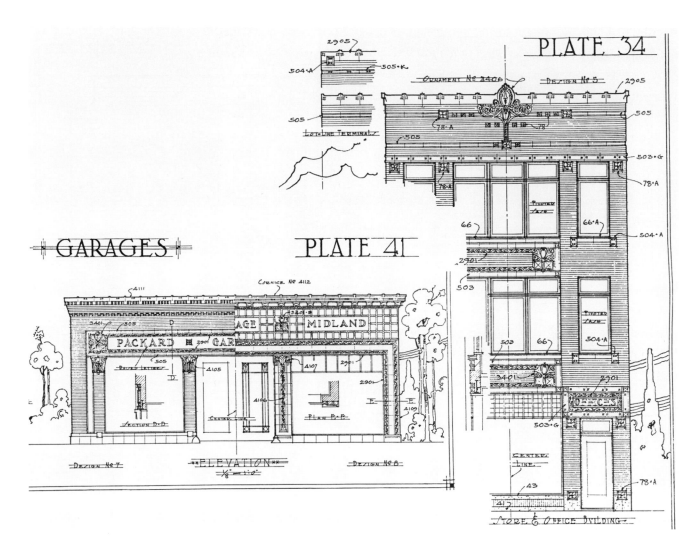

credit. As Midland's president and the only known registered architect with the company (although his registration lapsed during his tenure), Krieg was ultimately, if not directly, responsible. Draftsmen for design plates were not identified as anonymity was clearly a company policy. However, when the freehand printing on design plates is compared to that on shop drawings, where the draftsman was sometimes identified, it appears that two longtime employees, George J. Nejdl and George Johnson, drew most of the design plates. In addition, the ego of a draftsman seems to have emerged as the veiled letter "G" consistently appears on the line drawings of shrubs on design plates. The letter style and slant more closely resembled those of George Nejdl. Additional evidence, though not conclusive, suggests that both Nejdl and Johnson had design responsibilities at Midland.[41]

Design plates did not define the full extent of Midland's architectural design activities. Besides producing terra cotta, the Midland company provided design and architectural services. Not only did Midland produce Sullivanesque terra cotta, it designed Sullivanesque buildings. Midland served as the architect for some builders; its records indicate that it acted as architect or architectural designer for more than forty-five con-

Midland Terra Cotta Company catalog (c. 1924). Two of Midland's many Sullivanesque designs are shown here. Left: one-story garage, design no. 7 (design no. 8 mixes styles of ornament), plate 41. Right: three-story store and office building, design no. 5, plate 34.

structed buildings.[42] This was in addition to numerous small orders, such as minor re-modelings, where an architect was not involved. It appears that many of the building commissions employed terra cotta in historical styles; however, a number of the buildings were Sullivanesque.[43]

Occasionally, Midland was the designer for an architect. An example was the Pahl Building (1915) in Clinton, Iowa. The architect of record was Ladehoff and Sohn; however, as noted earlier, Midland records indicate, under the column for architect, "our sketch."[44] Evidently, Midland designed the front facade for the building, which, clad entirely in white-glazed terra cotta, appeared much like a facade shown in a plate from a company catalog.

Midland's advertisements often encouraged architects to avail themselves of Midland's services. For example, the February and March 1915 advertisements in the *American Carpenter and Builder* suggested: "Our designing department is at your service—send in your plans for ideas and estimates."[45] A year later, in the same journal, Midland advertising copy stated: "White enamel stock terra cotta—similar to that used on these buildings, can be had for immediate delivery. Send in your plans for ideas and estimates."[46] This practice was not condoned by the American Institute of Architects. However, for many journeyman architects, especially those without real design ability or training—which was common in the days of apprenticeship—Midland's design services were especially enticing. How much of an exterior facade design was from the commissioned architect and how much was the input of Midland, in most cases, will never be known. It is clear, however, that Midland influenced the design of many speculative commercial structures in mid-America.

A Masonic Temple (1914) in St. Joseph, Illinois, designed by Midland, had Sullivanesque qualities, but mixed styles of ornament were employed. The first truly Sullivanesque building designed by the Midland company while acting as "architect" was constructed in Martinsville, Indiana, for the Toner Brothers (1915).[47] Two stories high, the street facade was entirely clad in white-glazed terra cotta and was generally based on Midland's design no. 1, plate 36. This all-terra-cotta interpretation was a variation of the brick and terra-cotta two-story facade that appeared in the February and March 1915 issues of the *American Carpenter and Builder*. However, someone at Midland adjusted the design of the Toner Building for a wider site, reworked the second-story fenestration, and "customized" the front by adding a terra-cotta sign panel with blue-glazed letters. Still standing, the building facade is crisp and inviting although the fenestration has been modernized. Its progressive design contrasts with the eclectic building of the same vintage that stands adjacent to the north.[48]

Midland acted as architect for the dealership garages of the Overland Automobile Company in both Peoria and Rockford, Illinois. Both buildings were constructed in 1916 and still survive. However, the Rockford building has been converted to first-floor shops and second-story offices; furthermore, it has been debased by incongruous modernizations. The most serious vitiation has been the application of black paint over all exteri-

Toner Store (1915), Martinsville, Indiana; Midland Terra Cotta Company design. Photo: 1991.

or surfaces. The paint masks the terra-cotta reliefs and destroys the original play of contrasting materials and colors between face brick and white terra cotta. What was once an attractive facade, especially for a downtown automobile facility, has been unconscionably vandalized. The structure, as originally designed and constructed, was part of a photomontage of buildings featured in an advertisement for Midland in the August 1917 issue of *American Builder* (page 89).

Although not as attractive as the design at Rockford, the Peoria building was interesting and, more important, has survived relatively intact. It now houses a Salvation Army resale shop. Exterior walls are white-glazed brick and the terra-cotta ornamentation has a special green glaze for the otherwise stock pieces. The green color was rare for Midland and probably resulted from the company's attempt to match the lustrous color of Sullivan's terra cotta as produced by the American Terra Cotta and Ceramic Company. The American company was famous for its green glazes, especially when applied to its Teco pottery. Midland's glaze was more of a moss green and lighter in value; however, it was comparable to most of the preferred green glazes used for arts and crafts pottery of the period.[49] The one-story Peoria building is elongated with seven structural bays, and the bays at opposite ends of the facade have gently sloping parapets that approximate a gable shape while a similar parapet stretches across the center three bays. Sullivanesque ornamental medallions cap the rise of each inclined parapet.

Rhinelander, Wisconsin, is noted for its Purcell, Feick, and Elmslie First National Bank (1910–11); however, it is not the only Sullivanesque building in the small northern Wisconsin town. Midland designed a three-story building for O. A. Hilgermann in 1917 and the brick front facade, with terra-cotta ornamentation, still appears much as originally built, although the ground level has been remodeled.[50]

The Genoa Lumber Company (1919), located at 113 Main Street in Genoa, Illinois, was another Sullivanesque design by the Midland company. The roof parapet of the street facade followed the curved top chord of the long-span bow-string trusses. At street level, the front facade had three wide display windows separated by brick piers. Elaborate Sullivanesque terra cotta, featuring number 6500 series stock, enhanced the main facade. Badly damaged by fire and rebuilt with a second story, the structure does not approach its original handsome appearance despite the survival of some of the ornate terra cotta.[51]

In 1921, Midland provided architectural services for two automobile service garages. For R. C. Judd in St. Charles, Illinois, the Midland company developed a facade similar to that of the Genoa building. The parapet line again followed the curve of the roof. The Sullivanesque terra cotta included accent pieces of sculpted lion heads.[52] Another automobile garage, for H. H. Gunther in Galesburg, Illinois, combined terra-cotta ornament with brick for the two-story front facade. Sixty-five and a half feet wide, the facade was divided into three structural bays. Brick piers encased steel columns and were capped by a simple assembly of terra-cotta ornament. Brick spandrel panels were recessed four inches from the face of the piers and each spandrel segment had a rectangular panel framed by ornate borders of terra cotta. A popular medallion (two no. 4508 pieces), with supplemental pieces (4507 series and no. 4506), centered and capped the facade. Unfortunately, the building has been destroyed.[53]

Midland provided architectural designs for other buildings during 1921. Among these was a small building in Ortonville, Minnesota, for Carlson and Hasslen. It featured a major Sullivanesque assembly based on catalog plate 83. This set of pieces featured a central disc (no. 4508) with symmetrical flanking arms. The two horizontal extensions were composed of ornate rectilinear pieces of decreasing widths. The major horizontal axis was terminated by a larger ornate square (no. 4501) for each arm.[54] Another 1921 commission—a two-story store building for A. Quilici located at the intersection of Ellinwood with Center Street, in Des Plaines, Illinois—featured the same ornamental set.[55] The building was enhanced by construction of an adjacent complementary design (1923) for Quilici by Robert P. Ninneman, Architect (see chapter 8).[56] Unfortunately, both buildings for Quilici have been demolished. Another Sullivanesque

Garage (1921), St. Charles, Illinois; Midland Terra Cotta Company design. Photo: 1992.

design by Midland of the same year and in the same town, extant although altered, is a small two-story store building for a Mr. Winkelman on Northwest Highway. It closely resembled the design illustrated in Midland catalog plate 83 except the second-story band of fenestration was separated into individual window openings, which are now cluttered with incongruous shutters.[57]

Another 1921 Midland design stood in the North Shore Chicago suburb of Wilmette. The post office and store building had multiple storefronts stretching along Wilmette Avenue. Above the glass display windows was an uninterrupted wall in ashlar coursing of white-glazed terra cotta. Ornamental belt courses, accents, and focal pieces enlivened the wall and were composed to form a handsome Sullivanesque facade. With horizontal emphasis, the facade was balanced on a central focus comprised of ornate stock pieces similar to design number 1, plate 47, from the Midland catalog. At first glance, the entirely white facade seemed unassuming; however, the reliefs unfolded as one walked by. The wall surfaces danced with rich patterns and became a unique abstraction of urban-scale mosaics. Although architectonic, the white-glazed surfaces captured the essence of American ceramics during the arts and crafts period. The facade was destroyed (1978) during an extensive building remodeling and was replaced by a scaleless red brick wall and aluminum storefront.[58] Undoubtedly, client and architect were proud of the rebuilding, with its modern architecture; but it was dull and could have been located anywhere, while an important Sullivanesque facade was lost.

As noted earlier, shop drawings for Midland building designs, like most shop drawings for terra cotta, were accompanied by a "key elevation" drawing of small scale to show the entire facade intact and without breaks. These were usually drawn by George Nejdl, although George Johnson was sometimes responsible. In addition, for the Midland building designs, Nejdl or Johnson also drafted many of the construction details, wall sections, and partial detail elevations. For other orders, these mundane duties were usually performed by different draftsmen. After 1914, as revealed by a review of Midland shop drawings, these two men usually drew only key elevations and rarely undertook other drawing tasks on shop drawings for orders of architect-designed buildings.[59] This suggests that Nejdl and Johnson were design coordinators for most orders and probably the project designers for the Midland architectural commissions. Of the previously described Midland designs, George Johnson's name appeared on the drawings for the Overland Building in Peoria and the Winkelman Building in Des Plaines. George Nejdl's name appeared for all of the remaining works. For some projects—the Wilmette

A. Quilici Store Building, at left (1921; demolished 1986), Des Plaines, Illinois; Midland Terra Cotta Company design. Photo: 1986.

Post office and store building (1921; facade destroyed 1978), Wilmette, Illinois; Midland Terra Cotta Company design. Photo: 1978.

Post office and store building (1921; facade destroyed 1978), Wilmette, Illinois. Detail of terra-cotta facings and ornament at parapet based on Midland catalog plate 47, design No. 1. Photo: 1978.

Post Office and Store Building, for example—all of the shop drawings were entirely the work of Nejdl. It may be concluded that, until 1918, the designers for Midland's buildings were William G. Krieg, assisted by George J. Nejdl and, occasionally, George Johnson.[60] After 1918 and after Krieg left the position of president of Midland, it is not clear how responsibilities and roles were delegated. Krieg probably stayed with the company in an "architect" capacity until he established an independent architectural practice in 1922. If so, perhaps little changed in the architectural design department until that date. On the other hand, the Sullivanesque designs illustrated in later portfolio plates, especially plates 81 through 86, and the increased number of Midland designed Sullivanesque buildings, particularly in 1921, suggest a different hand and more expressive direction. Was this the direct hand of Krieg, now freed of administrative duties, or was Nejdl the prime architectural design talent with the company? Could noted designers have been hired on a freelance basis and remain anonymous? The complete list of characters and their roles at Midland will never be known. Company records have disappeared, except for a collection of shop drawings held by the Northwest Architectural Archives of the University of Minnesota Libraries.[61]

Around 1922, William Krieg resumed his own independent architectural practice.

Midland Terra Cotta Company catalog (c. 1924). Plate 86, stock terra-cotta garage front.

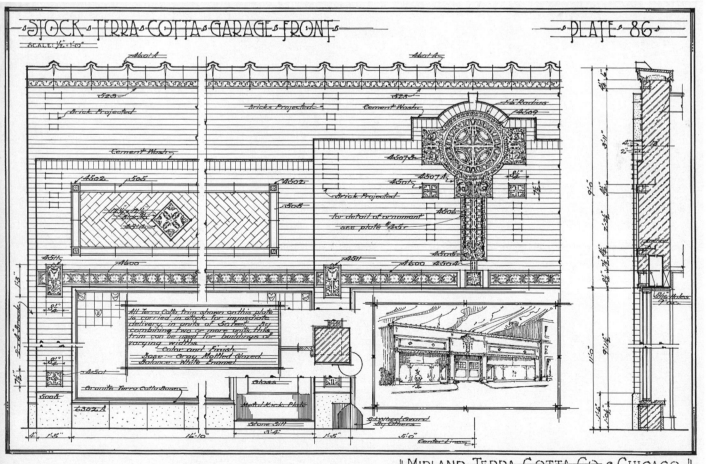

193

However, commissions were scarce and only a few Sullivanesque designs resulted. The most important of these was a large three-story apartment complex (1922) at the northeast corner of South Central Avenue and West Gladys Avenue on Chicago's West Side. Krieg articulated the two street facades by a series of rhythmic pavilions and arched entryways, and he matched Midland's Sullivanesque terra cotta with white-glazed brick and tapestry face brick. Despite some weaknesses, such as the awkward juncture of pavilions with entryways and some fussiness of adjacent ornamentation, the design had an exuberance and a sense of spontaneity not usually found in architectural design work. Unfortunately, Krieg was unable to sustain this quality, and a similar commission for an apartment hotel (1922–23) in suburban Oak Park resulted in a banal facade of English Gothic and Tudor design for F. F. Tunk and Company.[62]

The drawings for the Oak Park apartment building were completed under the title of a new firm. In late 1922, Krieg joined with John T. Hetherington (1858–1936) and his son, Murray D. Hetherington, and the firm name became Krieg, Hetherington, and Hetherington.[63] The firm, like many others in the 1920s, practiced design

Apartment building (1922), Gladys and Central Streets, Chicago; William G. Krieg, Architect. Photo: 1990.

Apartment building (1922), Chicago; William G. Krieg, Architect. Detail of terra-cotta ornament. Photo: 1990.

eclecticism. For example, a 1924 design of a two-story store and apartment for Ludwig Prohofer on Twenty-second Street (now Cermak Road) near Fiftieth Avenue in Cicero had a front facade with stepped parapet, reminiscent of old Dutch architecture.[64] During this time, however, Krieg faithfully utilized terra cotta from his old Midland company, with one exception. For the Beloit Water, Gas, and Electric Light Company Building (1923) in Beloit, Wisconsin, the firm used terra cotta from the American Terra Cotta and Ceramic Company.[65] In addition, handsome Sullivanesque ornament was mixed with motifs of other styles on this building.

In 1925, William Krieg's son, Arthur Walter Krieg (1905–72), graduated in architecture from the University of Illinois, and the following year the two formed a partnership as Krieg Associates, Architects. Most of their designs were still mired in eclecticism. However, a small industrial building in Chicago, at the southwest corner of West Forty-seventh Street and Hoyne Avenue, was a simple design that recalled earlier Sullivanesque associations. Built in 1927, the building was faced with brick and had Sullivan-like lion heads of stock Midland terra cotta as ornamental accents.[66] The Depression claimed the Kriegs' architectural firm. William G. Krieg left Chicago for California and Walter Krieg, after a time, relocated to Rockford, Illinois.[67] Both eventually returned to the Chicago area and again practiced architecture together. William G. Krieg died at his home in Riverside, Illinois, on April 13, 1944.[68]

William G. Krieg had become a member of the Illinois Society of Architects in 1910.[69] However, during his years as president of the Midland Terra Cotta Company,

Krieg let his membership in the society, as well as his architect's registration, lapse.[70] His name reappeared on the roll of architects for 1922 and he was reinstated as a member of the society in April of that year.[71] A review of historical documents of the architecture profession and the terra-cotta trade in Chicago indicates that Krieg's name very seldom appeared. In contrast, his counterpart at the American Terra Cotta and Ceramic Company, William D. Gates, was a major leader in the terra-cotta industry and was highly visible within the professional circle of architects in Chicago. Krieg did not have that kind of visibility. Yet he must have been a dynamic and forceful figure as well as versatile man. He helped form a new terra-cotta company, served as its first president, and created a niche for it in the highly competitive Chicago market. He maintained an office at the factory in Cicero rather than at the company headquarters in Chicago's Loop; therefore, he must have been closely involved with factory production. As the chief executive officer, he ultimately, if not directly, was responsible for creation of terra-cotta lines of Wrightian geometrical ornament and the more successful Sullivanesque series. The seven-year period during which William G. Krieg headed Midland was important as much of the built Sullivanesque work could be traced to his company at that time.

In 1922, Midland had the highest number of orders for terra cotta (409) in its history.[72] Many of these were for Sullivanesque terra cotta, as that booming construction year also saw the largest number of Sullivanesque architectural designs constructed.[73] However, architectural tastes in Chicago soon shifted to the popular taste of the country, which favored eclectic design. Midland's advertising, like that of other building material companies, then featured historical eclecticism. Midland still made Sullivanesque terra cotta but the vast majority of its orders were for historically derived ornament. In 1927, Midland's known orders for Sullivanesque terra cotta numbered only ten.[74]

As discussed previously, the modeler for Louis Sullivan's and George G. Elmslie's ornament was Kristian Schneider. His association with Chicago terra-cotta companies started with Northwestern and continued with the American company. Schneider completed the employment circuit of the trio of major terra-cotta companies in Chicago by becoming the chief modeler for the Midland company in 1930.[75] Thus, Midland, the producer of so much stock Sullivanesque ornament that imitated the designs of Sullivan and Elmslie and the handiwork of Schneider, finally secured the services of the revered modeler himself.[76] And it was in this same period that Midland manufactured Elmslie originals for the four schools in the Hammond, Indiana area. The architect for the schools, William S. Hutton, employed George G. Elmslie as design architect.[77] But, the opportunity to have a master modeler work on ornament designed by a master architect was short lived. With Schneider's death on August 11, 1935, just five months after the contract for the Thornton school terra cotta was signed,[78] Fritz Albert was hired to model Elmslie's ornament.

The Great Depression was especially severe for terra-cotta companies and their workers. Not only was construction curtailed but architectural tastes were changing,

Opposite: Beloit Water, Gas, and Electric Light Company Building (1923), Beloit, Wisconsin; Krieg, Hetherington, and Hetherington, Architects. Detail of a terra-cotta ornamental design for entryway walls. Photo: 1993.

which would alter choices of material. Ornamentation, a major feature to which terra cotta was ideally suited, became perceived as an antiquated frill. The Midland company was especially hard hit. For the years 1934 through 1938, Midland's annual orders for terra cotta totaled, respectively, 37, 35, 58, 43, and 38 orders. In 1939, Midland received a contract in January; its next and final order was in April for a structure at 7755 South Halsted, Chicago.[79]

For twenty-eight years, the Midland Terra Cotta Company was an integral part of the construction industry in Chicago and instrumental in promoting the Sullivanesque. Through production of terra cotta, free distribution of illustrative portfolio examples, and its own architectural services, Midland was a leading advocate of Sullivanesque design. Although not of the same caliber as Sullivan's work, Midland's ornamentation was a reasonable facsimile and considerably less expensive. Since Midland's Sullivanesque was more affordable, it was adapted for a wide range of buildings. Therefore, more people from a broader range of social and economic classes could enjoy the artistry of its ornamentation. The decorated modern architecture that Sullivan and his followers advocated and called an "Architecture for Democracy" may have been achieved, in the most democratic sense, by the Midland Terra Cotta Company.

CHAPTER 7

SULLIVANESQUE ARCHITECTS
IN CHICAGO

A SMALL NUMBER of Chicago architects were responsible for Sullivanesque designs during the lengthy second phase of the style (1911–30). The most important of this group included William G. Carnegie, A. L. Himelblau, and Levy and Klein. Several other lower-echelon Chicago architects were advocates of the Sullivanesque for a while. This conviction was significant at a time when more prestigious Chicago architectural firms with important clients and major commissions had reverted to design eclecticism based on historical European models. The Sullivanesque architects in Chicago were not leaders of the profession and their usual commissions were for smaller buildings in the city's neighborhoods. Prior to World War I, members of this group were inevitably trained by apprenticeship. However, after the war, when the largest concentrations of Sullivanesque buildings in Chicago were constructed (1922 was the peak), only a small number of architects were responsible, but most of them were college educated. However, they did not attend prestigious East Coast universities. They were educated almost exclusively in the city of Chicago, at the Armour Institute of Technology or the Chicago School of Architecture (which, as noted earlier, included classes at the Armour Institute and the Art Institute of Chicago), or downstate, at the University of Illinois at Urbana-Champaign.

Many Sullivanesque architects were from lower-income and/or ethnic backgrounds and were rising from ghetto-like conditions. Without fanfare, these advocates busied themselves with unspectacular commissions for clients of similar background. Without documented theoretical utterances, they designed in the Sullivanesque vein; however, they undoubtedly understood that the style was synonymous with American democracy. But at the same time, the crassness of American capitalism influenced their designs, as budget and utility were major concerns. These factors may have contributed to the acceptance of the Sullivanesque aesthetic but also eroded the quality of their architecture. Still, a wide range of heretofore unknown but vital designs in Chicago are available to explore, although demolitions and alterations have had a serious impact on this inventory.

Carl M. Almquist received his professional license (A 310) under the "grandfather clause" in the architectural licensing law. Almquist was prolific; he designed many buildings in Chicago's developing neighborhoods, including houses early in his career, and then, later on, small two- or three-story brick flats and, in lesser numbers, larger apartment buildings.[1] Occasionally there was a one-, two-, or three-story store building with flats; and, from 1915 on, these commercially oriented structures were Sullivanesque.

Among the first was a building (1915) for Dr. A. H. Keats, for which Midland's stock terra-cotta (order no. 557) was employed. This was followed by four additional Sullivanesque store designs in 1921 for Swanson and Erickson. The next year Almquist designed another store (now demolished) at the intersection of North Kedzie and Leland, and a two-story commercial building at 6960–64 North Clark. For Louis Erickson, Almquist designed a two-story commercial structure (1923). Although its appearance has been altered through storefront and second-floor window remodelings, the terra-cotta patterns survive.[2] Almquist's Sullivanesque designs for these commercial facades are characterized by ragged parapet profiles, repetition of aligned ornamental clusters of terra-cotta on brick upper wall surfaces, and window openings framed by terra cotta trim. Almquist's most successful Sullivanesque design was probably the two-story commercial building (1921) for Swanson and Erickson at 4745–47 North Kedzie Avenue. Large Chicago windows at the second floor were grouped as a horizontal banding; each window opening was in turn surrounded by decorative white-glazed terra cotta. Ornamental terra-cotta assemblies dominated the brick upper-wall surfaces. Large storefront windows stretched across the ground floor and were asymmetrically arranged to accommodate various entries, although the upper story was symmetrically composed.

The firm of Aroner and Somers was responsible for several superb examples of Sullivanesque architecture, including a theater, a laundry, and an apartment building with ground-floor stores. The Orpheus (c. 1912; demolished) was a creative design for what was then a new building type, the motion picture theater. Although some eclectic ornament was mixed with Sullivanesque, the result was still a highly original interpretation of the Sullivanesque style. The decorative front facade of terra cotta sheathed the underlying skeletal steel structure. The building was the subject of coverage in *The Brickbuilder* (October 1913), which included photographs of details of the Sullivanesque terra-cotta.[3] Ornamental trim was used as a running border on the front facade, and this

Swanson and Erikson Building (1921), North Kedzie Avenue, Chicago; Carl M. Almquist, Architect. The parapet's ragged profile and repeated ornamental clusters were characteristic of Almquist's designs. Photo: 1987.

swirling motif was replicated for use on Aroner and Somers's laundry and mixed-use buildings as well.

The Jewel Laundry (1912–13) seems inspired by the classical style because of the use of repeated pilasters and columns, but its "colonnade" was integrated into the white-glazed brick wall and incorporated Sullivanesque terra cotta. Terra-cotta borders framed the colonnade and additional ornament capped each column. Triangular ornamental accents were positioned at opposite ends of the front facade and aligned with the top of the colonnade. A polished granite base separated white-glazed brick from grade and the granite continued about the entryway to form a portal. Cripple columns rhythmically continued the colonnade over the portal. Terra cotta was supplied by the Northwestern Terra Cotta Company (order no. 12382).[4] The design of the Jewel Laundry was praised in an article in the journal *Brick and Clay Record*.[5]

Aroner and Somers were the architects for a mixed-use building (1914) on West Chicago Avenue for J. Penner; two floors of apartments were placed above ground-floor shops. The residential entry was centered in the facade and treated as a slightly recessed vertical panel, which was emphasized by a raised and stepped parapet with Sullivanesque ornament prominently featured. Flanking storefronts and apartment windows were collectively enclosed by an ornamental terra-cotta border. This border resembled the Northwestern pieces used at the Orpheus Theater and the Jewel Laundry; however, the terra cotta was from the Midland company.[6] A heavily ornamented parapet cap, entry ornament, and carefully positioned accents completed the incorporation of Sullivanesque terra cotta. Continuous horizontal bandings of unornamented terra cotta aligned with windowsills and heads. These bandings are terminated by the vertical borders of the ornamented terra cotta. The major exterior surface material was yellow face brick in running bond. Beautifully appointed with ornament, well-proportioned, and made subtly taut by the play of wall planes, the facade was an advanced design.

Formed around 1911, the firm of Aroner and Somers was responsible for the design of many simple buildings in Chicago's neighborhoods—mostly flats and small apartment buildings. By 1915, Aroner and Somers had dissolved their partnership.[7] Elbert S. Somers joined in a short-lived partnership, Brydges and Somers, and then practiced alone until 1921.[8] Jacob S. Aroner (d. 1924) subsequently designed many buildings but few seemed responsive to the Sullivanesque.[9] However, Aroner did employ some Sullivanesque stock terra cotta from Midland (order no. 22396) for a store building (1922) for E. Edelmann at 3618 Broadway. A few accent pieces, numbers 4501 and 4511, complemented the simple statement.[10]

The architect who utilized stock Sullivanesque terra cotta in the most creative and effective way was William G. Carnegie (1888–1969). For several years (1914–16) he was responsible for some notable Sullivanesque designs for inexpensive buildings in the Roseland neighborhood on the far South Side of Chicago. Born in Chicago, Carnegie spent much of his life in Roseland, which was west of the factory town of Pullman (1880–84; S. S. Beman, Architect). Carnegie's father, born in Scotland, was a building contrac-

J. Penner Building (1914–15), West Chicago Avenue, Chicago; Aroner and Somers, Architects. The apartment entrance was centered and flanked by storefronts, now remodeled. Photo: 1990.

tor. After only six months of high school, William went to work full time for his father, and the contracting firm's name became John L. Carnegie and Son.[11] However, William wanted to be an architect. After some coursework at the Art Institute of Chicago (Chicago School of Architecture) but mostly self-taught, he took the examination for architect's registration in Illinois. Carnegie's license (B 367) was issued on October 15, 1909.[12]

Carnegie's early commissions were competent but uninspired designs.[13] However, in 1914 the architect secured a prestigious commission and it became a major accomplishment of Sullivanesque design. The Roseland Safety Deposit Bank, at 11108–14 South Michigan, is an important but little known work. This design is remarkable considering its reliance on the use of standardized terra cotta, but with custom glazes, from the Midland Terra Cotta Company.[14] The construction incorporated an existing building in which the bank was housed. The design expanded around the existing structure and extended the frontage on South Michigan Avenue to an overall length of 107' 2".[15] An entrance for second-floor offices bisected the facade and was emphasized by a decorative terra-cotta eagle perched atop a shield entwined with Sullivanesque foliage, which was placed at the midpoint of the upper wall and parapet. The eagle was a Midland stock piece, number 2904B; however, it was customized with colorful glazes. It measured 4' 8" high with a wing span of 5' 4". To the north of the office entrance, the first floor was

J. Penner Building (1914–15), Chicago; Aroner and Somers, Architects. Detail of terra-cotta ornamentation. Photo: 1990.

occupied by the bank (a thirty-six-foot expanse) and a narrow rental store. Bank entry doors were framed by terra cotta set in a glass storefront. Centered above the bank entry and positioned on the upper wall surface was a cartouche of Sullivanesque ornament based upon Purcell, Feick, and Elmslie's prominent focal piece for their First National Bank Building (1910) in Rhinelander, Wisconsin. Carnegie repeated this motif on the southerly portion of the facade. These two clusters were placed above their respective ground-floor frontages, each centered above a second-floor window—the second-to-last from each end. The second-floor windows were collected together to appear as a continuous horizontal opening and were framed by a banding of Sullivanesque ornament. The white-glazed facade was subtly modulated by alternating heights of terracotta coursing. Luxfer prisms formed a pattern of glass squares above the wide display windows while low bulkheads of terra cotta, glazed to simulate granite at the bank and marble at the large shop, supported the display windows at street level.

In 1925, Carnegie was engaged to remodel the Roseland Safety Deposit Bank building. These changes included expansion of the bank into the small shop area and a new storefront for the large shop that put the entry door closer to Michigan Avenue. In the 1960s, the storefronts were "modernized": a projecting sign and aluminum canopy were installed above the sidewalk and a different bank occupied the premises. But these changes did not detract from the subtle beauty of the upper facade. Unfortunately, the successor bank has vacated the neglected building and the neighborhood is declining. This instability may not bode well for the future of the building.

In August and September 1915, Carnegie produced two Sullivanesque designs for small one-story shops. These were the Peter Foote Real Estate Office Building, on the southeast corner of East Seventy-ninth and Stony Island, and the Jurgensen Tea Company, 11743 South Michigan Avenue.[16] The front facade of the Foote Building (1915; demolished) curved to become tangential to the diagonally intersecting streets. Stock terra cotta was composed with brick masonry for both buildings. The street facades were inspired by a one-story storefront design that appeared about the same time in Mid-

Front elevation of Roseland Safety Deposit Bank (1914), Chicago, from working drawings; William G. Carnegie, Architect. Courtesy of David Carnegie.

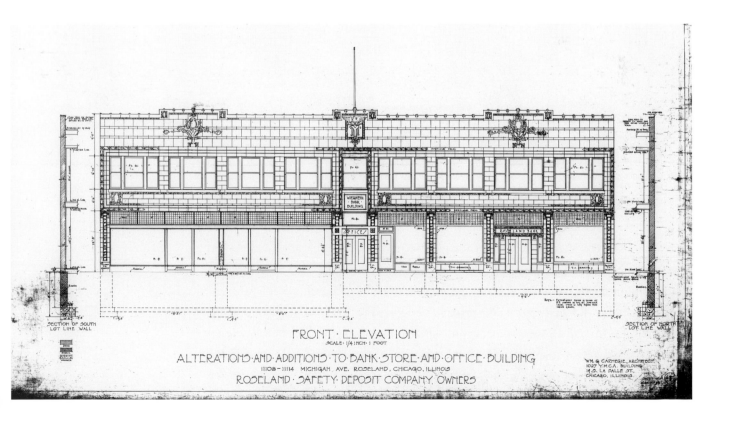

FRONT · ELEVATION
SCALE: 1/4 INCH: 1 FOOT
ALTERATIONS · AND · ADDITIONS · TO · BANK · STORE · AND · OFFICE · BUILDING
11108 - 11114 MICHIGAN · AVE. ROSELAND · CHICAGO · ILLINOIS
ROSELAND · SAFETY · DEPOSIT · COMPANY, OWNERS

Roseland Safety Deposit Bank (1914), William G. Carnegie, Architect. Detail of white-glazed terra-cotta facings and ornament. Photo: 1987.

land catalogs and advertisements; but Carnegie personalized his facades with paired terra-cotta eagles. The glass storefronts of the Jurgensen building have been replaced by concrete block in the building's conversion to a storefront church.

Photographs of Carnegie's Sullivanesque designs were featured, without attribution, in several Midland advertisements published in the *American Carpenter and Builder*. These were the Roseland Safety Deposit Bank, in the October 1915 issue; Peter Foote Real Estate, September 1916; and Jurgensen Tea Company, April 1918.[17] The Jurgensen building was also featured in an article that appeared in *American Builder* in December

1919. However, Carnegie was not mentioned.[18] A photograph of the same building, this time with Carnegie's name, appeared in the monograph *Architectural Terra Cotta: The Store*, published by the National Terra Cotta Society, which produced a number of books to promote terra cotta.[19] During this time, Carnegie was still active in professional organizations.[20]

In 1916, Carnegie's last built Sullivanesque design for a client was completed. This was the Dekker Brothers Market at 10646–48 South Michigan Avenue in Chicago's Roseland community. The building had two shops at street level, each of a different width, and these flanked an entrance to second-floor apartments. The front facade was treated as an envelope with red face brick, terra-cotta piers, upper-story terra-cotta bandings, and a central ornamental cluster.

Carnegie designed and built his own "house" (1916), which was actually an apartment building, in the Sullivanesque style. His family occupied the largest unit and the other units were leased to tenants. The four-story building, with exterior walls of brick and ornamented terra-cotta trim, was located in Roseland but was later demolished for a bank parking lot.[21] The year 1916 was crucial to Carnegie's experimentation with the

Peter Foote Real Estate Building (1915; demolished), E. Seventy-ninth and Stony Island, Chicago; William G. Carnegie, Architect. Photo: c. 1916, courtesy of David Carnegie.

Sullivanesque. He designed at least three additional Sullivanesque projects that year, but none was built. His garage and office building for the Redd Cab Company was a promising design. Offices were on the second floor above the garage entries and the building aligned with the street to convey a commanding presence. The rendering of a large apartment project suggested a Sullivanesque design of extraordinary strength and potential. An English basement formed a strong base; a vertical emphasis was created by three floors of stacked dwelling units; and the building was capped by a strong horizontal banding of terra cotta and strategically positioned terra-cotta focal pieces. Another project was a large, three-and-one-half-story apartment building. Terra-cotta use consisted of small accents connected by vertical strips composed to reinforce the verticality of the exterior wall.[22] Although still Sullivanesque, the design seemed to indicate a change in Carnegie's taste. In his later work, he completely embraced design eclecticism, tending to favor the verticality of the collegiate Gothic style.

The Dubin name has been recognized in Chicago architectural circles for more than eighty years, mostly in connection with modern architecture as the firm Dubin and Dubin and, later, Dubin Dubin Black and Moutoussamy. George Harold Dubin (1890–1958) was born in Denver, Colorado; however, he was educated in Chicago and graduated in 1914 from the University of Illinois at Urbana-Champaign with a bachelor of science degree in architecture.[23] By 1916, he was independently practicing architecture. One of his first known commissions (1916; demolished) was just a few doors away from his office, on the opposite side of the street. But the four-story building at 837–39 West Twelfth Street (now Roosevelt Road) for J. Weiss and P. Javshitz was a timid Sullivanesque design.[24] Around 1919, Dubin formed a partnership with an engineer, Abraham J. Eisenberg. The firm of Dubin and Eisenberg was responsible for many buildings in neighborhood shopping and apartment districts of Chicago. Some of these were Sullivanesque buildings designed between 1919 and 1923. All used Midland stock terra cotta.[25]

Dubin's two-story store for B. Schuhter at 3915 Roosevelt Road, Chicago, was built in 1920. Unfortunately, the building has now been badly altered as all of the original glazings have been replaced by incompatible materials. As in many Dubin designs, a terra-cotta disc (Midland number 4508) was the primary focus for the Sullivanesque facade. The disc measured 2' 6" and was expanded and "individualized" by additional ornamental pieces. Similarly, a one-story store building, three bays in width, built (1922) at 3715 Lawrence, featured the basic medallion but it was varied by differing combinations and positions of secondary pieces. Horizontal string courses and insets of terra cotta were composed in the brick upper wall surfaces for both buildings. Similar basic features were employed for a one-story store (1922; demolished) on North Avenue near Avers Avenue.[26]

Dubin and Eisenberg buildings anchored the southeast and northwest corners of the intersection of West Chicago and North Monticello Avenues. A one-story store building (1922) had a sixty-foot-long brick facade with terra-cotta string courses and

Opposite:

W. C. Jurgensen Tea Company Building (1915; altered), Chicago; William G. Carnegie, Architect. Except for terra-cotta end piers with sculpted eagles, the facade resembled a Midland catalog plate. Photo: c. 1916, courtesy of David Carnegie.

Dekker Brothers Market (1916), Chicago; William G. Carnegie, Architect. The original shop fronts shown here have been replaced but the upper facade of brick and decorative terra cotta remains relatively intact. Photo: c. 1916, courtesy of David Carnegie.

three ornamental groupings (based on Midland plate 47, design number 1) punctuated the horizontal parapet cap. The two-story building at the northwest corner did not include the usual terra-cotta string courses and bandings for the upper wall surfaces. Instead, only a Midland medallion and subset of accents were positioned in the facade. Therefore, the brick cladding seemed more massive and the terra-cotta insets were less integrated. (The reliance on just a few primary pieces of ornament, without ancillary treatments, was a mistake that was duplicated by some other architects.) The center portion of the parapet on the front facade was a gable-like shape that emphasized the terra-cotta cartouche but seemed forced and not very successful. Usually, Dubin's Sullivanesque designs had simple horizontal parapets relieved by terra-cotta ornamental clusters that projected above the parapet and engaged the sky.

George Dubin's brother, Henry, a 1915 graduate of the University of Illinois at Urbana-Champaign, joined the firm in 1919.[27] This date coincides with the firm's increase in output of Sullivanesque designs; but it is unclear if this was due to Henry Dubin's influence, although he did have increasing design responsibilities and was in the forefront of those seeking to reintroduce modern architecture to Chicago in the 1930s.[28] The Sullivanesque appeared only briefly in the total scope of the work from the Dubin and Eisenberg firm and its successors, but it is clear that George H. and Henry Dubin admired Louis Sullivan and his work. Henry Dubin (1892–1963), upon seeing the destruction of Sullivan's cast-iron ornament during a "modernization" (c. 1953) of

Redd Cab Company Project (1916), Chicago; William G. Carnegie, Architect. Architect's pencil rendering, courtesy of David Carnegie.

the Gage Building storefronts (1898–99) in Chicago, acquired some of the larger fragments. Segments of the ornament, cast by Winslow Brothers Iron Works, Chicago, were donated to several institutions, and two large panels are displayed in the entryway of the Architecture Building at the University of Illinois at Urbana-Champaign.[29]

With the possible exception of Louis Sullivan, A. L. Himelblau was the architect responsible for the largest number of Sullivanesque buildings in the city of Chicago. At least 56 of his buildings have been verified to have been Sullivanesque. At least 97 Himelblau-designed buildings used terra cotta for ornament; of this number, 52 have been demolished, leaving 45 extant.[30] Among the demolished structures, 20 have been verified to have been Sullivanesque, including a building that available drawings show to have been his most successful design. This was a 1924 store building located at 3310–24 South State Street. Of the other demolished structures, 2 were of eclectic styles and 30 were of unknown appearance.[31] Since terra cotta was employed for these 97 buildings, they were more expensive and important than his other commissions.

For his time, Himelblau was among the most prolific architects in Chicago. But the vast majority of his commissions were for low-budget simple buildings in Chicago's neighborhoods—mostly two- or three-flats and, occasionally, apartment buildings.[32] His two- and three-story dwellings were usually flat-roofed and had exterior walls of brick, sometimes red but usually yellow. These were simple, utilitarian designs, forming a kind of vernacular. His flats, on narrow lots and all aligned in the same way, created unified and pleasant street frontages. Often the front facade was shaped by bending the wall plane to create a vertically continuous "bay window" in the Chicago mode. Limestone banding and accents relieved brick surfaces. However, it was only in his designs with Sullivanesque terra cotta that his work ranged beyond a level of mere competency and achieved some artistic merit. Surprisingly well proportioned and pleasing designs often resulted, despite low budgets and use of stock terra cotta. His facade designs sometimes resembled Midland's catalog examples, especially early in his career, but more often than not, he created original variations and satisfying results.

Abraham L. Himelblau (1890–1944) was born in Waverly, Iowa, and at the age of ten moved with his family to Chicago.[33] Himelblau completed the studies of the Chicago School of Architecture. He became a registered architect (Illinois B 622) in 1914 and immediately formed a partnership with an engineer, Abraham J. Eisenberg. However, the partnership lasted less than a year and Himelblau thereafter practiced architecture in sole proprietorship until 1931, when the Depression forced him to retire.[34] In 1919 Eisenberg formed a partnership with the architect George H. Dubin.

Himelblau's first built Sullivanesque design was in 1915 for H. Emmermann and it was published in the September 1916 issue of the *Western Architect*. Located at 4310–22 North Clarendon Avenue and Junior Terrace, the building is U-shaped in plan with various entrances accessible from the landscaped court. The yellow brick–faced building has terra-cotta quoins that give it a Tudor expression; however, the terra-cotta ornament is Sullivanesque.[35] It was the only Himelblau building that used terra cotta from the American Terra Cotta and Ceramic Company (order no. 2655). His other buildings used stock terra-cotta from Midland.[36]

During the first six years of his practice, Himelblau used terra-cotta ornament on only six buildings.[37] One of these was a small two-story structure (1919) for Kaplan and Schachter on Roosevelt Road. A centered ornamental disc capped the main facade and a vertical ornamental "stem" extended down from the disc through a narrow brick pier and bisected the wide expanse of second-floor windows into paired openings. As in many of his buildings, the design has been compromised by deplorable alterations.

Beginning in 1921, Himelblau frequently used terra cotta and created many Sullivanesque designs. Why this sudden concentration occurred is not known. Perhaps it was because an increased number of commercial and mixed-use structures then constituted his practice. Many of these were one-story shops and service garages for commercial strips in Chicago's neighborhoods. For example, three buildings share similar characteristics. Each was one story high and had an extended street frontage with multiple structural bays and continuous storefronts. The masonry upper walls, which spanned the window void with supporting beams, were visually reduced in weight by shaped outlines and surfaces with ornamental patterns. Parapet walls were symmetrically shaped through the use of sloping segments and articulations. These configurations created interest and increased the scale of the building while unifying the entire breadth of the frontage. Upper wall surfaces were textured by various brick patterns and rhythmically placed terra-cotta focal pieces and/or accents. The commercial building (1921) for S. Dlott on Irving Park Road used a central medallion assembly as a major focus and capped the parapet wall. For a 1922 commercial building in suburban Oak Park, Himelblau used a similar arrangement; a dominating dual-medallion ornamental cluster centered on the facade and engaged with a sloping sector of parapet. Flemish bond brickwork provided a richly textured background as the unified upper wall stretched across seven structural bays. For a building (1923) on Chicago's Montrose Avenue, Himelblau again utilized a similar composition but the parapet was configured with a stylized central "gable" of shallow slope flanked by two horizontal segments.[38] Instead of major terra-cotta ornament, smaller clusters marched across the upper wall and aligned with terra-cotta column covers below. These clusters were, in turn, tied to the brickwork by aligned rowlock brick courses while terra-cotta accents provided additional points of reference and movement. In each building, the elongated upper wall was independent of the storefront within each structural bay. However, structural columns and upper wall surfaces had carefully considered relationships.

Two larger mixed-use structures by Himelblau share some features. The profiles of the parapets for both were comprised of gently curved segments connected by strictly horizontal alignments. Both buildings had facades of face brick with white-glazed stock terra cotta. Decorative terra cotta on both included horizontal bandings and upper wall ornament featuring Midland's number 4508 medallions. However, the facades of the two-story building at the northwest corner of Pulaski and West Adams Street included

Store building (1922), Oak Park, Illinois; A. L. Himelblau, Architect. Photo: 1992.

Store building (1923), 3639–47 Montrose Avenue, Chicago; A. L. Himelblau, Architect. Photo: 1991.

vertical lines of terra-cotta trim and column covers of decorative terra cotta joined with major terra-cotta bandings to suggest a structural grid superimposed across the brick facade. Counterpoint was provided by a smaller-scale grid formed by narrow terra-cotta bandings and vertical stripes aligned with window jambs, heads, and sills. For the other building, a three-story structure (1923; demolished 1991) on West Sixty-ninth Street, terra-cotta ornamental medallions (no. 4508) were prominent at the roof parapet.[39]

Two of Himelblau's later Sullivanesque designs exhibit the influence of Midland catalog's plate 47, design number 1. Centered on each building parapet was an ornamental medallion composed with other decorative components. For a two-story building (1925) on Irving Park Road, this was the only decorative feature to engage the sky although horizontal bandings, decorative accents, and column borders completed the terra-cotta embellishments. For another two-story mixed-use building, at 5910–14 West Roosevelt Road, Himelblau essentially used the same assemblage. However, because of the building's greater length, secondary ornament was also introduced, rising against the sky. In addition, the dominant bandings of terra cotta within the field of yellow brick provided more horizontal emphasis than in the earlier design. Built in 1927, the Roosevelt Road building was Himelblau's last known Sullivanesque design; despite a fire and insensitive modifications, it still exhibits his Sullivanesque vernacular.[40]

In 1923, Himelblau expanded the size of his office and started developing and contracting buildings as well as designing them. His investments expanded to fifteen prop-

Stores with flats (1927), Roosevelt Road, Chicago; A. L. Himelblau, Architect. Detail of terra-cotta ornamental cluster centrally positioned at the parapet. Photo: 1987.

erties; however, he lost all, including his practice, to the Depression. The bank, which took his properties, hired him to manage his former holdings.[41] He then lived in the Sovereign Hotel at 6200 Kenmore Avenue; he died in Michael Reese Hospital on December 17, 1944.[42]

In summary, most of Himelblau's numerous nonresidential buildings were Sullivanesque with terra-cotta ornamentation. However, his designs varied in the application of ornament. Some seemed excessive in their use of ornamental medallions, while others minimized the ornamental motifs and restricted Sullivanesque terra-cotta to subtle accents and string courses. His smaller buildings usually had ragged parapet profiles and excessive ornamentation that often seemed applied rather than integral, as in Sullivan's designs. This abundance of ornament was probably an attempt to call attention to these small buildings and make them meaningful. Conversely, Himelblau's larger buildings were ordinarily clean and simple, with uninterrupted horizontal parapets. However, most of his designs fell between these two extremes. In general, Himelblau's designs were successful—especially given the scope of his commissions.

Charles J. Grotz was representative of the struggling architects who designed in the Sullivanesque style for speculative work in Chicago neighborhoods.[43] Since his practice concentrated on residential work such as two-flats and apartments, budget limitations forced simple solutions and use of economical materials. For more lucrative commissions, he used terra-cotta embellishments. He had eleven projects in this category. Of this number, five buildings have been demolished and no records exist to determine their architectural style. Of the remainder, six were mixed-use and have been confirmed to have been Sullivanesque designs.[44]

The first of Grotz's Sullivanesque designs was in 1921 for J. Drew in Chicago.[45] The thirty-foot-wide brick front facade featured a prominent terra-cotta grouping on the parapet and was based on Midland plate 48, design number 4. The major Sullivan-inspired motif was a disc (no. 4508) engaged by flanking horizontal bars.

One of Grotz's more successful designs is located at the northeast corner of South Halsted and West Eight-first Streets. Built in 1922 by a contractor, William Graf, for George Valhakis, the two-story building included two shops at street level and apartments on the second floor.[46] The building has a rounded corner at the street intersection; therefore, the two red-brick street facades "flow" together, an effect heightened by the dominance of horizontal bandings of white-glazed terra cotta. Major bandings align with window heads of the storefronts and second-story openings while minor bandings align with second-floor windowsills and the parapet cap. In addition, secondary bandings were introduced in the upper wall between the parapet coping and the second-story window heads. These paired horizontals are in a "dot-dash" pattern with brick segmenting the terra-cotta trim. Ornate cruciform medallions of terra cotta were placed near the building corners. A fourth terra-cotta ornamental assembly was positioned near the halfway point of the Eighty-first Street side to help give prominence and identity to the apartment entrance. Although suffering from some settlement and lax maintenance, the building still is in use and demonstrates a simple but effective facade treatment.

A small two-story building (1922) on West Forty-seventh Street, now badly remodeled, was based on Midland plate 82. The Midland prototype paired ornamental assemblies that were spaced apart to create tension between the two decorative elements, but the plate illustrated a one-story shop. Grotz adopted the same ornamental theme but added a second-story apartment. Fenestration was asymmetrically arranged in the brick facade as window placement was based on the functional layout of the interior. However, the ground-floor storefront was symmetrically composed: the shop entry was adjacent to one party wall while the apartment entrance was opposite, and display windows were placed in between. Another Grotz building (1922; demolished), for J. Slader, repeated the same basic design with only minor variations.[47] Two additional commercial buildings had stock Sullivanesque terra cotta but were devoid of any major ornamental features. Instead, Grotz enlivened the brick facades with white-glazed terra-cotta string courses, window trim, column covers, parapet caps, and a few small accent pieces. Still standing, but with storefront alterations, a two-story building (1923) designed by Grotz for James Svejda is located at the northwest corner of West Fifty-first and South Winchester. Grotz used a similar approach for a one-story building (1924; demolished) that stood on West Fifty-first Street at South Paulina.[48]

George Valhakis Building (1922), Chicago; Charles J. Grotz, Architect. The ornamental assembly centered on the side street or long facade is above the entryway to second-floor apartments. Photo: 1991.

Maurice Lewis Bein attended architecture school at the University of Illinois, Urbana, and became a licensed architect in Illinois in 1920.[49] He opened his own office for the practice of architecture in Chicago around 1922 and designed a number of Sullivanesque buildings. The first of these was a simple one-story store (1922) for M. A. Bender on North Broadway, Chicago. Three terra-cotta assemblies, which stressed verticality from storefront lintel to parapet cap, subdivided the upper wall into even-numbered segments. Each segment had terra-cotta trim that defined a rectangular panel; within each panel, brick was laid in a basketweave pattern and a terra-cotta accent was centered. The Bender Building resembled Midland catalog plate 48, design number 1.

Although Bein continued to use Midland's stock terra cotta, his subsequent Sullivanesque facade designs were more original and didn't copy the "pattern-book" designs shown in Midland portfolio plates. Furthermore, he used yellow brick for these buildings instead of the range of red hues employed in his first design. The increased scale of these buildings must have prompted Bein's reliance on his own ingenuity. Midland's catalog representations were for simple, small buildings and were not directly applicable for the increased scale and greater complexity of Bein's commissions. Many of his projects were mixed use, which combined a number of shops with multiple dwelling units. Although these buildings were compatible with surrounding structures, Bein's were larger and therefore more important than most other buildings in Chicago's neighborhoods. Several projects had similar conceptual schemes but were varied in facade treatment. These three-story buildings were at 5934–44 West Roosevelt Road, northwest corner with Mason; 3619–27 Lawrence at Monticello (the I. S. Robins Building), southeast corner; and 3752–58 Montrose at Hamlin. The first two of these buildings were constructed in 1924; the one at Montrose and Hamlin was built a year later.[50]

Each of the three buildings was S-shaped in plan. Shops were on the ground floor of the leg that fronted on a major commercial street, that is, Roosevelt, Lawrence, and Montrose, respectively. Street-level entrances gave access to stairs to offices and/or apartments above the shops. Most dwelling units were grouped about a light and access court, which could be reached from the adjoining residential streets, that is, Mason, Monticello, and Hamlin, respectively. The conventional Chicago walk-up apartment building arrangement, U-shaped in plan and wrapped about an open-ended courtyard, was adopted and modified. In plan, a serviceway and lightwell separated the commercial wing from the paralleling middle leg of residential use. Multiple residential entryways, leading to an interior stair and flanking apartments on each floor, were reached from the landscaped court. With yellow brick and contrasting white-glazed terra-cotta trim and ornament, the facades were similar but each differed in appearance. The commercial street facade, with its upper masonry walls "undercut" by wide expanses of glass storefronts, was treated as an envelope. Exterior upper walls became vertical "screens," which were laced by terra-cotta trim and punctuated by decorative accents. For the residential side-street facades, traditional bearing-wall construction was utilized and appropriately expressed. Terra-cotta use was mostly restricted to focal pieces at the

parapet to strengthen the identification of entry locations. However, terra-cotta ornamental work encasing entry doorways was often historically derived, usually from the Georgian style.

Why this introduction of conflicting and inappropriate stylistic elements? Most likely it was Bein's concession to a client's desire to have a building of historical style. With a concentration of stylistic elements, recognizable in closeup but appearing scaled-down from a distance, the impression of traditionalism could be achieved but the modernity of Sullivanesque could dominate. Despite the continuity provided by the white-glazed terra cotta, however, the competing ornamental motifs diminished the success of Bein's designs.

The last of Bein's known designs, one in which the Sullivanesque overwhelmingly dominated, was an automobile sales and service building (1926) at 5539–45 North Clark Street. The design of the street facade was novel although not entirely successful. A grand archway was centered on the yellow brick facade and this two-story arch defined the vehicular entrance. However, the entrance was subsequently abandoned and infill now contradicts the importance of the archway. The superimposed arch engaged the brick walls at the second story but its piers were articulated at the ground floor by glass storefronts and the (original) entrance. Repeated arched window openings on the second floor formed a horizontal element that echoed the horizontality of the ground-floor glazing. Terra-cotta decorative elements, a large eagle set within the major archway and flanking medallions at the roof parapet, added ornamentation to the facade. Although portions of the facade are delightful, the overall impression is of a disjointed and awkwardly proportioned building.[51]

Mandel H. Hymowitz graduated in architecture (1915) from the University of Illinois and upon return to Chicago changed his last name to Harris.[52] He lived in his old neighborhood near Maxwell Street and its open market; but he moved westward in a series of changes of residence. Around 1922, Harris started his own architectural firm and designed a number of Sullivanesque structures.[53] In a year-and-a-half span, from April 1922 to October 1923, he had six commissions that utilized terra cotta; five are confirmed to have been Sullivanesque (the sixth has been demolished, and records are inadequate to determine its appearance). In 1928, he used terra cotta for two more structures; however, these designs were eclectic, with adaptations of classical motifs.[54]

The five Sullivanesque designs appeared similar at first glance. Each was a small, one-story store and/or garage structure that fronted directly on a street and shared party walls with adjoining buildings. Each used stock terra cotta, with a variation of Midland's standard medallion featured on each. Four of the five buildings had a parapet profile that was stepped and/or "notched." This manipulation of the parapet tended to dilute the Sullivanesque intent and confuse it with other styles, such as the collegiate Gothic. However, terra-cotta ornament and trim were usually well composed in the buildings. In addition, the ornament had an intrinsic beauty, and this, combined with the overall

Opposite: I. S. Robins Building (1924), W. Lawrence at Monticello, Chicago; Maurice L. Bein, Architect. A mixed-use building with shopfronts facing the neighborhood commercial street, Lawrence Avenue. Photo: 1990.

composition and proportions, created a satisfying design, especially considering the budget and program limitations of Harris's commissions.

Mention the name Jens Jensen and anyone familiar with Chicago architecture and planning immediately thinks of the noted Danish-born landscape architect who designed Humboldt, Garfield, and Columbus parks for Chicago's West Park District.[55] Some historians who run across the name Jens J. Jensen as the architect for neighborhood buildings in Chicago assume that the landscape architect practiced architecture as well.[56] However, the landscape architect and the architect were two different people. Although obscure, Jens J. Jensen designed some Sullivanesque buildings, and some ornamental fragments from his buildings and a collection of his drawings are in the depositories of the Chicago Historical Society.[57]

Jens J. Jensen's first Sullivanesque designs were done in 1922, about a year after he opened his practice. The first was a three-story mixed-use building, with shops fronting on North Robey (now Damen) and apartments above. This building for Jacob Miller extended along Argyle Street and wrapped around a narrow courtyard open to the street. Conventional exterior construction of yellow brick was relieved by terra-cotta bandings and accents from the Midland company. Two 1922 store buildings by Jensen, one at 4956–58 Milwaukee Avenue and the other in suburban Oak Park, resemble each other. Red brick walls are enlivened by terra-cotta bandings; second-floor window openings are encased by terra-cotta trim; and the front facade has a centered entrance for second-floor access with a focal piece of terra cotta centered above it at the parapet. A Midland medallion with T-shaped arms was used, but it deviated from catalog examples by the addition of terra-cotta "trailers" that dropped from the end of each arm, stalactite fashion, across the red brick. Both buildings still are attractive but the one on Milwaukee Avenue has been compromised by the installation of many oversized signs.

Although Jensen seemed to prefer the Sullivanesque style, he also indulged in eclecticism. Designs based on historic precedent appeared more frequently in his work after 1923. Most of these eclectic designs were for larger or more important projects, and terra-cotta ornament for these commissions was mostly supplied by the American Terra Cotta and Ceramic Company.[58] However, he periodically returned to the Sullivanesque for small, simple buildings. These were characterized by wide glass storefronts, intricate brickwork, and terra-cotta trim and ornamentation. Midland's stock 4508 medallion was usually prominently featured. On small buildings, this was centered on the facade at the parapet; on longer facades, multiple medallions appeared. Terra-cotta trim framed rectangular panels on the brick walls. Within this framework, various brick patterns, such as herringbone or paver bond, were used and expressed the nonstructural properties of the wall. Jensen usually used red brick or tapestry brick with a full range of red hues and tones. One of the larger examples of this basic facade composition was a commercial building (1925) for Charles Andrews, on the northwest corner of North Cicero Avenue and Cornelia Street. Similar solutions for small building facades can be found at 2239–41 North Cicero Avenue, 5326–28 North Kedzie, and 3750 West Sixty-

Shop drawing prepared by the Midland Terra Cotta Company for store building (order no. 22165), Oak Park, Illinois; Jens J. Jensen, Architect. Detail drawing of terra-cotta ornament above the ground-floor entrance to the second floor. Courtesy of Northwest Architectural Archives (NWAA), University of Minnesota.

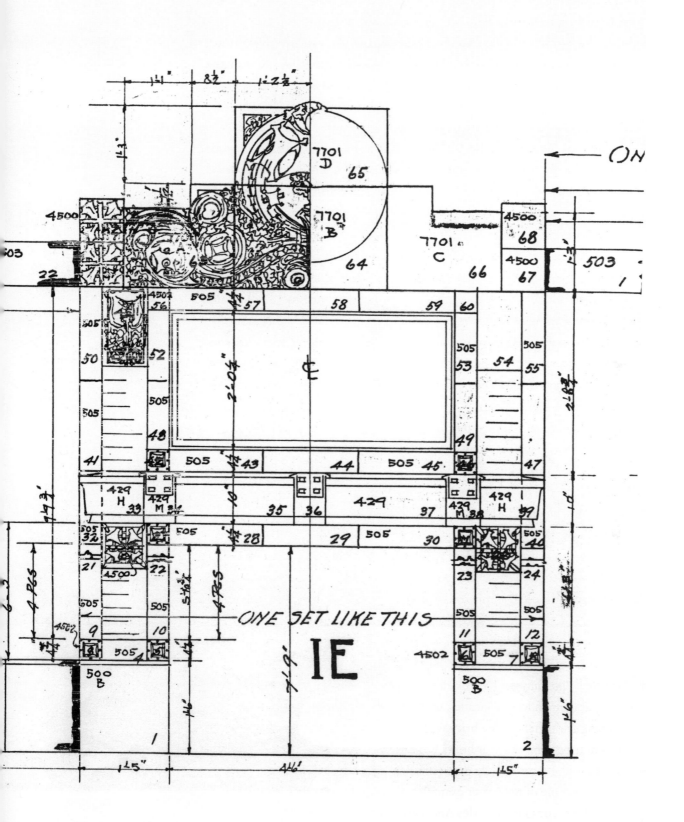

ONE SET LIKE THIS

IE

third Street. Of these, the Cicero building, for B. P. Silverman, was built in 1925 while the stores on Kedzie and Sixty-third Streets were constructed in 1927.[59]

Carl Osker Kuehne (1874–1950) was born in Germany but came to this country with his family while still a young boy. After public high school in Chicago, Kuehne studied architecture at the University of Illinois and graduated in 1897. Kuehne started his own office around 1911 and practiced architecture until 1924, when he became a businessman.[60] It appears that he didn't have many commissions during his years of architectural practice.[61] However, he did have five Sullivanesque designs constructed during a two-year span (1922–24).[62] The most successful was a one-story commercial building that was triangular in plan because the plot of land on which it stood was shaped as North Clark Street intersected on the diagonal with the gridded streets of Sheffield and Roscoe. The building's exterior has yellow brick piers and walls relieved by carefully positioned decorative terra cotta. Its parapet is predominantly horizontal, but short segments step above the parapet line and form a background for elaborate Sullivanesque terra-cotta ornament. Smaller terra cotta elements include ornamental pier caps and minor accents. The stepping of the parapet wall for short distances in order to receive and emphasize terra-cotta ornament was repeated on other Kuehne designs. However, for the small one-story commercial building (1923) at 4724–28 Lincoln Avenue, three stepped parapet segments were independent of the terra-cotta ornament positioned on

Charles Andrews Store Building (1925), Chicago; Jens J. Jensen, Architect. Detail of terra-cotta ornamentation and decorative brickwork. Photo: 1992.

the parapet wall, and these elements conflicted. The stock terra cotta was undersized for the facade, which resulted in problems of proportion and scale. A two-story store and office building, the North American Business Exchange (1922; demolished), stood at the northwest corner of North Avenue and North Halsted Street and had a different kind of facade composition. Kuehne used narrow borders and bandings of terra-cotta trim that orthogonally gridded the brick-faced building elevations. A projecting terra-cotta cornice, located at the roof line and below the brick parapet wall, provided a strong horizontal terminus for the composition.[63]

A partnership of two other University of Illinois graduates was responsible for a number of Sullivanesque designs, especially in the first two years of their association. Alexander Levy and William Klein are noted in American architectural history as the designers of some flashy 1920s movie theaters in the rococo revival style.[64] However, for neighborhood building commissions, which constituted most of their practice in their early years, Levy and Klein usually responded with a Sullivanesque design. Alexander Louis Levy (1872–1965) was an 1893 graduate in architecture of the state university and, after teaching in Chicago high schools for eight years, he started his architectural practice in 1904. William Julius Klein (1889–1971) graduated from the same university in 1911 and in 1918 became chief draftsman (replacing M. O. Nathan) for the Alexander L. Levy firm. In 1920, Klein became a partner and the firm's name was changed to Levy and Klein, Architects.[65]

Several buildings on Roosevelt Road were early Sullivanesque designs by Levy. At 707–9, a three-story building (1916–17; demolished) he designed had a wide expanse of window glass at the ground-floor storefront while the upper two stories had fenestration collected into a single large assembly. The parapet was horizontal except for a shaped segment that centered on the facade, and there were subtle protrusions of ornament. Sullivanesque motifs highlighted the ornamental terra cotta used for the storefront trim and pier capitals. However, ornament positioned higher on the upper story was based on the Gothic, with shields and coats-of-arms.[66]

Why this flaw in mixing ornamental motifs? Since Levy learned about historical styles as part of his university education, he obviously was aware that this would produce a conflict. Perhaps it was a way to appease a client who wanted an eclectic design, and the architect believed that the introduction of a few easily recognizable historical symbols would "mask" the predominately Sullivanesque motifs. Most likely, it was a practical and economical solution. It is possible that proper sizes of consistently styled terra cotta were not available or could not be obtained without delaying the project. In order to save time and money on a low-budget job, perhaps Levy used what was readily at hand and thought the mix would work. The scale and degree of relief of the terracotta surfaces would be similar and the viewing distances would be great, making stylistic differences less obtrusive. Levy was more concerned with the overall impact of the facade as a whole, rather than consistently using "correct" details. Levy, first working alone and then with Klein, adhered to Sullivanesque principles of composition for

building facades; however, overall ornamental effect was more important than unity and purity of detail. This inconsistent use of stylistic ornament was a flaw that sometimes recurred in the firm's other building designs.

After Klein became a partner, the renamed firm of Levy and Klein increased its output of Sullivanesque designs.[67] A large three-story mixed-used building (1921) for A. J. Levinson provided store and office frontage on the neighborhood commercial street (Lawrence) and apartment frontage on the intersecting residential street (Spaulding). The red brick facades were enlivened with ornamental treatments. The two upper stories had paired brick "pilasters" that were defined by vertical terra-cotta trimmings and terminated by decorative terra-cotta panels. A major feature, Midland's disc number 4508, adapted and modified, capped the building's clipped corner at the street intersection. This chamfered corner was reminiscent of the turreted corner in older Chicago neighborhoods.

A Levy and Klein building of similar size and use, for J. Blumenthal on Cermak Road in Cicero, an adjoining western suburb, had some of the same decorative features but these were composed with different and perhaps more successful results. Narrow terra-cotta trim was used extensively, mostly as vertical relief and to emulate paired pilasters. Third-floor spandrel panels were framed by terra-cotta trim and had centered ornament. Two major bandings of terra cotta circumscribed the facades: one established a base, with its ground-floor storefronts, while the other, which aligned with the third-floor window head, defined a terminating cap. Between these two broad bandings, the wall "disappeared" in a quilt-like pattern. Segments of the parapet profile were curved for relief and related to Midland stock discs, which were positioned near the ends of each parapet wall and also centered on the longer facade.

A three-story building (1921) the firm designed for Louis Cracko at 2017 West Lawrence in Chicago resembled Midland catalog plate 36, design number 1. A cluster of ornamental terra cotta on the upper wall dominates the narrow facade. In addition, upper-story windows are visually tied together by terra-cotta trim. A one-story store building (1922) at the northwest corner of Lincoln Avenue and Byron Street is another Levy and Klein design influenced by Midland precedent. Terra-cotta medallions and vertical supplemental ornament segment the lengthy brick wall while additional terra cotta is used as accents and parapet coping. Upper-wall brickwork is decorative, with string courses of rowlock and soldier brick as well as brick coursing laid in patterned Flemish bond. Additional Sullivanesque designs in 1922 by Levy and Klein include buildings at 7642 Sheridan Road (now demolished), 5347 North Clark Street, and 4651 Washington, the latter now altered for a storefront church. The ornamentation for all these buildings was white-glazed stock supplied by the Midland Terra Cotta Company, although Levy and Klein were adept at creating facades using stock components from other manufacturers as well.[68]

For at least three confirmed designs and probably others, Levy and Klein adapted stock terra cotta from the Northwestern Terra Cotta Company. The confirmed exam-

Opposite: One of the ornamental assemblies on the Clark Street facade of a store building (1924), Chicago; C. O. Kuehne, Architect. Photo: 1991.

ples are similar commercial buildings of two-story height built in 1922. All three were built for M. Astrahan and resemble each other with only minor variations. The terracotta work is generally understated, with smaller pieces integrated within the predominant wall of face brick. The facade compositions were achieved not by relying on sheer size and importance of ornamental terra cotta, but by creating an interplay of smaller pieces in studied positions within the wall plane, which results in a tension of the negative spacing between these points.[69]

The last known Sullivanesque buildings by Levy and Klein were designed in 1924. These were three mixed-use buildings with stores and apartments: at 6642–52 North Clark Street; on the southeast corner of East Seventy-ninth Street and South Vernon; and on East Seventy-ninth Street, at the northwest corner at Burnham.[70] Terra-cotta accents were composed on the facades and terra cotta trim was woven as bandings with the brick. Additional ornate terra cotta was positioned on the upper wall at the parapet; however, some of the ornamental motifs were based on baroque or rococo styles.

J. Blumenthal Building (1921), Cicero; Levy and Klein, Architects. Photo: 1992.

Louis Cracko Building (1921), Chicago; Levy and Klein, Architects. Detail of terra-cotta ornamental assemblies at parapet. Photo: 1990.

Sullivanesque principles did provide a basis for the facade compositions; however, these principles became lost in the frothy ornament and eclectic design in Levy and Klein's later projects.

When Casriel Halperin and Isadore H. Braun initially formed their partnership, they designed in the Sullivanesque style but they soon embraced eclectic design. The two architects had been classmates at the Chicago School of Architecture and had been employed by the architectural firm of Berlin, Swern, and Randall prior to their partnership.[71] *The Year Book for 1914–15*, published by the Chicago School of Architecture, listed Louis H. Sullivan as one of the school's critics in architectural design and included illustrations of student projects. Three projects of C. Halperin were depicted and they demonstrated that he was a strong student. One of his designs won a competition for a traveling scholarship. This was a large library that had both Gothic and Sullivanesque facade elements, but they seemed well integrated. Halperin's design for "A Pavilion of Music—in Colored Terra Cotta or Faience" was predominately in the Renaissance revival style, with some Sullivanesque overtones.[72] When Halperin and Braun opened their own architectural office (c. 1922), their first design was Sullivanesque.[73]

Midland's stock terra cotta was integrated with the brick surfaces of a seventy-five-foot-long wall located above glass storefronts for a commercial building developed by J. F. Dooley at 214–18 South Loomis Street and designed by Halperin and Braun. Terra-cotta fabrication began on October 29, 1921, and included trim (no. 505) to frame rectangular panels of brick; copings for the gently stepped parapet; 4", 8", and 12" square decorative accents for the piers and parapet; and a focal piece (no. 4508) 2' 6" in diameter that was centered on the parapet wall. Since the building has been demolished, only shop drawings give an indication of the building's appearance. Additional Sullivanesque designs by Halperin and Braun followed.[74] A one-story store building (1922) for Goldberg, Fried, and Cantor, located at the southeast corner of Devon and Magnolia, made a simple statement. Small-scale pieces for "panelization" of the brick and decorative insets comprised the ornamental terra-cotta work. A twenty-two-foot-wide one-story store (1922; demolished) for Leo Behrstock at 1250 South Kedzie used brick rowlock coursing and terra-cotta squares for panelization of the brick wall above storefront windows while Midland's number 4500 ornament provided both base and cap for two brick piers aligned with the party walls. A major terra-cotta assembly, featuring Midland's 4508 medallion, was centered on the upper wall surface and bisected it through the addition of rectangular supplemental pieces.[75]

By 1925, Halperin and Braun had turned to eclectic design although a 1926 remodeling, with a new storefront, provided an opportunity to rekindle the Sullivanesque. The small storefront at 4830 South Ashland demonstrated Halperin and Braun's use of stock terra cotta for original Sullivanesque facades.

M. O. Nathan (1891–1971) was a native of Iowa and graduated in architecture (1912) from the University of Illinois. Nathan worked in Des Moines, Iowa, before moving to Chicago, where he became Alexander L. Levy's chief draftsman and was introduced to the Sullivanesque in that office. After military service in World War I, Nathan worked in Detroit before returning to Chicago to open his own office (1921).[76] Among Nathan's Sullivanesque designs in Chicago were a store building (1922; demolished) for Isaac Frank at 5345 West Madison Street; Manor Garage and Auto Sales (1922 and 1923; demolished 1997) at 2901–15 Lawrence Avenue; a one-story store (1922) at the southeast corner of North Avenue and Tripp; and an automobile service building (1927) at 3727–29 Broadway. In 1947 he remodeled an existing Sullivanesque building (1923; Henry Newhouse, Architect) at 321–27 Pershing Road (Thirty-ninth Street) but respectfully retained the principal Sullivanesque features.[77] The store building at North Avenue and Tripp closely resembled designs recommended by the Midland Terra Cotta Company. Now demolished, the two-story automobile facility (1922) and addition (1923) on Lawrence featured horizontal lines and decorative terra cotta for bandings, supplemental ornamental accents, and window casings. The auto sales and garage structure on Broadway has a two-story facade of white-glazed brick and ornamental terra cotta. This late (1927) Sullivanesque design stressed the gently shaped profile of the parapet and the tactile play of gleaming white surfaces. It survives relatively intact with only some ground-floor alterations.

Another less well known Chicago architect, Erich J. Patelski, was responsible for a number of Midland-based Sullivanesque designs over a period of time. Patelski's use of stock Sullivanesque terra cotta could be seen on buildings such as the Michael Telechanski Building (1922), at the northeast corner of Twenty-sixth Street and Kedvale, and a three-story apartment building with shops for M. Margolis (1923) at North Damen Street and Leland.[78] Another apartment building, which overlooked Garfield Park, has been demolished but several Sullivanesque terra-cotta pieces from it are in the collection of the Commission on Chicago Historical and Architectural Landmarks.[79]

This review shows that Chicago had a number of Sullivanesque architects in addition to the well-known stars of the profession. Each produced an inventory of Sullivanesque designs over several years, although this was only a brief period for most. Almost all of these architects utilized stock terra-cotta ornament, and many of their designs were inspired by design plates from the Midland Terra Cotta Company. Most of these designs were for commercial uses; auto-related facilities, such as sales garages; and mixed-use buildings for the "streetcar" commercial strips of the city's neighborhoods. Walk-up apartment buildings and an occasional industrial structure completed the typical inventory. Perhaps the Sullivanesque designs by William G. Carnegie were the most successful in the use of stock ornament while the most prolific architect was A. L. Himelblau, followed by Levy and Klein.

CHAPTER 8

CHICAGO STREETS

A Sullivanesque Vernacular

IN ITS LAST YEARS, the Sullivanesque movement became almost exclusively a local style centered in Chicago. Sullivanesque designs that achieved various levels of success and used stock terra cotta were numerous in Chicago's neighborhoods, especially in areas developed between 1911 and 1930. Commercial streets that served as neighborhood convenience strips often boasted several such buildings.

The major leaders of the Sullivanesque, such as Sullivan himself and Elmslie, were no longer in leadership roles in the 1920s. Yet, nonresidential buildings of the Sullivanesque genre were still being built in Chicago. This could be attributed to the conservative nature of small-time developers and lenders who finally accepted the aesthetics and economical functionality of the Sullivanesque. They no longer found the style revolutionary or threatening for speculative investment. This acceptance of the Sullivanesque can be mostly attributed to the salesmanship and promotional efforts of several commercial interests. The two most important and influential of these were the Midland Terra Cotta Company and the Radford Architectural Company.[1]

The Radford Architectural Company was founded in Chicago in 1902 by six investors, four of whom were members of the Radford family. William A. Radford was president and treasurer of the company as well as the editor-in-chief of company publications. The secretary was Roland D. Radford, who was the other family member involved with the administration of the company. George W. Ashby was vice president and the only company investor who was a registered architect. Ashby was a principal in the architecture firm of Ashby, Ashby, and Schulze. In 1905 the Radford company started publishing a monthly journal called the *American Carpenter and Builder*; the name was shortened to *American Builder* in 1917.[2] Other Radford publications included books on construction and catalogs of building plans, from which drawings and specifications could be ordered. A 1909 *Portfolio of Plans* featured a number of Sullivanesque and Prairie School designs. All of these publications catered to a readership of marginal speculative developers, contractors, and architects. The monthly journal was especially concerned with economical construction of housing and new building types, such as auto sales and service garages, for commercial streets in city neighborhoods and central business districts of small towns. Although historically based eclectic designs appeared in these publications, the majority of projects were either utilitarian or simplified versions of the Sullivanesque for nonresidential buildings or Prairie School and bungalow designs for residential use.

Radford supported progressive design by publishing visual materials rather than editorials or articles of advocacy. It stressed matter-of-fact construction descriptions and methods. The pragmatic designs of commercial facades published in *American Carpenter and Builder* usually had simplified geometrical ornamental pieces incorporated, and a number of design plates had Sullivanesque characteristics. One of the more original designs, a three-story mixed-use building, appeared in April 1916 (p. 57) and seems to have anticipated the gridded curtain wall. The designers of these proposals were never identified, although George Ashby may have had major responsibility.[3] Ralph W. Ermeling, a Chicago architect for several commercial buildings with Sullivanesque ornament, most likely was the designer for some facade proposals.

Only two buildings with terra-cotta ornament are known to have been constructed as Sullivanesque designs by Ermeling. However, he influenced the Sullivanesque in other ways. Ermeling gained registration in 1915 and opened his own architectural office soon after.[4] His first Sullivanesque design, a small store with second-floor flat, for J. Kutten, was constructed in 1915–16. The street facade closely resembled plate 36, design number 1, in a Midland Terra Cotta Company catalog; Midland used this design plate in an advertisement promoting Sullivanesque stock terra cotta that ran in the February and March 1915 issues of the *American Carpenter and Builder* magazine. The terra-cotta order (no. 5345) for Ermeling's building was placed on December 11, 1915.[5] It appears that Ermeling simply adopted this basic design. His next Sullivanesque design was more original, although he again used Midland stock pieces.[6] For the two-story Crawford Building, at 1526–34 North Crawford (now Pulaski), the front facade was divided into five wide structural bays clad with brick and had terra-cotta trim, bandings, accents, and focal pieces. The parapet was horizontal for the three central bays but had a shaped profile at opposing end bays; second-floor windows were grouped as a horizontal banding for the width of each bay.

Ermeling's architectural practice was short lived.[7] He then worked for the *Ameri-*

can Carpenter and Builder. Ermeling's name began appearing on various articles and drawings in the journal as early as October 1915. Since that publication rarely identified the authors of articles or the delineators of drawings and only reluctantly identified some architects for buildings in published photographs, the editors must have thought Ermeling something special. His interior design ideas were featured under the title "Work of Ralph W. Ermeling, Architect" and included various design studies, mostly for interiors "in the Modern Straight Line Style."[8] The January 1917 issue had "A Fireplace Alcove," although by that date Ermeling's name was played down and relegated to fine

Store and flat for J. Kutten (1915), Chicago; Ralph W. Ermeling, Architect. Photo: 1992.

print.[9] This was an exceptional study and drew inspiration from the arts and crafts movement as well as from the work of Wright and Sullivan. The arched fireplace opening was surrounded by tile, and two ornamental accents of terra cotta were composed in this field. Two octagonal plaster-encased columns were decorated with a stencil pattern inspired by Sullivan but simplified in its geometry.

Ermeling wrote articles on construction practices published in the renamed journal, the *American Builder*, in January and April 1918. After that, his name doesn't appear there. However, a number of designs for hypothetical projects, without identification of the designer, were subsequently published. These must have been by Ermeling as the drawing techniques were the same and the lettering style matched that of his identified drawings. Furthermore, these designs had touches similar to those of Ermeling's two constructed Sullivanesque buildings. For example, the "Modern Store Building" appeared in the August 1915 issue of the *American Carpenter and Builder* (pages 42–45) and this design showed a three-story building, with store and apartments, suitable for many Chicago neighborhoods and for small cities. The partial elevation drawing showed Sullivanesque terra-cotta ornament and assembly patterns in detail.

Other Sullivanesque but simple designs that were published in the journal and appear to be from Ermeling's hand included: "Block of Store Buildings" (January 1916); "A Modern Daylight Factory" (March 1916); "Modern Business Block," "Three 2-Story Store Buildings," and "Five 1-Story Stores" (April 1916). The designs for speculative stores were rudimentary Sullivanesque works with some use of terra-cotta bandings and insets. The factory design was utilitarian, with some ornamental brickwork and terra-cotta accents to enliven the facade. The "Modern Business Block" was the most innovative as vertical terra-cotta trim was repeated to form mullions and was also laid over smaller-scale horizontal terra-cotta trim for the building facades. The design became an exercise in the play of rectangular grids in shallow relief. The vertical lines dominated and were terminated at the parapet by terra-cotta ornament. The facade treatment in the design proposal resembled that of Ermeling's Crawford Building but was more complex. Structure and other traditional building elements "disappeared" in the dominating grid patterns. The proposed design was still Sullivanesque but was an innovative stylization. It was not entirely successful, however, as a deceptive scale was introduced. In many ways, this 1916 proposal anticipated the latter-day Miesian curtain wall with vertical mullions and an emphasis on an abstracted, gridded surface. The caption accompanying the illustration matter-of-factly stated: "Suggestion for Modern Business Block Suitable for Any Growing City or Suburb. The Strong Vertical Elements of the Design Exaggerate the Height of the Building, Making It Seem Larger and Taller than it Really is."[10] Some of the designs by Sullivanesque architects, such as William G. Carnegie in Chicago and John Hanifen in La Salle, Illinois, with their use of vertical bandings of terra cotta and variations of gridded facades, must have been influenced by this proposal.

Ralph W. Ermeling was a talented architectural designer. However, information on him is scant, leaving much to conjecture. His association with the *American Carpenter and Builder* approximately coincided with the appearance of articles about terra cotta and Midland's advertisements in that journal. The examples of Sullivanesque designs by Ermeling (most published anonymously) undoubtedly influenced speculative developers and architects. Competent if not inspiring, these original but conservative designs for inexpensive buildings were examples meant to be imitated. However, a theoretical or philosophical statement or treatise never accompanied these published designs. The visuals stood alone, leaving the reader—the would-be developer or "small-time" architect—without guidance about how to respond to the images. Text, if any, concentrated only on the construction and functional aspects of the proposed design. Still, through the published designs in the *American Carpenter and Builder*, the obscure Ermeling was an important advocate of the Sullivanesque and his designs became patterns for a commercial vernacular.

In early 1914, the *American Carpenter and Builder* formed an alliance with the Midland Terra Cotta Company of Chicago. As noted earlier, the journal ran articles about Midland terra cotta while Midland had major advertisements in the journal. The advertisements featured designs that utilized Midland's stock terra cotta, many of them based on Sullivanesque ornamental themes.[11] Of course, since Midland was trying to sell its terra cotta, its designs were profusely ornamented. In contrast, plates prepared for the journal by Ermeling, Ashby, and staff members were more spartan and restrained in facade treatments and were generally simplified designs based on Sullivanesque and Wrightian geometrical themes. Together, Midland and the Radford Architectural Company, primarily through the *American Carpenter and Builder*, offered a range of Sullivanesque examples for speculative builders and architects to copy. With design plates from

Design for a "Modern Business Block Suitable for Any Growing City or Suburb," attributed to Ralph Ermeling, Architect. *American Carpenter and Builder* (Apr. 1916): 37.

the two companies and the availability of stock terra cotta, the journeyman architect had the direction and means to design attractive Sullivanesque facades for party-wall buildings. Many did so, and the result was a kind of commercial vernacular that at times verged on high art.

Among the early and successful Sullivanesque building designs based on Midland stock terra cotta and constructed in Chicago neighborhoods were two by Swen Linderoth (1860–1920). Linderoth came to Chicago in 1884 from Sweden and practiced architecture.[12] Usually, his commissions were small utilitarian buildings in South Side neighborhoods. It appears that only nine buildings were of sufficient budget and importance to be embellished with architectural terra cotta. Of this number, four are known to have been Sullivanesque, two were of other styles, and three have been demolished without leaving a visual record that would permit determination of appearance or style.[13]

Two of Linderoth's known Sullivanesque designs have been demolished; however, these were simple statements with minor terra-cotta accents and trim, much like design examples in the *American Carpenter and Builder*.[14] Two other known Sullivanesque designs by Linderoth—or rather, one building and a remnant of another—still exist. Both surviving examples were designed at approximately the same time (1915). One was modest, a small store with flat above, while the other was larger and an important design.

The smaller building was designed for Edward Bunde and was based on a Midland design promoting the use of stock terra cotta as advertised in the *American Carpenter and Builder* (February and March 1915).[15] Featured was a Sullivanesque ornamental assembly that formed an elongated rectangle with a horizontal axis; ornamental plaques anchored each end of this rectangular shape. A major focal piece, with vertical emphasis and intricate foliate, bisected the horizontal rectangular panel.

This same assembly was repeated six times and integrated with horizontal decorative terra-cotta bandings along the street facades for the larger building, constructed on the South Side for G. E. Anderson. The multiple horizontal bandings of white-glazed terra cotta anticipated later use of horizontal stripes or bandings for some modern architecture in Europe as well as for Frank Lloyd Wright designs in California, such as the Charles Ennis House (1923). Linderoth's handsome design was even more remarkable given the common materials employed (stock terra cotta, tapestry brick, and Chicago windows), but these elements were composed in an imaginative way. A photograph of the two-story building appeared in a Midland company advertisement published in the May 1916 issue of the *American Carpenter and Builder*; however, the architect was not cited. This building was almost square in plan and a bearing wall bisected it. There were shops on the ground level and a lodge hall above.[16] Unfortunately, the northern half of the building has been demolished; moreover, the surviving southern half has been badly altered and is in poor condition. The second-story Chicago windows have been removed and the openings filled in with concrete block. Located in a deteriorating, high-crime area, the building has been converted to a SRO (single room occupancy) hotel.

Still, if we keep in mind the 1916 published photograph and visualize the building without the desecrating changes, we can recognize that the exterior had merit. It must have been viewed as a progressive design when it was completed.

Linderoth founded the Linderoth Ceramic Company, which made porcelain mantels (large stoves based on historic Swedish models called Kackelofen), glazed bricks, tiles, vases, and other wares.[17] The company name changed to the Alhambra Ceramic Works with the introduction of a line of art pottery around 1906.[18] Linderoth was a supporter of the arts and crafts movement and used tiles and colorful glazed bricks on the interiors of his buildings. However, it wasn't until 1910 that he used terra cotta (a product his company didn't make); and in the Anderson Building he made good use of it.[19]

The English-born William G. Barfield had an active practice in Chicago for many years and at least two of his designs were Sullivanesque.[20] Of these two, the Roser Store and Apartment Building (1915) in the Ravenswood neighborhood had the larger and more elaborate facade. Terra-cotta plaques and accents were richly foliated in swirling patterns and glazed in "Teco green." The ornate pieces were supplied by the American Terra Cotta and Ceramic Company (order no. 2575) and appear to have been stock. Similarly, American supplied the ornamental terra cotta (order no. 2588) for Barfield's 1915 theater design in the western suburb of Downers Grove.[21] The small theater for E. A. Baxter had a simple but handsome facade of warm brick with carefully positioned Sullivanesque terra cotta and it greatly enhanced the south side of tree-lined Curtiss

Street.[22] Unfortunately, the theater closed and was converted to shops. The conversion included "modernized" claddings that covered the facade, and only a close inspection today reveals a few visible accents of terra cotta. The Roser Building survives relatively intact with only a bad tuck-pointing job marring its appearance.

Louis C. Bouchard, who had his architectural office in Adler and Sullivan's Schiller Building, designed many apartment buildings, and at least one was inspired by Sullivan. A four-story building was built in 1914 for William E. Nesbit at 1134 Farwell Avenue. Its utilitarian brick facade was punctuated by an elaborate entryway of green-glazed Sullivanesque terra cotta.[23] This building was published in the November 1915 issue of the *Western Architect.* Terra cotta was supplied by the Midland company; the entrance motifs were similar to plate 51, entrance number 2, from Midland catalog designs.

One of the rare, entirely terra-cotta facades for a commercial strip building in the Sullivanesque style stands in a suburban town just south of Chicago. This is a 1915 design

Roser Store and Apartment Building (1915), Chicago; William G. Barfield, Architect. Detail of apartment entrance. Photo: 1992.

William E. Nesbit Apartment
Building (1914), Chicago;
Louis C. Bouchard, Architect.
Detail of entrance. Photo: 1992.

by Albert S. Hecht for a Woolworth's Five and Ten Store in Blue Island.[24] It was immediately recognized as a successful design and a photo of the two-story building appeared often in promotional materials for terra cotta. Since stock terra cotta was featured (order no. 5185), Midland used a photograph of the building in its advertisements and the National Terra Cotta Society published a photo of it, although miscaptioned, in its promotional book, *The Store*.[25] Hecht's Blue Island building still has a vibrant richness on the upper facade although the ground-floor storefront has been insensitively modernized.

Anders G. Lund, one of the most prolific architects in Chicago, was responsible for hundreds of neighborhood buildings, including houses, residential flats, apartment buildings, and commercial structures.[26] Most of these were utilitarian and responsive to tight budgets and the conservative nature of neighborhood clients. However, these buildings were generally pleasing and appeared substantial due to their well-proportioned massings and the use of red face-brick for major facades. Occasionally, small terra-cotta accents, almost always flat-faced and without ornament, for economic reasons, were positioned to enhance the composition of the principal facade(s).

For his "prestigious" commissions, Lund employed Sullivanesque terra-cotta reliefs as ornamentation. These included a one-story building for two shops (1917) at 6508–10 South Halsted Street; a two-story building (1924) on West Forty-seventh Street near Union Street; a three-story apartment building (1922) at 7018 South Clyde; and stores with second-floor flats at 1503 West Fifty-first Street (1917) and 6326 South

Woolworth's Five and Ten Store (1915), Blue Island, Illinois; Albert S. Hecht, Architect. Although the storefront has been altered, the superstructure displays white-glazed terra-cotta facings and ornament. Photo: 1991.

Woolworth's Five and Ten Store (1915), Blue Island; Albert S. Hecht, Architect. Detail of terra-cotta facings and ornament. Photo: 1991.

Cottage Grove (1924). Now demolished, small buildings in Lund's Sullivanesque style were located on West Sixty-third Street (1923), near Kedzie, and at 438 West Seventy-ninth Street (1923).[27]

Pre–World War I Sullivanesque designs include several by Mead Walter (Illinois registration A 291).[28] One of these was part of a three-building complex (1905–6) for Lord's Department Store in the Chicago suburb of Evanston, at the corner of Davis Street and Orrington Avenue.[29] Walter's design for the McKee Building (1910) at 1134–38 Wilson Avenue exhibited design eccentricities, such as exaggerated proportions and rhythmic openings, that characterized his work.

The Henderson Building (1915) is a handsome Walter-designed building featuring

Three-story apartment building (1922), 7018 South Clyde, Chicago; A. G. Lund, Architect. This building is representative of Lund's neighborhood commissions. Lund used stock terra cotta but mixed Sullivanesque patterns with historical reliefs. Photo: 1992.

Henderson Building (1915),
Chicago; Mead Walter, Architect.
Detail of ornament at corner entry.
Photo: 1991.

heavily textured brick with terra-cotta bandings and ornament.[30] The building site is trapezoidal in shape because of the relationship of the diagonal Clark Street to the orthogonal grid orientation of Newport Avenue. Therefore, the building design was adapted to the acute angle of the street intersection by the introduction of subtle "turrets" or "towers" at the corners of the building. A series of narrow vertical windows separated by brick piers stretched from tower to tower across the second-story of the two street facades and created a rhythmic horizontal banding. The parapets slope subtly to a high point midway between towers. This refinement of shape created a tautness across the lengthy (109 feet) Clark Street facade. Terra-cotta bandings and ornament enhanced the appearance and unified the elongated facade. Unfortunately, some of the terra-cotta ornament has been recently painted in incongruous colors.

A three-story apartment hotel developed by Dr. B. Hotchkin, designed by Mead Walter in 1916, and built by Anderson Contracting in 1917 is unusual as the brick building facade acted as a foil for the centrally positioned cantilevered concrete balconies and ground-level entry canopy.[31] This canopy, which has a curved roof, seems to be balanced on two large octagonal columns that have oversized stylized capitals of ornate Sullivan-esque foliated patterns.

All of the buildings described so far have housed commercial or retail space, mixed-use with retail and residential or office space, auto sales and/or service, or apartments and flats. However, warehouses and industrial buildings were also designed in the Sul-livanesque style. Many of these fronted on commercial streets and were adjacent to other buildings. Most were tight to the public sidewalk in the street right-of-way. Therefore, these structures helped define the street. Since the facades facing the street were the primary exposed portions of the building, the designers utilized Sullivanesque compo-sitional techniques and elements to create handsome facades that were responsive to the urban setting and created a positive image for both building and occupant.

Eclectic designs for warehouses were specialties of George S. Kingsley, who was born on October 18, 1869, in Cleveland, Ohio. Kingsley opened his own office in Chi-cago in 1894.[32] Although he designed other structures, he became noted for his ware-houses and gained a reputation of long standing as a specialist in that building type. One of his early warehouses was a handsome Sullivanesque design at Sheridan Road and Sheffield Avenue in Chicago. The E. M. Hebard Storage Warehouse was built in two stages. The first phase, with clock tower, is at the southeast corner of Sheri-dan and Sheffield and was built in 1911. Five stories high with basement, the build-ing is of fireproof construction and has overall dimensions in plan of 50 by 150 feet. The building structure is concrete with arched-tile spans, topped with concrete for a level finish floor, and brick exterior walls.[33] The facades are embellished with custom-made Sullivanesque terra cotta from the Midland company.[34] Two years later, in 1913, the building was doubled in size by construction of an addition to the east, without a tower. Kingsley employed the same Sullivanesque terra-cotta ornament and place-ments. Still in use, with only the removal of one of its monumental clocks to alter its original appearance, the building is a stately, unified constant in a neighborhood that is changing around it.

The success of the Hebard building design must have established Kingsley's repu-tation, for a succession of warehouse designs in Chicago followed. None seemed to repeat the Sullivanesque ornamentation although most were simple masses and well proportioned. For example, the four-story Wenter and Drechaler Storage Warehouse (1914) in Oak Park, Illinois, had a brick facade enlivened with terra-cotta ornament loosely derived from the Sullivanesque.[35] As time went by, Kingsley's approach became even more eclectic, with designs ranging in style from Gothic to classical revival. Kings-ley's most celebrated design was probably the W. C. Reebie and Brother Warehouse (1923) on North Clark Street in Chicago, a building encased in glazed terra cotta in a colorful Egyptian revival style.[36]

John Ahlschlager and Son designed many handsome warehouses and industrial

244

structures. The firm's most clearly Sullivanesque design was the Schulze Baking Company Building, which was published in the *Western Architect*.[37] This large five-story structure at the northwest corner of East Garfield Boulevard and South Wabash Avenue, Chicago, was constructed in 1914 and expanded in 1919. The custom-made terra cotta, in an ivory-colored glaze with blue-glazed accent pieces, was the product of the Midland Terra Cotta Company. Repairs to the terra cotta were undertaken in 1949, 1952, and 1958 with American company replacements, which may explain why some parts of the terra-cotta work appear inconsistent and more Gothic than the dominant Sullivanesque.[38]

The success of the Schulze Baking Company Building evidently made the Ahlschlager firm "experts" in this building type as Ahlschlager designed at least two additional bakeries.[39] One was a handsome Sullivanesque design of brick and terra cotta for the Wagner Baking Company (c. 1919) in Detroit, Michigan. This large four-story building followed the curvature of the intersecting streets' right-of-way. Photographs and an article about the project were published in the architectural journal *National Builder*.[40]

The architect Edward A. Hogenson designed some factories and at least two—both in Cicero, Illinois—had Sullivanesque facades. The one at Fifty-fourth Avenue and Fourteenth Street was built in 1923 and has been demolished. However, the Lusterlite Enamels factory (1926) at 1425 Fifty-fifth Court remains.[41] Its structure is expressed and its horizontality is emphasized by Midland's terra-cotta ornamental bandings, accent pieces, and column capitals. Several special panels, with colorful glazes, complete the composition and complement the dark brick and white-glazed stock terra cotta.

Another factory (1927) in Cicero, on South Fifty-fifth Avenue, has a handsome Sullivanesque cartouche positioned above the main street entrance in the one-story brick facade; but the architect is unknown. Jens J. Meldahl was the architect for a handsome industrial building (1917; demolished) for the American Tag Company, which stood at 6135–45 South State Street, Chicago. An appealing array of Sullivanesque terra cotta was composed in the yellow brick facade that fronted tight to the street.[42]

One of the larger industrial buildings in the Sullivanesque style was the Glass Novelty Company on Chicago's West Side. Glass Novelty was touted as the largest manufacturer of children's furniture in the world. Designed by Sidney Minchin and built in 1925, the three-story structure was clad with brick for piers and spandrels; fenestration included large expanses of steel factory-sash. The Sullivanesque facades had horizontal bands of terra cotta that tied a two-story wing to the main three-story mass. Elaborate focal pieces were aligned on the third-floor spandrel of the main building and the parapet of the two-story wing. Still standing, the building exhibits the utilitarianism of an industrial structure tempered by Sullivan-like ornament from Midland stock.[43]

Some Sullivanesque designs that may remain in Chicago and vicinity warrant recognition even if very little or nothing is known about their architectural designers. One

Opposite: E. M. Hebard Storage (1911 and 1913), 957 N. Sheridan Road at Sheffield and Byron, Chicago; George S. Kingsley, Architect. Photo: 1992.

Overleaf: Schulze Baking Company Building (1914; expanded 1919), Chicago; John Ahlschlager and Son, Architects. The building still houses bakery operations. Photo: 1987.

of the more successful of all designs using stock Sullivanesque ornament was the Quilici Store, a three-story mixed-use structure with two floors of apartments, built in 1923 with Robert P. Ninneman as architect. Unfortunately, the building, which stood at 709 Center Street in suburban Des Plaines, was demolished in 1986. It was notable for its relationship to an adjacent two-story Sullivanesque store and office (1921; demolished 1986) located at the corner of Center and Ellinwood Streets and designed by the Midland Terra Cotta Company.[44] Together, the intricate street facades, with brick, horizontal

Glass Novelty Company (1925), Chicago; Sidney Minchin, Architect. Photo: 1988.

bandings, and ornamental reliefs of terra cotta, created a unified and vital urban image made possible through application of the Sullivanesque.

The two-story building designed by Albert A. Schwartz (1923) for Dr. Thomas H. Kelly, on East Seventy-fifth Street on Chicago's South Side, was a relatively inexpensive neighborhood building. But the street facade is a sophisticated envelope or skin that achieved the dematerialization of the external wall sought in principle by adherents of the Chicago School, the Prairie School, and the Sullivanesque. Horizontality was emphasized and a "panelization" of the wall was achieved through a liberal use of glass and terra-cotta trim, bandings, and ornamental accents. By this treatment, the brick cladding becomes visually weightless and seems to hover above the void of storefront windows. The right touches of delicate ornament, exacting proportions, and a strong com-

Quilici Store and Apartments (1923; demolished 1986), Des Plaines, Illinois; Robert P. Ninneman, Architect. Ninneman related his design for the building (at the right) to an earlier store building, at left (1921; demolished 1986), by the Midland Terra Cotta Company. Photo: 1986.

position of components resulted in a design that was a handsome and creative interpretation of the Sullivanesque. Although the ground floor is marred by remodelings, the building retains its integrity and seems appropriate for the New Sanctuary Church now occupying the storefront structure.[45]

It seems that two successful Sullivanesque buildings by Robert P. Ninneman and Albert A. Schwartz, respectively, may be aberrations. The demolished building in Des Plaines, by Ninneman, and the South Side Chicago building, by Schwartz, are two of the three known designs by these architects. The designers demonstrated talent but, as so often is the case in the architecture profession, the architects may have lacked connections or the ability to secure additional commissions to further their independent practices. Other Chicago architects such as Albert E. Colcord, Jacques J. Kocher, and Edward G. McClellan were also responsible for some Sullivanesque designs, but again, little is known about these men.

Sullivanesque designs by Albert E. Colcord included two on Cottage Grove Avenue: a two-story building for T. J. Sekema (1922) and a store building for L. G. Wagner (1922; demolished). Confirmed Sullivanesque designs by Jacques J. Kocher included

Building for Dr. Thomas H. Kelly (1923), East Seventy-fifth Street, Chicago; Albert A. Schwartz, Architect. The handsome facade was composed with stock terra cotta. Photo: 1991.

a building for R. H. Holmes (1921; demolished) at 6449–55 South Halsted Street and a service garage for M. Pearlman (1921) at 6912–20 Stony Island. The one-story garage has been badly remodeled but the upper wall surface retains the original exuberance of alternating horizontal bandings of brick and terra cotta capped by a decorative medallion.[46] Edward G. McClellan's known designs include several late examples on South Ashland Street. The buildings are similar but of uneven quality. In these examples, second- and third-floor apartment window openings were bordered by terra cotta and these, in turn, were grouped by an encompassing outline of terra cotta. A centrally positioned ornamental cluster, based on Midland's catalog plate 47, design number 1, capped each facade. The building for Elmer Olson at 8740–44 South Ashland was built in 1927 while the one at 8524–26 was built in 1928. A small one-story store for H. Jensen (1922) at 1534 East Seventy-fifth Street predated the South Ashland buildings. All three buildings have been marred by subsequent remodelings.[47]

Not unexpectedly, building construction in Chicago had slowed during World War I. After the war, however, construction accelerated. Hundreds of Sullivanesque buildings were being constructed in the city, although elsewhere Sullivanesque designs had become rare. As indicated previously, the number of Sullivanesque buildings peaked in 1922.[48] Building construction in Chicago was booming that year, and the promotion and advertising of the Sullivanesque by local terra-cotta companies and trade journals made an impact. Furthermore, in conjunction with the national convention of the American Institute of Architects held in June 1922 in Chicago, twelve studies by Louis Sullivan for his ornament were displayed at the Burnham Library of the Art Institute of Chicago. This was a preview of Sullivan's book *A System of Architectural Ornament: According with a Philosophy of Man's Powers*, first published in 1924 by the AIA.[49] The exhibition and accompanying publicity provided additional exposure to the Sullivanesque.

Many different architects designed one or more Sullivanesque buildings, especially in 1922. But most were eclectic designers who experimented with the Sullivanesque as they did with designs based on historical precedent, and they soon moved on to other styles. A number of these designers were minor architects with neighborhood clients and were susceptible to those clients' changing tastes and demands. Others were young architects and firms just starting practice after World War I. Most struggled, shifted directions, and/or relocated, but a few firms prospered and grew. Such was the case for Rissman and Hirschfield.

Maurice Barney Rissman (1893–1942) was born in New York City but was educated in Chicago.[50] Leo Saul Hirschfield was born on September 26, 1892, in Chicago.[51] Rissman and Hirschfield were classmates at the Armour Institute of Technology in Chicago and both graduated in 1915. Organized in 1919, the architectural firm of Rissman and Hirschfield had several handsome Sullivanesque designs among its early commissions. The firm's design of a store and office building (1922) for M. Shooman on North Milwaukee Avenue at Monticello remains a superb example. The Milwaukee

Avenue facade was clad entirely in white-glazed terra cotta while the Monticello side bore a contrasting but compatible combination of brick cladding and white-glazed terra-cotta ornamentation. The terra cotta was comprised of stock Sullivanesque reliefs supplied by the Northwestern Terra Cotta Company.[52] Two distinct decorative elements adorned the upper wall surfaces and alternated in a rhythmic progression across each facade. The larger assembly was based on the cartouche from Purcell, Feick, and Elmslie's bank building in Rhinelander, Wisconsin, and emphasized flowing foliate on a field of irregular outline. The other ornamental piece was smaller in area and stressed geometric shapes. It featured two circular discs placed as polar opposites on a large rectangular plaque that bore curving plantlike shapes introduced as a secondary theme. Decorative terra-cotta bandings extended across the street facades, joining brickwork and terra-cotta surfaces. The building was wedge-shaped in plan as Milwaukee Avenue diagonally cut through the dominating rectangular street grid and the resulting intersections created odd, triangular sites. The "prow" of the building was blunted by a narrow sliver of wall clad in terra cotta and festooned with ornament.

M. Shooman Building (1922), Chicago; Rissman and Hirschfield, Architects. Photo: 1992.

Rissman and Hirschfield provided a similar solution for another irregularly shaped lot in their design for a two-story building (1923) commissioned by Nathan Schoenberg and located at North Lincoln Avenue and Montana Street. However, for this building, with ground-floor shops and upper-story apartments, the exterior walls were face brick. A narrow wall segment joined the Lincoln Avenue and Montana facades although here the acute angle of the street intersection approached ninety degrees. Terra-cotta ornament and bandings relieved large expanses of brick and provided horizontal emphasis and decorative counterpoint. The same rectangular shields with circles and stylized foliate that were used on the Milwaukee Avenue building were incorporated here as the dominant ornamental feature. However, some were placed vertically as well as horizontally and were further modified by decorative appendages.

Stock Sullivanesque terra cotta, this time from the Midland company, was employed by Rissman and Hirschfield for another neighborhood mixed-use structure, at 1344 Devon Avenue. Intended for retail and apartment uses, the building was constructed in 1922 but has been destroyed. Terra cotta use in the building was limited and the overall effect was not as successful as that of the designs that used Northwestern stock.[53] Increasingly, Rissman and Hirschfield relied on historic precedent for mixed-use buildings in Chicago neighborhoods. As the firm grew and large apartment buildings became a staple of its practice, eclectic design became pervasive.[54]

Among the few known designs in Chicago by the architect Harry B. Aarens were three small one-story commercial buildings that incorporated Midland's stock Sullivanesque terra cotta. For street-facing facades, Aarens employed white-glazed stock pieces to configure ornamental designs based on plate 82 from a Midland catalog. These ornamental assemblies, combined with patterned brickwork, created attractive facades for simple buildings of mundane use. Two especially handsome buildings were constructed in 1925 just a few doors apart on North Kedzie Avenue. Of the two, the one at 3751–55 has retained its integrity. The original glass storefront and its framework of masonry and ornament display the contrast of void and patterned solid surface that characterized Sullivanesque designs. A service garage (1926) on Belmont Avenue has these same characteristics despite some alterations and an array of distracting signage. The only other known Aarens building design with ornamental terra cotta in Chicago was eclectic.[55] By 1930, Aarens had relocated to the West Coast and was designing expensive houses in the Spanish revival style.[56]

The partnership formed in 1923 by Sigmund V. Ablamowicz and M. F. Winiarski resulted in a number of designs that used Sullivanesque terra cotta from the Midland company for small buildings of the 1920s commercial strips in Chicago.[57] These included two-story buildings with dwelling units above shops, built at 1538 and 1937 Chicago Avenue in 1926 and 1925, respectively, near the firm's office. Sullivanesque terra-cotta trim and accents were combined with yellow brick for each building, and each featured a frequently used Sullivanesque medallion (no. 4508) as a central focus on the front facade. Both buildings survive. However, a one-story retail building (1926) of Sullivanesque style by Ablamowicz and Winiarski, located at Milwaukee and Miltmore Streets, has been demolished.[58]

David Theodore Bjork (1883–1967) was representative of builder-architects who, given an opportunity to design a project as well as build it, adopted the Sullivanesque. Born in Chicago, Bjork studied civil engineering at the University of Illinois (1900–1901) and at the University of Michigan.[59] By 1913 he was secretary of Bjork Brothers Construction Company, Architects and Engineers.[60] Bjork's design for the store and apartment building (1923; demolished 1993) for A. Frazier was constructed at the southeast corner of North Clark Street and Highland Avenue.[61] With its richly embossed ornament and street facades clad entirely in white terra cotta, the small building bordered on the bizarre, in part because of its basic configuration in plan. The alignment of the adjacent streets shaped the ground plan into a parallelogram; however, the acute angle at the street intersection was truncated with the insertion of an additional narrow wall. Therefore, the building's perimeter was five-sided, and not one of its five interior angles measured 90 degrees. This peculiar shape was emphasized on the facades by a multitude of horizontal lines: some were subtle, such as the mortar joints of the large-scale terra-cotta units, and others were more emphatic, such as the string courses on the upper facade. These string courses aligned heads and sills of all windows, with the exception of a small bathroom window. Patterns of Sullivanesque ornament were embroidered on the modular grid of terra cotta for the upper wall and parapet. With the building's white-on-white "embossing," one had to look closely to appreciate its curious but intriguing facades; but with a wealth of detail and pattern, it was both a naive and wonderful little building.

Frank William Cauley (1898–1984) designed a tiny Sullivanesque structure in 1924 as one of his first commissions after opening his office earlier that year.[62] The small, now-altered one-story store for Oscar Abrams on Chicago's far North Side matched Midland terra cotta with brick. The front facade featured a Midland semicircular cartouche centered on the parapet. A companion piece of the same design was positioned on the narrow wall that "clipped" the corner and angled away from the street at 45 degrees. Midland accents (no. 4500 series) and string courses completed the facade composition. Cauley's subsequent commissions were eclectic designs, including a number of residences in Evanston, Illinois.[63]

After World War I, Commercial Avenue was a developing retail and social spine for the south Chicago neighborhood near the Chicago Rolling (steel) Mills South Works on Lake Michigan, a growing community of blue-collar workers.[64] F. William Fischer designed many of the buildings in the growing area, especially along Commercial Avenue.[65] One of these was a Sullivanesque design for Frazer Brothers at 9036–42 South Commercial. This two-story building, named the Henryetta Block, was built in 1924 by James Hamilton, a contractor.[66] On the brick upper wall, two Midland ornamental assemblies, one near each end, joined terra-cotta string courses to the parapet coping, with a Midland Sullivanesque disc located at the midpoint. Fischer's building is still handsome despite some storefront remodelings and an accumulation of garish, over-sized signs.

Two commercial buildings by Albert J. Fisher (1863–1938) utilized terra-cotta or-nament and are based on Midland examples of Sullivanesque design.[67] Both are two-story retail structures on Chicago's North Side and were built in 1917.[68] The plan of the larger building was angled, shaped by its through-lot. The parcel of land abuts the two bordering streets of (3009–11) Lincoln Avenue and (3012–18) North Southport,

A. Frazier Building (1923; demolished 1993), Chicago; David T. Bjork, Architect. Photo: 1992.

A. Nelson Building (1922),
Chicago; Koenigsberg and
Weisfeld, Architects. Detail of
stock terra-cotta medallion.
Photo: 1992.

which form an acute angle. The principal facade, approximately forty-eight feet long, faced Lincoln and was composed of yellow brick combined with Midland's stock white terra cotta. The major ornament, positioned on the parapet, was comprised of an eagle and shield with entwined floral motifs. The building is still in use but the storefronts have been altered. Fisher's other Sullivanesque example is located at 1938 Irving Park Road and was constructed for J. J. Hoellin. Clad with white-glazed brick matched with white terra cotta, the twenty-two-foot-wide front facade was topped with a variation of a Midland medallion (number 4508) centered on the upper parapet. Although the building scale has been disturbed by modern window replacements and the brickwork has deteriorated, the building still glistens in its humdrum surroundings.

A graduate of the Armour Institute of Technology, Arthur Jacobs (1890–1947) was responsible for several Sullivanesque designs.[69] In 1921, Jacobs designed a one-story commercial building for A. Guthman on Chicago's far North Side. Jacobs clad the simple post-and-beam steel structure with brick and introduced Midland stock terra-cotta ornamental pieces for column capitals and accents. The accents were aligned on the upper wall above the columns, echoing the rhythm of the structural bays. More compelling was Jacob's design for a commercial structure (1923) in suburban Cicero. The long facade of the one-story building fronts on what is now Laramie (formerly Fifty-second Avenue) and contains a series of storefronts. Again, the steel frame was clad with brick; however, the parapet was shaped with a large central section that gently sloped up to the center point, like a stylized pediment. Several Midland discs were stacked in pairs at the central "pediment" and were differentiated from one another by varying combinations of supplemental terra cotta. The vertically paired discs combined into one assembly and achieved sufficient scale to create a primary focus and helped unify the lengthy facade.[70]

The firm of Koenigsberg and Weisfeld was formed in 1920 with offices at 155 North Clark Street, Chicago. Born in 1889 in Russia, Nathan Koenigsberg became a registered architect in Chicago in 1915. Leo H. Weisfeld, also born in 1889, was a 1913 graduate of the University of Illinois and received his license to practice architecture in 1918.[71] Their firm was responsible for at least three known Sullivanesque designs.[72] Two of these were one-story retail structures clad in brick with terra-cotta trim and ornamentation. Each featured a cartouche comprised of Midland stock pieces composed with a medallion (no. 4508) and paired finials. One structure was built (1922) at 4107 North Milwaukee Avenue for Dr. Harry Sered; it has been demolished. It featured one cartouche centered on the fifty-foot-long main facade. Another Koenigsberg and Weisfeld design (1926), also now demolished, once stood at 5138–46 West Division Street. Although in poor condition, a one-story commercial building (1922) for A. Nelson is still standing at the corner of North Damen Avenue and Lee Street. The front facade has four bays with a small shop sequestered in each and features ornamental assemblies centered above paired shops.

Among the many designs by the architect Benedict J. Bruns were at least four in the Sullivanesque style. Three were commissioned by the William Geschech Company. In the Charel Building (1922–23), a shop occupied the corner while the entry lobby for second-floor apartments was accessed from the side street. A pent roof softened the Sullivanesque qualities of ornate terra-cotta bandings, trim, and pier capitals composed with brick facades. The Lawfrank Building (1922–23), on Lawrence at Avers, was larger than the Charel Building and also differed from it in ornamentation. Its terra-cotta features and bandings in decorative reliefs were finished in mottled beige glazes to imitate granite.[73] The Burtonian Building (1922) featured Midland's stock pier capitals (no. 7704) and other terra-cotta trim pieces for bandings and panels, including a special panel emblazoned with the Burtonian name.[74] Bruns based his facade design for a small one-story store for Fred Hein (1924) at 1966 North Halsted Street on Midland's plate 36. This drawing was the basis of a 1915 advertising campaign to promote Midland's stock Sullivanesque terra cotta.[75]

Anton Charvat, John N. Coleman, Julian Floto, Frank L. Fry, and Paul Hansen were among the Chicago architects who tried Sullivanesque design. Anton Charvat (d. 1923) designed a small one-story store at 3916 West Twenty-sixth Street for L. Klein. It closely resembled a Midland archetype; but the warm beige glaze of the terra cotta, mottled to resemble granite, elevated it beyond ordinary stock.[76] The Jordan Building (1916–17; demolished 1986) was designed by John N. Coleman and stood at 3539–49 South State Street in an African-American neighborhood, now the historic district called Bronze-

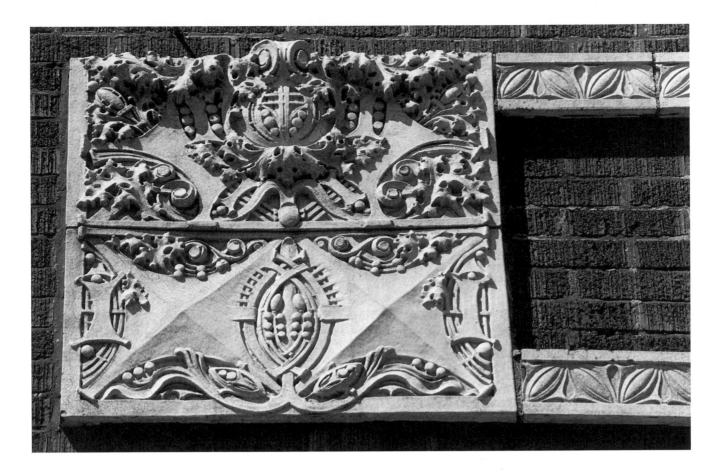

Fred Hein Store (1924), Chicago;
Benedict J. Bruns, Architect.
Detail of terra-cotta end plaque
on upper wall. Photo: 1991.

ville. A fragment of Midland's stock Sullivanesque terra cotta was salvaged from the building—which was named for musician-songwriter Joseph J. Jordan—and is now displayed, along with other architectural artifacts from works of Wright, Sullivan, and others, in the grand stair atrium of the Art Institute of Chicago.[77] In the Edison Park neighborhood of northwest Chicago, Julius Floto (1864–1950) designed a distinctive interpretation of the Sullivanesque. The two-story building (1922) on the northwest corner of Oliphant and Edison (now Northwest Highway) was designed for Charles Staack. Wide decorative trim pieces surrounded the window openings on the major facade. Additional terra cotta of white-glazed trim and bandings, but of narrower dimension, tied the Oliphant Street facade to the principal frontage, and ornamental accents complemented the facade treatments. Frank L. Fry (1860–1939) designed a one-story store building in 1922 at the intersection of Roosevelt Road and South California Avenue. Sullivanesque cartouches of terra cotta positioned on the upper facade distinguished this otherwise simple structure.[78] One of the more exuberant Sullivanesque neighborhood structures was designed in 1921 by Paul Hansen for a large garage. Now destroyed, it stood on Broadway near Grace Street. It was a virtual display of the Midland Terra Cotta Company's stock Sullivanesque terra cotta (order no. 21113), as almost every standard component was utilized. The (no. 4508) disc ornament was most prominent.[79]

Another demolished North Side building, a small store (1921) that stood on the southeast corner of Diversey and Lincoln, was designed by Clarence Hatzfeld. It featured Midland ornament (order no. 21152) arrayed on a brick facade.[80] Hatzfeld was the architect for many buildings of eclectic design, but he was responsible for at least one additional Sullivanesque building. This was a commercial structure remodeling at 11429–31 South Michigan Avenue, and it is extant, although altered. The two-story commercial building, which now houses a furniture store in Chicago's Roseland community, has an exceptional Sullivanesque facade and was the result of Hatzfeld's major alteration (1920) of an 1898 building.[81] The composition of brick upper wall surfaces and ornate terra cotta has strength and beauty. Large window openings at the second floor were framed by broad panels of terra cotta and refined with touches of decoration. The parapet was raised at the center bay and capped with an ornamental plaque that featured a sculpted eagle and foliate motifs. Although insensitively remodeled in the past decade with new storefront and boarded-over upper-story windows, the facade still exhibits the best design characteristics of the Sullivanesque. Furthermore, it anticipates the art deco and demonstrates how Sullivanesque compositions and elements could evolve into that style.

Originating in the French decorative arts, the art deco was translated into American architecture through the use of angular geometric building forms, with decorative motifs providing focal points and references to human scale. It should be noted, however, that art deco skyscraper massings were influenced by the set-back requirements

Commercial building (1920), 11429–31 S. Michigan Avenue, Chicago; alteration of 1898 building; Clarence Hatzfeld, Architect. Detail of Midland stock terra cotta. This ornament and the composition illustrate the Sullivanesque as a precursor of the art deco style. Photo: 1991.

of New York's zoning ordinance and the drawings of Hugh Ferriss, not by Sullivan's simple geometric volumes. However, many art deco designs for low-rise commercial buildings did seem to be influenced by Sullivanesque compositions. They had similar geometrical massings composed as simple, bold forms and they incorporated and positioned decorative ornament in a similar fashion. But the art deco ornamental motifs broke with Sullivanesque convention and were usually less elaborate. They were based on simple geometrical designs and/or images of stylized human figures or animals.

D. D. Meredith, William A. Nicholson, and Douglas S. Pentecost were among the many obscure architects responsible for one or more Sullivanesque designs. Meredith designed a one-story commercial building (1923) located at North Clark Street and Hollywood Avenue. The crenelated parapet projects a Gothic image for the simple building; but two elaborate terra-cotta assemblies on the Hollywood facade are prominent examples of Midland's Sullivanesque compositional pieces. The overall composition of the facade for another Meredith-designed (1923) building of three-stories on North Clark is not well resolved, although some of the terra-cotta ornament is handsome in its own right. The Joseph Spiker Building (1917), designed by William A. Nicholson, seems somewhat more successful as the terra-cotta patterns and ornament unify the facade and help express the three structural bays. The building, located at 11717 South Michigan Avenue, has ground-floor shops and second-story apartments. An example of Douglas S. Pentecost's interpretation of the Sullivanesque was realized in three-story flats (1916) for a Doctor Stewart, located at 1311–13 Pratt Street.[82]

Good examples of commonplace Sullivanesque buildings were designed by architects William Schultz, William Sevic, and Maurice Spitzer. These are a store and flat (1926) at 4939 South Ashland, by Schultz; Sevic's Fuhrman and Forster Company (1924), at 1647–49 South Blue Island; and a one-story commercial building (1922) at 5049–57 North Clark Street designed by Spitzer for Bender and Luckman.[83] There are other minor Sullivanesque examples in Chicago, by other largely forgotten architects and anonymous designers. Some buildings are disappointing, but others suggest that the beauty of the Sullivanesque could make the commonplace more uncommon, meaningful, and attractive.

The use of stock terra cotta even in low-budget buildings, with varying interpretations by different architects, contributed to the success and importance of the Sullivanesque style. With the guidance of Louis Sullivan's examples, designs published in professional journals and catalog plates, and the availability of decorative components, the journeyman architect could produce attractive facade designs. As noted earlier, many Sullivanesque designs, especially in the Midwest, can be traced to the influence of the architect William Krieg and his Midland Terra Cotta Company. The economy of stock terra cotta allowed the Sullivanesque to continue in Chicago and nearby locales while the cost of ornament became prohibitive elsewhere. The Sullivanesque waned in other regions partly because talented people were needed to design and reproduce the ornament, but the artisans skilled in its reproduction were concentrated in Chicago. The

Store building (1923), corner of
Clark and Hollywood, Chicago;
D. D. Meredith, Architect. Detail
of terra-cotta focal piece.
Photo: 1992.

costs for shipping terra-cotta ornament to distant locations became exorbitant. Economics was a major reason the Sullivanesque became a regional and then a local style.

In many ways, the Sullivanesque paralleled the fortunes of Louis Sullivan. The initial phase of the style was an optimistic time in which Adler and Sullivan enjoyed great success. The publication of their high-rise designs motivated other architects to apply Sullivan's ideas to their own commissions for similar building types, especially the skyscraper. At that time, information was disseminated much more slowly than it is today, so there was a considerable time lag between the completion of an Adler and Sullivan building and the appearance of its influence in the buildings by others. With the eventual decline of his practice, Sullivan's commissions were reduced in number to a few small buildings. Similarly, the later stage of the Sullivanesque was more obscure and was relegated mostly to projects for smaller buildings.

Louis Sullivan died in 1924. His death and the coverage his career received from the popular press and professional journals spurred renewed interest in his life and work. More architects attempted the Sullivanesque as an experiment or as a tribute. By 1930, however, interest in Sullivan's designs and ornament had diminished and the Sullivanesque decades were over. But Sullivanesque facade designs, inspired by journal and catalog examples of mass produced terra cotta, still give focus and distinction to inexpensive, utilitarian buildings in Chicago's commercial strips and throughout the Midwest. In some ways, the Sullivanesque may have been a true architecture of democracy.

EPILOGUE

THE DEPRESSION and World War II temporarily suspended most building construction in America and finally quieted any remaining Sullivanesque inclinations. After the war, America embraced the optimism of modern design. International Modernism, as originated by the Bauhaus in Germany and dispensed by its displaced students and faculty, such as the architects Walter Gropius, Marcel Breuer, and Mies van der Rohe, became the norm. New and different building materials, such as exposed concrete, painted or stainless steel, and aluminum claddings, were preferred by modern architects, and there was a greater emphasis on the use of glass. Ornamentation was discarded as unnecessary and inappropriate. Terra cotta was "dated" and was rejected because of its associations with revivals of historical styles. Terra-cotta companies that survived the lean years of the Depression and the war could not survive changes in taste and demand. In the 1920s there were forty-eight companies manufacturing terra cotta in America, but there were only two major companies left in 1987 (these were the Ludowici Celander Company, Inc., in the East and the Gladding, McBean, and Company on the West Coast).[1] Today, most demand for architectural terra cotta is for replacements on old buildings.

Because terra cotta is in limited supply, and because of its artistic merit as well, salvaged architectural terra cotta is now sought by collectors. In Chicago, for example, architectural salvage companies find that terra cotta—especially pieces of Sullivanesque ornament—is in great demand. Collectors have had to be wary of past claims that Sullivan himself designed stock Sullivanesque terra cotta for the Midland company. As noted earlier, Sullivan would not have done this and there is no evidence to support the claim. Although the quality of some of Midland's designs suggests that someone very familiar with Sullivan's work may have been involved, the designer's name will probably remain unknown.

The Sullivanesque, although inspired by nature, was an urban architecture. It was intrinsically part of the street. It defined space, whereas buildings of International Modernism, especially in America, became objects in space. The setback, plaza, or suburban setting separated the mid-twentieth-century modern building from its context, symbolically as well as physically, and, when combined with the stark abstractness of scaleless Modernism, further alienated people and nature from architecture. The buildings of modern architecture, as freestanding objects, became shaped like sculpture, and form became decoration. As the Chicago architect Richard Bennett once advised young designers: "You can decorate your structure but don't let your structure become decoration."[2] In Robert Venturi's analogy of the "decorated shed" versus the "duck,"[3] the Sullivanesque building was the decorated shed and many examples of modern architecture became "ducks" of indescribable shapes. Form became function.

The design pluralism of today, with such directions as deconstructionism, postmodernism, "high-tech," modern revival, and "sculpted" architecture, still tends to separate architecture from context. Forms can be assertive and unrestrained when free of the constraints of the built environment. Too often, the need for a building to relate to its physical, cultural, and societal context is ignored and the total urban environment suffers. Perhaps, what is needed today is a return to the philosophy of the Sullivanesque and the arts and crafts movements, wherein the building was part of a greater whole, societal interests were greater than those of the individual, and craft was primary. Even more important, the urban context needs to be stabilized and restored. The current "new urbanism," grounded in replication of the traditional city, in which the Sullivanesque was integral, is valid and has promise, although the architectural images of the new urbanism, with its nostalgic motivations and eclectic reproductions, are questionable.

The great success and tragic decline of Louis Sullivan has been a moving and powerful saga in architectural history. Today, more than seven decades after his death, Sullivan the man remains a heroic figure for many architects. His work, especially his ornament, is even more fascinating and admired. It is no wonder that some architects, especially in Chicago, have reevaluated his design principles and resurrected his building forms. For example, Ben Weese's design (1980) for the Community Bank of Lawndale, Chicago, is indebted to Sullivan in organization and image. With symmetrical facade compositions, arched entrance, horizontally banded windows, and color-contrasting brick used to frame the field of face brick, the building is linked to a sixty-year Chicago precedent—only the terra-cotta ornament is missing. Perhaps if terra-cotta facilities and modelers had been readily available to Weese, complete ornamentation might have appeared as well.

While with Harry Weese and Associates, Architects, Ben Weese recycled the Sullivanesque terra-cotta ornament of Frank Lloyd Wright from the Francisco Terrace (1895; demolished 1974). This terra cotta was salvaged by Ben Weese, John Baird, and Devereux Bowly for reuse in a new Francisco Terrace (1978) residential development on West Lake Street in Oak Park, Illinois.[4] For the 1981 renovation of an eighteen-story apartment hotel (1929; Oldefest and Williams, Architects) at 1211 North LaSalle Street, Chicago, Ben Weese had the famed muralist Richard Haas paint trompe l'oeil Sullivanesque facades on the barren party and rear walls of the LaSalle Tower. Thus, the freestanding building became a jewel amidst the confusion of urban renewal in Near North Chicago.[5] The great archway from Sullivan's Transportation Building for the Columbian Exposition and the grand bull's-eye window from his Grinnell, Iowa, bank are featured in the composition for the end walls of the LaSalle Tower. Haas called his illusionistic murals *Homage to the Chicago School.* Weese and Haas demonstrated that Sullivanesque design and ornamental features are timeless and their scale could be increased to monumental proportions without diminished value or importance; the illusion is complete and beautiful. For the interior of the Young Hoffman Gallery in Chicago, Haas utilized Sullivan-like motifs. Repetitive patterns, based on Sullivan's elevator grill designs for the Stock Exchange Building, are featured on one wall while decorative arches frame a window opening.[6]

Ben Weese was not the only Chicago architect to recycle salvaged Sullivanesque terra cotta. The Midland stock ornament on a one-story commercial building (1922; Jacobson, Architect) that occupied the south side of the 4300 block of Armitage Avenue was salvaged when building sections of street frontage were cleared for a parking lot. The rear portions of the building were saved and remodeled (1992) into a neighborhood convenience center. The stock Sullivanesque terra cotta, with white and custom-blue glazes, was reused on the new facade. Unfortunately, the project is another example of the "suburbanization" of the city, as a parking lot fronts the commercial strip building and separates it from the street. This void replaced the building portion and facade that previously had respected and defined the street. Pedestrian orientation and human scale were lost. Although the original facade and ornamental compositions designed by an obscure architect are gone, the reused pieces and assemblies capture the original spirit and distinguish an otherwise nondescript example of suburban typology.

Other examples of recycled Sullivanesque terra cotta in Chicago include pieces salvaged from Adler and Sullivan's Schiller/Garrick Theater Building and placed in the facade of the Second City Theater building, 1616 North Wells Street in Old Town. In addition, smaller but similar pieces were used in garden walls for old rowhouses in the Lincoln Park West neighborhood. The Art Institute of Chicago has reconstructed the great entry arch of Adler and Sullivan's Stock Exchange (1893; demolished 1971). The trading room from the Chicago Stock Exchange was recreated (1977) by the architect

John Vinci in Skidmore, Owings, and Merrill's Columbus Drive addition to the Art Institute. The thirty-foot-high trading room is alive with Sullivan's decorative designs: decorative column capitals, stenciled wall patterns in multiple hues, and stained glass.[7]

In addition to Ben Weese, other current Chicago architects who have been inspired by Sullivanesque imagery include James Nagle and Christopher H. Rudolph. Geometric forms, brick massings, contrasting trim, and accents that appear like ornament, but without any decorative reliefs, have appeared in the work of these architects. James Nagle of Nagle, Hartray, and Associates, has been the most consistent in the use of Sullivanesque aesthetics. A nine-story building for the elderly (1981) in Taylorville, Illinois, and the twelve-story Ramada Renaissance Hotel (1985) in Springfield, Illinois, are Nagle designs that incorporated Sullivanesque arches, masonry massings, and methods of facade composition. Perhaps the most literal designs by Nagle were the First Bank of Oak Park (1987), Oak Park, Illinois, and the Rudich Townhouse (1986), in Chicago's Lincoln Park. The base treatment of the two-story store for Mitchell's Jewelry (1985) in Arlington Heights, Illinois, by Christopher H. Rudolph was influenced by Purcell, Feick, and Elmslie's bank design in Rhinelander, Wisconsin. Bulkheads under display windows and an arch that framed the entryway were of stone and contrasted with the brick walls above. This treatment closely resembled that at Rhinelander. Some of the townhouse complexes designed by Pappageorge and Haymes, Architects, follow the Sullivanesque vernacular for facade composition. For example, Greenview Passage (1987), Chicago, has three-story front facades composed with upper-story symmetry above asymmetrical arrangements of the ground-floor entry and garage doors. Brick walls are "dematerialized" by the architect's use of horizontal bandings of masonry in contrasting colors and small but colorful inset panels, which are analogous to ornamental terra-cotta accents.

Modern architecture, which started in Chicago, lost humanistic content over time and under the influence of intercontinental transformations. In reaction, postmodernism emerged in the early 1980s with a reexamination of historical precedent. Architects rejected contemporary modernism, with its scaleless and inhuman abstractness, and began searching for intrinsic humanistic qualities and references to human scale. However, postmodernism soon degenerated into a new eclecticism, its historical motifs usurped and misappropriated. East Coast architects, some of whom saw the new eclecticism as an opportunity for self-promotion and advancement, mimicked historical European styles with contorted and meaningless results. Wouldn't it be much more meaningful for Chicago architects to rediscover their roots? The Chicago School, the Prairie School, and the Sullivanesque were indigenous to the region and culture. These architectures responded to human needs as well as to functionalism and structural expression. It seems appropriate and fundamental to understand earlier Chicago architectural movements, such as the Sullivanesque, in order to achieve the original intent of postmodernism.

There has been renewed interest in architectural terra cotta. This interest was

LaSalle Tower, Chicago; Ben Weese, Architect. This 1981 remodeling of a 1929 building features trompe l'oeil murals by Richard Haas on the rear and end walls, entitled *Homage to the Chicago School of Architecture*. Photo: 1993.

strongly signaled by the Contemporary Terra Cotta Competition, sponsored by the National Building Museum in 1985. From 110 submissions, six were honored by the jurors. One, by H. Stow Chapman, could be considered Sullivanesque as the decorative designs had plant forms, based on the honeysuckle, emerging from a geometrical framework of circular and rectangular shapes.[8] Despite renewed interest in terra cotta and admiration of the modeled intricacies and lustrous polychromes of the material, widespread usage is unlikely. Lack of production facilities and skilled workers are among the many obstacles to a revival of the terra-cotta industry.

Louis Sullivan remains the master who was most closely associated with terra-cotta ornament. He was able to exploit its potential as a medium for artistry, producing buildings and ornament that are now often viewed as architectural manifestations of poetry. Yet these designs were also an inspiration for modern architecture. Sullivan's buildings motivated many designers of his time, a number of whom tried to emulate his work. Not pale copies, the imitative work became a vibrant form of vernacular architecture. The Sullivanesque thus emerges as a decorated modern architecture and a uniquely American contribution to the history of architecture.

APPENDIX

An Inventory of Sullivanesque Buildings

THIS INVENTORY of built Sullivanesque designs is based on extensive field surveys, review of available drawings, and comprehensive research in journals, books, and records. Building department records, city directories, and other local references were consulted. The inventory is as complete as possible although omissions are inevitable.

The inventory comprises two lists. The first is organized by state and city, excluding Chicago and its suburbs, which are covered in the second list. The state list has subheadings by city; the Chicago list is divided into city sectors, with buildings grouped under street names. The following is noted about each building: (1) name or description; (2) address or location; (3) ranking; (4) name of architect; (5) year built; (6) remarks. Known demolitions are noted under remarks, as are instances of destruction by fire or other accident. Information has been compiled since 1990 but constant urban change may render some rankings and conditions obsolete.

The rankings of buildings are: 1 = superior; 2 = excellent; 3 = good; 4 = fair; 5 = poor. The rankings are somewhat subjective and are not intended to indicate a preference for the retention or expendability of a building. The ranking suggests the degree to which a building adheres to the Sullivanesque style. A minimal use of Sullivanesque ornamentation or the introduction of mixed styles would reduce the ranking. Most buildings have been changed in some way. If alterations have compromised the integrity of the original design, the ranking is likewise reduced. In some cases, the ranking is given as a ratio (for example, 1:3), which indicates the ranking of the original design in relation to the ranking after remodelings or alterations.

Abbreviations used in the listings include: alts. for alterations; apts. for apartments; attr. for attributed to; bldg. for building; brk. for brick; C.I. for cast iron; cor. for corner; DEMO for demolished; hs. for house; int. for interior; t.c. for terra cotta. "Stock t.c." indicates stock terra cotta supplied by the Midland Terra Cotta Company; however, the addition of (NWT) indicates that the supplier was the Northwestern Terra Cotta Company while (Am) indicates the supplier was the American Terra Cotta and Ceramic Company.

I. INVENTORY BY STATE AND CITY OR OTHER GEOGRAPHICAL UNIT

Name/Description	Address (if known)	Rank	Architect	Year	Remarks
ARIZONA					
Douglas					
Hotel Gadsden	—	1:4	Trost & Trost	1906–7	part int. only; fire (1928) & reblt. differently
Phoenix					
YMCA	—	2	Trost & Trost	1907	hip roof
Tucson					
Owls Club	300 N. Main St.	3	Trost & Trost	1900	
CALIFORNIA					
Los Angeles					
Wilson House	7 Chester Place	3	—	c. 1895	Mission & Sulliv.
House	1507–9 S. Hoover	3	—	c. 1900	
Philharmonic Aud./ Temple Bapt. Ch.	427 W. 5th St.	2	Chas. F. Whittlesey	1906	alt. (1938)
Apartment bldg.	235 San Juan	4	attr. Marsh & Russell	c. 1905	
Richmond					
Firehouse No. 3	—	3	—	c. 1916	gable roof w/ ornate fascia
San Francisco					
Gingg House	35 Lopez Ave.	2	Glenn Allen	1915	stucco w/ ornament
COLORADO					
Denver					
A. T. Lewis & Son Dept. Store	1531 Stout	1	Harry W. J. Edbrooke	1917	6 stories; now res. lofts
Pueblo					
Opera House Block	—	1	Adler & Sullivan	1890	Fire & DEMO (1922)
FLORIDA					
Jacksonville					
Morocco Temple	219 N. Newnan St.	3	H. J. Klutho	1910–11	mixed styles/now altered
St. James Bldg.	117 W. Duval St.	1	H. J. Klutho	1911–12	interior has been altered
Nolan Garage	937 N. Main St.	2:5	H. J. Klutho	1911–12	facades destroyed
Burbridge Hotel	—	2	H. J. Klutho	1911	DEMO (1981)
Florida Life Ins. Co.	117 N. Laura St.	1	H. J. Klutho	1911–12	
Criminal Court & Jail Expansion	Liberty St.	1	H. J. Klutho	1913–15	DEMO (1968)
Jackson-Hoyt Bldg.	Bay & Laura St., NW cor.	3:4	H. J. Klutho	c. 1915	alts. detract
Panama Pk. Elem. School	580 Lawton Avenue	2	H. J. Klutho	1915	
East Jacksonville School No. 3	1016 E. Ashley St.	2	H. J. Klutho	1917	DEMO (1981)
Wilkie/Napier Apts.	1530–36 Riverside	3	H. J. Klutho	1923	
Masonic Temple	410 Broad St.	2	Mark & Sheftall	1912–16	
Palatka					
James Hotel	—	2	H. J. Klutho	1916	cast-stone ornament
IDAHO					
Boise					
Union Pacific RR Depot	UPRR	4	—	1924	mixed styles

Name/Description	Address (if known)	Rank	Architect	Year	Remarks
IDAHO (continued)					
Caldwell					
Houston School	—	4	W. A. McGee & Son, Bldr.	c. 1918	hip roof
Nampa					
Union Pacific RR Depot	UPRR	4	—	1924	mixed styles
ILLINOIS—Downstate (see separate listing for Chicago & Chicago Suburbs)					
Albany					
First Trust & Savings Bank	Highway 84	2	J. G. Legal & Co.	1921	now library
Alton					
Store addition	419 E. Broadway	4	—	1928	t.c. accents
Brighton					
Village Hall	—	4	J. L. Rinaker	c. 1914	DEMO
Carbondale					
Virginia Bldg.	114 N. Illinois Ave.	4	—	1914	2 stories
Champaign					
Dallenback Bldg.	204 N. Neil St.	4	N. S. Spencer & Son	1916	mixed styles
Store bldg.	6th & John, NE cor.	4	attr. Berger & Kelly	1925	stock t.c. accents
Charleston					
Norfolk Bldg.	7th & Monroe, NE cor.	4	—	1913	2 stories
(Chicago & Chicago Suburbs—see separate listing)					
Eldorado					
First National Bank	—	2	H. E. Boyle & Son	1923	stock t.c.
Fairbury					
Masonic Temple	downtown	4	C. H. Schnetzler	1921	2-story brick w/ white t.c.
Farmington					
Moose Lodge	164 N. Main St.	3	Aldrich & Aldrich	1925	now Zellmer's Theatre
Franklin Grove					
Citizens State Bank	Elm & South St., NE cor.	4	Midland T.C. Co.	1920	now insurance office
Freeport					
E. Bergston Jewelry	12 Chicago Avenue	3	W. G. Walker	1915	remodeled 1880s bldg.
Galena					
Commercial bldg.	Main St.	4	—	c. 1922	stock t.c. accents
Galesburg					
McCullom Bros. Candy Co.	465 Mulberry	2	Aldrich & Aldrich	1917	3-story factory
Stanley Oberg Bldg.	788 N. Seminary	4	Aldrich & Aldrich	1917	1-story store
Killeen Buick Co.	79–87 N. Cherry	3	Aldrich & Aldrich	1920	DEMO
H. H. Gunther Garage	170 S. Seminary	2	Midland T.C. Co.	1921	DEMO
G. G. Glavis Bldg.	206–8 Tremont	4	Aldrich & Aldrich	1917	
Foley Mortuary	164 N. Broad St.	3	Aldrich & Aldrich	1925	2-story brick w/ t.c.
G. W. Thompson	—	4	Aldrich & Aldrich	1916	
Genoa					
Genoa Lumber Co.	113 Main St.	1:4	Midland T.C. Co.	1919	(1) before fire, (4) now rebuilt
Hoopeston					
J. H. Dryer Bldg.	E. Main & Bank, NW cor.	3:4	J. F. McCoy	1914	remodeling detracts
Kankakee					
Garage	183 S. Indiana Ave.	3	—	c. 1918	altered
Lawrence Babst Bldg.	256 E. Merchant	3	L. F. W. Steube	1918	to be demolished
Fortin Bros. Garage	—	4	C. D. Henry	1919	DEMO
Garage	—	2	attr. Midland T.C. Co.	1923	DEMO

Name/Description	Address (if known)	Rank	Architect	Year	Remarks
ILLINOIS —Downstate (continued)					
Knoxville					
Tate Hardware	Main St.	4	Aldrich & Aldrich	1915	1 story; stock t.c.
LaSalle					
Max Erlenborn Bldg.	636 First St.	2	John Hanifen	1921	DEMO
J. E. Skelly Bldg.	3d & Joliet, NE cor.	2	John Hanifen	1924	DEMO
Store for John Cummings	—	4	John Hanifen	1924	
McLellen Store Alterations	735 First St.	3	John Hanifen	1926	remodeled
Commercial bldg.	First & Gooding, NW cor.	4	John Hanifen	1938	
Fitch Laundry	427–29 First St.	1:2	attr. John Hanifen	c. 1924	some alts.
LaSalle Theatre	—	4	Victor Andre Matteson	c. 1912	DEMO
Manlius					
First State Bank	E. Maple St.	2	Parker N. Berry	1916	vacant w/ 2d fl. apt.
Marengo					
School	Grant Rd. & Rt. 20	2	Adler & Sullivan	1883	DEMO (1993)
Moline					
Berglund Bldg.	1317–21 Fifth Ave.	4	—	c. 1920	3-story brick w/ t.c.
Oregon					
Lyons Bldg.	3d & Washington, NW cor.	4	—	c. 1915	altered; now hdw. store
Bank bldg.	4th & Washington, SE cor.	4	—	c. 1916	now Rock River Bank
Orion					
Garage	downtown	4	Midland T.C. Co.	1919	geometrical ornament
Ottawa					
T. R. Godfrey Bldg.	—	3	White & Hanifen	1914	stock t.c.
Jordan Hardware	208 W. Main St.	4	John Hanifen	1919	stock t.c.
Paris					
Pearman's Store	108 W. Court St.	2	Welch, Wilmarth Co.	1924	storefront intact w/ Luxfer prism glass
Peoria					
Overland Automobile Gar.	804 W. Main @ Douglas	2	Midland T.C. Co.	1916	green-glazed t.c.
Commercial bldg.	707–11 Adams S.W.	1	—	c. 1916	DEMO (1999)
Store bldg.	115 Perry S.W.	4	—	1919	small 1-story store
Mohammed Temple	—	4	Hewitt & Emerson	c. 1914	Egyptian & Moorish influences
Princeton					
Adeline Prouty Home	501 Park Ave. E.	4	Parker N. Berry	1917	mainly Prairie School
Princeton Dry Goods	902 N. Main St.	1:2	Parker N. Berry	1915–16	somewhat altered
Princeton Hotel	500 S. Main St.	4	Aldrich & Aldrich	1915	small t.c. accents
Rochelle					
Township Public Library	4th Ave. & 7th St., NE cor.	1	Claude & Starck	1912	addition (1989) relates
Bert Comstock Bldg.	400 Cherry @ N. Main	4	Peterson & Johnson	1915	2-story brk. w/ white t.c.
Rockford					
Martin W. Floberg Bldg.	120–34 N. Church St.	2	Peterson & Johnson	1923	2-story brk. w/ white t.c.
Overland Auto Garage	206–12 N. Church St.	1:4	Midland T.C. Co.	1916	alterations detract
R & S Bldg.	309 S. Main St.	4	Frank A. Carpenter	1911	Viennese influence
St. Joseph					
Masonic Temple	228 Lincoln	4	Midland T.C. Co.	1914	2-story brk. w/ white t.c.
Savanna					
F. G. Sullivan Bldg.	523 Main St.	1	John Ladehoff	1915	storefront intact w/ Luxfer prism glass
Springfield					
Educa. wing, First Presby. Church	Capitol & 7th, NW cor.	3	—	c. 1912	some alterations

Name/Description	Address (if known)	Rank	Architect	Year	Remarks
ILLINOIS—Downstate (continued)					
Wordon					
Wordon School	Kell & Shirley St., SW cor.	3	M. B. Kane	c. 1923	brick w/ white t.c. trim
INDIANA					
Anderson					
Brock & Brock Bldg.	21 W. 11th St.	3:4	E. R. Watkins	1916	stock t.c., remodeled
Evansville					
Farmer's Dairy Co.	317–19 N. Main @ Michigan	4	A. E. Nevcks	1921	now Koch Dairy Co.
Fellwock Auto Co.	408 N.W. 4th (?)	2	Clifford Shopbell	1922	probably DEMO
Fort Wayne					
Store bldg.	—	1	J. M. E. Riedel	1922	probably DEMO
Remodeling	—	3	A. M. Strauss	1925	
Gary					
J. J. Verplank	7612 Greenview	4	J. J. Verplank	1915	stock t.c.
Hammond					
Oliver Morton School	Marshall & 171st	1	Hutton w/ Geo. Elmslie	1936–37	DEMO (1991)
Thomas A. Edison School	Calumet @ 170th	1	Hutton w/ Geo. Elmslie	1936–37	DEMO (1991)
Washington Irving School	4727 Pine St.	1	Hutton w/ Geo. Elmslie	1936	addition (1953) relates
Indianapolis					
Williams Bldg.	611 N. Capitol	2	J. Edwin Kopf	1916	4 stories, stock t.c.
Martinsville					
Toner Bros. Store Bldg.	61 N. Jefferson St.	1	Midland T.C. Co.	1915	white t.c. facade
Mechanicsburg (Boone Co.)					
Mechanicsburg Bank	Highway 39	3:4	D. A. Bohlen & Son	1913	badly altered to cafe
Michigan City					
Archer Block	710 Franklin Square	3	attr. F. F. Ahlgrin	1914	stock t.c.
Vreeland Garage Bldg.	—	4	L. C. Bernard	1924	mixed styles
Mishawaka					
Theater for Roy Robleder	210–14 Main St.	3	Myrle E. Smith	1923	polychrome t.c., mixed styles, to be DEMO
Mount Vernon					
Edward Wade Bldg.	W. 2d St.	4	Clifford Shopbell	1923	stock t.c.
New Castle					
H. F. Burke Bldg.	105 S. 12th St.	4	H. E. Wallace	1919	stock t.c. accents
Poseyville					
Bozeman-Waters National Bank	William @ Locust, NE cor.	1	Clifford Shopbell	1924	interior altered
Richmond					
McConaha Bldg.	—	2	Nicol & Dietz	1918	rich ornament
South Bend					
2-story store	224 Colfax	2	—	c. 1922	stock t.c.
S. Bend Tribune	223–25 Colfax @ Lafayette	4	Austin, Shambleau, & Wiser	c. 1920	Gothic influences
3-story store	122 S. Michigan	4	—	c. 1923	badly altered
Urbana					
High School	—	4	—	c. 1920	
Walkerton					
Farmer's State Bank	708 Roosevelt	4	C. E. Kendrick	1917	stock t.c.
West Lafayette					
Purdue State Bank	State & South Sts.	1	Louis Sullivan	1914	wedge-shaped plan

Name/Description	Address (if known)	Rank	Architect	Year	Remarks
I O W A					
Algona					
Henry C. Adams Bldg.	State & Moore St., NW cor.	1:2	Louis Sullivan	1913–14	now badly altered
John Goeders Bldg.	123 E. State St.	4	Midland T.C. Co. & Wm. Schulze	1920	simple stock t.c.
Burlington					
Bock's Florist	310 N. 3d St.	2	Geo. W. Washburn	1924	stock t.c.
Scotten Bldg.	720 Jefferson @ 8th St.	3	—	c. 1915	stock t.c.
Burt					
Smith Bros. Bldg.	117 Walnut	4	H. R. Cowan	1915	now post office
Cedar Rapids					
Peoples Savings Bank	101 3d Ave. SW @ 1st St. SW	1	Louis Sullivan	1909–11	restored
St. Paul's Methodist Episcopal Church	1340 3d Ave. SE @ 14th St. SE	1	Louis Sullivan	1913–14	completed w/o Sullivan
Charter Oak					
Farmer's Store	Main St.	2	E. L. Barber	1919	stock t.c.
Clinton					
Henry Pahl	402–6 S. 2d St.	2	Ladehoff & Sohn	1915	white t.c. facade
Snow White Drug Store	512 S. 2d St.	3	Ladehoff & Sohn	1917	white-glazed brick w/ t.c.
Van Allen Bldg.	200 5th Ave. S.	1	Louis Sullivan	1913–15	4 stories
Schall's Candy Co.	501 N. 2d St.	1:2	—	1917	windows altered
Iowa State Savings Bank	122 Main Ave.	1	Harry R. Harbeck	1914	orig. entry removed
Clutier					
Farmer's State Bank	—	4	W. J. Brown	1915	
Des Moines					
French Way Cleaners	413 Euclid	4	Fred A. Harris	1916	Wright influence
Dubuque					
Joseph Fuhrman	—	3	J. F. Leitha	1922	probably demolished
Grinnell					
Merchants Natl. Bank	4th Ave. & Broad St., NW cor.	1	Louis Sullivan	1914	now Poweshiek Nat. Bank
Jefferson					
D. Milligan Co.	—	1	Midland T.C. Co.	1915	DEMO
Luna					
Consolidated School	Highway 52	4	William L. Alban	c. 1916	simple t.c. accents
Mason City					
Commercial Sav. Bank	21–23 S. Federal	4	—	1917	DEMO
Bagley & Beck Bldg.	20 S. Federal	2	Hansen & Waggoner	1927	virtually destroyed by mall
Knights of Columbus	202–4 S. Federal	3	—	1906	DEMO
Muscatine					
Laurel Bldg.	101 E. 2d St.	4	—	c. 1916	6 stories
Ottumwa					
Store bldg.	—	4	Midland T.C. Co.	1922	stock t.c.
Sioux City					
Woodbury County Courthouse	Douglas @ 7th St.	1	Purcell & Elmslie w/ Wm. L. Steele	1916–18	off. tower over crt. blk.
Insurance Exchange Bldg.	507 7th St. @ Pierce	4	—	c. 1919	6 stories, mixed styles
Morey's & People's Hotel	618–20 4th St.	2	—	c. 1920	DEMO
Raymond's & Hill Hotel	614–16 4th St.	2	—	c. 1918	DEMO
3-story store bldg.	512 4th St.	1	—	c. 1918	white t.c. facade
Sioux City Journal	421–23 Douglas	1	Wm. L. Steele	c. 1922	DEMO

Name/Description	Address (if known)	Rank	Architect	Year	Remarks
IOWA (continued)					
Sioux City (continued)					
S. S. Kresge	425 4th @ Pierce	1	Wm. L. Steele	1917	DEMO
Exchange Bldg. & Livestock Nat. Bank	Cunningham Drive, S. of Chicago Ave.	2	Wm. L. Steele	c. 1920	altered
Williges Bldg.	613 Pierce	1	Wm. L. Steele	1930	cream-color t.c.
Fishgall's	521 4th St.	4	—	c. 1920	white t.c. facade
Everist House	27 McDonald Drive	2	Wm. L. Steele	1916–17	Sulliv. w/ Prairie
Waukon					
M. J. Barthell Bldg.	18 Allamakee	4	—	1914	2 stories
Wesley					
Ben Felt Store	106 Main St.	4	Midland T.C. Co.	1915	white-glazed brk. & t.c.
KANSAS					
Pittsburg					
Besse Hotel	121 E. 4th	4	Wm. T. Schmitt w/ Hawk & Parr	1926	mixed styles, now apts.
Salina					
Lincoln School	210 W. Mulberry St.	3	Wm. T. Schmitt	1915–17	mixed styles
Topeka					
Capital Bldg. & Loan Assoc.	—	1	Geo. G. Elmslie	1922	DEMO (1968)
C. M. Knowlton Drugs	—	3	N. P. Nielsen	c. 1910	
KENTUCKY					
Louisville					
Store & apt.	716 E. Broadway	2	Weakley & Hawes	1924	stock w/ cream glaze
Olympic Bldg.	223–29 W. Breckinridge	1	E. P. Lynch	1926	stock t.c.
Kaufman Bldg.	4th St. Galleria	2	Mason Maury	c. 1908	remodeled; now inside galleria
William R. Belknap School	1810 Sils Ave.	3	J. Earl Henry	c. 1916	
LOUISIANA					
Baton Rouge					
Bldg. entrance remodeling	—	?	R. Spencer Soule	1922	t.c. entry only
New Orleans					
ICRR Passenger Station	1001 S. Rampart St.	2	Adler & Sullivan	1892	DEMO (c. 1954)
MICHIGAN					
Benton Harbor					
Store bldg.	—	2	Midland T.C. Co.	1924	DEMO
Store bldg.	301–3 Washington St.	4	—	c. 1918	1 story
Sheffield Bldg.	153–55 Washington St.	4	—	1918	
Baker Vasoler Co.	205 W. Main St.	3	—	1914	addition (1915)
Breckenridge					
First State Savings Bank	228 E. Saginaw	1:3	Joseph Rosatti of Cowles & Mitscheller	1913	badly remodeled
Detroit					
J. Sparling & Co.	Woodward Ave.	4	Stratton & Baldwin	1906	6 stories
A. T. Rayl Co. Bldg.	Woodward & Grand River	3	Baxter O'Dell & Halprin	1915	7 stories, red t.c.
National Theater	—	4	Albert Kahn	c. 1919	
Wagner Baking Co.	—	3	John Ahlschlager & Son	c. 1919	

Name/Description	Address (if known)	Rank	Architect	Year	Remarks
MICHIGAN (continued)					
Flint					
C. Smith Bldg.	Saginaw St. (10th-12th)	2	Geo. Bachman	1915	stock t.c.
Grand Rapids					
Remodeling of (1880) hotel	226 Pearl St. N.W.	4	—	c. 1916	columns; now Israel's Interiors
Holland					
Store bldg.	42–44 E. 8th St.	2:3	—	c. 1928	altered; now Steketee's
Kalamazoo					
Desenberg Block	251 E. Michigan Ave.	1	Adler & Sullivan	1885–87	early example
Gazette Telegraph	S. Burdick & Lovell	2	M. C. J. Billingham	1916	DEMO
Kalamazoo Masonic Temple	309 N. Rose	4	Spier & Rohns	1913–15	converted (1987–88) to Rose St. Market
Niles					
Store bldg.	224 Main St.	2:3	Kawneer Co.	1923	stock t.c.; altered
Pontiac					
Rundel Substation	—	4	Commonwealth Power Co.	1924	stock t.c.
Saginaw					
Hotel bldg.	105 Washington @ Genesee, SW cor.	2	Schmidt, Garden, & Martin	1915	6 stories
Warehouse	S. Water @ Genesee, SW cor.	4	—	c. 1925	6 stories
Sault Saint Marie					
High School	—	4	—	c. 1918	mixed styles
Stambaugh					
Store bldg.	—	2	David E. Anderson	1921	stock t.c.; 1 story
MINNESOTA					
Adams					
First National Bank	4th & Main, NE cor.	1	Geo. Elmslie w/ Strauel	1924	polychrome t.c.
Creamery	Main St.	4	—	1927	altered
Aitkin					
Store	2d St. N.W. @ Minn. Ave. N.W.	3	—	c. 1914	polychrome t.c.
Albert Lea					
Skinner & Chamberlain Dept. Store	221–25 S. Broadway	1	Wm. Alban	1924	stock t.c. (Am)
Bemidji					
Commercial bldg.	304 3d St.	4	—	c. 1910	altered
Blooming Prairie					
F. Werwerka store	Main St.	3	Buechner & Orth	1916	stock t.c., like Midland plate
Crookston					
High School	—	4	Bert D. Keck	c. 1912	
Detroit Lakes					
Carnegie Public Library	1000 Washington Ave.	1	Claude & Starck	1913	sympathetic add. (1990)
Duluth					
George H. Crosby Res.	2029 E. Superior	3	I. Vernon Hill	1902	hip roof
F. A. Patrick & Co.	S. 5th Ave. nr Commerce	2	Palmer, Hall, & Hunt	1902	7 stories
Elgin					
Farmers & Merchants Bank	E. Main & 1st Ave. N.E.	4	Midland T.C. Co.	1915	now post office

Name/Description	Address (if known)	Rank	Architect	Year	Remarks
MINNESOTA (continued)					
Eveleth					
Manual Training School	Roosevelt Ave. nr Jones	3	Bray & Nystrom	1914	Wright influence
Granville					
First National Bank	—	1	Purcell, Feick, & Elmslie	1910–11	DEMO
Grand Meadow					
Exchange State Bank	Main & RR Ave., NW cor.	1	Purcell, Feick, & Elmslie	1910	some alts.
Grand Rapids					
Village Hall	Pokegama Ave. N @ 5th St. E.	3	Holstead & Sullivan	1928–29	transitional design
Hector					
Farmers & Merchants State Bank	206 Main St.	1	Purcell & Elmslie	1916	stucco & polychrome t.c.
LeRoy					
First State Bank of LeRoy	Main St.	2	Purcell & Elmslie	1914	brick box w/ arch
Luverne					
First National Bank	E. Main & N. Cedar	3	W. E. E. Greene	1917	mixed styles, now city hall
Madison					
Madison State Bank	218 6th St.	1	Purcell & Elmslie	1913	DEMO
Mankato					
First National Bank	229 Front St.	1	Ellerbe & Round	1913	polychrome t.c.
Zimmerman & Bangerter	Second St. (?)	2	H. C. Gerlach	1916	DEMO
Minneapolis					
Flour Exchange	310 4th Ave. S.	4	Long & Kees	1892–93	Romanesque transition
Advance Thresher & Emerson-Newton	700 3d St. S.	2	Kees & Colburn	1900 & 1904	2 bldgs. appear as one
Chamber of Commerce	400 4th St. S.	1	Kees & Colburn	1900–2	now Grain Exchange Bldg.
Deere & Webber Co. wrhse	800–18 Washington Ave. N.	2	Kees & Colburn	1902	6 stories
P. R. Brooks Res.	1600 Mount Curve	1	Edwin H. Hewitt	1905	hip roof
Parlin & Orendorff Plow	Washington Ave. N. @ 7th Ave.	3	Bertrand & Chamberlain	c. 1910	DEMO
Great Northern Implement	616–22 3d St. S.	4	Kees & Colburn	1910–11	Romanesque influence
Westminster Presby. Church Sunday School	12th & Nicollet Ave. S.	3	Purcell, Feick, & Elmslie	1911	int. intact; ext. altered
Parker Residence	4829 Colfax Ave. S.	1	Purcell, Feick, & Elmslie	c. 1912	Prairie w/ Sullivan. entry
Purcell House	2328 Lake Place	1	Purcell & Elmslie	1913	Prairie & Sullivanesque
Studebaker Garage	Hennepin @ Laurel	4	Kees & Colburn	c. 1913	3 stories
L. S. Donaldson Co. garage	13th Ave. @ 8th St.	2	Kees & Colburn	1915	DEMO
Telephone Exchange	2726–30 W. 43d St.	3	Downes & Eads	1915	now commercial bldg.
E. N. Hegg Bldg.	2930 Nicollet Ave. S.	2	Purcell & Elmslie	1915	DEMO
Morry					
School (grades 1–12)	—	4	G. L. Lockhart	c. 1916	2½ stories w/ hip roof
Ortonville					
Carlson & Brewster Bldg.	—	3	Midland T.C. Co.	1921	stock t.c.
Owatonna					
National Farmers' Bank	101 Cedar @ Broadway	1	Louis Sullivan	1907–8	sympathetic int. alt. (1958) by H. H. Harris
Minnesota Mutual Fire Ins.	129 Broadway E.	1	Jacobson & Jacobson	1922 & 1929	altered & additions

Name/Description	Address (if known)	Rank	Architect	Year	Remarks
MINNESOTA (continued)					
Rochester					
IOOF Lodge Hall & stores	1st Ave. S.E. & 2d St. S.E.	2	—	c. 1917	polychrome t.c.
St. Paul					
factory bldg.	—	4	Schmidt Garden & Martin	c. 1919	
M. Burg & Sons	2402 University	2	W. R. Wilson	1917	7 stories
W. A. Tilden, garage	63–71 E. 3d	2	John M. Alden	1922	DEMO
Virginia					
Horace Mann School	5th Ave. W. 900 blk.	3	Bray & Nystrom	1914 & 1924	Wright influence
Winona					
J. R. Watkins Medical Products	150–78 Liberty St.	2	George W. Maher	1911	Maher's most Sullivanesque bldg.
Merchants Bank of Winona	102–4 3d St. E.	1	Purcell, Feick, Elmslie	1911–12	some int. alt. & add.
MISSISSIPPI					
Ocean Springs					
Louis Sullivan Cottage	—	2	Adler & Sullivan	1890	Shingle style influence
James Charnley Cottage	—	2	Adler & Sullivan	1890	Shingle style influence
MISSOURI					
Kansas City					
Newbern Hotel (Peacock)	525 E. Armour Blvd.	1	Ernest O. Brostrom	1921 & 1925	altered Peacock Apts.
Scarritt Bldg. & Arcade	818 Grand & 819 Walnut	1	Root & Siemens	1906–7	11 stories w/ galleria
Edison Shop	—	2	Purcell & Elmslie	c. 1912	interiors, now destroyed
Commercial bldg.	Walnut, west side 1000 blk.	3	—	c. 1910	5 stories
Marceline					
Santa Fe RR Depot	Santa Fe RR	4	—	c. 1920	simple t.c. accents
St. Louis					
Wainwright Bldg.	7th & Chestnut, NW cor.	1	Adler & Sullivan	1891	int. altered
Charlotte D. Wainwright Tomb	Bellefontaine Cemetery	1	Adler & Sullivan	1892	
Union Station	Market & 18th St.	2	Link & Cameron	1892	Romanesque exterior
Union Trust	7th & Olive, NW cor.	1	Adler & Sullivan	1893	remodeled
St. Nicholas Hotel	8th & Locust	1	Adler & Sullivan	1893	DEMO (1961)
Roberts, Johnson & Rand Shoe Co.	1509 Washington @ 15th	1	Theodore C. Link	1910	10-story office bldg.
Raleigh Residence (apts.)	3708 (?) Washington	4	—	c. 1912	DEMO (1996)
Bar and apt.	N. Broadway @ Dooridge	4	—	c. 1912	green-glazed t.c. accents
Store and apt.	2646 Cherokee	2	—	c. 1922	polychrome t.c.
Store and apt.	2744 Cherokee	3	—	c. 1922	2 stories
Rear entry addition to Cinderella Theater	2743 Cherokee	3	—	c. 1922	a small addition
Store bldg.	3524 Gravois	3	—	c. 1926	like a Midland plate
NEBRASKA					
North Platte					
Commercial bldg.	Dewey St., 500 blk. W. side	4	—	c. 1912	2 stories, stock t.c.
Omaha					
Apartment complex	17th @ Howard (?)	2	Drake Realty Const. Co.	1919	19 bldgs., 4½ stories

Name/Description	Address (if known)	Rank	Architect	Year	Remarks
NEW JERSEY					
Atlantic City					
Apartment bldg.	—	2	Seward G. Dobbins	1924	stock t.c.
NEW YORK					
Buffalo					
Guaranty/Prudential Bldg.	Church & Pearl St., SW cor.	1	Louis Sullivan	1894–95	
So. Side Bank of Buffalo	2221 Seneca St.	1	Harold Jewett Cook	1921	altered; Fleet Bank
New York					
Bayard/Condict Bldg.	65–69 Bleecker St.	1	L. Sullivan w/ L. P. Smith	1897–98	
Syracuse					
Robert Gere Bank Bldg.	121 E. Water St.	3	Charles E. Colton	1894	Romanesque influence
NORTH DAKOTA					
Bismarck					
Bismarck Tribune	—	4	—	c. 1910	
First National Bank	—	3	Purcell, Feick, & Elmslie	c. 1909	interiors & storefront
Fargo					
Addition to hotel for T. F. Powers	—	3	Wm. F. Kurke	1919	stock t.c.
F. W. Cook Bldg.	—	4	Ashelman & Gage	c. 1911	3 stories
Ford Motor Co. Factory	Broadway @ N. 5th	4	John Graham	1914	now printing plant
Jamestown					
White Bldg.	1st Ave. S. & 2d St.	3	—	1917	2 stories
OHIO					
Bucyrus					
L. D. Pickering Bldg.	—	4	Wm. Unger	1917	mixed styles, stock t.c.
Cincinnati					
Queen City Livery	950 Gest	4	Ben DeCamp	1917	stock t.c.
Cleveland					
St. Clair Market	St. Clair @ E. 106th	2	H. T. Jeffery	1917	stock t.c.
Wilshire Bldg.	201–11 Superior	—	—	1882	
Rockefeller Bldg.	Superior & W. 6th, NW cor.	3	Knox & Elliot	1903	
Newark					
Home Bldg. Assoc. Bank	W. Main & N. 3d, NW cor.	1	Louis Sullivan	1914–15	t.c. facades
Sidney					
People's Savings & Loan Association Bank	Court St. & Ohio Ave., SE cor.	1	Louis Sullivan	1917–18	new addition to south
OKLAHOMA					
Muskogee					
Graham Bldg.	—	2	Dickman & Niemann	1920	stock t.c.
Oklahoma City					
Pioneer Bldg.	Third & Broadway	2	Williams & Wells	1907–8	7 stories
Colcord Bldg.	Grand @ Robinson, NW cor.	1	Wm. Wells	1909–10	12–14 stories
Edward H. Graham Hs.	300 E. Park Pl.	4	Wm. Wells	c. 1909	DEMO
House	229 N.E. 11th St.	4	Wm. Wells	c. 1910	probably DEMO

Name/Description	Address (if known)	Rank	Architect	Year	Remarks
OKLAHOMA (continued)					
Tulsa					
McCullough Mausoleum	—	2	Rush, Endacott, Rush	1920	designed by Bruce Goff
St. Paul's Methodist Epis. Church	Boston Ave. @ 13th	2	Bruce Goff for R.E.R.	1926–29	important transitional des.
OREGON					
Portland					
Auditorium Bldg.	920 S.W. 3d Ave.	3	F. Manson White	1894	4 stories
SOUTH DAKOTA					
Aberdeen					
Store bldg.	—	4	Geo. Fossum	1926	stock t.c.
Canton					
T. T. Sexe, 2-story store	—	4	Perkins & McWayne	1920	stock t.c.
Huron					
IOOF Bldg.	336 Dakota Ave. S.	4	F. C. W. Kuehn	1914	
K. P. Bldg.	60 3d St. S.W.	4	F. C. W. Kuehn	1919	
Lake Andes					
Charles Mix County Courthouse	—	1	Wm. L. Steele	1917	
Mitchell					
G. L. Branson & Co. Bank	200 N. Main	1	Purcell & Elmslie	1916	1 story
Logan Store Bldg.	N. Main St.	2	Purcell & Elmslie	1916	adjoins bank, now altered
J. N. Crow Bldg.	—	4	F. C. W. Kuehn	1912	
Sioux Falls					
Sioux Falls Natl. Bank	100 N. Phillips	4	—	1917–18	mixed styles
Medical & Surgical Clinic	—	3	Perkins & McWayne	1919	
Yankton					
Forbes Hall of Science	Yankton College	1	Geo. Elmslie w/ Wm. L. Steele	1929	now federal prison
Look Hall (Men's Dorm)	Yankton College	2	Geo. Elmslie w/ Wm. L. Steele	1931	now federal prison
TENNESSEE					
Greenville					
Virginia Hall	Tusculum College	3	Louis Sullivan	1901	simple dormitory
TEXAS					
Alice					
Jim Wells County Courthouse	—	2	Atlee B. Ayres	1912	conc. ornament
Athens					
Masonic Hall & store bldg.	—	3	Midland T.C. Co.	1918	2 stories, 25' frontage
Brownsville					
Cameron County Courthouse	—	4	Atlee B. Ayres	1912	interior rotunda only
Cameron					
First Methodist Church	—	2	Waller, Silber & Co.	1921	Prairie influence
Cleburne					
Johnson County Courthouse	—	2	Lang & Witchell	1912	transitional

Name/Description	Address (if known)	Rank	Architect	Year	Remarks
TEXAS (continued)					
Dallas					
Campbell Hotel	Harwood & Elm	4	Lang & Witchell	c. 1906	5 stories
Central Fire Station	Main St. (?)	2	Lang & Witchell	1908	DEMO
Clem Lumber Co.	—	4	—	c. 1916	
Commonwealth Nat. Bank	—	4	Lang & Witchell	c. 1912	DEMO
Cotton Exchange Bldg.	—	3	Lang & Witchell	c. 1913	DEMO
Deere/Kingman-Texas	501 Elm Pl. @ Record St.	4	Hubbell & Green	1902	now JFK Museum
Garage/Republic Auto Sup.	2210 Commercial St.	2	—	c. 1916	2 stories
Hippodrome Theater	—	4	Lang & Witchell	c. 1910	mixed styles
Huey & Philp Hardware Co.	—	4	Lang & Witchell	c. 1908	4 stories
M. K. & T. RR Offices	Commerce @ Market	4	H. A. Overbeck	1912	mixed styles
A. R. Phillips Apts.	—	4	Hubbell & Greene	c. 1910	w/ porches
Sanger Bros. Store	Main @ Lamar	3	Lang & Witchell	1910	now jr. college
Sears Roebuck Wholesale	1409 S. Lamar St.	4	Lang & Witchell	1913	Prairie influence
Southwestern Life Ins. Co.	Main @ Akard	4	Lang & Witchell	1911–13	DEMO
Trinity Methodist Church	Pearl @ McKinney St.	4	James E. Flanders	1903	DEMO (1985)
Wholesale bldg. for Boren & Stewart	—	4	Lang & Witchell	c. 1908	4 stories
El Paso					
Caples Bldg.	—	4	Trost & Trost	1909	
Donan Residence	—	3	Trost & Trost	1908	DEMO (c. 1965)
Douglas Grey Residence	1205 N. El Paso St.	2	Trost & Trost	1906	orn. porch frieze
Mills Bldg.	San Jacinto Plaza	2	Trost & Trost	1910–11	concrete, altered & painted brown
Mt. Sinai Synagogue	—	4	Trost & Trost	1916	
Posener Bldg.	—	4	Trost & Trost	1911	DEMO
Rio Grande Valley Bank	—	4	Trost & Trost	c. 1909	
Roberts-Banner Bldg.	Mesa @ Mills St.	4	Trost & Trost	1910	
YMCA	—	1	Trost & Trost	1907	DEMO (1961)
Fort Worth					
Flatiron Bldg.	1000 Houston @ Ninth	4	Sanguinet & Staats	1907	7 stories; mixed styles
North Ft. Worth High Sch.	—	4	Sanguinet & Staats	1918	Prairie influence
Gainesville					
Cooke County Courthouse	—	4	Lang & Witchell	1910	interior lobby only (classical ext.)
Houston					
Armor/Hogg Bldg.	Louisiana @ Preston, SE cor.	1	Barglebaugh & Whitson	1919	7 stories
Kingsville					
Kleberg County Courthouse	—	4	Atlee B. Ayres	1914	t.c. orn. entry porch
Laredo					
C. Papas Bldg.	—	4	Midland T.C. Co.	1918	geometrical ornament
McAllen					
New Palace Theater	—	2	Fred D. Jacobs	1925	stock t.c.
Paris					
First National Bank	—	4	Griffith & Barglebaugh	1916	6 stories
Pittsburg					
First Methodist Church	—	3	James E. Flanders	1904–5	w/ ornament
Plainview					
C. E. White Seed Co.	—	2	L. A. Kevy	1917	stock t.c.

Name/Description	Address (if known)	Rank	Architect	Year	Remarks
TEXAS (continued)					
Refugio					
Refugio County Courthouse	—	2	Atlee B. Ayres	1917	concrete ornament
Seguin					
Plaza Hotel	—	4	Leo M. J. Dielmann	1916	concrete ornament
Stamford					
St. John's Methodist Ch.	—	4	James E. Flanders	1910	minor ornament
Waco					
Auto Showroom & Garage	906 Austin St.	2	Miton W. Scott	1925	stock t.c.
Raleigh Hotel	—	1	Lang & Witchell	1912	10 stories
UTAH					
Salt Lake City					
Dooley Block	111 W. 2d St. South	2	Adler & Sullivan	1890–91	DEMO (1965)
VIRGINIA					
Honaker					
3-story store bldg.	—	4	H. C. Davis, Contractor	1923	mixed styles; stock t.c.
WASHINGTON					
Hoquiam					
Public Library	621 K St.	3	Claude & Starck	1910	
Seattle					
Oriental Block	606–10 2d Ave.	2	Bebb & Mendel	1903	6 stories w/ NWT t.c.
Schwabacher Hdw. Co./ Pacific Marine	First Ave. S. @ S. Jackson, SW cor.	3	Boone & Corner	1905	
Maynard Bldg.	119 First Ave. S.	4	A. Wickersham	1892	Romanesque transition
WEST VIRGINIA					
New Haven					
Mason County Bank	—	4	Batey & Halloran	1920	stock t.c.
WISCONSIN					
Bailey's Harbor					
Maxwelton Braes	Bonnie Brae Road	4	Elmslie w/ von Holst	1930	mixed styles
Baraboo					
High School	Ash St. & 1st St.	1	Claude & Starck	1927	now civic center
Beloit					
Beloit Light & Power Bldg.	Public Ave. & Pleasant St.	4	H. H. & Krieg	1923	mixed styles, side entry excellent
Columbus					
Farmers' & Merchants' Union Bank	James & Broadway	1	Louis Sullivan	1919	additions relate
Darien					
American Milk Co., dairy	Highway 14	4	Co. Const. dept.	1917	badly altered, now tire warehouse
Evansville					
Eager Free Library	39 W. Main	1	Claude & Starck	1908	rear addition (1996)
Grade School	S. 1st St.	4	Claude & Starck	1921	no ornamentation

Name/Description	Address (if known)	Rank	Architect	Year	Remarks
WISCONSIN (continued)					
Fond du Lac					
Store bldg. & theater	27–39 S. Main St.	4	—	c. 1925	mixed styles, colorful glazes on t.c.
Green Bay					
Community Bldg.	—	3	F. C. Klawiter	1921	stock t.c.
Kenosha					
Graham Bldg.	5038 6th Ave.	3	Midland T.C. Co.	1926	white t.c. facade
2-story shop & apt.	7505–7 Sheridan Rd.	4	—	c. 1922	stock t.c.
La Crosse					
Commercial bldg.	421 Main St.	4	—	c. 1910	4 stories
Store bldg.	507 Main St.	3	Percy D. Bentley	1913	3 stories; pent roof
Lancaster					
Municipal Bldg.	Madison & Cherry, SE cor.	1	Claude & Starck	1919	3-story offices & theater
Madison					
Josephine Crane Bradley House	106 N. Prospect	1	Louis Sullivan	1909	now fraternity house
Lincoln School	Prospect & Forest St.	1	Claude & Starck	1915	now apartment bldg.
Manitowoc					
Store bldg.	—	4	Wm. J. Raeuber	1926	mixed styles, stock t.c.
Commerce Bldg.	—	2	Wm. J. Raeuber	1925	DEMO
Store bldg.	Buffalo @ N. 9th, SE cor.	3	Wm. J. Raeuber	c. 1925	2 stories; stock t.c.
Merrill					
T. B. Scott Library	E. 1st St. (Highway 64)	1	Claude & Starck	1911	now w/ additions
Milwaukee					
Butter Bldg.	1217–31 W. Mitchell	2	—	c. 1924	2 stories
Das Deutsche Haus	—	?	Adler & Sullivan	1890	a remodeling; fire & DEMO (1895)
A. L. Gebhardt Co.	416 N. Water	3	Clare C. Hosmer	c. 1918	3 stories
Milwaukee Journal	333 W. State St.	4	Frank D. Chase	1924	transition art deco
Commercial bldg.	808 N. Planketon	4	—	c. 1918	
Monroe					
Lincoln School	—	1	Claude & Starck	1915	fire & DEMO (1975)
Neenah					
Jandrey Grove Co.	124 W. Wisconsin	2	Sindahl-Matheson	1915	remodeled
Neenah Club	114 E. Wisconsin	4	—	c. 1914	
Plymouth					
Curtis Hotel	E. Main & Caroline, SW cor.	4	E. A. Juul	1922	DEMO
Prairie du Sac					
Store bldg.	Water St. nr Galena	3:4	—	c. 1920	altered; now Masonic Temple
Racine					
Off. bldg. for M. Tidyman	610 Main St.	1	Edmund B. Funston	1915	now Badger Bldg.
Dr. C. H. Hann Residence	Grand @ 11th St.	4	Wm. F. Burfiend	1914	stock t.c.
Zahn's Dept. Store	5th St. & Wisconsin, SE cor.	3:4	Wm. F. Burfiend	1914	altered
Rhinelander					
First Natl. Bank Bldg.	8 W. Davenport St.	1	Purcell, Feick, & Elmslie	1910	mixed-use bldg.
O. A. Hilgerman Bldg.	Brown, east side nr King	2	Midland T.C. Co.	1917	stock t.c.

Name/Description	Address (if known)	Rank	Architect	Year	Remarks
WISCONSIN (continued)					
Sauk City					
Store & apt.	807 Jackson	4	Midland T.C. Co.	c. 1918	mixed styles
Sheboygan					
Store for Mullen Tire Co.	—	4	Edward A. Juul	1926	mixed styles, stock t.c.
Store bldg.	723 New York	3	Juul & Smith	1919	stock t.c.
Stanley					
North Western Lumber Co.	2d St. & Broadway	2	Purcell & Elmslie	1916	Land Office, 2 stories
Tomah					
Library	716 Superior Avenue	1	Claude & Starck	1916	now w/ additions
Two Rivers					
Addition to 2-story bldg.	—	4	Wm. J. Raeuber	1925	probably DEMO
Valders					
Store bldg.	222–24 S. Calumet Rd.	3	Juul & Smith	1921	to be DEMO
WYOMING					
Cheyenne					
Gas station	16th & Pioneer	4	—	c. 1920	mixed styles
PUERTO RICO					
San Juan					
Bank of Nova Scotia	—	2	Antonín Nechodoma	c. 1920	
CANADA					
Toronto					
Robert Simpson Co.	Yonge @ Queen St. W.	4	Edmund Burke	1894–95	additions, mixed styles
Winnipeg					
Fairchild Block	Princess St.	2	Rugh & Atchison	1907	6 stories

II. INVENTORY FOR CHICAGO & SUBURBS

CHICAGO: Center City (Loop & Nearby Areas)

Lake Michigan to Halsted St. (800 W); Roosevelt Road (1200 S) to Chicago Ave. (800 N). Listed by street within the center city area.

Name/Description	Address (if known)	Rank	Architect	Year	Remarks
Adams (200 S)					
Chapin & Gore Bldg.	63 E.	1	Richard E. Schmidt	1904	altered & restored (1996)
M. Ryerson Charities	318 W.	2	Adler & Sullivan	1886	DEMO (c. 1929)
Walker Warehouse	W. @ Wacker, SW cor.	1	Adler & Sullivan	1887–89	DEMO (1953)
Canal (500 W)					
Factory for Eli Felsenthal	63–71 N.	3	Adler & Sullivan	1889	DEMO (c. 1908)
Crane Co. Factory	S. @ Roosevelt, SW cor.	3	Adler & Sullivan	1890–91	DEMO
Crane Co. Foundry & Shop	S. @ Roosevelt, SE cor.	3	Louis Sullivan	1899–1900	DEMO
Crane Co. Office	S. @ Roosevelt, NW cor.	2	Louis Sullivan	1904	DEMO
Chicago (800 N)					
Sol Blumenfeld Res.	8 W.	2	Adler & Sullivan	1883–84	DEMO (1963)
Montgomery Ward Warehouse	604 W.	1	Richard E. Schmidt	1906–8	concrete construction
Montgomery Ward Office	619 W.	4	Willis J. McCauley	1930	relates to warehouse
Clark (100 W)					
Bldg. for Reuben Rubel	309 S.	2	Adler & Sullivan	1883	DEMO
Store for B. Goldberg	@ Flournoy	2	A. L. Himelblau	1922	DEMO
Desplaines (700 W)					
F. A. Kennedy Bakery	27–33 N.	3	Adler & Sullivan	1884	DEMO (1970)
Jackson (300 S)					
Comm. bldg. for E. L. Brand	nr State	2	Adler & Sullivan	1883–84	DEMO
R. W. Sears Bldg.	17–23 W. @ Plymouth	3	George C. Nimmons	1911	white-glazed t.c.
Commercial bldg.	33 W. @ Dearborn, SE cor.	4	—	c. 1910	5 stories
Larrabee (600 W)					
Selz, Schaub & Co. Factory	N. @ Superior, NE cor.	3	Adler & Sullivan	1888–87	DEMO (c. 1939)
La Salle (150 W)					
Stock Exchange Bldg.	30 N.	1	Adler & Sullivan	1893–94	DEMO (1971)
Warehs. for W. & C. Peck	N. @ W. Wacker, SE cor.	3	Adler & Sullivan	1886	DEMO (c. 1928)
Warehs. for J. W. Oakley	N. @ Hubbard, SW cor.	3	Adler & Sullivan	1891–92	DEMO (c. 1976)
Madison (0)					
Remodeling: McVickers' Thr.	25 W.	—	Adler & Sullivan	1885, 1891	DEMO
Remodel: Inter-Ocean Publ.	W. @ Dearborn, NW cor.	—	Adler & Sullivan	1889	DEMO (1941)
Michigan (100 E)					
Montgomery Ward Bldg.	6 N.	4	Richard E. Schmidt	1897–99	altered
Gage Bldg. facade	18 S.	1	Louis Sullivan w/ Holabird & Roche	1898–99	1st fl. altered (1953)
Auditorium Bldg.	430 S. @ Congress	1	Adler & Sullivan	1887–89	now Roosevelt U.
Monroe (100 S)					
Arch from Stock Exchange	E. @ Columbus, Art Inst.	1	Adler & Sullivan	1893	salvaged & displayed
Trading Rm., Stock Exch.	E. @ Columbus, Art Inst.	1	Adler & Sullivan	1893–94	restoration (1977): Vinci
Remodeling: Haverley's Thr.	57 W.	—	Adler & Sullivan	1884	DESTROYED: fire (1900)
Rothschild Store	212 W.	2	Adler & Sullivan	1881	DEMO
Knisely Factory Bldg.	551–57 W.	3	Adler & Sullivan	1884	DEMO (c. 1960)
Ontario (628 N)					
Charles P. Kimball Res.	22 E.	2	Adler & Sullivan	1883	DEMO (1964)
Plymouth (31 W)					
Plymouth Bldg.	416–18 S.	2	Simon B. Eisendrath	1899	C. I. Storefront

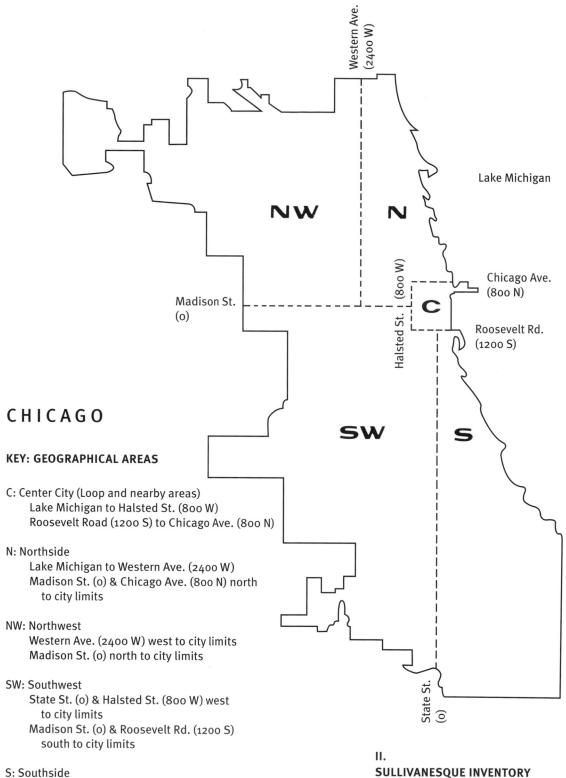

Western Ave.
(2400 W)

Lake Michigan

NW **N**

Chicago Ave.
(800 N)

Halsted St. (800 W)

C

Madison St.
(o)

Roosevelt Rd.
(1200 S)

CHICAGO

KEY: GEOGRAPHICAL AREAS

SW **S**

C: Center City (Loop and nearby areas)
    Lake Michigan to Halsted St. (800 W)
    Roosevelt Road (1200 S) to Chicago Ave. (800 N)

N: Northside
    Lake Michigan to Western Ave. (2400 W)
    Madison St. (o) & Chicago Ave. (800 N) north
      to city limits

NW: Northwest
    Western Ave. (2400 W) west to city limits
    Madison St. (o) north to city limits

SW: Southwest
    State St. (o) & Halsted St. (800 W) west
      to city limits
    Madison St. (o) & Roosevelt Rd. (1200 S)
      south to city limits

S: Southside
    Lake Michigan & state line to State St. (o)
    Roosevelt Road (1200 S) south to city limits

State St.
(o)

**II.
SULLIVANESQUE INVENTORY
CHICAGO, ILLINOIS
SECTOR MAP: GEOGRAPHICAL AREAS**

Name/Description	Address (if known)	Rank	Architect	Year	Remarks
CHICAGO: Center City (continued)					
Randolph (150 N)					
Ryerson Bldg.	16–20 E.	2	Adler & Sullivan	1884–85	DEMO (1939)
Schiller/Garrick	64 W.	1	Adler & Sullivan	1891–92	DEMO (1961)
Remodeling: Hooley's Thr.	124 W.	—	Adler & Sullivan	1884–85	DEMO (1926)
Chicago Cold Storage	W. @ Chicago River	2	Adler & Sullivan	1890–91	DEMO (1902)
Roosevelt (1200 S)					
Remodeling: Crane Co. Mill	W. nr Canal	—	Adler & Sullivan	1886–87	DEMO
Commercial bldg.	727–29 W.	4	—	c. 1920	DEMO (2001)
Commercial bldg.	801 W. @ S. Halsted, SW cor.	4	J. T. Fortin	1916	DEMO (2001)
Rush, N. (100 E)					
Remodeling: McCormick Hs.	675	—	Louis Sullivan	1898	DEMO (1954)
State (0)					
Remodeling: Springer Bldg.	126–46 N. @ Randolph	—	Adler & Sullivan	1888	DEMO (1990)
Addition: Schlesinger & Mayer	S. @ Madison, SE cor.	—	Adler & Sullivan	1890	DEMO (1902)
Schlesinger & Mayer	S. @ Madison, SE cor.	1	Louis Sullivan	1899 & 1902–3	now Carson's
People Theater	525–29 S.	2	Adler & Sullivan	1884	DEMO
Superior (732 N)					
J. M. Brunswicke-Balke	W. @ Orleans, SW cor.	3	Adler & Sullivan	1881–91	DEMO by fire
Van Buren (400 S)					
M. A. Meyer Bldg.	307 W.	1	Adler & Sullivan	1892–93	DEMO (1968)
Wabash (45 E)					
Jeweler's Bldg.	15–19 S.	1	Adler & Sullivan	1881–82	remodeled
Revell Bldg.	131 S. @ Adams, NE cor.	1	Adler & Sullivan	1881–83	DEMO (1968)
Edison Shop	229 S.	1	Purcell, Fieck, & Elmslie	1912	DEMO (1967)
Office bldg.	422 S.	3	Wm. Brinkmann	c. 1902	
Wirt Dexter Bldg.	630 S.	2	Adler & Sullivan	1887	6 stories
Munn Bldg.	815–19 S.	4	Christian A. Eckstrom	1909	now The Loftrium
Wacker (360 W)					
Troescher Bldg.	15–19 S.	1	Adler & Sullivan	1884–85	DEMO (1978)
Washington (100 N)					
Levi Rosenfeld Bldg.	@ Halsted, SE cor.	2	Adler & Sullivan	1881	DEMO (1958)
Western Methodist Publish.	12–14 W.	1	Harry B. Wheelock	1899	DEMO (1990)
Scoville Bldg.	619–21 W.	2	Adler & Sullivan	1884	DEMO (1973)
Rosenfield Bldg.	W. @ Halsted, SE cor.	2	Adler & Sullivan	1882–83	DEMO (1958)
Wells (200 W)					
Frankenthal Bldg.	141 S.	2	Adler & Sullivan	1882	DEMO

CHICAGO: North Side

Lake Michigan to Western Ave. (2400 W); Madison St. (0) and Chicago Ave. (800 N) north to city limits.
Listed by street location within that area.

Name/Description	Address (if known)	Rank	Architect	Year	Remarks
Ada, N. (1332 W)					
Garage bldg.	172–74	3	—	c. 1920	altered
Addison, W. (3600 N)					
Store bldg.	1027	4	—	c. 1915	stock t.c., 1 story

Name/Description	Address (if known)	Rank	Architect	Year	Remarks
CHICAGO: North Side (continued)					
Armitage, W. (2000 N)					
Store bldg.	1301–15 @ Spaulding	3	—	c. 1921	stock t.c., 1 story
Ashland, N. (1800 W)					
Hammond Library	44	2	Adler & Sullivan	1882	DEMO (1963)
American Theatre	nr Madison	2	H. H. Mahler	1913–14	DEMO
Astor, N. (50 E)					
Edward G. Pauling Res.	@ Scott (1240), NE cor.	2	Adler & Sullivan	1886	DEMO (1913)
James Charnley Res.	1365	1	Adler & Sullivan	1891	Wright des.; now SAH
Balmoral, W. (5400 N)					
Apt. bldg.	1408 @ Edgewood	4	—	c. 1916	2 stories
Beacon, N. (1338 W)					
Apt. bldg.	4451–57 @ Sunnyside	4	—	c. 1915	SE cor.
Belden, W. (2300 N)					
Ann Halsted Res.	440	3	Adler & Sullivan	1883	
Belmont, W. (3200 N)					
Commercial bldg.	1100–10 @ Seminary	3	Charles Liska	1922	1 story; altered
Garage bldg.	1931–33	3	H. B. Aarens	1926	alt.
Birchwood, W. (7500 N)					
Store for Oscar Abrams	1910–14	3	Frank W. Cauley	1924	1 story; altered
Bosworth, N. (1532 W)					
Mrs. H. L. Schmitz Apt. Bldg.	nr Jonquil (7700 N)	4	Albert Lang	1915	
Broadway, N.					
E. Edelmann Store Bldg.	3618	4	J. S. Aroner & Co.	1922	
Auto Service Bldg.	3727–29	3	M. O. Nathan	1927	white-glazed brk. & t.c.
Garage bldg.	near Grace	1	Paul Hansen	1921	DEMO
L. Dehmlow store & flats	3906	3	S. M. Eichberg	1915	C. B. Johnson & Son, Bldr.
B. L. Morris Bldg.	3926–28	4	A. L. Himelblau	1922	
M. A. Bender Bldg.	4025–27	3	Maurice L. Bein	1922	1 story, stock t.c.
A. E. Cook Dept. Store	4700–18 @ Leland	3	—	1912	4 stories
Store bldg.	5354–56	4	—	c. 1928	mixed styles
Store bldg.	6120	4	L. M. Mitchell	1921	
Burton, W. (1500 N)					
Albert F. Madlener Hs.	4 @ N. State, NW cor.	1	Richard E. Schmidt	1902	now Graham Fnd.
Chicago, W. (800 N)					
Store bldg.	1538	3	S. V. Ablamowicz	1926	2 stories, stock t.c.
Store bldg.	1937	4	S. V. Ablamowicz	1925	2 stories, stock t.c.
Store bldg. w/ apts.	2315–17	2	—	1922	3 stories
Store bldg.	2316–18	4	—	c. 1924	badly altered
Store bldg.	2320	3	—	c. 1917	altered: S. Tigerman; now Ukrainian Modern Art Museum
J. Penner Bldg.	2323–29	1	Aroner & Somers	1914–15	apts. w/ stores
Store bldg.	2335–39	4	—	c. 1922	1 story
Clarendon, N. (800 W)					
Apt. bldg.	4022–24	4	—	c. 1915	4 stories
H. Emermann Apts.	4310–22	3	A. L. Himelblau	1915	stock t.c. (Am)
Apt. bldg.	4338–46	4	Samuel N. Crowen	1905	mixed styles
Clark, N.					
Garage & store bldg.	2128–30	2	L. G. Hallberg & Co.	1922	DEMO
Dlott & Silverman	2453–67	3	A. L. Himelblau	1922	stores, offices, apts.
John Hammon Bldg.	2872	4	—	1917	
J. Goldberg Bldg.	2901–11 @ Surf	4	A. L. Himelblau	1922	DEMO

Name/Description	Address (if known)	Rank	Architect	Year	Remarks
CHICAGO: North Side (continued)					
Clark, N. (continued)					
Store bldg. for J. Goldberg	2939–49	4	A. L. Himelblau	1922	DEMO
Store bldg.	3420 @ Roscoe	3	C. O. Kuehne	1924	1 story, yellow brick
Bldg. for Mrs. Henderson	3438–48 @ Newport	1	W. Mead Walter	1915	brk. piers & t.c.
Links Hall	@ Sheffield & Newport	4	Oscar Johnson & Son	1916	2 stories
Epstein & G. Store	3464–66	3	attr. M. H. Harris	1922	altered
Martin Ryerson Tomb	4001, Graceland Cem.	2	Adler & Sullivan	1889–90	black granite
Getty Tomb	4001, Graceland Cem.	1	Adler & Sullivan	1890	w/ bronze gates
Bender & Luckman Stores	5049–55	2	M. Spitzer	1922	elaborate t.c. w/ brk.
Commercial bldg.	5151	4	—	c. 1915	2 stories
Commercial bldg.	5347–49	3:4	Levy & Klein	1922	2 stories; altered
Bldg. for John Hammer	5501–3 @ Catalpa	4	Oscar Johnson & Son	1915	
Capital Garage	5541–45	3	Maurice L. Bein	1926	dominating arch, alts.
Harry Last Store Bldg.	5701 @ Hollywood	3	D. D. Meredith	1923	good focus orn.
Paul Hesse Bldg.	5828–30	4	C. W. Westerlind	1924–25	3 stories
A. Frazin Store & Apts.	6323–25 @ Highland	2	David T. Bjork	1923	DEMO
H. Finder Store Bldg.	6534–38	3	A. L. Himelblau	1922	added signs detract
Stores & apts.	6640–52	4	Levy & Klein	1924	stock t.c.
Store bldg.	6962–64	2:3	C. M. Almquist	1922	altered
Commercial bldg.	@ Touhy, SE cor.	4	attr. Levy & Klein	c. 1920	stock t.c. (NWT)
Cleveland, N. (500 W)					
Leon Mannheimer Res.	2147	2	Adler & Sullivan	1884	
Damen, N. (2000 W, formerly Robey)					
Store bldg. for A. Nelson	736–42	3	Koenigsberg & Weisfeld	1922	stock t.c.
Store bldg.	1704	4	Anton A. Tocha	1924–25	1 story
Store for Balsom & Harris	4429–31	3	M. H. Harris	1922	altered; t.c. painted
Stores & apts.	4654–58 @ W. Leland	4	—	c. 1922	stock t.c.
Store bldg. for A. Epstein	4949–53	3	M. H. Harris	1922	1 story, stock t.c.
Jacob Miller Bldg.	4956–60 @ Argyle	4	attr. to Jens J. Jensen	1922	stores & apts.
Devon, W. (6400 N)					
Goldberg, Fried, & Cantor Bldg.	1225–27 @ Magnolia	3:4	Halperin & Braun	1922	altered; t.c. painted
Bldg. for Dr. A. H. Keats	1547 Devon	2	C. M. Almquist	1915	facade DESTROYED
Diversey, W. (2800 N)					
Store for E. Dichs	@ Lincoln, SE cor.	2	Clarence Hatzfeld	1921	DEMO
Farwell, W. (6382 N)					
Apts. for Wm. E. Nesbit	1134–36	3	Louis C. Bouchard	1914	elaborate entry
Foster, W. (5200 N)					
Leon Bldg.	1905–15 @ Wolcott	3	—	c. 1915	stores & apts.
Granville, W. (6200 N)					
Bldg. for E. I. Mitchell	nr Broadway	3	L. E. Russell	1915	
Greenleaf, W. (7032 N)					
Jewel Laundry	1730	2	Aroner & Somers	1913	t.c. w/ white-glazed brk.
Halsted, N. (800 W)					
Store for Fred Hein	1966	1	B. J. Bruns	1924	like a Midland plate
Store bldg.	2812–16	3	A. L. Himelblau	1923	stock t.c.
Store bldg.	@ Cornelia, NE cor.	3	A. L. Himelblau	1922	stock t.c.
Flat Iron Laundry	3629–31	3	—	1911	2 stories
Hutchinson, W. (4232 N)					
Edwin J. Mosser Hs.	750	1	Geo. W. Maher	1902	

Name/Description	Address (if known)	Rank	Architect	Year	Remarks
CHICAGO: North Side (continued)					
Irving Park, W. (4000 N)					
Comm. bldg. for L. Dlott	912–20	2	A. L. Himelblau	1921–22	stock t.c.
J. J. Hoellin Bldg.	1938	3	A. J. Fisher & Son	1916–17	t.c. w/ white-glazed brk.
Kenmore, N. (1038 W, formerly Alexander)					
Hotel for D. B. Hotchkin	5511	2	W. Mead Walter	1916	unusual entry canopy
Kingsbury, N.					
Euston & Co. Factory	1440–1500	3	Louis Sullivan	1899–1900	
Lake, W. (200 N)					
Store & flat: Richard Knisely	2147 W. Lake	3	Adler & Sullivan	1883	DEMO (1958)
Larrabee, N. (600 W)					
People's Gas Lt. & Coke Co. off.	nr North Ave.	1	Elmslie w/ von Holst	c. 1926	DEMO (c. 1968)
LaSalle, N. (150 W)					
Homage to Chicago School (mural)	1211	1	Richard Haas, painter, w/ Weese Seegers Hickey Weese	1981	Mural of Sullivan motifs
Lawrence, W. (4800 N)					
Store bldg.	1700–2 @ Paulina	4	—	c. 1924	alt.; Paulina side O.K.
Store bldg.	1704–16	3:5	—	c. 1924	facade DESTROYED
Leavitt, N. (2200 W)					
Holy Trinity Rus. Or. Church	1121	1	Louis Sullivan	1902–3	stucco-clad w/ tower
Lincoln					
Comm. bldg. for F. Kaufman	2310–12	3	Adler & Sullivan	1883, 1887	remodeled
Stores & apts.	2452–56 @ Montana	2	Rissman & Hirschfield	1922	stock t.c. (NWT)
M. L. Evan & Son Bldg.	3007–11	3	A. J. Fisher	1917	t.c. eagle w/ shield
Grossman Bros.	3231 @ Ashland	3	Theo. Stueben	1915	DEMO
Commercial bldg.	3854–60	3	Levy & Klein	c. 1922	stock t.c. (NWT)
Stores for M. Factor	3900–3904 @ Byron	3:4	Levy & Klein	1922	1 story; altered
Garage	4216	4	—	c. 1922	1 story
Krause Music Store facade	4611 N. Lincoln	1	Louis Sullivan	1922	w/ Wm. G. Presto, Arch.
Store bldg.	4716	2	Oscar Johnson	1922	alt.: Leland Thr.
Mixed-use for Jacob Lasker	4717–27	2	Grossman & Proskauer	1913–14	incl. thr., apts., stores
B. G. Elser Addition	4729–47	2	Grossman & Proskauer	1913–14	apts. & stores
Store for Henry A. Habel	4718	4	Oscar Johnson	1923	all white-glazed t.c.
Store bldg.	4724–28	4	Carl O. Kuehne	1923	1 story, 3 stores
Lincoln Park West (300 W)					
Ann Halsted Townhouses	1826–34	2	Adler & Sullivan	1884–85	
Apt. bldg.	2236–58 @ Belden	1	Simon B. Eisendrath	1910	ornate entrances
Lunt, W. (7000 N)					
Store bldg.	@ Glenwood, NW cor.	3	A. L. Himelblau	1921	stock t.c.
Magnolia, N. (1232 W)					
Apt. bldg.	@ Sunnyside, SE cor.	4	—	c. 1915	green-glazed t.c.
Milwaukee					
Store bldg.	1012	3	J. J. Cerny	1925	altered
Morse, W. (6900 N)					
Garage for P. C. Winn	1238–52	4	James Burns	1921	
Store bldg.	@ Glenwood, NW cor.	3	Arthur Jacobs	1921	originally 9 stores
North, W. (1600 N)					
Hyman Bros. Store	617 W. North	3	Hugo Schmidt	1923	DEMO

Name/Description	Address (if known)	Rank	Architect	Year	Remarks
CHICAGO: North Side (continued)					
North, W. (1600 N) (continued)					
N. Am. Business Exchange	@ Halsted, NW cor.	2	Carl O. Kuehne	1922	DEMO, t.c. @ Art Inst.
Store bldg. remodeling	1921	4	—	1924	t.c. storefront to exist. bldg.
Store bldg.	2321	3	—	c. 1922	altered
Paulina, N. (1700 W)					
Henry W. Schoenfeld Store	near Howard	2	Ralph C. Harris	1921	DEMO
Garage bldg.	7630–34	4	Percy T. Johnstone	1917	2 stories
Store bldg.	7638–48	2	Carl M. Almquist	1921–22	remodeled, now clinic
Bosert & Cohlgraff Store	7639–45	3	Midland T.C. Co.	1922	stock t.c.
Store bldg.	7647–51	3	Carl M. Almquist	1921	stock t.c.
Apt. bldg.	@ Jonquil, SE cor.	4	—	c. 1922	fake t.c. "ornament"
Pratt, W. (6800 N)					
Bldg. for Dr. Stewart	1311–13	3	D. S. Pentecost	1916	4-story apt. bldg.
Ridge					
Apt. bldg. w/ stores	@ Victoria, SE cor.	4	—	c. 1920	4 stories
Store bldg.	5825–33 @ Ardmore	4	—	c. 1920	altered
Sheridan					
Union Van Lines	957 @ Sheffield, SE cor.	1	Geo. Kingsley	1911, 1913	now United Van
Store bldg.	4920–24	4	Andrew Sandegren	c. 1915	mixed styles
Store bldg.	6748	4	—	c. 1922	marred by pt. & signs
Bldg. for A. Eisenstein	7642 Sheridan	2	Levy & Klein	1922	DEMO
Stratford Place, W. (3480 N)					
Geo. M. Harvey Hs.	600	2	Adler & Sullivan	1888	frame const.
Webster, W. (2200 N)					
Apt. bldg.	327–33	4	—	c. 1915	mixed styles
Wilson, W. (4600 N)					
McKee Bldg.	1134–38	4	W. Mead Walter	1910	2 stories
Other					
Helen Husser Res.	Buena Pk. (neighborhood)	1	Frank Lloyd Wright	1899	DEMO (1925)

CHICAGO: Northwest

Western Ave. (2400 W) to city limits; Madison St. (0) north to city limits. Listed by street location within that area.

Name/Description	Address (if known)	Rank	Architect	Year	Remarks
Armitage, W. (2000 N)					
Store bldg.	4343 @ Kostner	2	Jacobson	1922	partly DEMO, t.c. reused in new const.
Belmont					
Allen Sachs Bldg.	nr Lawndale (3700 W)	4	Joseph H. Klafter	1915	
California, N. (2800 W)					
Garage bldg.	@ Palmer	3	—	1922	
Central Park, N. (3600 W)					
Apt. bldg.	4417–21	4	C. O. Kuehne	1924	stock t.c.
Chicago, W. (800 N)					
Laundry bldg.	2621	2	S. N. Crowen	1925	DEMO
Store bldg.	3621–25 @ Monticello	3	Dubin & Eisenberg	1922	stock t.c.
Store bldg.	3632–38 @ Monticello	3:4	Dubin & Eisenberg	1923	altered
Theater for P. H. Sloan	3644	4	H. Zimmerman	1915–16	
Store bldg. for B. Z. Mory	@ Lotus (5432 W), SE cor.	3	A. L. Himelblau	1922	
Linnie Brown Store & Flat	5551–53	3	Wm. C. Miller	1922	

Name/Description	Address (if known)	Rank	Architect	Year	Remarks
CHICAGO: Northwest (continued)					
Cicero, N. (4800 W)					
Myer Linger Store	156–58	4	Ludgin & Leviton	1922	
Store bldg.	644–48	4	—	c. 1916	altered
B. P. Silverman Bldg.	2239	3	Jens J. Jensen	1925	stock t.c.; altered
Store bldg.	2957–59 @ Wellington	4	—	c. 1922	2 stories
Store bldg.	@ Barry, NE cor.	2	A. L. Himelblau	1925	DEMO
Stores & apts.	@ Roscoe, NW cor.	4	—	c. 1924	2 stories
Charles Andrews Store	@ Cornelia, NW cor.	2	Jens J. Jensen	1925	stock t.c.; altered
Store & flat for James Kutter	4238–40	2	Ralph W. Ermeling	1915	like Midland plate
Store bldg. for B. Z. Mory	@ Lotus, SE cor.	3	A. L. Himelblau	1922	DEMO
Diversey, W. (2800 N)					
Store bldg.	5008–10	3	Joseph H. Klafter	1926	stock t.c.
Division, W. (1200 N)					
Store bldg.	5138–46	2	Koenigsberg & Weisfeld	1926	stock t.c.
A. Goldberg Bldg.	5616–24 @ Parkside	2	A. L. Himelblau	1922	storefronts altered
Store bldg. for E. Miller	5733 @ Massasoit	3	A. L. Himelblau	1922	stock t.c.
Store bldg.	5847–59 @ Mayfield	3	A. L. Himelblau	1922	stock t.c.
B. Handler Stores	—	3	A. L. Himelblau	1921	stock t.c.
Elizabeth, N. (1232 W)					
Adolph & Wm. Loeb Apts.	157–59 @ W. Randolph	2	Adler & Sullivan	1891–92	DEMO
Elston					
Store bldg.	@ Central Pk., NW cor.	4	A. L. Himelblau	1922	DEMO
Elston-Crawford Bldg.	4346–56	3	A. L. Himelblau	1923	
Francisco, N. (2900 W)					
Francisco Terrace	253–57	2	Frank Lloyd Wright	1895	DEMO (1974)
Franklin Blvd., W. (500 N)					
Bunte Bros. Candy Factory	3301	3	Schmidt, Garden, & Martin	1921	now Westinghouse H.S.
Fullerton, W. (2400 N)					
Store bldg.	4306–10	4	A. L. Himelblau	1922	
Store bldg. for J. Stevens	4413–17	3	A. L. Himelblau	1922	DEMO
C. & H. Chipain Store	nr Laramie (5200 W)	3	Jens J. Jensen	1925	DEMO
Commercial bldg.	6920	3	—	1925	
Irving Park, W. (4000 N)					
Commercial bldg.	@ Ravenswood, SW cor.	3	Jens J. Jensen	1923–24	
Bldg. for A. Silverman	3020	3:4	A. L. Himelblau	1921	altered
Store bldg.	3408–10	3	—	1923/25	fire, to be DEMO
Store & apts.	3445–49	2	A. L. Himelblau	1925	stock t.c.
N. Asvos Store Bldg.	3940–42	3	Jens J. Jensen	1922	DEMO
People's Gas Lt. & Coke Co. office	4839	1	Elmslie w/ von Holst	1926	2 stories
R. Finder Store	5314	2	A. L. Himelblau	1922	stock t.c.
Kedzie, N. (3200 W)					
Store bldg.	3705–7	3	attr. H. B. Aarens	1924–25	altered
Store bldg.	3751–55	2	H. B. Aarens	1925	well preserved
A. J. Goldberg Bldg.	4201–5 @ Berteau	4	A. L. Himelblau	1922	altered
Swanson & Erickson Bldg.	@ Leland, NE cor.	2	Carl M. Almquist	1921–22	DEMO
Swanson & Erickson Bldg.	4745–47	1	Carl M. Almquist	1921	2 stories
Store bldg.	5326–28	3	Jens J. Jensen	1927	1 story, altered

Name/Description	Address (if known)	Rank	Architect	Year	Remarks
CHICAGO: Northwest (continued)					
Lawrence, W. (4800 N)					
Store for Louis Erickson	2415	3	Carl M. Almquist	1923	badly altered
Commercial bldg.	2421	3	Carl M. Almquist	1923	altered
Louis Cracko Store	2617	3	Levy & Klein	1922	
L. Wallen Bldg.	2647	3	Levy & Klein	1922	stock t.c. (NWT)
Bldg. for Chas. F. Hilland	2719	4	Edward Benson	1915	
Manor Garage/Auto Sales	2901–15	4	M. O. Nathan	1922	DEMO (1997)
Spaulding Bldg. for A. I. Levinson	@ Spaulding, SE cor.	2	Levy & Klein	1921	stores & apts.
Dr. A. M. Sowler Bldg.	@ Monticello	4	E. J. Sherry	1915	mixed styles
T. S. Robins Bldg.	3619–27 @ Monticello	2	Maurice L. Bein	1924	stock t.c.
Store for Swanson & Erickson	3642	2	Carl M. Almquist	1921	altered
Store bldg.	3715–19	2:3	Dubin & Eisenberg	1922	altered
The Lawfrank Bldg.	3832–44 @ Avers	3	B. J. Bruns	1922–23	stores & apts.
Charel Bldg.: Wm. Jeschek	4035 @ Keystone	3	B. J. Bruns	1922	stores & apts.
Madison (o)—see Chicago: Southwest listing					
Milwaukee					
Herman Braunstein Store	nr North Ave.	2	Adler & Sullivan	1884	DEMO (1968)
Store bldg.	2104	4	L. J. Allison	1923	2 stories
Commercial bldg.	3015–25 @ Monticello	1	Rissman & Hirschfield	1922	stock t.c. (NWT)
Commercial bldg.	3255	4	—	c. 1922	2 stories
Auto sales bldg.	3261–65	4	A. M. Ruttenberg	1925	mixed styles
Bldg. for Dr. H. Sered	4107	2	Koenigsberg & Weisfeld	1922	DEMO ?
Commercial bldg.	4253–57	3	attr. Levy & Klein	1922–23	stock t.c. (NWT)
Store & apt.	4412–14	4	James Guske	1922	
Store bldg.	4767–69	4	I. S. Stern	1925	some alts.
Kneipp & Kneggel Stores	4902–4	4	Jens J. Jensen	1922	1 story w/ 3 stores
J. & R. Sone Stores	4935–39 @ Gale	3	Wm. Schulze	1922	1 story w/ 3 store bays
Store & office bldg.	4956–58	3	Jens J. Jensen	1922	added signs detract
Monticello, N. (3632 W)					
Apt. bldg.	4700–2 @ Leland	4	—	c. 1922	4 stories
Montrose, W. (4400 N)					
Store bldg.	@ Artesian, NW cor.	4	Wm. C. Presto	1924	remodeled
Delevitt, Epstein, & Geiser	3040–50	3	M. H. Harris	1922	
Bowling Alley: A. D. Schuller	3318–22 @ Christiana	2:4	Wm. C. Presto	1924–25	badly altered
Burtonian Bldg.	@ Bernard (3432 W)	3	B. J. Bruns	1922	stores & flats
Store bldg./garage	3639–45	3	A. L. Himelblau	1923	
Stores & apts.	3752–58 @ Hamlin	2	Maurice L. Bein	1925	
E. Newman Bldg.	3910–14	3	A. L. Himelblau	1923	
North, W. (1600 N)					
Store bldg. for Philip Rosen	3325–29	2	attr. Ed. Steinborn	1922	DEMO
S. Dulkin Store Bldg.	nr Avers (3832 W)	3	Dubin & Eisenberg	1922	DEMO
S. Dulkin Store, Off. & Apts.	@ Springfield, SW cor.	3	Joseph Klafter	1922	
Furniture Salesroom	4221–23 @ Tripp	3	Edward Steinborn	1923	
Stores & apts.	5333 @ Lorel	3	Ernest N. Braucher	1923	2 stories
Bldg. for Philip Huthert	5339	4	G. W. Ashby	1915	
Bldg. for Linnie Brown	5551	3	Wm. C. Miller	1922	2 stories
Store & apt. bldg.	5845–49	3	attr. Levy & Klein	c. 1922	stock t.c. (NWT)

Name/Description	Address (if known)	Rank	Architect	Year	Remarks

C H I C A G O : Northwest (continued)

Northwest Highway (formerly Edison)

Name/Description	Address (if known)	Rank	Architect	Year	Remarks
Store & apt. for Chas. Stasch	@ Oliphant, NW cor.	3	Julian Floto	1922	2 stories

Pulaski (4000 W, formerly Crawford)

Name/Description	Address (if known)	Rank	Architect	Year	Remarks
Crawford Bldg. (S. Kutten)	1524–32	2	Ralph Ermeling	1916	2 stories
Garage for the Bandur Co.	2939	4	attr. John Campbell	1918	2 stories
Store bldg.	3323	4	Ohrenstein & Hild	1926	
Auto sales bldg.	3400	3	attr. L. I. Simon	c. 1925	mixed styles

Randolph, W. (150 N)

Name/Description	Address (if known)	Rank	Architect	Year	Remarks
Store bldg./garage	1325	3	—	c. 1919	1 story; altered

Rockwell, N. (2600 W)

Name/Description	Address (if known)	Rank	Architect	Year	Remarks
Louis Sigel Apts.	4632–36 @ Eastwood	4	A. L. Himelblau	1921	
Roser Stores & Apts.	4644–52	2	Wm. G. Barfield	1915	green-glazed t.c. (Am)
Commercial bldg.	4649–51	4	—	c. 1915	
Store bldg. for G. K. Hall	4653–57	4	Andrew E. Norman	1915	

Sacramento, N. (3000 W)

Name/Description	Address (if known)	Rank	Architect	Year	Remarks
Idell Apts. (M. W. Goldstein)	2d lot N. of Thomas St.	3	A. L. Himelblau	1922	4 stories

Sawyer, N. (3232 W)

Name/Description	Address (if known)	Rank	Architect	Year	Remarks
Apt. bldg.	5404	4	Steinborn & Simon	1923–24	2 stories

School, W. (3300 N)

Name/Description	Address (if known)	Rank	Architect	Year	Remarks
Store for B. J. Morris	@ Harding, NW cor.	4	A. L. Himelblau	1922	stock t.c.

Spaulding, N. (3300 W)

Name/Description	Address (if known)	Rank	Architect	Year	Remarks
R. S. Cook Apt. Bldg.	Ainslie to Argyle	4	Levy & Klein	1922	
Apt. bldg.	@ Argyle	3	Levy & Klein	1922	

Walnut, W. (234 N)

Name/Description	Address (if known)	Rank	Architect	Year	Remarks
E. C. Waller Apts.	2840–58	4	Frank Lloyd Wright	1895	DEMO

Washington, W. (100 N)

Name/Description	Address (if known)	Rank	Architect	Year	Remarks
Zion Temple	@ Ogden, SE cor.	2	Adler & Sullivan	1885	DESTROYED (fire, 1930)
Rosen & Fishell Store	4651	4	Levy & Klein	1922	converted to church
Galbraith & Bowers	4658–60	2	—	1923	1-story auto sales
Store bldg.	4748–50	4	J. L. Koster	1922	altered

Western, N. (2400 W)

Name/Description	Address (if known)	Rank	Architect	Year	Remarks
Store bldg.	6948	4	United Cigar Co.	1926	25' frontage
Store bldg.	7012–16	4	attr. Midland T.C. Co.	1924–25	stock t.c.
Commercial bldg.	@ Lawrence	4	C. O. Kuehne	1924	

Wilson, W. (4600 N)

Name/Description	Address (if known)	Rank	Architect	Year	Remarks
Apts. for R. Fleishman	2557–59 @ Rockwell	4	Daniel J. Schaffner	1915	3 stories

C H I C A G O : South Side

Lake Michigan and Indiana state line west to State St. (o); Roosevelt Road (1200 S) south to city limits.
Listed by street location within that area.

Name/Description	Address (if known)	Rank	Architect	Year	Remarks

Baltimore, S.

Name/Description	Address (if known)	Rank	Architect	Year	Remarks
Commercial bldg.	13310	2	—	c. 1930	reused P. Berry t.c.
Interstate National Bank	13310 (?)	1	Parker Berry	1917–18	DEMO

Calumet, S. (344 E)

Name/Description	Address (if known)	Rank	Architect	Year	Remarks
Roloson Townhouses	3213–19	2	Frank Lloyd Wright	1894	
Joseph Deimel Res.	3143	2	Adler & Sullivan	1886–87	

Clyde, S. (2100 E)

Name/Description	Address (if known)	Rank	Architect	Year	Remarks
August Anthony Apt. Bldg.	7018	4	A. G. Lund	1922	4 stories

Name/Description	Address (if known)	Rank	Architect	Year	Remarks
CHICAGO: South Side (continued)					
Commercial, S. (3000 E)					
People's Gas Lt. & Coke Co. office	8933	1	Elmslie w/ von Holst	1925–26	1 story
Grossman & Starck Bldg.	8951–55	4	Franz Roy	1923	2 stories
Frazer Bros. Bldg.	9036–42	2	F. Wm. Fischer	1924	added signs detract
Cottage Grove (800 E)					
L. G. Wagner Store	6236	3	A. E. Colcord	1922	DEMO
Store & office bldg.	6326	4	A. G. Lund	1924	24' frontage
T. J. Sekema Bldg.	6544–48	3	A. E. Colcord	1922	2 stories
Ellis, S. (1000 E)					
Michael Reese Hospital	2789	4	Richard E. Schmidt	1905	
Levi Eliel/Holzheimer Res.	3538	2	Adler & Sullivan	1886	DEMO (1961)
Mrs. Abraham Kohn Res.	3541	2	Adler & Sullivan	1885–86	DEMO
Dankmar Adler Res.	3543	2	Adler & Sullivan	1885–86	DEMO
Eli B. Felsenthal Res.	3545	2	Adler & Sullivan	1885–86	DEMO
Gustav Eliel Res.	4122	2	Adler & Sullivan	1886	
Forrestville, S. (532 E)					
Francis Apts.	4304	1	Frank Lloyd Wright	1895	DEMO (1971)
Garfield, E. (5500 S)					
Schulze Baking Co.	40 @ Wabash	1	John Ahlschlager & Son	1913–14	5-story factory
Greenwood, S. (1100 E)					
Dr. Allison Harlan Res.	4414	1	Frank Lloyd Wright	1892	DEMO (1963)
Indiana, S. (200 E)					
Store & factory bldg.	2536	2	E. P. Steinberg	1925	
Flats for Max Rothschild	3200	2	Adler & Sullivan	1882	DEMO (1978)
Houses for Max Rothschild	3201–5	2	Adler & Sullivan	1883	DEMO (1976)
3 Res.: Max Rothschild	@ 32d, SW cor.	2	Adler & Sullivan	1884	DEMO (1984)
Kehilath Anshe Ma'ariv Syn.	3301 @ 33d, SE cor.	1	Adler & Sullivan	1889–91	now Baptist church
Lake Park, S. (400 E)					
Albert W. Sullivan Res.	4575	1	Adler & Sullivan	1891–92	DEMO (1970)
Marquette Road, E. (6600 S)					
Store bldg.	@ Normal Ave. (500 W)	4	—	c. 1916	1 story
Michigan, S. (100 E)					
Mrs. Henry Horner Res.	1705	2	Adler & Sullivan	1886	DEMO
Anna McCormick Res.	1715	1	Adler & Sullivan	1884	DEMO (1970)
Morris Selz Residence	1717	1	Adler & Sullivan	1883	DEMO (1967)
Standard Club	@ 24th, SW cor.	2	Adler & Sullivan	1887–88	DEMO (1931)
Auto sales bldg.	2522	2	—	1923	stock t.c. (NWT)
Leopold Schlesinger Res.	2805	2	Adler & Sullivan	1884–85	DEMO
Abraham Kuh Res.	3141	2	Adler & Sullivan	1885	DEMO
Louis E. Frank Res.	3219	2	Adler & Sullivan	1884	DEMO (1968)
Commercial bldg.	10341	3	—	1918	
Harry Dekker Bldg.	10646	2	Wm. G. Carnegie	1916	some alts.
Roseland Safety Deposit Bank	11108–14	1	Wm. G. Carnegie	1914	storefronts altered
Commercial bldg.	11431 @ 114th Pl.	1:2	Clarence Hatzfeld	1920	altered
Jos. T. Spiker Bldg.	11717–21	2	Wm. Nicholson	1917	
W. C. Jurgenson Store	11739–41	1:2	Wm. Carnegie	1915	remodeled to church
Oakwood, E. (3946 S)					
Apt. hs.	—	4	Dwight H. Perkins	c. 1902	ornate entrance

Name/Description	Address (if known)	Rank	Architect	Year	Remarks
CHICAGO: South Side (continued)					
Pershing Road, E. (3900 S)					
Store bldg.	321–27 @ Calumet	3	Newhouse & Bernham	1923	remodeled (1947): Nathan
Store bldg.	@ Langley, NW cor.	3	Albert Anis	1923	50' frontage
Prairie, S. (300 E)					
Addition: Wirt Dexter Res.	1721	2	Adler & Sullivan	1889	DEMO
Henry Stern Res.	2915	2	Adler & Sullivan	1885	DEMO (1959)
Samuel Stern Res.	2963	2	Adler & Sullivan	1885	DEMO (1959)
Ira A. Heath Res.	3132	2	Adler & Sullivan (?)	1889	
Martin Barbe Res.	3157	1	Adler & Sullivan	1884	DEMO (1958)
Flats for Max M. Rothschild	3200	2	Adler & Sullivan	1882–83	DEMO (1978)
State, S. (0)					
Store bldg.	3310–24	1	A. L. Himelblau	1924	DEMO
Store bldg., 1 story	4824–32	2	Wm. L. Hoffman, Jr.	1923–24	DEMO
American Tag Co.	6143	2	J. J. Meldahl	1917	DEMO
Stony Island, S. (1600 E)					
Transp. Bldg. @ Colum. Expo.	6301:Jackson Pk.	1	Adler & Sullivan	1891–93	DEMO, temp. Fair bldg.
Store & garage for I. Perlman	6912–20	2	Jacques J. Kocher	1921	1-story brk. w/ t.c.
Peter Foote Store Bldg.	@ 79th	1	Wm. G. Carnegie	1915	DEMO
Store & offices	@ 79th, SW cor.	4	Wm. H. Lautz	1922	
Wabash, S. (45 E)					
Int. alt.: Arthur Block	2131	-	Adler & Sullivan	1886	DEMO (1964)
Henry Leopold Res.	2516	3	Adler & Sullivan	c. 1882	DEMO
Sigmund Hyman Res.	2624	3	Adler & Sullivan	c. 1882	DEMO
Benjamin Lindauer Res.	3312	2	Adler & Sullivan	1885	DEMO (1958)
Hugo Goodman Res.	3333	2	Adler & Sullivan	1885–86	DEMO
Abraham Strauss Res.	3337	1	Adler & Sullivan	1884	DEMO (c. 1953)
3 Res.: Victor Falkenau	3420–24	1	Adler & Sullivan	1888–90	DEMO (1958)
Woodlawn, S. (1200 E)					
Isidore Heller Hs.	5132	1	Frank Lloyd Wright	1897	
14th, E. (1400 S)					
Stable for Mandel Bros.	nr Michigan, @ alley	3	Adler & Sullivan	1884	DEMO
21st, E. (2100 S)					
Remodel: Sinai Temple	@ Indiana, SW cor.	—	Adler & Sullivan	1891–92	DEMO
35th, E. (3500 S)					
Marcus C. Stearns Res.	@ Lk. Pk., NW cor.	2	Adler & Sullivan	1885	DEMO
36th, E. (3600 S)					
Mrs. Mary M. Lively Res.	533	2	Adler & Sullivan	1887	DEMO
Store bldg.	@ Cottage Grove	3	Joseph H. Klafter	1924	1 story
39th, E. (3900 S)					
Store bldg.	@ Calumet, SE cor.	2	Henry L. Newhouse	1923	
ICRR Station	@ ICRR	3	Adler & Sullivan	1886	DEMO
43d, E. (4300 S)					
D. Rosenheim Store	nr Greenwood	3	R. Harold Zook	1923	DEMO
ICRR Station	@ ICRR	3	Adler & Sullivan	1886	DEMO
47th, E. (4700 S)					
Commercial bldg.	525 @ Forrestville	4	—	c. 1915	
Eli Felsenthal Bldg.	701–3	1	Louis Sullivan	1905	DEMO (1982)
Apt. bldg. w/ stores	1120–26	3	—	1915	U-shaped plan
51st, E. (5100 S)					
Bldg. w/ four stores	@ Indiana	3	Rawson & Eisenberg	1925	

Name/Description	Address (if known)	Rank	Architect	Year	Remarks
CHICAGO: South Side (continued)					
53d, E. (5300 S)					
Store bldg.	1350–64	4	—	c. 1920	
Store bldg.	1369	4	Olson & Berg	1922	1 story
67th, E. (6700 S)					
N. Johannsen Bldg.	@ Blackstone, NW cor.	4	Swen Linderoth	1916	DEMO
75th, E. (7500 S)					
Bldg. for Dr. Thos. H. Kelly	742–46	1	Albert A. Schwartz	1923	now church
Store bldg.	1534	4	Edward McClellan	1922	1 story; stock t.c.
Store bldg.	1716	4	C. W. Lampe & Co.	1922	
Store bldg.	2116–20	4	—	c. 1916	1 story; stock t.c.
Store bldg. for B. A. Lewis	@ Oglesby	4	Levy & Klein	1923	
79th, E. (7900 S)					
Stores & apts.	@ Vernon, SE cor.	4	Levy & Klein	1924	
J. S. Glickauf Bldg.	2728–32 @ Burnham	4	Levy & Klein	1923	stores & apts.
Expo. Bldgs. @ Cheltenham Beach	@ Lake Michigan	—	Adler & Sullivan	1886	DEMO (c. 1900)
103d, E. (10300 S)					
Offices for Fred'k H. Bartlett	nr M. L. King	2	Thos. R. Bishop	1916	DEMO
119th, E. (11900 S)					
Store bldg.	5–11	4	—	c. 1920	1 story

CHICAGO: Southwest

State St. (o) & Halsted (800 W) west to city limits; Madison St. (o) south to city limits. Listed by street location within that area.

Name/Description	Address (if known)	Rank	Architect	Year	Remarks
Archer					
Hyman Goldstein Store	4239–41	3	Albert M. Ruttenberg	1922	mixed styles
Bldg. for Bartlett Realty	4800 block	2	—	1924	DEMO
Ashland, S. (1600 W)					
Reuben Rubel Res.	320	2	Adler & Sullivan	1884	DEMO (1958)
Store bldg. for Thomas Slader	4716	3	Chas. J. Grotz	1922	
Store alterations	4830	3	Halprin & Braun	1926	
Store bldg.	4939	3	Wm. Schulze	1926	
Elmer Olson Bldg. (2d)	8524–26	4	E. McClellan	1928	
Commercial bldg.	8623–25	4	—	c. 1928	3 stories
Elmer Olson Bldg. (1st)	8740–44	4	E. McClellan	1927	
Blue Island					
Fuhrman & Forster Co.	1647–49	3	Wm. Sevic	1924	1st fl. altered
Central Park, S. (3600 W)					
Apt. bldg.	@ Gladys, NE cor.	2	Wm. G. Krieg	1922	
Cermak, W. (2200 S, formerly 22d St.)					
Rubin Bros. Bldg.	2129	3:4	A. L. Himelblau	1923	altered
Cicero, S. (4800 W)					
Bldg. for Muskow & Lazowsky	519–21	3	Raphael N. Friedman	1915	stock t.c.
National Laundry Co.	749–59	4	Samuel N. Crowen	1925	mixed styles
Halsted, S. (800 W)					
Store for Landfield	5226–28	3	Joseph Cohen & Co.	1924	
Store bldg. for R. H. Holmes	6449–55	2	J. J. Kocher	1921	DEMO
Store bldg.	6503	2	Albert Anis	1923	DEMO

Name/Description	Address (if known)	Rank	Architect	Year	Remarks
C H I C A G O : Southwest (continued)					
Halsted, S. (800 W) (continued)					
Store bldg. for J. E. Temple	6508–10	2	A. G. Lund	1917	some alts.
A. J. Surey Store Bldg.	6514	4	Chas. A. Strandel	1915	2 stories
Furniture bldg.	6821	3:4	Wm. H. Lautz	1922	stock t.c.; altered
Bldg. for G. E. Anderson	@ 69th, NW cor.	1:3	Swen Linderoth	1915	altered; 1/2 DEMO
Stores & apts.	6919–21	3	attr. Chas. Archer	c. 1927	
Store bldg.	7106	3	Kocher & Larson	1923–24	DEMO
F. Wolf Bldg.	7534–38	3	A. L. Himelblau	1922	stock t.c.
Store bldg.	7708–12	2	Thos. R. Bishop	1922	DEMO
Store for I. Lasker	7747–49	2	Thos. R. Bishop	1922	
Geo. Valhackis Bldg.	8059 @ 81st, NE cor.	2	Chas. J. Grotz	1922	stock t.c.
Harrison, W. (600 S)					
M. Welensky Store Bldg.	3839–41	3	A. L. Himelblau	1922	DEMO
Store & flat	4015	4	E. H. Braucher	1924	
Store bldg.	near Lotus	3	A. L. Himelblau	1923–24	DEMO
Independence, S. (3800 W)					
Store for H. Goldblatt	@ Harrison	2	A. L. Himelblau	1921	DEMO
Kedzie, S. (3200 W)					
Leo Behrstock Bldg.	1250	2:4	Halprin & Braun	1922	altered
Store bldg.	1302	3:4	attr. Ed Steinborn	c. 1925	altered
B. Goldman Store Bldg.	@ W. 15th, NE cor.	3	A. L. Himelblau	1921	DEMO
Store bldg.	3803–9	3	A. L. Himelblau	1922	altered
K. Sidder Store	@ 54th Pl., NE cor.	3	Levy & Klein	1924	
Loomis, S. (1400 W)					
J. F. Dooley Bldg.	214–18	3	Halperin & Braun	1921–22	DEMO
Madison, W. (0)					
Wm. Brizzolara Bldg.	@ Sangamon	3	Joseph T. Fortin	1922	DEMO
Auto Sales Bldg.	2808–10	3	A. L. Himelblau	1921	DEMO
Store bldg.	4111	3	A. L. Himelblau	1921–22	DEMO
Sullivan Bldg.	5130	4	Paul Gerhardt	1921	
Isaac Frank Bldg.	5345	3	M. O. Nathan	1922	DEMO
Store bldg.	5403–9	4	—	c. 1924	fake t.c. "ornament"
Philip M. Yarwitz Bldg.	5667	3:4	W. F. Pagels	1923	altered
Apt. bldg.: Newman, Baskerville	5712	2	Purcell & Elmslie	1913	
Bldg. for Mrs. Finder	5722	4	A. L. Himelblau	1921–22	altered
Store & apt. bldg.	5902 @ Mayfield	3	Fred Lindquist	1925	3 stories
Polk, W. (800 S)					
Factory for Wright & Lawther	@ Beach, NE cor.	3	Adler & Sullivan	1883	DEMO
Pulaski, S. (4000 W)					
Store bldg. w/ apts.	158 @ Adams, NW cor.	4	A. L. Himelblau	1923	2 stories
Store bldg. w/ apts.	@ Adams, NE cor.	4	A. L. Himelblau	1922	2 stories
Store bldg.	@ Van Buren, NW cor.	2	A. L. Himelblau	1922	1 story
Store bldg.	1422	2	A. F. Rusy	1923	DEMO
Store bldg. for A. Chapman	@ Eddy, SE cor.	3	A. L. Himelblau	1923	
Roosevelt Road, W. (1200 S)					
Bldg. for Weiss & Javshitz	837–39	4	Geo. H. Dubin	1916	DEMO
Store bldg. for M. Bank	1140	3	Edward Steinborn	1925	DEMO
The Orpheus Theater	— Roosevelt ?	4	Aroner & Somers	c. 1912	mixed styles, DEMO
M.G.M.H. Investment	@ Paulina, SW cor.	4	Levy & Klein	1923	
Store bldg.	2802 @ California	3	attr. Frank L. Fry	c. 1922	altered

Name/Description	Address (if known)	Rank	Architect	Year	Remarks
CHICAGO : Southwest (continued)					
Roosevelt Road, W. (1200 S) (continued)					
Bldg. for A. Pink	3425	2	Alex. L. Levy	1915	DEMO
Bldg. for Kaplan & Schuhter	3712	2:3	A. L. Himelblau	1919	badly altered
B. Schuhter	3915	3:4	Dubin & Eisenberg	1920	badly altered
Store & apt. bldg.	5910–14	2:3	A. L. Himelblau	1927	altered
Stores & apts.	5934–44 @ Mason	3	Maurice L. Bein	1924	some alterations
Throop, S. (1300 W)					
W. Chicago Clubhouse	119	3	Adler & Sullivan	1886	DEMO (1953)
12th Place, W.					
Jewish Manual Trn. School	554	2	Adler & Sullivan	1889–90	DEMO (1954)
15th, W. (1500 S)					
Standard Elevator Co. Factory	1515	3	Adler & Sullivan	1891	
16th, W. (1600 S)					
H. Goldblatt Store	3237–47 @ Sawyer	3	A. L. Himelblau	1922	stock t.c.
Store bldg.	@ Springfield, NW cor.	3	A. L. Himelblau	1922	altered
S. Pikowski Bldg.	@ Springfield, SW cor.	3	A. L. Himelblau	1922	stock t.c.
Store bldg.	5747–49	3	Joseph Cohen & Co.	1926	
26th, W. (2600 S)					
D. Kapson Store Bldg.	3325	3	Levy & Klein	1921	
Store bldg.	3508–12	3:4	Chas. Vedra	1923	marred by sign panel
P. Karlosky Store	3916	4	J. B. Rezney	1921	mixed styles
L. Klein Store Bldg.	3920–22	3	Anton Charvat	1923	"granite" t.c. finish
M. Telechanski Bldg.	4070–78 @ Kendale	4	Erich J. Patelski	1922	some alterations
Glass Novelty Co.	4418 @ Kostner	3	Sidney Minchen	1925	factory bldg.
47th, W. (4700 S)					
Emil Frau Bldg.	nr Union (700 W)	4	A. G. Lund	1924	altered
Store & apt.	1936	3	Chas. J. Grotz	1922	2 stories; stock t.c.
Office bldg. & shelter	2101 @ Hoyne	4	Wm. G. Krieg	1927	
Store bldg.	@ Western	3	Chas. J. Grotz	1924	
51st, W. (5100 S)					
Joe Kanske Store	1503	4	A. G. Lund	1917	2 stories, altered
Store bldg.	@ Paulina	3	Chas. J. Grotz	1924	1 story
E. Kaufman Store & Flat	1915	4	Jesse E. Scheller	1923	storefront altered
Jas. Svejda Store Bldg.	1934 @ Winchester	4	Chas. J. Grotz	1923	storefront altered
C. E. Wach Bldg.	1951	3	Ed F. Wach	1921	storefront altered
63d, W. (6300 S)					
Later Bros. Store Bldg.	nr Kedzie (3200 W)	3	A. G. Lund	1923	
Store bldg.	3750–52	3	Jens J. Jensen	1927–28	1 story
69th, W. (6900 S)					
M. Schultz Store & Apts.	917–19	3	A. L. Himelblau	1923	DEMO; 3 story
S. Rosenzweig Garage	@ Sangamon, SE cor.	3	Dubin & Eisenberg	1923	
Store bldg.	2614–16	2	Scott-Larson Co.	1928	
79th, W. (7900 S)					
Store bldg.	438	4	A. G. Lund	1923	2 stories
Store for J. J. Curtin	936–38	3:4	Robert S. Smith	1922	altered
Store bldg.	@ Racine, NW cor.	4	—	c. 1920	2 stories
Edward Bundie Bldg.	1243	3	Swen Linderoth	1915	2 stories
Bldg. for Adolph C. Larsen	@ Throop (1300 W)	4	Swen Linderoth	1915	
Store for Sam Sorte	1326–28	3	Wm. H. Lautz	1922	DESTROYED (fire, 1989)
87th, W. (8700 S)					
L. Pihl Bldg.	1338–40	4	W. Owen	1925	2 story

Name/Description	Address (if known)	Rank	Architect	Year	Remarks
Antioch					
C. J. Roeschlein Store	—	3	F. J. Teich	1922	
Aurora					
Aurora Watch Co. Factory	603 S. LaSalle	3	Adler & Sullivan	1883–84	DESTROYED (fire, 1989)
American National Bank	1 S. Broadway @ Galena	1	George Elmslie	1922	L. Fournier, Assoc. Arch.
Old 2d National Bank	37 River St. @ Downer	1	George Elmslie	1924	gable roof
Newhall/Keystone Bldg.	24–36 N. Stolp	1	George Elmslie	1922–23	4 stories
Graham Bldg.	33 N. Stolp	1	George Elmslie	1924–26	8 stories
Healy Chapel (Funeral Hm.)	5 E. Downer Pl.	1	George Elmslie	1927–28	Sulliv. & Prairie
Berwyn					
Stores & apts.	6318–24 Cermak	2	—	c. 1922	3-story yellow brk. w/ t.c.
Parthenon/Berwyn Theater	Cermak @ Ridgeland, NW cor.	4	E. P. Rupert	1923	mixed styles
Store bldg.	6634 Cermak	3	—	c. 1922	2-story yellow brk. w/ t.c.
Store & apt. bldg.	6301–5 Roosevelt	3	—	c. 1922	3-story yellow brk. w/ t.c.
Blue Island					
Store bldg. for Teresa Klein	13042–44 Western	1	Albert S. Hecht	1915	ground fl. remodeled
Calumet City					
Thornton Twp. High School	755 Pulaski Road	1	Elmslie w/ Wm. Hutton	1934	
Chicago Heights					
Victoria Hotel	Illinois @ Halsted, NW cor.	1	Adler & Sullivan	1892–93	DEMO (1961)
Cicero					
Residence	1634 S. Austin	4	Ira C. Saxe	1925	t.c. accents & trim
Commercial bldg.	5210 Cermak	4	A. L. Himelblau	1923	
Norbert Krametbaur Bldg.	5639 Cermak	3	Rezny & Krippner	1922	DEMO
Store bldg.	Cermak @ 57th Ave., NE cor.	4	—	c. 1922	altered, 57th side O.K.
J. Blumenthal Bldg.	5701 Cermak @ 57th	3	Levy & Klein	1921	stores & apts.
Store & apts.	Cicero @ 16th St., SW cor.	4	—	c. 1922	
Store bldg.	2007–11 Cicero	2:4	M. H. Harris	1923	badly altered
Windy City Bowling Assoc.	Cicero @ 21st St., SE cor.	4	Adolph Lonek	1922	vac., to be DEMO
Commercial bldg.	2125–27 Cicero	4	Filas & Vittner	1922	DEMO
Store & apt. bldg.	Laramie @ 22d Pl., NW cor.	4	—	c. 1922	3 stories, stock t.c.
Store bldg.	2340 Laramie @ 23d Pl.	3	A. L. Himelblau	1922	altered
Store bldg.	Laramie @ 24th Pl., NW cor.	2:3	Arthur Jacobs	1922	storefronts altered
Bartelstein Bldg.	2336 Laramie @ 24th St.	3	A. L. Himelblau	1922	DEMO
Store bldg.	5132 25th St.	4	J. J. Cerny	1927	white-glazed brk. & t.c.
Store bldg.	5406 25th St.	4	—	c. 1922	altered; t.c. eagle
Factory bldg.	1829 55th Ave.	3	—	1927	1 story, stock t.c.
Lusterlite Enamels	1425 55th Court	3	E. A. Hogenson	1926	factory bldg.
Des Plaines					
A. Quilici Store Bldg.	1505 Ellinwood @ Center	2	Midland T.C. Co.	1921	DEMO (1986)
Quilici Stores & Apts.	705–9 Center St.	1	Robert P. Ninneman	1923	DEMO (1986)
B. H. Winkelman Store	1514 Miner (NW Hwy)	3	attr. Midland T.C. Co.	1921	altered
Downers Grove					
Theater for E. A. Baxter	1009 Curtis	2:4	Wm. G. Barfield	1915	badly altered
Store bldg.	—	4	Robert S. Smith	1926	1 story
Evanston					
The Evanston (apts.)	502–10 Lee @ Hinman	2	John D. Atchison	1901	3 stories

Name/Description	Address (if known)	Rank	Architect	Year	Remarks
SUBURBAN CHICAGO (continued)					
Evanston (continued)					
James Patten Res.	1426 Ridge	1	Geo. W. Maher	1901	DEMO (c. 1938)
Univ. Bldg. (store & off.)	Chicago @ Davis, NW cor.	2	Geo. W. Maher	1905–6	transitional design
Swift Hall of Engineering	Northwestern Univ.	3	Geo. W. Maher	1908–9	transitional design
Commercial bldg.	1016 Davis	4	E. O. Blake	1915	white-glazed brk. & t.c.
Lord's Dept. Store	625 Davis	4	Mead Walter	c. 1907	
Joliet					
J. P. Stevens Bldg.	—	4	C. W. Webster	1916	
B. Berkovitz Store	717 N. Chicago (?)	2	C. W. Webster	1926	
A. O. Marshall School	Harwood @ Stirling	4	Ashby, Ashby, & Schulze	c. 1916	Wright influence
Oak Park					
Edw. W. McCready Hs.	231 N. Euclid	2	Spencer & Powers	1907	Prairie w/ Sulliv. entry
Service station addition	Euclid @ Madison, NE cor.	4	M. E. Zaldokas	1923	
Store bldg.	201–9 Harrison	2	A. L. Himelblau	1922	brk. patterns & t.c.
Store bldg.	334 Harrison	4	attr. A. L. Himelblau	c. 1922	stock t.c.
John Farson House	217 S. Home	1	Geo. W. Maher	1897	Sulliv. & Prairie
Garage bldg.	Lake @ Lincoln, SE cor.	4	Edw. N. Nordlie	1926	
Francisco Terrace (2d)	Lake @ N. Linden	2	Harry Weese & Assoc.	1978	reuse of FLW t.c.
Store bldg.	729 Madison	4	Max Lowel Cable	1922	
Commercial bldg.	809 Madison	4	—	c. 1924	now printing co.
Commercial bldg. w/ apts.	1047–53 Madison @ WI	4	Wm. F. Pagels	1924	stock t.c.
Stores & apts.	200–12 Marion @ Pleasant	4	Thos. R. Bishop	1922	mixed styles
Masonic Hall & Stores	126–34 Oak Park Ave. S.	3	Jens J. Jensen	1922	stock t.c.
G. H. Schneider & Co. Bldg.	137–47 Oak Park Ave. S.	4	A. A. Packard	1922	2 stories
Sullivan Lane Townhouses	425–9 Oak Park Ave. S.	3	James Edward Collins	1989	brk. & stucco w/ Sulliv. orn.
Store bldg.	835 Oak Park Ave. S.	4	—	c. 1922	
Commercial bldg.	6126–34 Roosevelt	4	—	c. 1925	3 stories
Commercial bldg.	6136 Roosevelt	4	—	c. 1924	1 story, altered
Store & office bldg.	721–23 South Blvd.	2	A. A. Packard	1924	stock t.c.
Apt. bldg.	715–17 Washington	4	—	c. 1922	U-shaped plan
River Forest					
William Winslow Hs.	515 Auvergne	1	Frank Lloyd Wright	1893	
Chauncey Williams Res.	530 Edgewood Pl.	2	Frank Lloyd Wright	1895	ornament @ entry
Riverside					
Henry Babson Res.	230 N. Longcommon	1	Louis Sullivan	1907	DEMO (1960)
Alterations: Babson Res.	230 N. Longcommon	-	Geo. Elmslie	1925	Sullivan hs. des., DEMO
Henry Babson Service Bldgs.	320 Riverside Dr.	1	Purcell & Elmslie	1915–16	remodeled (1955); 7 apts.
St. Charles					
Garage for R. C. Judd	11 S. 2d Ave.	2	Midland T.C. Co.	1921	now altered for offices
Waukegan					
Bldg. for Fred Bishoff	—	3	C. W. Webster	1916	stock t.c.
Wilmette					
The Boulevard (stores & apts.)	1101–7 Central @ 11th	4	—	c. 1915	
Frank Scheidenhelm Hs.	804 Forest Ave.	3	Geo. W. Maher	1902	Sulliv. trim
Post Office & Store	1150 Wilmette Ave.	1	Midland T.C. Co.	1921	facade DESTROYED
Commercial bldg.	1157–61 Wilmette Ave.	4	—	c. 1922	stock t.c.
Winnetka					
Warehouse for E. C. Iredale	—	4	W. C. Carlson	1921	DEMO

NOTES

CHAPTER 1:
NATURE PATTERNS IN THE URBAN LANDSCAPE

1. Louis Sullivan, "The Tall Office Building Artistically Considered," *Lippincott's Magazine* 57 (Mar. 1896), as quoted in *Louis Sullivan: The Public Papers*, ed. Robert Twombly (Chicago: University of Chicago Press, 1988), 108. Sullivan's essay was reprinted in other publications as well.

2. One of the more convincing arguments is put forth by James Grady in his essay "C. R. Mackintosh and Louis Sullivan: A Comparison of Celts," *Architectural Prospect* 4, no. 106 (Winter 1956): 10–15.

3. Edgar Kaufmann Jr., *Louis Sullivan and the Architecture of Free Enterprise* (Chicago: Art Institute of Chicago, 1956), 15.

4. Paul E. Sprague, *The Drawings of Louis Henry Sullivan* (Princeton: Princeton University Press, 1979), 4, 6.

5. Ibid., 3, 5, 7.

6. Louis Sullivan, *Kindergarten Chats and Other Writings* (New York: Wittenborn, Schultz, 1947), 189.

7. Louis H. Sullivan, *A System of Architectural Ornament: According with a Philosophy of Man's Powers* (1924; New York: Eakins Press, 1967), n.p. This was originally published by the AIA. The previous quotation is from the same source.

8. Ibid., plate 9.

9. See Lauren S. Weingarden's essay, "Louis Sullivan's System of Architectural Ornament," in *Louis H. Sullivan: A System of Architectural Ornament*, foreword by John Zukowsky and Susan Glover Godlewski (New York: Rizzoli, 1990), 12.

10. Leon Lefevre, *Architectural Pottery* (London: Scott, Greenwood and Son, 1900), 364.

11. The term "terra cotta" once referred to a variety of different clay products. After 1910, the term was understood to refer to the material for building claddings and ornament. Before the turn of the century, these same building components in terra cotta were called "architectural terra cotta." In addition, several Chicago companies manufactured "terra-cotta fireproofing." Essentially, these companies produced variations of hollow tile, and in the 1880s, the material was called "porous terra cotta" or "terra-cotta lumber." Today, these materials are generally known as "structural clay tile." None of these products, which are mentioned in histories of Chicago construction, should be confused with architectural terra cotta.

12. F. W. Fitzpatrick, "American Architecture," *Western Architect* (Sept. 1913): 75–77.

13. For the nineteenth-century industrial city, Chicago architects pioneered structural and technical innovations in construction and created original designs responsive to functional needs. This movement is now called the Chicago School (c. 1883–c. 1906). The vitality of the Chicago School

waned, and progressive design was furthered by a second generation of architects led by Frank Lloyd Wright. These architects focused on smaller-scale buildings, especially free-standing houses in Chicago suburbs. Now known as the Prairie School (c. 1893–c. 1916), this movement produced an innovative style for suburban residences. In suburbia, the house was an object in space, a sculptural piece in an open setting. With horizontal lines, wide overhanging roofs, and spacious flowing interiors, Prairie School residential designs, expanded in plan and section, expressed interlocking mass and space. A number of books have explored these two movements; the widely recognized primers are Carl Condit, *The Chicago School of Architecture* (Chicago: University of Chicago Press, 1964); and H. Allen Brooks, *The Prairie School* (New York: Norton, 1972).

14. I established these parameters through extensive field surveys and I cross-referenced my findings to dates of orders listed in Statler Gilfillen, ed., *American Terra Cotta Index* (Palos Park, Ill.: Prairie School Press, 1974) and other sources, such as building permit records and references. I conducted all field surveys referred to in the notes.

15. Ronald E. Schmitt, "Sullivanesque Architecture and Terra Cotta," in *The Midwest in American Architecture*, ed. John S. Garner (Urbana: University of Illinois Press, 1991), 164–65.

CHAPTER 2: EARLY SULLIVANESQUE

1. Louis H. Sullivan, *Autobiography of an Idea* (New York: Press of the American Institute of Architects, 1924), 255–56. One Sullivan biographer, Robert Twombly, asserts that these events occurred two years later than Sullivan recalled. See Robert Twombly, *Louis Sullivan: His Life and Work* (Chicago: University of Chicago Press, 1986), 96, 98.

2. Sullivan worked for Furness and Hewitt, Architects, in Philadelphia for only a short time, from early summer to fall of 1873, before the Panic of 1873 hit the firm hard and cost Sullivan his job. Sullivan arrived in Chicago just before Thanksgiving 1873 to join his parents, who had moved to Chicago from Boston. Many characteristics that have been attributed to Sullivan could apply to Furness. Furness was highly creative, individualistic, eccentric, outspoken, and could be critical of colleagues and their work. Born in Philadelphia, Frank Furness (1839–1912) learned about architecture in the New York office of Richard Morris Hunt. Schooled in classical styles, Furness instead produced "Victorian Gothic" designs in a highly original and personal expression after he opened his own office (1867) in Philadelphia. Characterized by bold forms and sometimes exaggerated scales, his designs were idiosyncratic and didn't lend themselves to easy classification. Furness was dismissed by earlier architectural historians and critics because of his association with the Victorian Gothic; but he has been rediscovered by later generations. See James F. O'Gorman, *The Architecture of Frank Furness* (Philadelphia: Philadelphia Museum of Art, 1973), for more on Frank Furness.

3. I made these assessments of facade compositions after thoroughly reviewing Adler and Sullivan buildings or photographs of them. A photographic record of early buildings was prepared by Ralph Marlowe Line and is now in the collection of the University of Illinois at Urbana-Champaign (UIUC). I also have an extensive collection.

4. Twombly, *Louis Sullivan: His Life and Work*, 168. Twombly quoted Adler, "The Chicago Auditorium," *Architectural Record* (Apr.–June 1892): 415–34.

5. "Painting and Decorating: Plastic and Color Decoration of the Auditorium," *Industrial Chicago: The Building Interests*, vols. 1 and 2 (Chicago: Goodspeed, 1891), 2:490. This statement by Sullivan was reprinted in Twombly, *Louis Sullivan: The Public Papers*.

6. Louis Sullivan, "Ornament in Architecture," *Engineering Magazine* 3 (Aug. 1892), reprinted in Twombly, *Louis Sullivan: The Public Papers*, 80.

7. Two impost blocks survive in collections, one at the University of Illinois at Urbana-Champaign (where it is displayed behind the Architecture Building) and another at the Graham Foundation, Chicago.

8. Commission on Chicago Historical and Architectural Landmarks (now Commission on Chicago Landmarks [hereafter, CCL]), plaque in front of Getty Tomb, designated a city landmark in 1971, Graceland Cemetery, Chicago, Illinois.

9. Barbara Lanctot, *A Walk through Graceland Cemetery* (Chicago: Chicago School of Architecture Foundation, 1977), 39.

10. William H. Jordy, "The Tall Building," in *Louis Sullivan: The Function of Ornament*, ed. Wim de Wit (New York: Norton, 1986), 71.

11. *Commercial and Architectural St. Louis* (St. Louis: Dumont Jones, 1891), 162, 163, 197.

12. Hugh Morrison, *Louis Sullivan: Prophet of Modern Architecture* (New York: Norton, 1962), 279.

13. John A. Bryan, *Missouri's Contribution to American Architecture* (St. Louis: St. Louis Architectural Club, 1928), 353.

14. George McCue and Frank Peters, *A Guide to the Architecture of St. Louis* (Columbia: University of Missouri Press, 1989), 42–43.

15. Sullivan's mother died in 1892, and so Louis Sullivan occupied the house from about 1892 to 1896. He was displaced by his brother, Albert, who moved his family into the house. A squabble over the house soured the relationship between the two brothers. Twombly, *Louis Sullivan: His Life and Work*, 208–9.

16. *The Northwestern Terra Cotta Company*, company catalog (Chicago: Northwestern Terra Cotta Co., c. 1908), 41. A copy of this catalog in the library of the University of Illinois at Urbana-Champaign (UIUC) bears a dated inscription: "Donated to the Architecture Library on May 21, 1908 by Mr. Fritz Wagner, Jr."

17. Morrison, *Louis Sullivan*, 175–76.

18. See Kirsten Kingsley, "Reuse of the Gage Building" (master's thesis, School of Architecture, University of Illinois at Urbana-Champaign, 1990).

19. The fragment at the Art Institute of Chicago was the gift of Dubin, Dubin, and Black, Architects, in memory of Henry and Anne Dubin, 1964.

20. Hugh C. Miller, *The Chicago School of Architecture* (Washington, D.C.: United States Department of the Interior, National Park Service, 1973), 16.

21. The initial 1898 design on Madison Street was nine stories high and three bays wide. A nine-story expansion was proposed for the State-Madison corner. In the summer of 1902, the owners approved proceeding with construction but wanted twelve stories. Sullivan redesigned the building for twelve floors. He also accommodated the client's desire to maintain operation of the old store buildings on the site through the Christmas season. The second stage of construction was, in turn, phased with north and south halves. In October 1902, foundation construction commenced. "Wells" (concrete piers) for the new building were dug by hand in the vacated basements of the existing buildings. Occupancy continued above. Sullivan said: "It was not considered expedient to sink more than five or six wells at one time as the operation of a greater number would require a larger gang of men than could have been used effectively." Foundation construction proceeded around the clock. On January 6, 1903, demolition of the buildings at the corner of State and Madison commenced. Because of construction delays in fabrication of the intended steel columns, cast-iron columns were substituted. By April 1903, the building superstructure, including white-glazed terra-cotta cladding, was complete. Store operations moved from the south half of the site to the completed wing. The buildings on the southern half of the site were then demolished and the remainder of the building constructed. The projected three-story addition atop the nine-story initial phase was never undertaken. Steel beams for the building were fireproofed by "porous terra cotta" (structural clay tile). The steel beams supported a floor system of tile segmented arches, and a concrete topping provided a level floor surface. The design of the Schlesinger and Mayer Building was a unified whole and a remarkable achievement, given the difficulties of multiphase construction. "The New Schlesinger and Mayer Building, Chicago," *The Brickbuilder* 12 (1903): 101–4.

22. *Western Architect* 31 (1922): 3–4. Originally published in *Lippincott's Magazine*, Mar. 1896. It was also reprinted in other publications, including Sullivan's *Kindergarten Chats and Other Writings* (1947) and Twombly, *Louis Sullivan: The Public Papers*.

23. Henry F. Withey, *Biographical Dictionary of American Architects (Deceased)* (Los Angeles: New Age Publishing, 1956), 333–34.

24. After partnership with B. W. Fisk, Kees formed a partnership in 1884 with Frank B. Long (1842–1912). Long and Kees rapidly became a powerful architectural force in Minneapolis. The firm adopted H. H. Richardson's Romanesque style and employed it in prestigious commissions. Long was originally from New York but at age seventeen moved with his family to Illinois. His architectural training began in the Chicago office of Cochrane and Peerqunard and he practiced architecture in Chicago before relocating to Minneapolis. "Long and Kees: Founding Fathers," *Architecture Minnesota* 18, no. 6 (Nov.–Dec. 1992): 37–39; Withey, *Biographical Dictionary of American Architects (Deceased)*, 131–32.

25. In addition to ornamental terra cotta by the American Company, the building used Norman pressed bricks manufactured by the Columbus Brick and Tile Company in Ohio. *Western Architect* (Supplement 1903): n.p.

26. *Western Architect* 1 (1902), unnumbered plate.

27. Craig MacIntosh and Ilga Eglitis, *Minneapolis Cityscape: An Artist's View* (Wayzata, Minn.: MACILO Publishing Co., 1986), 56–57.

28. A photograph of these buildings appears in John R. Borchert, David Gebhard, David Lanegran, and Judith A. Martin, *Legacy of Minneapolis: Preservation amid Change* (Minneapolis: Voyageur Press, 1983), 44.

29. Gilfillen, *Index*, 2 (order no. 1211).

30. David Gebhard and Tom Martinson, *A Guide to the Architecture of Minnesota* (Minneapolis: University of Minnesota Press, 1977), 38.

31. Using Gilfillen, *Index*, I compiled an inventory of terra-cotta orders for Kees and Colburn buildings. I identified thirty-nine orders from the American Terra Cotta and Ceramic Company and three from Midland. From field work and a sampling of available shop drawings for Kees and Colburn buildings that I studied at the Northwest Architectural Archives (NWAA), University of Minnesota Libraries, St. Paul, I determined that only in the L. S. Donaldson Company garage (Midland order no. 558) was Sullivanesque ornamentation utilized to any degree.

32. Review of issues of *Western Architect* and *Architectural Record* (1902–24).

33. Hewitt formed a partnership with Edwin H. Brown in 1911, and for the next nineteen years, Hewitt and Brown were responsible for many eclectic designs. Withey, *Biographical Dictionary of American Architects (Deceased)*, 281.

34. Sherman Paul, *Louis Sullivan: An Architect in American Thought* (Englewood Cliffs, N.J.: Prentice-Hall, 1962), 57, 58, 157. Paul says that in an open letter published in *Interstate Architect and Builder* 2, no. 7 (Dec. 8, 1900): 8–9, Sullivan complained that his ornamental designs were being plagiarized. The letter was accompanied by a design by Sullivan and an illustration of a bronze door for the Cathedral of the Sacred Heart in Duluth, Minnesota, by Tenbusch and Hill, Architects.

35. *Loop Area—Chicago's Landmark Structures: An Inventory* (Chicago: Landmarks Preservation Council and Service, 1974), 16.

36. Architectural salvage establishments in Chicago offered the terra cotta for sale. Salvage One had a large assembly. Architectural Artifacts, Inc., still had a few ornate panels as of summer 2001.

37. Harry Bergen Wheelock was born July 12, 1861, in Galesburg, Illinois. After the death of his parents, George I. and Sylvia M. (Field) Bergen in 1869, he was adopted by Otis L. Wheelock, a Chicago architect. Harry B. Wheelock was educated in Chicago schools and studied civil engineering for two years (1881–83) at the University of Michigan. He married Irene Francis Grosvenor of Monroe, Michigan, on June 15, 1886. Their family included two children. The same year that he was married, Wheelock assumed his adoptive father's architectural practice. Harry B. Wheelock lived in Evanston and designed a number of buildings for that suburb, including Covenant Methodist Church and numerous houses. He died in 1934. Albert Nelson Marquis, ed., *The Book of Chicagoans, 1917*, 2d ed. (Chicago: A. N. Marquis, 1917), 721; Margery Blair Perkins, *Evanstoniana* (Evanston, Ill.: Evanston Historical Society, 1984), 172.

38. *Sixteenth Annual Exhibition of the Chicago Architectural Club, Exhibition Catalog* (Chicago: Art Institute of Chicago, 1903), 39, 41.

39. Thomas J. Noel and Barbara S. Norgren, *Denver: The City Beautiful and Its Architects, 1893–1941* (Denver: Historic Denver, Inc., 1987), 129, 195–96.

40. Leonard K. Eaton, *Gateway Cities and Other Essays* (Ames: Iowa State University Press, 1989), 99–101.

41. Bernard C. Greengard, "Hugh M. G. Garden," *Prairie School Review* 3, no. 1 (1966): 17.

42. During the time Schmidt was initiating his professional practice, he wed Anna Comstock on June 11, 1890, in Chicago. The Schmidts had two children, Kathryn and Richard E. Schmidt Jr. Marquis, *Book of Chicagoans, 1917*, 600.

43. Schmidt was in partnership with Theodore O. Fraenkel from 1890 to 1895; subsequently, Schmidt became sole principal of the firm. Through his father's contacts, Schmidt secured the commission for Alexian Brothers Hospital (1896), Chicago. Carter Manny, *Madlener House: Tradition and Innovation in Architecture* (Chicago: Graham Foundation for Advanced Studies in the Fine Arts, 1988), 25–29, 38.

44. Albert Nelson Marquis, ed., *Who's Who in Chicago and Vicinity, 1931*, 5th ed. (Chicago: A. N. Marquis, 1931), 351.

45. American Institute of Architects (AIA), *American Architects Directory* (New York: AIA and R. R. Bowker, 1955), 189.

46. Manny, *Madlener House*, 13, 14.

47. Ibid., 16, 17, 36.

48. Historic American Buildings Survey (HABS), *Historic American Buildings Survey: Chicago and Nearby Illinois Areas* (Park Forest, Ill.: Prairie School Press, 1966), 5, 6.

49. Condit, *Chicago School of Architecture*, 188.

50. William Herbert, "An American Architecture," *Architectural Record* 23 (Feb. 1908): 113–22.

51. HABS, *Historic American Buildings Survey*, 6.

52. Lee Bey, "Orchestra Hall Fine Tuned," *Chicago Sun-Times*, Sept. 7, 1997, 30.

53. Art Institute of Chicago, *Chicago Architects Design* (New York: Rizzoli, 1982), 62.

54. Condit, *Chicago School of Architecture*, 197.

55. Gilfillen, *Index*, 37 (order no. 2619).

56. In 1914, Garden became a U.S. citizen. Garden's autobiographical entry in Marquis's *Who's Who* noted his only pastime: "Recreation: sculpture." Garden married Sally Plows of Chicago on July 22, 1915. They had one daughter. Marquis, *Who's Who in Chicago and Vicinity, 1931*, 351.

57. Norbury L. Wayman, *St. Louis Union Station and Its Railroads* (St. Louis: Evelyn F. Newman Group, 1987), 21, 25.

58. McCue and Peters, *Guide to the Architecture of St. Louis*, 42–43.

59. Ibid., 59.

60. Link worked in a number of cities, including Pittsburgh, Philadelphia, New York, and St. Louis. Starting in 1883, Link was in a number of architectural partnerships in St. Louis. When he won the Union Station design competition, he was in partnership with Edward A. Cameron (1861–99), a two-year association that was dissolved in 1893. After World War I, Link moved to the South, where he was the architect for buildings in Mississippi and Louisiana. Withey, *Biographical Dictionary of American Architects (Deceased)*, 373–74.

61. Kansas City Chapter of the American Institute of Architects, *Kansas City* (Kansas City, Mo.: AIA, 1979), 51.

62. Walter C. Root was born in Atlanta and educated there and in New York. Upon graduation from City College of New York, he moved to Chicago and worked for his brother, John Wellborn Root. The firm of Burnham and Root had major commissions under construction (now all demolished) in Kansas City, Missouri, during a two-year period starting in 1886. These were the Board of Trade; the large, eight-story Midland Hotel; and the American National Bank Building. Walter C. Root moved to Kansas City to oversee construction of these buildings. He stayed and opened his own office. In 1896, he joined in partnership with George M. Siemens. Withey, *Biographical Dictionary of American Architects (Deceased)*, 526.

63. The state pavilion for Kentucky at the World's Columbian Exposition in Chicago (1893) was designed by Maury and Dodd, but it conformed to the Beaux-Arts classicism of the fair. C. Julian Oberwarth, *A History of the Profession of Architecture in Kentucky* (Louisville: State Board of Examiners and Registration of Architects, 1987), 21, 46.

64. Author's field survey; the Galleria, Oxford Properties, stands on Fourth Street between Liberty Street and Muhammad Ali Boulevard.

65. Oberwarth, *History of the Profession of Architecture in Kentucky*, 21, 46.

66. Walter Carry, "Henry John Klutho" (master's thesis, University of Florida School of Architecture, 1955); Robert

C. Broward, *The Architecture of Henry John Klutho: The Prairie School in Jacksonville* (Jacksonville: University of North Florida Press, 1983), 52.

67. Broward, *Architecture of Henry John Klutho*, 10–13, 50–52.

68. Ibid., 86–88, 123, 295.

69. Wayne W. Wood, *Jacksonville's Architectural Heritage* (Jacksonville: University of North Florida Press, 1989), 52.

70. Ibid.

71. *Western Architect* 20, no. 6 (June 1914) and no. 8 (Aug. 1914), unnumbered plates.

72. Florida Association, American Institute of Architects, *A Guide to Florida's Historic Architecture* (Gainesville: University Press of Florida, 1989), 73.

73. Broward, *Architecture of Henry John Klutho*, 212–15.

74. Ibid., 311–15, 327, 338.

75. Trost moved (c. 1888) to Chicago, perhaps to be part of the architectural renaissance that was then occurring there and to be nearer to his family in Toledo, Ohio. Trost became active in the Chicago Architectural Sketch Club and won second prize in a club-sponsored design competition judged by Louis Sullivan, John Wellborn Root, and William Le Baron Jenney. Trost undoubtedly heard Sullivan lecture at the club. One of Trost's ventures in Chicago was to form the American Art Metal Works with Emil Henry Seeman (1865–1945) in 1891. However, the company folded after about a year. Seeman went to work for Adler and Sullivan. It has been speculated that Trost then also worked for Adler and Sullivan. If so, it was probably indirectly, as a subcontractor for ornamental iron work. According to research by Trost's biographer, Lloyd C. Engelbrecht, Trost designed for the Chicago Ornamental Iron Company from 1892 to 1896 and became a vice president of the company. Lloyd C. Engelbrecht and June-Marie F. Engelbrecht, *Henry C. Trost: Architect of the Southwest* (El Paso, Tex.: El Paso Library Association, 1981), 11–12.

76. Lloyd C. Engelbrecht, "Henry Trost: The Prairie School in the Southwest," *Prairie School Review* 6, no. 4 (1969): 11–15.

77. Engelbrecht and Engelbrecht, *Henry C. Trost*, 51–57.

78. G. H. Edgell, *The American Architecture of Today* (1928; reprint, New York: AMS Press, 1970), 81, 83.

79. Engelbrecht and Engelbrecht, *Henry C. Trost*, 85–87.

80. Trost and Trost went on to design several notable buildings. These were not Sullivanesque in style but, as Sullivan advocated, creative designs in the spirit of the place. This is especially true of the Hotel Franciscan (1922–23; demolished 1972) in Albuquerque, New Mexico. The hotel was inspired by the architecture of the Pueblo Indians and constructed in concrete. It transcended mere replication of the native style and gained acclaim, as it was published in many journals and books, including *Western Architect* (Jan. 1924) and Edgell, *American Architecture of Today*, 340.

81. Ronald Lanier Ramsey, "William Wells: Towers in Oklahoma," *Prairie School Review* 8, no. 4 (1971): 5, 6. According to Ramsey, Wells listed his address with the Chicago School in 1901–2 as: "c/o Frank Lloyd Wrights [*sic*], Oak Park." In what way Wells knew, worked, and/or lived with Frank Lloyd Wright is not known.

82. William Wells was never among any of the classes of architectural graduates listed in the *Integral*, the yearbook for the Armour Institute. (However, an F. D. Wells was listed with the class of 1908 in both the 1906 and 1907 editions of the *Integral*.)

83. *The Chicago Architectural Annual* (Chicago: Chicago Architectural Club, 1902) listed W. A. Wells as a nonresident member and identified his address as the First National Bank Building, Moline, Illinois. "The State of Illinois List of Architects" as of January 1, 1903, included William A. Wells (B 123) and gave his address as 41 M. & L. Blk., Rock Island, Illinois. See *State of Illinois Third Biennial Report of the Board of Examiners of Architects* (Chicago: State of Illinois Board of Examiners of Architects, 1903), 49.

84. Ramsey, "William Wells," 6, 7.

85. In 1907, the population was 32,452 and it swelled to 64,205 by 1910. *Twenty-first Annual Report of the Oklahoma City Chamber of Commerce* (Oklahoma City: Chamber of Commerce, 1910), 14, 20.

86. *Twenty-first Annual Report of the Oklahoma City Chamber of Commerce*, 20.

87. Ramsey, "William Wells," 8, 9.

88. It should be remembered that Colcord was a vice president and served on the board of the organization. *Twenty-first Annual Report of the Oklahoma City Chamber of Commerce*, 3, 15.

89. Jay C. Henry, *Architecture in Texas, 1895–1945* (Austin: University of Texas Press, 1993), 43–44.

90. *Western Architect* 20, no. 7 (July 1914), unnumbered plates.

91. Henry, *Architecture in Texas*, 52–53.

92. Ibid., 55, 56.

93. Ibid., 50.

94. *Western Architect* 20, no. 7 (July 1914), unnumbered plate.

95. Henry, *Architecture in Texas*, 57.

96. *The Northwestern Terra Cotta Company*, company catalog, 27.

CHAPTER 3: LATER SULLIVANESQUE

1. Broward, *Architecture of Henry John Klutho*, 221, 330.

2. Robert Twombly, "Chronology," in *Louis Sullivan: The Function of Ornament*, ed. Wim de Wit (New York: Norton, 1986), 214.

3. The American Terra Cotta and Ceramic Company office, which Sullivan used, was initially at 1808 Prairie Avenue, Chicago; after 1921, it was at 1701 Prairie Avenue.

4. Larry Millett, *The Curve of the Arch: The Story of Louis Sullivan's Owatonna Bank* (St. Paul: Minnesota Historical Society Press, 1985), 89–90.

5. In 1940, the original interior brick walls and teller counters, with seven teller wickets, were removed. The interior was both restored and modernized in 1956–58. Harwell Hamilton Harris was the architect and did a sympathetic job. In 1976, David Bowers of Val Michelson and Associates, Architects, of St. Paul was hired to upgrade the building regarding banking functions while respecting and restoring the original work. This took six years to complete. *An Architectural Symphony*, pamphlet (Owatonna: Norwest Corp, c. 1984), n.p. The commercial and office wing along E. Broadway was incorporated into the bank during a 1997 renovation with David Bowers and Tom Zumwalde as architects. *Owatonna Journal-Courier*, May 12, 1997, spec. ed., 2.

6. Sharon S. Darling, *Chicago Ceramics and Glass* (Chicago: Chicago Historical Society, 1979), frontispiece.

7. My detailed review of orders verifies this. Gilfillen, *Index.*

8. Robertson wrote about the building he compared to Sullivan's: "A typical American Bank Building, The First National Bank, Hoboken by Kenneth Murchison. This type is dignified and well handled, but contributes little to the progress of architectural design." Howard Robertson, *The Principles of Architectural Composition* (London: Architectural Press, 1924), 141.

9. Joseph Siry, "Louis Sullivan's Building for John D. Van Allen and Son," *Journal of the Society of Architectural Historians* 49, no. 1 (Mar. 1990): 67–90.

10. *Kindergarten Chats* was first published as a series of articles that appeared weekly in *Interstate Architect and Builder* between Feb. 16, 1901, and Feb. 8, 1902, according to Elaine Hedges, "Introduction," Louis H. Sullivan, *Democracy: A Man-Search* (Detroit: Wayne State University Press, 1961), x.

11. Thomas S. Marvel, *Antonín Nechodoma: Architect, 1877–1928* (Gainesville: University Press of Florida, 1994), 4–17, 19–21, 25–26.

12. Ibid., 43, 60, 63, 69.

13. The name of the building and the street address were not on the drawings. Study of shop drawings at NWAA.

14. Midland Terra Cotta Company order numbers were 23219 for the Honaker, Virginia, building and 2084 for the Mason County Bank. Study of shop drawings at NWAA.

15. Henry, *Architecture in Texas*, 52, 66, 67.

16. Ibid., 61–64.

17. Study of shop drawings at NWAA.

18. Henry, *Architecture in Texas*, 68.

19. Review of orders for terra cotta listed in Gilfillen, *Index*, 419.

20. *A. D. Profiles 16: Bruce Goff* 48, no. 10 (1978): 6.

21. These projects were displayed in the exhibition *The Architecture of Bruce Goff, 1904–1982: Design for the Continuous Present*, Art Institute of Chicago, June 9–Sept. 4, 1995.

22. Born into a family of Chicago architects, Harry W. J. Edbrooke studied architecture at the University of Illinois and at the Armour Institute, from which he graduated in 1898. His father, Willoughby J. Edbrooke, was an architect in partnership with F. P. Burnham. In Denver, Harry became a designer for his uncle, Frank E. Edbrooke (1840–1921), who was the architect for some important progressive designs in that city, such as the Brown Palace Hotel (1892). Some of these designs, such as the ten-story Gas and Electric Building (1910), 910 Fifteenth Street, were Sullivan-inspired but not literally Sullivanesque. The Gas and Electric Building featured ten thousand exterior light bulbs composed amidst the terra-cotta work of the two street facades. After Frank E. Edbrooke retired in 1913, Harry Edbrooke headed the practice. Noel and Norgren, *Denver*, 129, 195–96.

23. David H. Sachs and George Ehrlich, *Guide to Kansas Architecture* (Lawrence: University of Kansas Press, 1996), 198.

24. Midland order no. 20120 for Graham Building and no. 922 for the hotel addition. Study of shop drawings at NWAA.

25. The Drake Realty Company also pioneered concrete construction for low-cost housing in Omaha. *American Builder* (Feb. 1920): 70.

26. Raymond DeCamp Weakley was born (1877) in Cincinnati and practiced architecture in St. Louis from 1905 to 1917. After serving in the army (1917–21), he moved to Louisville and formed a partnership with Henry F. Hawes. American Institute of Architects, *American Architects Directory* (New York: AIA, 1956), 588.

27. Inventory prepared by author from orders listed in Gilfillen, *Index*; field surveys; and shop drawings, NWAA.

28. The building was covered thoroughly in G. L. Lockhart, *Public Schools: Their Construction, Heating, Ventilation, Sanitation, Lighting, and Equipment* (St. Paul, 1918).

29. Henry served as City Architect for Schools until 1918, when he returned to private practice as a partner with Hugh Nevin. Withey, *Biographical Dictionary of American Architects (Deceased)*, 279.

30. Don Hoffmann, "Ernest Olaf Brostrom," *Prairie School Review* 6, no. 3 (1969): 26.

31. By 1932, Brostrom and Drotts were listed at 216 East Tenth Street but they had offices on different floors. *Polk's City Directory for Kansas City, 1932* (Kansas City, Mo.: Gate City Directory Company, 1932), 2509. In 1913, Brostrom was listed at 1119 McGee Street. *The Architect's Directory and Specification Index for 1913–14* (New York: William T. Comstock, 1913), 73. He later had an office in room 212 of the Reliance Building. *The Western Blue Book and Buyers Reference* (Chicago: Blue Book Publishers, 1918), 26.

32. See *Western Architect* (Feb. 1924), plates 1–4.

33. See "The Peacock Apartments," *American Builder* 41, no. 1 (Apr. 1926): 304.

34. George Ehrlich, *Kansas City, Missouri: An Architectural History, 1826–1976* (Kansas City, Mo.: Historic Kansas City Foundation, 1979), 68–70.

35. See *Western Architect* (Nov. 1927), plates 196–98.

36. Author's field surveys.

37. Study of shop drawings, Midland Terra Cotta Company (order no. 711), NWAA.

38. Study of shop drawings, Midland Terra Cotta Company (order no. 741 for the Cincinnati building and no. 7110 for the one in Bucyrus), NWAA.

39. Listing of architects, *Western Blue Book and Buyers Reference*, 24. Also, study of Midland shop drawings (order nos. 6156, 5145) at NWAA.

40. Review of orders listed in Gilfillen, *Index;* author's field surveys and study of available shop drawings at NWAA.

41. Kathryn Bishop Eckert, *Buildings of Michigan* (New York: Oxford University Press, 1993), 374.

42. Author's field survey and comparison of Grand Rapids building to photographic details of column capitals for the Edison Shop, *Western Architect* (Jan. 1913).

43. Shop drawings, American order no. 3497, NWAA.

44. Gebhard and Martinson, *Guide to the Architecture of Minnesota*, 240.

45. Gerlach and his son, Henry C. Gerlach Jr., entered into partnership after his son's graduation in 1922 from the University of Minnesota. The son was listed in the *Annual of the Department of Architecture, University of Minnesota, 1922,* 3. Announcement of partnership appeared in *Western Architect* (Aug. 1922): vii.

46. Author's field survey and study of Midland shop drawing (order no. 6170) at NWAA.

47. Greene was identified as the architect on the Midland shop drawings (order no. 734) at the NWAA. Author's inventory prepared from listing of orders in Gilfillen, *Index;* field surveys; and shop drawings, NWAA. The architect for the Luverne bank building, W. E. E. Greene, was an obscure figure. Greene later worked for the Curtis Company, woodwork manufacturers in Clinton, Iowa. Greene was the architect for a subdivision of exclusive homes (in the Tudor style) developed by Curtis and named Castle Terrace (c. 1926), also in Clinton. Ronald E. Schmitt, *The Architecture of Clinton, Iowa* (Clinton, Ia.: City of Clinton Department of Community Development, 1980), 78.

48. Gebhard and Martinson, *Guide to the Architecture of Minnesota*, 182, 211, 383.

49. Alan Lathrop, curator, NWAA, personal interview by author, July 13, 1989.

50. Nothing is known about W. R. Wilson; the name doesn't appear on rosters of Minnesota architects at that time. Rosters consulted included those in *Architects' Directory and Specification Index for 1913–14* and *Western Blue Book and Buyers Reference* (1918).

51. Mark Hammons, "Ongoing Concerns," *Architecture Minnesota* 15, no. 5 (Sept./Oct. 1989): 28.

52. Gilfillen, *Index,* 52, 302.

53. Major additions and expansions also took place in 1951, 1967, 1978, and 1985 and created a large complex. Terra cotta from the original building was utilized on the facade of the 1985 addition, which was designed by Setter, Leach, and Lindstrom. Hammons, "Ongoing Concerns," 28–31.

54. Author's inventory prepared from field surveys; Gilfillen, *Index;* city directories; and available records, City of Sioux City Department of Urban Renewal, c. 1970.

55. Manufacturer unknown but it was not the American Terra Cotta and Ceramic Company or Midland Terra Cotta Company, as determined from a review of Gilfillen, *Index,* and records of both companies on file at NWAA.

56. These included the Orpheum Theater (1907), 218 Sixth Avenue South, and the Langan Building (1914), 317–25 South Second Street. Prior to this commission, Ladehoff had formed a partnership with Frank Sohn. It is possible that Sohn had an influence in the firm's embracing of the Sullivanesque but more likely it was Ladehoff's decision. Several old-time contractors recalled this scenario. Ladehoff and Sohn offices were at 217 Sixth Avenue South, Clinton. Very little is known of Sohn. He had been in Clinton for a short time and had attempted to establish his own practice before joining Ladehoff. Schmitt, *Architecture of Clinton, Iowa,* 27, 96.

57. Author's review of order listed in Gilfillen, *Index,* 347 (order no. 594).

58. Shop drawing (order no. 594), Midland Terra Cotta Company, NWAA.

59. Midland Terra Cotta Company catalog (Chicago: n.d.), plate 36.

60. Advertisements, *American Carpenter and Builder* (Feb. 1915): 86–87, and (Mar. 1915): 104–5.

61. Inventory prepared from orders listed in Gilfillen, *Index,* 363 (order no. 735), and field surveys.

62. Ladehoff designed a number of structures with white-glazed brick and terra cotta, as did the Clinton architect John Morrell. This preference was noted in an article that appeared in the Chicago-based journal *National Builder,* which carried photographs of Ladehoff's Pahl Building and the Snow White Drug Store. Two additional Clinton buildings by Morrell, the six-story Wilson Building (1912–14) and City Garage (1916), were also illustrated. However, neither architectural firm was identified—such was the architects' anonymity. See "A White City," *National Builder* 62, no. 12 (Dec. 1919): 48–49.

63. Economic conditions in Clinton were poor at the time as the city had lost population. Clinton owed its original prosperity to sawmill industries that were located at the crossing of an east-west rail line with the Mississippi River, which provided a waterway system for floating logs down from the north woods. Once the logging industry had depleted the forests, the sawmills closed. The city tried to diversify economically and industrially but it wasn't until 1930 that Clinton's population exceeded that of 1910. (U.S. census population figures for 1910 = 25,577; 1920 = 24,151; 1930 = 25,726.) The advent of World War I may have been a factor in the 1917 dissolution of the Ladehoff and Sohn partner-

ship. What became of Frank Sohn is not known. Ladehoff then worked for Clinton Engineering Company, a contracting firm owned by Gus Ladehoff, his brother. In 1918, another brother, Arthur Detlef H. Ladehoff, joined the company after graduating in engineering from the University of Illinois. John Ladehoff resided at 1309 West Pleasant Street in Clinton until 1924, when he moved to Davenport, Iowa, to take a position with the Rock Island Sash and Door Company. Schmitt, *Architecture of Clinton, Iowa*, 10.

64. Midland shop drawings, NWAA.

65. At that date, Steinway Hall in downtown Chicago housed many Chicago School and Prairie School architects (Tomlinson's office was across the corridor from the city office of Frank Lloyd Wright). Listings in *The Chicago Architectural Annual* (Chicago Architectural Club, 1902). Jervis R. Harbeck was listed as a member of the Chicago Architectural Club, with an office at 1107 Steinway Hall, the same office listing as Webster Tomlinson. *The Chicago Architectural Annual* for 1903 lists Jervis R. Harbeck as a nonresident member at 123 Theodore Street, Detroit, Michigan. Frank Lloyd Wright was not a member of the club; however, Grant Carpenter Manson, *Frank Lloyd Wright to 1910: The First Golden Age* (New York: Van Nostrand Reinhold, 1958), 215, lists Wright's Chicago office as 1106 Steinway Hall for the years 1901–7.

66. Phil H. Feddersen, personal interview by author, Clinton, Iowa, 1980. Feddersen is an architect in Clinton and a distant relative of Harbeck.

67. Schmitt, *Architecture of Clinton, Iowa*, 56.

68. Author's inventories prepared from Gilfillen, *Index;* field surveys; and study of available shop drawings at NWAA.

69. Karl Marshall Waggoner was born January 19, 1894, in Decatur, Illinois. Son of a Decatur architect, C. S. Waggoner, Karl attended Millikin University and later studied architecture at the University of Illinois, from which he graduated in 1917. He passed his Illinois architect's registration in November 1924, moved to Iowa, and became a partner in the Hansen and Waggoner firm in Mason City. Franklin W. Scott, ed., *Semi-Centennial Alumni Record of the University of Illinois* (Chicago: Lakeside Press, 1918), 702.

70. [Ronald E. Schmitt], Environmental Planning and Research, Inc., *Mason City, Iowa: An Architectural Heritage* (Mason City: Department of Community Development, City of Mason City, 1977), 25.

71. Author's inventories prepared from Gilfillen, *Index;* field surveys; and study of available shop drawings at NWAA.

72. [Robert J. Cook], Environmental Planning and Research, Inc., *Historic Architecture of Muscatine, Iowa* (Muscatine: Citizens Advisory Council for the Improvement of Muscatine, 1977), 17.

73. Morrison, *Louis Sullivan*, 301, 304, 305.

74. A complete listing of Purcell and Elmslie's buildings is given in David Gebhard, *A Guide to the Existing Buildings of Purcell and Elmslie* (Roswell, N.M.: Roswell Museum and Art Center, 1960).

75. Kristin Visser, *Frank Lloyd Wright and the Prairie School in Wisconsin* (Madison, Wisc.: Prairie Oak Press, 1992), 186–87.

76. Author's field surveys and study of shop drawings at NWAA.

77. Funston was born May 19, 1868, in Champaign County, Illinois. It is not known if Funston designed additional Sullivanesque projects. Previously, he had been in partnership with A. Arthur Guilbert as Guilbert and Funston, Architects. Funston married Ella May Kephart in 1905 and they had a daughter. Scott, *Semi-Centennial Alumni Record of the University of Illinois*, 65.

78. The exhibition was held at the Art Institute of Chicago, April 4–May 1, 1918. The exhibition and catalog were the joint effort of the Chicago Architectural Club, the Illinois Society of Architects, and the Illinois Chapter of the American Institute of Architects.

79. H. Allen Brooks, "Percy Dwight Bentley at La Crosse," *Prairie School Review* 9, no. 3 (1972): 5–17.

80. Author's inventory prepared from orders listed in Gilfillen, *Index;* field surveys; and study of available shop drawings, NWAA.

81. Ibid.

82. Ibid.

83. Junior League of Evansville, *Reflections upon a Century of Architecture: Evansville, Indiana* (Evansville: Junior League of Evansville, 1977), 63.

84. Harris was born 1868 in Louisville, Kentucky. He first served in the office of the Evansville architect Frank J. Schlotter (1864–1943) and had an architectural partnership with Henry Weiss prior to the formulation of Harris and Shopbell, Architects. *Western Architect* 12 (Nov. 1909): 11.

85. Two moderate-sized houses were reminiscent of the Tudor-like prairie houses of Spencer and Powers. Each house had an upper story of stucco panels and wood trim that successfully reduced the visual weight of the wall, an effect found also in Japanese architecture. The third design was titled "A Homelike Plaster House." See *Keith's Magazine* 17 (Apr. 1907): 234–35; 17 (May 1907): 294; 18 (July 1907): 23; and 18 (Aug. 1907): 81–82.

86. A residence (1916) for the mayor of Evansville, Benjamin Bosse, was a Prairie School house with limestone piers, leaded glass windows, and gable roofs with green tiles. Related to the Prairie School, but more understated, was the 1918 design for the municipal market for the city of Evansville. The now badly deteriorated market contrasts sharply with photographs of the newly completed complex that appeared in the March 1919 issue of *Western Architect*. Although devoid of ornamentation, Shopbell's municipal market represented the philosophical intent of architectural design advocated by Louis Sullivan. It captured a midwestern spirit and was an American interpretation of a civic institution rooted in the tradition of the European central market. Junior League of Evansville, *Reflections upon a Century of Architecture*, 26; *Western Architect* 22 (Mar. 1919), plates 15, 16.

87. Shop drawing, Midland Terra Cotta Company (order no. 22324), NWAA.

88. Gilfillen, *Index*, 41, 291, 296.

89. Craig Robert Zabel, "The Prairie School Banks of Frank Lloyd Wright, Louis H. Sullivan, and Purcell and Elmslie" (Ph.D. diss., University of Illinois at Urbana-Champaign, 1984), 495.

90. Frank E. Fowler established an office at 505 Central Union Bank Building in Evansville, Indiana; Thole stayed in the Furniture Building; and Clifford Shopbell was listed at 301 American Trust Building, Evansville. Clifford Shopbell, who was a registered architect in both Indiana (registration no. 55) and Illinois (B 482), established an independent office in Evanston, Illinois, as early as 1926, although he still maintained an office in Evansville. By 1933, however, Shopbell had left Evansville and his professional address was listed as the North Shore Hotel in Evanston, Illinois. Little is known of Fowler and Thole; their names last appeared in the *Roster of Registered Architects for Indiana* in 1946. *Roster of Registered Architects* (State of Indiana Board of Registration for Architects, Dec. 1, 1931), 7, 13, 14; Junior League of Evansville, *Reflections upon a Century of Architecture*, 63. Commencing with the Dec. 1, 1931, *Roster of Registered Architects*, Shopbell was listed as a "non-resident architect" with the Evanston, Illinois address. *Roster of Registered Architects* (State of Indiana Board of Registration for Architects) for 1931, 1933, 1934, 1935, 1938, 1944, 1945, 1946, 1948. The address for Frank E. Fowler (registration no. 197) for the years 1944–46 was 615 East Chandler, Evansville, Indiana; Edward J. Thole (registration no. 32), at the same time, was listed at 707 Court Building, Evansville, Indiana.

91. Inventories prepared from orders listed in Gilfillen, *Index*; author's field surveys; and study of available shop drawings at NWAA.

92. Determined by author's inventories prepared from orders listed in Gilfillen, *Index*; extensive field surveys; and/or study of available shop drawings at NWAA.

93. Two Galesburg, Illinois, examples were: Dr. G. E. Luster Residence (c. 1894) at 756 North Broad Street; and an 1898 residence, 427 North Prairie. Richard C. Welge, *Remnants of the Nineteenth Century Landscape: Knox County, Illinois* (Knoxville, Ill.: Knox County Historical Sites, Inc., 1979), 80–81.

94. Born January 30, 1889, in Galesburg, Harry G. Aldrich studied at the local school, Knox College, and received his bachelor of science degree in 1910. He then went to Urbana to study architecture at the University of Illinois. After graduation in 1913, Harry worked as a draftsman in St. Louis for the firm of Patterson and Davidson. He was married in 1915 and his family included two children. Alumni Records, Archives, UIUC. Offices were in the Mail Building, 135 S. Cherry, Galesburg, where they remained for several decades. Address of Aldrich and Aldrich verified from listings of registered architects, *State of Illinois Board of Examiners of Archi-*

tects, 1913 (Norman K. Aldrich was listed at 86 South Cherry, Galesburg, for 1907–13); Illinois Society of Architects, *Handbook for Architects and Builders* (Chicago: Illinois Society of Architects, 1915–25); *Colville's Galesburg City Directory, 1929–30* (Detroit: R. L. Polk, 1929), 430; all listed Aldrich and Aldrich at the Mail Building.

95. Author's inventory of Aldrich and Aldrich buildings compiled from eleven orders from Midland company listed in Gilfillen, *Index* (none were listed from the American company; Northwestern listings not available); also, study of available shop drawings from NWAA.

96. Hanifen died on January 12, 1938, in Chicago's Presbyterian Hospital. John Hanifen and his wife, Helene, had two children. *Illinois Society of Architects Monthly Bulletin* 22, nos. 8–9 (Feb.–Mar. 1938): 12; C. J. Roseberry, *The University of Illinois Directory for 1929* (Urbana: University of Illinois, 1929), 389.

97. By 1913, Hanifen had passed the architect's registration examination and had received his Illinois license (B 464). He then formed a partnership with Kesson White. One of the firm's designs, the T. R. Godfrey Building (1914) at 208 West Main Street in Ottawa, made timid use of Sullivanesque terra-cotta accents. These decorative insets provided focal points about a second-story window grouping. By 1916, White and Hanifen had dissolved their partnership; White moved to Chicago and Hanifen retained the Ottawa office. "List of Architects," corrected to January 1, 1913, *State of Illinois Eighth Biennial Report of the Board of Examiners of Architects* (Chicago: Secretary's Office, 1913), 38. Hanifen was not in the January 1, 1911, "List of Architects," *State of Illinois Seventh Biennial Report of the Board of Examiners of Architects* (Chicago: Chicago Architects' Business Office, 1911). White received his license (A 82) under the "grandfather" provision in the state architectural licensing law. Under this provision, architects who had been practicing prior to the July 1, 1897, enactment of the Illinois architectural registration law could be licensed without examination and were permitted to continue the practice of architecture. The firm of White and Hanifen had offices in the Nertney Building, Ottawa, Illinois. *State of Illinois First Biennial Report of the Board of Examiners of Architects* (Chicago: Secretary's Office, 1899), 44; *Architects' Directory and Specification Index for 1913–14* (New York: Wm. Comstock, 1913), 55; Illinois Society of Architects, *Handbook for Architects and Builders* (1916), 45, 47.

98. Shop drawings (order no. 21018), Midland Terra Cotta Company, NWAA.

99. Shop drawings (order no. 24253), Midland Terra Cotta Company, NWAA.

100. Shop drawings (order nos. 9130, 24260, 26005), Midland Terra Cotta Company, NWAA.

101. Author's field survey and study of shop drawings (Midland order no. 21068), NWAA.

102. Paul Kruty, *Prairie School Architects: The Illinois Connec-*

tion, exhibition at I Space Gallery, Chicago (University of Illinois at Urbana-Champaign), 1994, exhibition panel.

103. Author's field surveys and study of shop drawings at NWAA.

104. Author's field surveys.

105. Author's inventory prepared from orders listed in Gilfillen, *Index*, and field surveys.

106. Gilbert Axell Johnson (b. March 12, 1892) became sole proprietor. For more than forty-five years, the firm of Peterson and Johnson and its successors had offices in 406 Swedish American Bank Building, 501–3 Seventh Street, Rockford. AIA, *American Architects Directory* (1955), 278.

107. Author's field survey and study of Midland shop drawings (order no. 23108), NWAA.

108. Author's field surveys.

CHAPTER 4: SULLIVAN'S FORMER EMPLOYEES

1. Frank Lloyd Wright, *Genius and the Mobocracy* (New York: Duell, Sloan, and Pearce, 1949), rear flap of dust jacket.

2. Manson, *Frank Lloyd Wright to 1910*, 13. Manson is probably correct in asserting that Wright spent fewer than two years at the University of Wisconsin, although most published accounts, including Wright's recollections, indicate he had three and a half years of university training. He did not receive a degree.

3. Silsbee was born (1848) in Salem, Massachusetts, and practiced architecture in Syracuse, New York, prior to his move to Chicago in 1882. *Industrial Chicago*, 2:628–29. After a short time with Silsbee, Wright requested a pay raise but was denied. Therefore, he changed employers and worked for the Chicago architectural firm of Beers, Clay, and Dutton. He soon left, however, and returned, with an increase in salary, to Silsbee's firm. In Silsbee's office were other draftsmen who would later contribute to progressive architecture and have later associations and/or rivalries with Wright. These included George Elmslie, George Maher, Cecil Corwin, and Henry Fiddelke. Henry-Russell Hitchcock, *In the Nature of Materials* (New York: Duell, Sloan, and Pearce, 1942), 4–6.

4. At that time, the Adler and Sullivan offices were in the Bordon Block. Designed by Adler and Sullivan, the Bordon Block (1879–80; demolished 1916) was located at the northwest corner of Randolph and Dearborn Streets, Chicago.

5. Wright, *Genius and the Mobocracy*, 45.

6. Both occupied the east end of the building, facing Lake Michigan. A consultation room separated Sullivan's office from that of Adler, which faced south. A fourth office, at the west end of the tower, was reserved for Paul Mueller, an engineer. A large, open drafting room, with space for approximately thirty employees, stretched along the northern wall between Wright's and Mueller's rooms. Twombly, *Louis Sullivan: His Life and Work*, 183.

7. Wright, *Genius and the Mobocracy*, 51.

8. An addition, to the south, marred the house but it was removed in 1988 during restoration by Skidmore, Owings, and Merrill, Architects, for the SOM Foundation. The Charnley House is now the national headquarters for the Society of Architectural Historians.

9. For example, Manson writes: "There is an indication that Sullivan took a direct interest in this design; Elmslie remembered Sullivan at work sketching the foliated ornament in the lunette over the front door, but, again, internal evidence, other than the extreme richness of embroidered detail inside (so much so that the little rooms have an almost 'Turkish' look), corroborates the continued assumption that most of the design was Wright's." Manson, *Frank Lloyd Wright to 1910*, 29.

10. Twombly, *Louis Sullivan: His Life and Work*, 209.

11. Condit, *Chicago School of Architecture*, 135.

12. William Allin Storrer, *The Architecture of Frank Lloyd Wright: A Complete Catalog*, 3d ed. (Cambridge, Mass.: MIT Press, 1984), 10–18.

13. David A. Hanks, *The Decorative Designs of Frank Lloyd Wright* (New York: E. P. Dutton, 1979), 10. A panel survives in a private collection in Chicago.

14. Wright, *Genius and the Mobocracy*, 66.

15. Wright's client, William H. Winslow, and Winslow's brother, Francis, owned Winslow Brothers, manufacturers of ornamental iron and bronze. The company was the supplier of metalwork for many Sullivan designed buildings, most notably the Schlesinger and Mayer Store Building (1899, 1902). It was while Wright was with Adler and Sullivan that he met William Winslow. Leonard K. Eaton, "Witt, Winslow and the Winslow House," *Prairie School Review* 1, no. 3 (1964): 12–13. See also, Frank Lloyd Wright, *An Autobiography* (New York: Longmans Green, 1932), 113.

16. W. R. Hasbrouck, "Frank Lloyd Wright's First Independent Commission," *Prairie School Review* 1, no. 3 (1964): 7.

17. Donald P. Hallmark, "Richard W. Bock, Sculptor—Part II: The Mature Collaborations," *Prairie School Review* 8, no. 2 (1971): 8–9.

18. Manson, *Frank Lloyd Wright to 1910*, 76–78.

19. Wright, *Genius and the Mobocracy*, 55.

20. Ibid., 56.

21. The Odd Fellows Temple project for Chicago was published in *Industrial Chicago*, 2:593–95. Sullivan wrote and illustrated an article for a Chicago magazine; see "The High Building Question," *The Graphic* 5 (Dec. 19, 1891): 405.

22. Brooks, *The Prairie School*, 18–20.

23. Wright articulated his "gradually deepening conviction that in the Machine lies the only future of art and craft." Frank Lloyd Wright, "The Art and Craft of the Machine," *Catalogue of the Fourteenth Annual Exhibition of the Chicago Architectural Club* (Chicago: Chicago Architectural Club, 1901), n.p. This address, first given on March 6, 1901, at Hull-House, Chicago, at a meeting of the Chicago Arts and Crafts Society, was widely excerpted and reprinted in other publications.

24. Morrison, *Louis Sullivan*, 226.

25. Albert Nelson Marquis, ed., *Who's Who in Chicago and Vicinity, 1936*, 6th ed. (Chicago: A. N. Marquis, 1936), 298. Also, Albert Nelson Marquis, ed., *Who's Who in Chicago and Vicinity, 1941*, 7th ed. (Chicago: A. N. Marquis, 1941), 250. Both *Who's Who* listings give 1873 as Elmslie's birth year, which conflicts with the year usually given, 1871. The year 1871 is probably correct, based on "age 81" given in newspaper obituaries. Obituaries include *Chicago Daily News*, Apr. 25, 1952, and *Chicago Tribune*, Apr. 25, 1952. These newspaper obituaries appear in *Architect's Scrapbook*, Burnham Library, Art Institute of Chicago, 716. They are also on microfilm; see microfilm project, Burnham Library, Art Institute of Chicago, and University of Illinois at Urbana-Champaign (c. 1952), 323. Elmslie, like Frank Lloyd Wright, may have attempted to make himself appear younger by giving a different date in the *Who's Who* publications, or newspaper writers could have deduced the wrong years. Craig Zabel writes that records at the Northwest Architectural Archives (NWAA) suggest Elmslie's birth may have been 1868 or 1869. See Zabel, "George Grant Elmslie and the Glory and Burden of the Sullivan Legacy," in *The Midwest in American Architecture*, ed. Garner, 2.

26. David Gebhard, "Purcell and Elmslie," *Macmillan Encyclopedia of Architects*, vol. 3 (New York: Free Press, 1982), 500.

27. Wright, *Genius and the Mobocracy*, 77.

28. David Gebhard, *Drawings for Architectural Ornament by George Grant Elmslie, 1902–1936* (Santa Barbara: University of California, Santa Barbara, 1968), 2.

29. Zabel, "George Grant Elmslie and the Glory and Burden of the Sullivan Legacy," 10–11.

30. Purcell was employed with John Galen Howard in San Francisco. In 1906, Purcell toured Europe with a former college classmate, George Feick Jr. During their travels, they met with progressive European architects, including Henrik P. Berlage, Ferdinand Boberg, and Martin Nyrop. While in practice, Purcell became active in local groups dedicated to the arts and crafts movement, including the Handicraft Guild of Minneapolis. At the same time, he wooed Edna Summy and they married in December 1908. Mark Hammons, "Purcell and Elmslie, Architects," in *Art and Life on the Upper Mississippi: 1890–1915*, ed. Michael Conforti (Newark, Del.: University of Delaware Press, 1994), 221–23, 226, 227, 232, 274.

31. Marquis, *Who's Who in Chicago and Vicinity, 1936*, 298. It might be assumed that the date of the marriage, October 12, 1910, is correct as it appeared in George Grant Elmslie's *Who's Who* autobiographical entry. Millett (*Curve of the Arch*, 127) reported the wedding date as September 14, 1910. Elmslie reported his birthday as "Feb. 20, 1873" in *Who's Who* whereas most sources, including obituaries, gave 1871 as his birth year; therefore, the October 12 wedding date may be in dispute as well.

32. Millett, *Curve of the Arch*, 127–30.

33. The first two banks were built under the firm name of Purcell, Feick, and Elmslie.

34. Purcell, Feick, and Elmslie, "The Statics and Dynamics of Architecture," *Western Architect* 19, no. 1 (Jan. 1913), reprinted as *A Reissue from the Prairie School Press: The Architecture of Purcell and Elmslie*, with a new introduction by David Gebhard (Park Forest, Ill.: Prairie School Press, 1965), 23.

35. Study of working drawings, microfilm project of Burnham Library, Art Institute of Chicago, and University of Illinois (c. 1952).

36. Author's inventory of terra-cotta orders for Purcell and Elmslie, prepared using Gilfillen, *Index*.

37. The 1911 "List of Architects Licensed to Practice in the State of Illinois" identified the New York Life Building, Minneapolis, as the address for William G. Purcell. In the 1913 listing, Purcell's address is listed as the Auditorium Building; Elmslie is listed for the first time and his address is 5759 Madison Avenue, Chicago. However, the 1915 edition lists the Auditorium Building, Minneapolis, as the address for both Purcell and Elmslie. Review of biennial reports, *Board of Examiners of Architects*, various editions; and study of working drawings, microfilm project of Burnham Library, Art Institute of Chicago, and University of Illinois.

38. William Gray Purcell, "Walter Burley Griffin, Progressive," *Western Architect* 16 (Sept. 1912): 93–94; idem, "Spencer and Powers, Architects," *Western Architect* 20 (Apr. 1914): 35–39.

39. For example, William Gray Purcell and George G. Elmslie, "The American Renaissance?" *The Craftsman* 21, no. 4 (Jan. 1912): 430–35; and W. G. Purcell and G. G. Elmslie, "H. P. Berlage: The Creator of a Democratic Architecture in Holland," *The Craftsman* 21, no. 5 (Feb. 1912): 547–53.

40. Hammons, "Purcell and Elmslie," 258.

41. Woodbury County Board of Supervisors, *Woodbury County Court House* (Sioux City, Iowa: Woodbury County Board of Supervisors, 1966), 7. This publication marked the fiftieth anniversary of the contract for the courthouse. The publication comprised reprints from *Western Architect* (Feb. 1921); a state examiner's report, 1918; and a brief history of Woodbury County by John F. Schmitt. This publication summarized (pp. 7, 40, 47) the parties responsible for the design and the emerging of the courthouse: "An organization was effected whereby Mr. Steele was to be executive head, Mr. Elmslie was to have charge of the planning and designing; Mr. Paul D. Cook, the structural engineering; and Mr. B. A. Broom, the mechanical engineering." Officially, William L. Steele was identified as architect for the courthouse and Purcell and Elmslie were listed as associate architects. Steele's 5 percent fee ($40,291.93) of construction cost included the services of Purcell and Elmslie.

42. Author's inventory prepared from orders listed in Gilfillen, *Index*, 38.

43. Woodbury County Board of Supervisors, *Woodbury County Court House*, 35, 41, 47. Page 47 contained a reprint of

the State Examiner's Report: General Summary of Contracts, May 28, 1918. Alfonso Iannelli was paid $4,950; John W. Norton received $8,500 for his murals; and Kristian Schneider was paid $710 for his additional freelance work for iron and bronze ornamental work.

44. Woodbury County Board of Supervisors, *Woodbury County Court House*, 9.

45. Hammons, "Purcell and Elmslie," 236, 237, 269–70.

46. Shuana J. Francissen, "An American Architect, George Grant Elmslie," *Historic Illinois* 9, no. 2 (Aug. 1986): 1–4.

47. Ibid., 2, 4.

48. Gilfillen, *Index*, 65 (order no. 3721).

49. Ira J. Bach, *A Guide to Chicago's Historic Suburbs* (Chicago: Swallow Press, 1981), 325–26.

50. Richard A. Haussmann, ed., *About Our Building: The Old Second National Bank, Aurora, Ill.* (Aurora, Ill.: Old Second National Bank, n.d.), 7, 10–12.

51. Ibid., 14. In the list of firms furnishing labor and materials for the building, only the Advance Terra Cotta Company is listed; American is not. This is verified by a compilation of American orders from Gilfillen, *Index*. The Old Second National Bank does not appear in the orders for Elmslie's terra cotta from American. However, Kristian Schneider is listed as "Ornament Modeler" as he freelanced for this bank.

52. Craig Zabel, "George Grant Elmslie: Turning the Jewel Box into a Bank Home," in *American Public Architecture: European Roots and Native Expressions*, Papers in Art History from the Pennsylvania State University, ed. Craig Zabel and Susan Scott Munshower (State College, Pa.: Pennsylvania State University, 1989), 222–23.

53. Among the first of many architectural historians to cite this resemblance was Donald L. Hoffmann, "Elmslie's Topeka Legacy," *Prairie School Review* 1, no. 4 (1964): 22–23.

54. Review of orders (no. 3345) listed in Gilfillen, *Index*, 55.

55. See William Steele, "The Capital Building and Loan Association Building," *Western Architect* (Sept. 1924): 99–100, plates 1–11.

56. The college is now defunct and the buildings are part of a minimum-security federal prison.

57. For example, Elmslie wrote in 1934: "If there is one thing we do not want, as self-respecting citizens of this assemblage of varied United States, it is an International Style. A real style, as rationally conceived, and arising in response to conditions of social, religious, and economic life, is national or racial. It is also on account of a particular environment regional, local, communal, and personal." George G. Elmslie, "Functionalism and International Style," *Illinois Society of Architects Monthly Bulletin* 19, nos. 6–7 (Dec. 1934–Jan. 1935): 3.

58. Elmslie, "Functionalism and International Style," 3.

59. Morrison, *Louis Sullivan*, 279.

60. Hermann Valentin von Holst was born June 17, 1874, in Freiburg, Baden, Germany. He came to the United States at the age of eighteen. He studied at the University of Chica-go for one year before transferring to MIT, from which he graduated in 1896. He gained employment with the Boston architectural firm of Shepley, Rutan, and Coolidge; however, he was placed in its Chicago branch. The firm had major commissions in Chicago, including the Public Library (1891–97) and the Art Institute (1891–93). In 1905, von Holst started ed his own practice. He formed a partnership with James L. Fyfe as von Holst and Fyfe, Architects, which lasted until 1917. Thereafter, von Holst practiced alone. Around 1935, he moved to Boca Raton, Florida, although he continued to maintain a Chicago office. Marquis, *Book of Chicagoans, 1917*, 697; idem, *Who's Who in Chicago and Vicinity, 1931*, 1005; idem, *Who's Who in Chicago and Vicinity, 1936*, 1040.

61. Building permit records and Resource Form (dated 9–9–87), CCL. Northwestern Terra Cotta Company order no. 25329, recorded in an untitled, unpublished list of Northwestern terra-cotta orders compiled by Timothy Samuelson.

62. Building permit records and Resource Form (dated 5–9–85), CCL.

63. Study of working drawings of building projects, microfilm project of Burnham Library, Art Institute of Chicago, and University of Illinois (c. 1952).

64. Author's inventory prepared from orders listed in Gilfillen, *Index*, 175, 465–67.

65. Sharon S. Darling, *Teco: Art Pottery of the Prairie School* (Erie, Pa.: Erie Art Museum, 1989), 175.

66. The attribution for the Thornton School comes from Brooks, *The Prairie School*, 309, and for the Edison School from Richard Guy Wilson, "Themes of Continuity," in *Modern Architecture in America: Visions and Revisions*, ed. Richard Guy Wilson and Sidney K. Robinson (Ames: Iowa State University Press, 1991), 192.

67. The Morton attribution comes from Talbot F. Hamlin, "George Grant Elmslie and the Chicago Scene," *Pencil Points* (Sept. 1941): 585.

68. George Grant Elmslie, "Autobiographical Sketch," undated manuscript in Elmslie Papers, microfilm project of Burnham Library, Art Institute of Chicago, and University of Illinois (c. 1952).

69. According to information provided by Hammond School administrative personnel in personal interview by author, May 17, 1996, a new school was being considered to replace it.

70. Ronald E. Schmitt, "George G. Elmslie's Culminating Designs," in *George G. Elmslie Architectural Ornament from the Edison and Morton Schools, Hammond, Indiana*, ed. Paul Kruty and Ronald E. Schmitt (Champaign, Ill.: School of Architecture, University of Illinois, 1998), 20.

71. Order no. 4920. Author's inventory prepared from orders listed in Gilfillen, *Index*, 98.

72. At this time, he used his full name, George Grant Elmslie, in signing his papers and articles. Previously, he was listed on working drawings and building identifications as George G. Elmslie.

73. "Advanced to Fellowship in 1947," *Journal of the American Institute of Architects* 7, no. 5 (May 1947): 230, 236. In addition, Louis Sullivan was posthumously awarded the 1943 Gold Medal of the AIA. Elmslie was to receive the award on Sullivan's behalf in a ceremony on May 9, 1946, but was unable to attend for health reasons. Instead, his speech was read. See "To Louis Henri Sullivan: The Gold Medal of the American Institute of Architects," *Journal of the American Institute of Architects* 6 no. 1 (July 1946): 4.

74. Obituary, *Chicago Tribune*, Apr. 25, 1952.

75. The list of employees was compiled from many corroborating sources. However, the single source for John T. Lang was the *Chicago Sun-Times*, Dec. 15, 1997, 16; the single source for W. F. Kleinpell and Charles F. Whittlesey (1867–1941) was Paul Clifford Larson, ed., *The Spirit of H. H. Richardson on the Midland Prairies* (Ames: Iowa State University Press, 1988), 156. A listing of Adler and Sullivan employees included H. C. Trost. However, this is unverified.

76. "Obituary: Parker Noble Berry," *Western Architect* (Jan. 1919).

77. Berry graduated as valedictorian and class president from Princeton Township High School in 1906. He then worked for his father, John Wesley Berry, a contractor and owner of a planing mill. Donald L. Hoffmann, "The Brief Career of a Sullivan Apprentice: Parker N. Berry," *Prairie School Review* 4, no. 1 (1967): 7, 14.

78. Roseberry, *University of Illinois Directory for 1929*, 73. The obituary for Parker Berry published in the *Western Architect* (Jan. 1919) noted that he was a 1909 graduate of the University of Illinois.

79. Hoffmann, "Brief Career of a Sullivan Apprentice," 8, 9.

80. Brian A. Spencer, ed., *The Prairie School Tradition* (New York: Whitney Library of Design, 1979), 118. The pencil drawing on tracing paper is in the collection of the Burnham Library, Art Institute of Chicago.

81. Original blueprints in author's collection, acquired from estate of Ralph Marlowe Line.

82. Review of order listings (no. 2406) from Gilfillen, *Index*, 31.

83. Shop drawing (order no. 605), Midland Terra Cotta Company, NWAA.

84. Hoffmann, "Brief Career of a Sullivan Apprentice," 11.

85. Shop drawings (order no. 7105), Midland Terra Cotta Company, NWAA. Although the building was intended to be U shaped in plan, only the west dormitory wing was realized as an addition to an old two-story house. The house was finally demolished around 1986 and an expansion constructed. Berry's proposed forms were not respected in the expansion. The new architecture's only recognition of the original building's simple but powerful domestic image came in an attempt to duplicate the stucco wall finish.

86. Author's field survey and inventory prepared from orders listed in Gilfillen, *Index*, 41.

87. *Western Architect* (Nov. 1918), plates 13, 14.

88. Spencer, *Prairie School Tradition*, 117. The pencil drawing on tracing paper is in the collection of the Architecture Department, Art Institute of Chicago.

89. His father, Robert Chiyon Steele, was born on March 13, 1846, in Chester County, Pennsylvania. His mother, Mary E. La Barthe Steele (born November 30, 1852), was a native of Springfield, Illinois. At the University of Illinois, William Steele was active in many student organizations, including the Architect's Club and several other clubs; Sigma Chi fraternity; and the University Glee Club. He was also a board member of the College of Engineering publication, *The Technograph*, and an illustrator for the 1896 yearbook, *The Illio*. However, he was most proud of his association with the university band. He played cornet, received a special music scholarship, composed a class song, and served as one of the first leaders of the fledgling band. His experiences as a university band leader, including performances at the 1893 World's Columbian Exposition, in Chicago, were recounted occasionally in correspondence and university alumni publications. Scott, *Semi-Centennial Alumni Record of the University of Illinois*, 96; William L. Steele, "Those Band Boys of the '90s," *News of Illinois Bandsmen* (n.d.), reprinted in the *Alumni News* (University of Illinois), June 1933, 319. Alumni Records, Archives, UIUC.

90. On April 30, 1901, in St. Louis, Missouri, Steele married Mariana Green. Known as Mary, she was a native of Champaign, Illinois, and an 1895 graduate of the University of Illinois in Liberal Arts and Sciences. Alumni Records, Archives, UIUC.

91. Mark L. Peisch, *The Chicago School of Architecture: Early Followers of Sullivan and Wright* (New York: Random House, 1964), 80.

92. In addition to the Schlesinger and Mayer Department Store, Sullivan's commissions during Steele's tenure included several industrial structures and an office building for the Crane Company in Chicago. Morrison, *Louis Sullivan*, 201–2.

93. William Steele moved his family, which by then included a baby daughter (b. June 10, 1903), to Pittsburgh, Pennsylvania, but they remained for less than six months. Mariana Green Steele, "Graduate's Record: University of Illinois" (Aug. 10, 1905), Alumni Records, Archives, UIUC. The various alumni forms for William Steele seemed to have been completed in haste. His file has some discrepancies in dates over the years. Most of his autobiographical material in alumni records, especially the later material, omits any mention of Pittsburgh.

94. Steele was a member of the board of trustees for the Sioux City Public Library for the years 1906–9, which established connections that led to architectural commissions for three branch libraries some years later. He was a member of the Sioux City Academy of Science and Letters and numerous civic organizations. Active in the Catholic church, Steele was president of the Catholic Charitable Society of Sioux

City, choir director at Sacred Heart Church, and a member of the Knights of Columbus. Steele must have been a fine orator as he was in demand as a public speaker; he frequently was the commencement speaker for local high schools and for nursing programs at area hospitals. Alumni Records, Archives, UIUC.

95. Steele chaired a commission to develop a building code for the city of Sioux City, 1913–14, and became principal author for the city's first building code. He served on the Board of Examiners for City Building Inspector, 1914–18. He also carried his organizational skills and leadership into the profession statewide. He was instrumental in getting the state of Iowa to adopt registration laws for architects. At the February 6–7, 1917, convention of the Iowa chapter of the American Institute of Architects, held in Des Moines, William L. Steele was elected president. Alumni Records, Archives, UIUC.

96. William L. Steele, "The Capitol Building and Loan Association at Topeka, Kansas," *Western Architect* (Sept. 1924): 99–100, plates 1–11.

97. Withey, *Biographical Dictionary of American Architects (Deceased)*, 569.

98. These children were: Melissa (b. November 6, 1905), William La Barthe Jr. (b. August 25, 1907), Harriet Gertrude (February 27, 1909–June 8, 1910), Jane Raymond (b. March 26, 1910), Sarah (Sallie) Green (b. February 7, 1914), and Philip Joseph (b. April 23, 1916). When the Steeles moved to Sioux City, they established residency at 2024 Douglas Street but by 1911 had moved to 2512 Jackson Street, where they resided until eventually leaving Sioux City for Omaha, Nebraska. Alumni Records, Archives, UIUC.

99. Peisch, *Chicago School of Architecture*, 80.

100. "Mr. Steele was to be executive head, Mr. Elmslie was to have charge of the planning and designing, Mr. Paul D. Cook, the structural engineering, and Mr. B. A. Broom, the mechanical engineering. The work was soon under way and acceptance by the Board of Supervisors of preliminary sketches was secured on March 23rd, 1915." *Western Architect* 30 (Feb. 1921): 13. This article was reprinted in Woodbury County Board of Supervisors, *Woodbury County Court House*, 7; H. Allen Brooks, ed., *Prairie School Architecture* (Toronto: University of Toronto Press, 1975), 130.

101. Kruty, *Prairie School Architects*, exhibition panel.

102. Terra cotta was from the American Terra Cotta and Ceramic Company; author's inventory prepared from orders listed in Gilfillen, *Index*, 42.

103. Schmitt, "Sullivanesque Architecture and Terra Cotta," 171.

104. Withey, *Biographical Dictionary of American Architects (Deceased)*, 569–70.

105. Study of working drawings, microfilm project of Burnham Library, Art Institute of Chicago, and University of Illinois (c. 1952).

106. Formal announcement (received Feb. 13, 1928), Alumni Records, Archives, UIUC.

107. In 1929, Steele resided at 3812 Davenport in Omaha. Associated architects in his firm were Louis W. Smetana of Omaha and George B. Hilgers of Sioux City. In 1946, William L. Steele retired due to poor health. In 1947, Steele resided in apartment 19 at 2315 Harvey Avenue, Omaha. That year, Steele and his wife moved to Neillsville, Wisconsin, to live with their daughter, Sallie, and her husband, Thomas S. Noble. There, Steele's wife, Mariana, died of pneumonia on January 28, 1948. After a long illness, William L. Steele died the following year, on March 4, 1949. Alumni Records, Archives, UIUC.

108. Gordon D. Orr Jr., "Louis W. Claude: Madison Architect of the Prairie School," *Prairie School Review* 14, Final Issue (1981): 6, 23.

109. Frank Lloyd Wright was born in 1869 at Richland Center and Claude was born in 1868 at Devils Lake, near Baraboo, Wisconsin. Wright moved (c. 1880) with his family to Madison. He began attending classes in 1885 at the University of Wisconsin and worked for Allen D. Conover of Conover and Porter, Architects and Engineers. Wright left Madison for Chicago in spring 1887. Manson, *Frank Lloyd Wright to 1910*, 2.

110. Orr, "Louis W. Claude," 7.

111. Ibid., 13.

112. *Historical and Architectural Walking Tour of Evansville's Historic District* (Evansville, Wisc.: Education Committee of the Evansville Historic Preservation Commission, 1983), n.p., entry 40.

113. Visser, *Frank Lloyd Wright and the Prairie School in Wisconsin*, 142.

114. Architectural Decorating Company, *Book of Designs: Plastic Ornaments* (Chicago: Architectural Decorating Company, 1928), 106.

115. This sympathetic expansion was the work of a Wausau, Wisconsin, architectural firm, Shavie and Murray. Visser, *Frank Lloyd Wright and the Prairie School in Wisconsin*, 237.

116. A massive wing, wider than the length of the original, was constructed in 1989 at the rear of Claude and Starck's building. Architects from the Chicago architectural firm of Frye Gillan Malinaro attempted to match the original brick; they reproduced the decorative frieze, wrapping it around their flat-roofed addition and aligning it with the original. The connection between the two buildings was complicated; the frieze on the narrowed "neck" of the new addition was slipped under the existing building's hip roof. It was a difficult assignment to provide for current and future needs while respecting Claude and Starck's handsome building. Author's field survey (1989).

117. A 10,000-square-foot addition was built in 1990 according to a design by the Minnesota architectural firm of Meyer, Scherer, and Rockcastle. "Detroit Lakes Public Library," *Architecture Minnesota* (Sept./Oct. 1991): 28–29.

118. A major addition (1980), designed by the Madison, Wisconsin, architectural firm of Potter, Lawson, and Pawlowsky, expanded the Tomah library. Visser, *Frank Lloyd Wright and the Prairie School in Wisconsin*, 209.

119. Orr, "Louis W. Claude," 22. Orr says that the drawings were dated 1919, but the order (no. 3279) for terra cotta from the American Terra Cotta and Ceramic Company was not placed until 1922. Gilfillen, *Index*, 53.

120. Author's field surveys and analysis.

121. A review of the terra-cotta order ledger in Gilfillen, *Index*, did not verify this assumption. However, several order numbers are lacking data; one of those may have been for that time frame. Orr, "Louis W. Claude," 20, 21, previously made these assumptions as well and they seem valid.

122. Spencer, *Prairie School Tradition*, 161.

123. This was confirmed by a thorough review of orders listed in Gilfillen, *Index*, 33, 41, 74.

124. See Orr, "Louis W. Claude," 24–33, for a (partial) list of buildings. As Orr notes, there are many other buildings he does not list. Several buildings designed by Claude and Starck that were not identified by Orr have been identified from records of the American Terra Cotta and Ceramic Company and the Midland Terra Cotta Company in Gilfillen, *Index*. In Madison, Wisconsin, these include: Madison Gas and Electric, Power House (1903–4); Castle and Doyle Coal Company (1921); Contagious Hospital (1924); Baseball Stadium, grandstand (1925); University Cooperative (1925); store alterations at 15 E. Main (1928); F&W Grand Store at 15–19 W. Main (1928); Herschleder Store at 531 State (1928); and Crane Company Warehouse on Williams Street (1929). In Lancaster, Wisconsin, Claude and Starck designed the Grant County Asylum (1913). After the partnership was dissolved in 1929, Claude designed the alterations and remodeling for a store and office building in Boscobel, Wisconsin (1930–31).

125. According to Presto's autobiographical entry in *Who's Who*, he "began in employ of Nimmons & Fellows, architects, 1910; later successively with Schmidt, Garden & Martin, architects, Leonard Construction Co., and Louis H. Sullivan, architect; conducting business in own name since Dec. 1920." Albert Nelson Marquis, ed., *Who's Who in Chicago*, 4th ed. (Chicago: A. N. Marquis, 1926), 705; Marquis, *Who's Who in Chicago and Vicinity, 1931*, 788. William Presto's parents were Oscar and Ida C. (Johnson) Presto. William Presto was a second lieutenant in the U.S. Army Quartermaster Corps in World War I. After his discharge from army service, Presto married Sylvia M. Nelson of Chicago on New Year's Eve, 1918.

126. Commission on Chicago Historical and Architectural Landmarks, *Krause Music Store* (Chicago: Commission on Chicago Historical and Architectural Landmarks, 1977), 3.

127. Review of American order (no. 3213), Gilfillen, *Index*, 52.

128. Author's list of William C. Presto's work was compiled from orders listed in Gilfillen, *Index*, and *The Economist*, numerous editions and pages.

129. Field work by author for a number of inventoried known buildings reveals this. However, many of Presto's buildings have been demolished and the designs remain unknown.

130. Building permit no. A98299 information, CCL.

131. Author's field surveys, 1987.

132. Ottenheimer's former partner, Henry J. Schlacks (1867–1938), seemed to reject completely Sullivan's message. Except for serving as associate architect to Claude and Starck for the Wilmette, Illinois, library, Schlacks doesn't seem to have had any association with the Sullivanesque or any other progressive design approach. Instead, he was an eclectic designer who favored the Gothic style. Perhaps his numerous commissions for Catholic churches prompted this choice. In a departure, however, his design for the Wilmette Village Hall (1910; demolished) featured a classical colonnade that marched around a flat-roofed building. Schlacks was born in 1867 in Chicago and lived in the city his entire life except for two years at MIT and travel abroad. Henry J. Schlacks died on January 6, 1938. *Illinois Society of Architects Monthly Bulletin* 22, nos. 8–9 (Feb.–Mar. 1938): 12.

133. Some urban designs and a gymnasium project of Ottenheimer, Stern, and Reichert were published in the *Western Architect* (Dec. 1914).

134. Twombly, *Louis Sullivan: His Life and Work*, 430, 432, 434.

135. Alice Sinkevitch, ed., *AIA Guide to Chicago* (New York: Harcourt Brace, 1993), 62.

136. Ibid., 189.

137. *Illinois Society of Architects Monthly Bulletin* 20, nos. 8–9 (Feb.–Mar. 1936): 8.

138. Esther McCoy, *Five California Architects* (New York: Reinhold, 1960), 61.

139. Withey, *Biographical Dictionary of American Architects (Deceased)*, 504, compared to lists of Illinois registered architects in *State of Illinois Biennial Report of the Board of Examiners of Architects* (1899–1915), and Illinois Society of Architects, *Handbook for Architects and Builders* (1915–25).

140. Author's field surveys, inventory prepared from orders listed in Gilfillen, *Index*, shop drawing, Midland Terra Cotta Co. (order no. 22214), NWAA.

141. Among the few draftsmen who were with Sullivan during his years of decline, several, such as Parker N. Berry and William C. Presto, attempted their own Sullivanesque designs. Others did not and were associated with eclectic architecture. These included Adolf O. Budina and Homer Sailor. Adolf Otto Budina (1891–1975), a 1914 graduate of the University of Illinois, worked for Sullivan and was Sullivan's last employee, leaving in the summer 1917. Budina later worked for John Eberson, a Chicago architect noted for his eclectic but distinctive movie theater designs. Homer Grant Sailor (1887–1968) earned a degree in architecture from the

Armour Institute and was employed by Louis Sullivan from 1911 to 1917. Sailor then opened his own office and, around 1925, formed a partnership as the firm of Sailor and Hoffman. Sailor's nonresidential commissions paid homage more to the famous Chicago theater architects Rapp and Rapp than to Sullivan. The superficial opulence of the great movie houses must have had an impact as Sailor seemed to revel in terra-cotta appliqués that mixed baroque and rococo ornament. The Great Depression was undoubtedly the major reason why Sailor left architecture for politics in 1931. However, he also experienced a conflict in design principles; for most of his practice he disavowed the tenets he had learned under Sullivan. Kruty, *Prairie School Architects*, exhibition panel; Art Institute of Chicago, *Chicago Architects Design*, 72.

CHAPTER 5: ORNAMENT

1. "Decorators, Painters and Paint Dealers," *Industrial Chicago*, 2:742.

2. Comparison of ornament photographed in the building for the Sioux City Journal with that illustrated in a catalog from the Decorator's Supply Company, which identified ornament no. 3434 as "Sullivanesque Style." The plaster piece was 11 ½" high and projected 4 ¾". Its list cost (c. 1925) was seventy cents per linear foot. Decorator's Supply Company, *Illustrated Catalog of Plastic Ornaments* (Chicago: Decorator's Supply Company, c. 1925), 161.

3. Comparison of ornament photographed with that illustrated in the catalog. The Architectural Decorating Company identified no. 3024A as a "Sullivanesque Style" panel ornament, measuring 27" x 36". Its cost in 1928 was ten dollars per panel. Architectural Decorating Company, *Book of Designs*, 106.

4. Dennis McFadden, "A Wright Restoration," *Inland Architect* 34, no. 5 (Sept./Oct. 1990): 37.

5. Decorator's Supply Company, *Illustrated Catalog of Plastic Ornaments*, 3.

6. Ibid., 94, 130, 132, 141, 151, 161, 187, 189, 190, 199.

7. In 1891, the company was headed by S. Strahan, president, and R. C. Foster, secretary and treasurer. Oscar Spindler was born on August 31, 1861, in Modlau, Germany, and educated in that country. He immigrated to the United States in 1887. After a year in Utica, New York, he went to Chicago and secured a position with the Decorator's Supply Company. "Decorators, Painters and Paint Dealers," 742.

8. Marquis, *Book of Chicagoans*, 1917, 638. Oscar Spindler married Salome Weigard of Chicago in 1888. Their family included a son, Raymond W., and a daughter, Ilse A. For more than fifteen years, the Spindlers resided at 3976 Lake Park Avenue, Chicago. Under Spindler's tenure, the position of secretary-treasurer for the Decorator's Supply Company was filled by a native Chicagoan, William Thomas Foster (b. January 12, 1869). Foster began working for the company in 1885 and remained there for more than forty-five years. He married Helen M. Hanifan in 1892 and they had three chil-

dren. Marquis, *Book of Chicagoans*, 1917, 242. Oscar Spindler was a member of the Chicago Architectural Club, the Art Institute of Chicago, and the Palette and Chisel. Marquis, *Book of Chicagoans*, 1917, 638; idem, *Who's Who in Chicago and Vicinity*, 1936, 953.

9. Officers of the Architectural Decorating Company were R. O. Schmidt, president; F. J. Hahn, vice president; Charles Dodd, secretary; and C. Bauer, treasurer. *Handbook for Architects and Builders* (Chicago: Chicago Architects' Business Association, 1911), 26. By 1915, Bauer was vice president; Dodd assumed the duties of secretary and treasurer; and Schmidt retained the position of president. Illinois Society of Architects, *Handbook for Architects and Builders* (1917), 260.

10. Architectural Decorating Company, *Book of Designs*, 8.

11. Ibid., 48, 67, 106, 107, 123, 219.

12. Timothy Samuelson, *Conflict and Creativity: Architects and Sculptors in Chicago, 1871–1937* (Chicago: Arts Club of Chicago, 1994), 4.

13. Hanks, *Decorative Designs of Frank Lloyd Wright*, 209. There is some uncertainty that Spierling and Linden did the interior finishes for Sullivan's Owatonna Bank. Millett (*Curve of the Arch*, 96) makes no reference to Spierling and Linden but refers to Louis J. Millet: "The precise extent of Millet's contribution to the bank is uncertain, although there can be no doubt that he had a large hand in creating the intricate color scheme of the banking room. It is known that he personally supervised final decorative work in the bank under Sullivan's direction." Lauren S. Weingarden (*Louis Sullivan: The Banks* [Cambridge, Mass.: MIT Press, 1987], 51) notes that Millet acted as colorist and consultant for the interior ornamental fresco patterns at the National Farmers' Bank, Owatonna, Minnesota. In addition, the bank pamphlet entitled *An Architectural Symphony* identifies Louis Millet as the person "who designed the great leaded glass windows and assisted Sullivan with the arch stencils and interior color work." There was no mention of Spierling and Linden.

14. Illinois Society of Architects, *Handbook for Architects and Builders* (1915), 256. Spierling and Linden were advertised as "Interior Decorators and Furnishers" and had offices and studios at 1216 South Michigan Avenue, Chicago. Marquis, *Who's Who in Chicago and Vicinity*, 1931, 920. Spierling was born on August 6, 1856, in Germany and went to Chicago at age twelve. After apprenticing in the decorator's studio of F. N. Atwood from 1875 to 1877, Spierling returned to Germany for study at the Art Trade School in Munich. Upon return to the United States, Spierling worked in New York until 1881, when he relocated to Chicago and worked for a year with P. M. Almini. The following year, Spierling formed a partnership with Linden, which lasted until 1929 when Spierling retired and the firm's name was changed. In 1882, Spierling married Caroline A. Behr of Chicago. The Spierling family included five children. Marquis, *Who's Who in Chicago and Vicinity*, 1936, 953.

15. Darling, *Chicago Ceramics and Glass*, 122.

16. Louis J. Millet "was born and educated in New York City before receiving additional training in Paris at the Ecole des Beaux-Arts and in the architectural section of the Ecole des Arts Décoratifs. From 1881 through 1899, Millet was in partnership with George L. Healy. Both men were friends of Sullivan; the three had known each other in Paris." Robert Judson Clark, ed., *The Arts and Crafts Movement in America, 1876–1916* (Princeton: Princeton University Press, 1972), 60.

17. Darling, *Chicago Ceramics and Glass*, 104–5.

18. Hanks, *Decorative Designs of Frank Lloyd Wright*, 209.

19. I have reviewed advertisements published between 1911 and 1925 by companies promoting ornamental plaster-work, plastic decoration, or architectural sculpture. Their names and particular skills included: Joseph Dux, "Architectural Sculptor, Stone and Wood Carving, Ornamental Patterns, Designing, Modeling"; Plastic Relief Manufacturing Company, "High Class Composition and Plaster Ornaments"; Robert N. Hughes, "Architectural Sculptor and Plasterer"; R. Palmquist and Company, "Plain and Ornamental Plastering"; A. Zettler, "Plastic Decorations, ornamental plaster"; J. T. Tudor, "Ornamental Plastering"; McNulty Brothers Company, "Architectural Sculptors"; and Chicago Ornamental Cement and Plaster Company, Carl J. Nilsson, Designer, "All kinds of Architectural Designs, Garden Decorations, Light Posts." Illinois Society of Architects, *Handbook for Architects and Builders* (1911–25), consecutive editions, various pages.

20. Donald P. Hallmark, "Richard W. Bock, Sculptor—Part I: The Early Work," *Prairie School Review* 8, no. 1 (1971): 9.

21. Millett, *Curve of the Arch*, 97.

22. Oskar Gross was born November 28, 1870, in Vienna, Austria. The son of an architect, his parents were Rudolph and Jeannette (Kurzweil) Gross. Gross was a 1897 graduate of the Royal Academy of Fine Arts, Vienna, and he also studied in Munich and Paris. He came to the United States in 1902. Marquis, *Book of Chicagoans, 1917*, 283.

23. Alice Coe McGlauflin, ed., *Who's Who in American Art* (Washington, D.C.: American Federation of Arts, 1938–39), 220.

24. Born on November 19, 1879, in Utica, New York, Allen E. Philbrick attended high school in Elgin, Illinois, and studied in Paris and at the School of the Art Institute of Chicago, where he also taught. His parents were Albert Francis and Elizabeth (Fox) Philbrick. He married Edith L. Kellogg of Chicago on June 24, 1908, and they had two children, Jane William and Allen Kellogg. Philbrick painted a portrait of Peter B. Wright, the first portrait for the American Institute of Architects gallery in Chicago. Marquis, *Book of Chicagoans, 1917*, 537.

25. Other muralists for Midway Gardens included Jerome S. Blum and William P. Henderson. See Paul Kruty, *Frank Lloyd Wright and Midway Gardens* (Urbana: University of Illinois Press, 1998), 144–56.

26. John A. Holak, "Richard W. Bock and His Museum at Greenville College," *Illinois Magazine* (Jan.–Feb. 1986): 13–14.

27. Hallmark, "Richard W. Bock, Sculptor—Part II," 9, 27, 28.

28. Richard Walter Bock, born in Schloppe, Germany, came to the United States at age five although he later returned to Europe to study at the Berlin Academy and the Ecole des Beaux-Arts, Paris. McGlauflin, *Who's Who in American Art*, 62. For more on Bock, see Dorathi Bock Pierre, ed., *Memoirs of an American Artist: Sculptor Richard W. Bock* (Los Angeles: C. C. Publishing, 1989).

29. Joseph Griggs, "Alfonso Iannelli," *Prairie School Review* 2, no. 4 (1965): 6, 14, 15.

30. Emil Robert Zettler's parents were August and Johanna (Ziller) Zettler. He married in 1922, but his wife, Mary Potter Jurey, died in 1927; Zettler was married again in 1931, to Edythe Louise Flack. He had three children. Marquis, *Who's Who in Chicago and Vicinity, 1941*, 928.

31. Darl Rastorfer, "Terra Cotta: Past to Present," *Architectural Record* (Jan. 1987): 110.

32. "Terra Cotta: Historical 'Baked Earth' an Early Office Building Staple," *Dodge Construction News* (June 27, 1988): 36.

33. Michael T. Miske, *Restoration and Maintenance of Architectural Terra Cotta*, pamphlet, reprint from *Masonry* (Masonry Contractors Association of America, n.d.).

34. Virginia Guest Ferriday, *Last of the Handmade Buildings* (Portland, Ore.: Mark Publishing, 1984), 32–35.

35. "A Visit to a Modern Terra Cotta Plant," *Clay Worker* 76, no. 3 (Sept. 1921): 233.

36. Ferriday, *Last of the Handmade Buildings*, 37.

37. Lefevre, *Architectural Pottery*, 366.

38. Paul N. Hasluck, *Terra Cotta Work* (London: Cassell, 1905), 13.

39. "Visit to a Modern Terra Cotta Plant," 234.

40. Ferriday, *Last of the Handmade Buildings*, 38.

41. Hasluck, *Terra Cotta Work*, 16.

42. Nancy D. Berryman and Susan M. Tindall, *Terra Cotta* (Chicago: Landmarks Preservation Council of Illinois, c. 1984), 6.

43. "Visit to a Modern Terra Cotta Plant," 234.

44. Gary F. Kurutz, *Architectural Terra Cotta of Gladding, McBean* (Sausalito, Calif.: Windgate Press, 1989), 10.

45. Darling, *Chicago Ceramics and Glass*, 168.

46. See Darling, *Chicago Ceramics and Glass*, 161–65, for history of the Chicago Terra Cotta Company. For further detail, see *Clay Record* 36, no. 3 (Feb. 14, 1910): 36; 37, no. 4 (Aug. 30, 1910): 32; 37, no. 5 (Sept. 15, 1910): 27.

47. The Winkle Terra Cotta Company was founded in 1883 by Joseph Winkle (1837–1914). Winkle was born in Staffordshire, England, and immigrated to the United States in 1859. The factory of the Winkle Terra Cotta Company was located at 5739 Manchester Road, St. Louis. See Mary M. Stiritz and Lawrence Giles, "Winkle Terra Cotta Compa-

ny," in *St. Louis Architectural Terra Cotta: An Installation of Historic Architectural Artifacts* (St. Louis: Missouri Botanical Garden, 1985), n.p. Adler and Sullivan buildings listed in Bryan, *Missouri's Contribution to American Architecture*, 353.

48. Three companies in Chicago made some form of "terra-cotta lumber." These were the Pioneer Fire Proof Construction Company (est. 1880), the Wright Fireproofing Company (est. 1879), and the Illinois Terra Cotta Lumber Company (est. 1885). Darling, *Chicago Ceramics and Glass*, 170–71; *Industrial Chicago*, 2:414–15, 789.

49. Capital stock of $500,000 was raised for the company; the organizers were G. A. Johnson, Stanley K. Gage, and Walter B. Rix. *Brick and Clay Record* 41, no. 7 (Oct. 1, 1912): 278.

50. Machinery for the new plant was installed in March 1913 and production started a few months later. The Advance company's first advertisement in the Illinois Society of Architects' *Handbook for Architects and Builders* appeared in 1913 and its last in 1918. The company seems to have lapsed into obscurity although it was listed in Chicago directories as late as 1925, with offices at 203 South Dearborn Street. Other than the names of its founders, only a name of a ceramic engineer, J. B. Krehbiel, has surfaced. *Brick and Clay Record* 42, no. 3 (Feb. 1, 1913): 189; *Clay Worker* 69, no. 3 (Mar. 1918): 479; *Donnelley's Directory: A Catalog of Chicago District, 1925* (Chicago: Reuben H. Donnelley, 1925), 272. The Advance company was also listed in the 1922 *Donnelley Directory* but with offices at 115 South Dearborn Street, Chicago.

51. *Clay Record* 36, no. 1 (Jan. 15, 1910): 32. By 1916, Federal wasn't listed in Chicago directories and had retreated to the East Coast.

52. *The Northwestern Terra Cotta Company*, company catalog, 13, 41.

53. Joseph Siry, *Carson-Pirie-Scott* (Chicago: University of Chicago Press, 1988), 229.

54. Darling, *Chicago Ceramics and Glass*, 168.

55. Hottinger married Catherine Rouse of Chicago in 1871. They had six children, one of whom, Adolf F. Hottinger (b. March 31, 1872), became the chief chemist and, in 1916, treasurer of the Northwestern company. *Industrial Chicago*, 2:736; Marquis, *Who's Who in Chicago*, 435.

56. Twombly, *Louis Sullivan: His Life and Work*, 387, 399.

57. *Industrial Chicago*, 2:737; *Brick and Clay Record* 40, no. 7 (Apr. 1, 1912): 333.

58. *Western Architect* (Jan. 1920): 20. This issue of the journal contained an obituary for Fritz Wagner but it was not the usual write-up; instead, it only extolled Wagner's demeanor and his support for the Chicago Architectural Club.

59. Samuelson, *Conflict and Creativity*, 23.

60. Ibid., 9.

61. Siry, *Carson-Pirie-Scott*, 174.

62. National Register form, CCL, handwritten notation.

63. "Obituary," *Clay Record* 37, no. 12 (Dec. 30, 1910): 27.

64. Darling, *Teco*, 170.

65. Ibid., 174.

66. Darling, *Chicago Ceramics and Glass*, 200.

67. Paul Evans, *Art Pottery of the United States* (New York: Feingold and Lewis, 1987), 195.

68. Darling, *Chicago Ceramics and Glass*, 72.

69. Verified by review of *Sweets Catalogue of Building Construction*, various editions (1906, 1907, 1910, 1914, 1916, 1918, 1923, 1926–27). Northwestern was the only Chicago terra-cotta company to be listed in each of these editions.

70. Illinois Society of Architects, *Handbook for Architects and Builders*, all editions up to 1926; *The Economist*, various editions (1910–26).

71. The January 1921 issue of the *American Builder* was an exception. This was a special edition devoted to the many hotels designed by the Chicago architect Walter W. Ahlschlager, and these hotels were clad with Northwestern wares. A two-page advertising spread for the Northwestern Terra Cotta Company was included and seems to have been the only time the company was represented in that journal. *American Carpenter and Builder*, later titled *American Builder* (1911–25).

72. *Brick and Clay Record* 40, no. 6 (Mar. 15, 1912): 260–62, 320.

73. *The Northwestern Terra Cotta Company*, company catalog, 3.

74. Ibid.

75. "Northwestern routinely sold white terra cotta blocks that were somewhat crudely modeled after Sullivan's highly refined designs, such as the Felsenthal Store." Pauline Saliga, ed., *Fragments of Chicago's Past* (Chicago: Art Institute of Chicago, 1990), 149.

76. Northwestern's manufacture of terra cotta for these buildings was verified in the untitled, unpublished list of Northwestern terra-cotta orders compiled by Timothy Samuelson.

77. Field surveys by the author and verified in Samuelson's untitled, unpublished list of Northwestern terra-cotta orders. Architects and owners were identified from building permit information maintained by the Commission on Chicago Landmarks.

78. Field surveys by the author and verified in Samuelson's untitled, unpublished list of Northwestern terra-cotta orders. Architects and owners were identified from building permit information maintained by the Commission on Chicago Landmarks. Information for 2522 S. Michigan was incomplete; the owner's name was illegible and the architect not listed. However, I believe that the architects may have been Rissman and Hirschfield.

79. *Northwestern Terra Cotta* 1, no. 2 (Dec. 1937), n.p.

80. Darling, *Chicago Ceramics and Glass*, 203.

81. Gilfillen, *Index*, various pages. I prepared a comprehensive list of designs by Sullivan, Purcell and Elmslie, Parker Berry, and William Steele and compared it to order listings of the American Terra Cotta and Ceramic Company. Sulli-

van's and Purcell and Elmslie's commissions matched almost completely with American records; Berry's and Steele's had a much lower correlation. Terra-cotta orders by American for Sullivan's banks included those in Owatonna, Minnesota (no. 1689); Grinnell, Iowa (no. 2405); Newark, Ohio (no. 2463); West Lafayette, Indiana (no. 2466); Sidney, Ohio (no. 2816); and Columbus, Wisconsin (no. 2916). The Van Allen Building in Clinton, Iowa (no. 2277), and the facade for the Krause Music Store, Chicago (no. 3213), were other Sullivan designs for which American made the terra cotta.

82. Martin W. Reinhart, "Norwegian-born Sculptor, Kristian Schneider: His Essential Contribution to the Development of Louis Sullivan's Ornamental Style," paper presented at the Norwegian American Life of Chicago Symposium, October 23, 1982, Norway Center, Chicago.

83. Darling, *Teco*, 175.

84. William D. Gates's parents were Simon S. and Sylvia (Day) Gates. Albert Nelson Marquis, ed., *The Book of Chicagoans, 1911* (Chicago: A. N. Marquis, 1911), 261.

85. Darling, *Teco*, 16.

86. Evans, *Art Pottery*, 278.

87. Darling, *Teco*, 35.

88. Marquis, *Who's Who in Chicago*, 329.

89. Occasionally, the Chicago Architectural Club took an excursion to Gates's plant. One such outing occurred on Saturday, July 15, 1911, and a "thanks" was printed in the journal, *Brick and Clay Record:* "The Chicago Architectural Club feels greatly indebted to Mr. W. D. Gates for the splendid outing which the club enjoyed as the guests of The American Terra Cotta Co., at Terra Cotta." *Brick and Clay Record* 39, no. 2 (July 15, 1911): 58.

90. Darling, *Teco*, 24.

91. *Sixteenth Annual Exhibition of the Chicago Architectural Club*, n.p.

92. List of Chicago architects compiled from names of designers identified in catalog. Catalog, *Teco* (1905), various pages.

93. *Common Clay* 1, no. 4 (Oct. 1920): 11.

94. Shop drawings, American order no. 3497, NWAA. The use of numbers to identify terra-cotta accent pieces was different than the usual reference marks used for terra-cotta work; the number indicates a stock identification.

95. Among these identified draftsmen were: Heitmann and C. Kallim for Sullivan's Van Allen Store (1913) in Clinton, Iowa; Hetrick and Elmzen for the Home Building Association (1914), Newark, Ohio; Tharp for People's Savings and Loan (1917), Sidney, Ohio; and M. J. Ritt and Nordberg, the Farmers' and Merchants' Bank (1919), Columbus, Wisconsin. Other draftsmen employed with the American Terra Cotta and Ceramic Company sometime during the period 1914–24 included: Allen, Alstrom, Bierdeman, Churan, Goffeney, Hoff, F. G. Kartowicz, G. Kirnson, L. Ritt, E. Studer, and Thomas. John R. E. Bjorklund headed the drafting department. This group was identified through a study of avail-

able shop drawings, NWAA. Usually only initials or a last name were given. Initials cannot be identified and therefore are not given in the text. The initials "G.S." appeared on shop drawings for the four Sullivan projects discussed. It appears that none of these draftsmen was a registered architect while employed at American. "Lists of Registered Architects," Illinois Society of Architects, *Handbook for Architects and Builders* (1915, 1921), various pages.

96. Advertisement for American Terra Cotta and Ceramic Company, *The Brickbuilder* 23 (Dec. 1914): ix.

97. "Lions in Architecture," *Common Clay* 1, no. 1 (July 1920): 12.

98. "Who's Who in the American Terra Cotta Co.," *Common Clay* 1, no. 4 (Oct. 1920): 13.

99. Willard Connely, *Louis Sullivan: The Shaping of an American Architecture* (New York: Horizon Press, 1960), 285.

100. American's offices were in the thirteen-story Chamber of Commerce Building (1888–89; Baumann and Huel, Architects) at the southeast corner of LaSalle and Washington Streets. In 1911, offices were relocated to the People's Gas Building, 122 South Michigan Avenue at Adams Street. The January–February 1922 issue of *Common Clay* reported: "tiring of the limited space afforded by Loop accommodations, we went house hunting and bought the Hibbard Residence at 1701 Prairie Avenue." The company also acquired space at 1808 Prairie Avenue as former mansions were converted into business offices. By 1927, American's front offices were back in the Loop at 228 North LaSalle. The drafting department had been housed in the Chicago offices until 1913, when it was moved to the factory location. Gates spent most of his time at the Chicago offices and traveled to the factory about once a week. He maintained a weekend retreat in an old farmhouse at the factory site but his principal residence was in suburban Hinsdale. *Common Clay* 4, no. 1 (Jan.–Feb. 1920): 13; Darling, *Teco*, 17, 26.

101. In 1911, capital stock increased from $200,000 to $500,000. *Brick and Clay Record* 40, no. 1 (Jan. 1, 1912): 66.

102. In 1913, preferred stock was issued and capital raised from $500,000 to $700,000. *Brick and Clay Record* 42, no. 10 (Apr. 1913): 774.

103. *Common Clay*'s "Who's Who" column in the early 1920s featured Ernest Clark, plant superintendent; Fritz Wagner Jr., sales manager and the son of Fritz Wagner of the Northwestern Terra Cotta Company; and L. M. "Bert" Munshaw, chief chemist, who joined the company in 1901 and, along with Elmer E. Gorton, helped develop the beautiful glazes used for Teco and terra-cotta wares. In addition, long-time plant workers who had risen to positions of responsibility were often featured in *Common Clay*. These included: pressing foremen Fred Rose and Fred Shuman; fitting room foreman Charles Nelson; and shipping foreman Otto Schwarz. Other people important in the history of the American Terra Cotta and Ceramic Company were W. H. Edwards and John G. Crowe. After the 1887 reorganization,

Edwards became secretary and treasurer of the American company. Later, Nathan Herzog became treasurer. When Gates relinquished presidency of the company, Harry J. Lucas assumed that role, but only for a few months. Soon, Crowe filled that position. Crowe joined the company in 1893 and had served stints as vice president and treasurer. Albert Sheffield was the company secretary in the 1920s. Duane F. Albery was an assistant chemist with the company for four years, after graduation from Ohio State University. He resigned in 1913 to form his own pottery works, Albery Novelty Pottery, in Evanston, Illinois. After two years, Albery left for the East Coast although he later returned to Chicago and worked for the Northwestern Terra Cotta Company before becoming plant superintendent at American.

104. *Common Clay* 1, no. 2 (July 1920): 13.

105. Darling, *Teco*, 19, 27, 42. According to Darling, the earliest work of the American company was modeled by A. LaJeune and a German potter named Gotterman.

106. The children were William Paul, Ellis Day, Margaret (Mrs. Price Williams), Neil Hurlbut, Major Earl, and Sylvia Day (Mrs. R. T. Evans). Marquis, *Who's Who in Chicago*, 329.

107. William Paul (1879–1920) worked as a chemist with the company and helped develop Teco lines. W. Paul Gates became company secretary in 1903. He left in 1908 for the Pacific Northwest and later worked for several terra-cotta companies on both coasts. Ellis (1880–1923) also worked as a chemist for the company and assisted in developing various glazes. In 1903, Ellis D. Gates became treasurer of the company, succeeding Nathan Herzog. Ten years later, Ellis relocated to Mobile, Alabama, where he opened a building supply company. Sharon Darling reported that Neil H. Gates (1884–1971) "was secretary-treasurer of the firm for many years. Major Earl (1886–1970) was the inventor of pulsichrome (a machine that sprayed glazes) and held several patents. He served as superintendent and later general manager of the plant." In 1922, Major Earl Gates formed a new company, the Clay Service Corporation, based in Chicago. With Justus C. Chancellor and Chancellor's son (junior) as investors, the company dealt in clay and machinery used in clay production. Darling, *Teco*, 20, 39, 172; *Brick and Clay Record* 42, no. 4 (Feb. 15, 1913): 239, and 60, no. 12 (June 27, 1922): 1014.

108. John William Leonard, ed., *The Book of Chicagoans* (Chicago: A. N. Marquis, 1905), 228; Marquis, *The Book of Chicagoans, 1911*, 261; idem, *Who's Who in Chicago*, 329.

109. The first headquarters for the National Terra Cotta Society were in the People's Gas Building, Chicago, which was where the American Terra Cotta and Ceramic Company offices were then located. This choice of office location was not surprising since Gates was secretary of the new society. At the same time, he served as president of the Illinois Clay Manufacturers Association as well as president for the Chicago Clay Club. These industry-wide responsibilities must have influenced Gates's decision to relinquish his managing presi-

dency position at American in 1913 and become chairman of the board of directors for the company. Gates had active roles in other industrial organizations, including the Terra Cotta Division of the National Brick Manufacturers Association and the American Ceramic Society. He served terms as president for both organizations. *Brick and Clay Record* 40, no. 7 (Apr. 1, 1912): 333; 40, no. 4 (Feb. 15, 1912): 182; 40, no. 1 (Jan. 1, 1912): 160. In 1922, Gates was a driving force in the establishment of the Association of Arts and Industries. As reported by *Brick and Clay Record*, this was "the amalgamation of two societies that were interested in the promotion of arts such as drawing, painting, sculpture, modeling, metal work, pottery decoration, and so forth. Among the list of directors is none other than William D. Gates." The first offices of the association were at 230 East Ohio Street, Chicago. *Brick and Clay Record* 60, no. 9 (May 16, 1922): 781.

110. Marquis, *Who's Who in Chicago*, 329.

111. Darling, *Teco*, 63.

112. The Indianapolis Terra Cotta Company was incorporated in 1883 as a successor to Stilz, Joiner, and Company and it too was reorganized several times (1899, 1904) because of financial difficulties. Benjamin D. Walcott served as the company president during this time, until his death on September 21, 1916. After the American takeover, the Indianapolis plant was managed by George H. Lacey. Lacey had been born in England and had practiced as an architect in London before coming to the United States. He joined the Indianapolis Terra Cotta Company in 1896 after previous employment with several East Coast terra-cotta companies. *Common Clay* 2, no. 3 (Mar. 1921): 3; Gilfillen, *Index*, 291; *Common Clay* 2, no. 3 (Mar. 1921): 15.

113. Author's fieldwork and check of orders from Gilfillen, *Index*, 296, 302.

114. The American Terra Cotta Corporation struggled but updated its Terra Cotta, Illinois, works. A 400-foot continuous tunnel kiln replaced the old periodic kilns in 1936. This kiln probably saved the company as it was used for annealing steel during World War II, which became a principal activity of the company after the war, although clay products were made until 1966. Teco wares, relegated to garden pottery, ceased production in 1941. In 1972, after a merger, the company name was changed to TC Industries, Inc., and Gates's old terra-cotta works became the site of an updated factory for heat-treating and the production of construction equipment. Darling, *Teco*, 70–73.

115. Exact counts are impossible due to incomplete listings, but it is possible to compile a reasonably accurate range per year. Gilfillen, *Index*, 189.

CHAPTER 6: STOCK SULLIVANESQUE AND THE MIDLAND TERRA COTTA COMPANY

1. Marquis, *Book of Chicagoans, 1911*, 399; idem, *Book of Chicagoans, 1917*, 394. Krieg's home was listed at 1615 South Trumbull Avenue, Chicago, in both entries. On June 3, 1896,

Kreig married Clara J. Patz in Chicago. They subsequently had three children, Amelia, Arthur, and Clarice.

2. Krieg located his office at 84 Washington Street in the Loop while the office of Frederick E. Gatterdam remained at 163 Randolph Street. Gatterdam's practice concentrated on industrial buildings with emphasis on breweries. He later moved to Texas and died there. Obituary, *Illinois Society of Architects Monthly Bulletin* 28–29, nos. 12–1 (June–July 1944): 8.

3. Marquis, *Book of Chicagoans, 1911*, 399.

4. Darling, *Chicago Ceramics and Glass*, 187.

5. Gilfillen, *Index*, 315. Thirty thousand dollars' worth of capital stock was owned by H. V. Shepard, H. D. Lewis, and W. N. Shepard. *Clay Record* 37, no. 10 (Nov. 30, 1910): 32.

6. *Brick and Clay Record* 39, no. 3 (Aug. 1, 1911): 91.

7. Adjacent, to the east, was the Grant Works of the National Malleable Castings Company; there was still vacant prairie to the west and south, although a small scrap yard occupied some of the southerly frontage along West Sixteenth Street. Sanborn Map Company, *Chicago*, vol. 20 (Chicago: Sanborn Map Co., 1917), map 38 (Cicero).

8. *The Economist* (Jan. 14, 1911): 161.

9. *Brick and Clay Record* 38, no. 11 (May 1911): 548.

10. Two buildings of equal length (245 feet) were spaced 150 feet apart and parallel to each other, but one was two stories high while the other was only one story. Oriented with the long axis north-south, both buildings used wood-lattice trusses for column-free interiors and had roof monitors with wire-glass clerestory windows that punctuated the gently curved arched roofs. The two-story building, with elevator, was 75 feet wide and contained the pressing and finishing operations. The one-story building, 60 feet wide, was to the east and housed fitting and shipping functions. Kilns and a covered service walkway were located between the two buildings and linked them. A third building, with an east-west alignment, near West Sixteenth Street, was separated from the pressing and finishing building by 70 feet and a railroad siding although the two structures were connected by a concrete-pipe tunnel. This building was compartmentalized by a variety of functional spaces as a four-story mill rose from the center of the building and divided it into flanking one-story wings. The west wing housed a laboratory and clay storage while the east wing contained a generating plant, boiler house, coal storage, and carpentry shop. A small, one-story office building, with hip-roof, stood to the west of the pressing and finishing building. This office structure was later replaced by a larger two-story building constructed west of it. The Schultz company was a Chicago concern founded 1896 by Albert L. Schultz (b. 1862 in Germany) and located at 1675 Elston Avenue. *Brick and Clay Record* 39, no. 3 (Aug. 1, 1911): 91.

11. In little more than a year, the company literally moved up, in April 1911, as it vacated its fifth-floor location (rooms 522–23) for more spacious quarters on the eleventh floor. In

August 1912 its offices were in rooms 1120–22 of the Chamber of Commerce Building. *Brick and Clay Record* 39, no. 3 (Aug. 1, 1911): 115. In 1914, Midland secured the order (no. 4200) for the architectural terra cotta that complemented the brick exterior cladding of a sixteen-story office tower, the Lumber Exchange Building at 11 South LaSalle Street, designed by Holabird and Roche. Midland moved its offices into the completed building, which served as a good promotional tool and demonstration of the company product besides providing convenient and prestigious office space. By May 1915 the company occupied suite 1515 of the Lumber Exchange Building. *Building Age* (Apr. 1914): 32; *American Carpenter and Builder* (May 1915): 103. In 1921, the building was expanded by a six-story addition, which raised its height to twenty-one stories. Holabird and Roche were again the architects; however, Midland didn't receive the terra-cotta contract for the expansion. This slight may have been due to Midland's relocation of its offices back to the Chamber of Commerce Building by June 1920. *American Builder* (June 1920): 67; *Clay Worker* 75, no. 1 (Jan. 1921): 51.

12. The land was purchased for $18,000 from John Walker. *Brick and Clay Record* 39, no. 12 (Dec. 15, 1911): 478.

13. Review of "List of Licensed Architects," Illinois Society of Architects, *Handbook for Architects and Builders* (1915–25).

14. While an officer with Midland, Mendius held memberships in the Chicago Architectural Club and the Art Institute of Chicago. He was also a family man. Mendius married Elline Bruhhs of Chicago on June 3, 1903, and they had three children: Caroline Louise (Mrs. W. O. Heinze), Fred H., and Jack Richard. Marquis, *Who's Who in Chicago*, 598; idem, *Who's Who in Chicago and Vicinity, 1931*, 669.

15. By 1936, Mendius resided in Burbank, California. Marquis, *Who's Who in Chicago and Vicinity, 1936*, 691.

16. Marquis, *Book of Chicagoans, 1917*, 552. Born on March 3, 1887, in Elkhart, Indiana, Primley graduated from Harvard University in 1909. While Primley served with Midland, he was also associated with the Wisconsin Granite Company and became its president in 1914. Primley married Kathleen F. Drumm of Montreal, Canada, on November 21, 1911. He and his wife resided at 903 Forest Avenue, Evanston, Illinois; around 1930, they moved farther north to Hubbard Woods. Marquis, *Who's Who in Chicago and Vicinity, 1941*, 674.

17. Gilfillen, *Index*, 315.

18. An article in the *Clay Worker* told of the National Brick Manufacturer's Association 1918 national convention in Indianapolis, Indiana. Henry Krieg and B. S. Radcliffe attended and represented Midland. *Clay Worker* 69, no. 2 (Feb. 1918): 135–37.

19. *Clay-Worker* 69, no. 6 (June 1918): 763.

20. Study of Midland shop drawings, NWAA.

21. Ibid. I have studied hundreds of shop drawings and recorded names and initials, with dates. Midland shop drawings had a title block that usually included boxes labeled

"draftsman," "checked," "sent to shop." Names and/or initials were to be filled in at each box. Risch's handwriting had a distinctive letter "R" and, although this initial often appeared only in the "checked" and/or "sent to shop" box, it was clearly his. Neither his first name nor first initial ever seems to have appeared. Another draftsman, who was with the company for more than ten years, was identified as "Paul L."; his last name has not been determined. Draftsmen who were with Midland for a period of two to six years but left before 1918 were: Alstrom, Bergman, Bradfield, Miner, T. Paulson, Robert Silvestri, A. H. Slepicka, and J. D. Zimmerlin. After 1918 and before 1924, the group of draftsmen included Baird, Baumel, H. F. Bossert, J. Duboski, Ekenberg, A. J. Harder, F. Kiest, J. N. Petersen, J. Rehder, Rigali, F. G. Rossi, and Seibert.

22. I compared the list of draftsmen, compiled from identifications on shop drawings, with the "List of Licensed Architects," Illinois Society of Architects, *Handbook for Architects* (1911–24, various editions).

23. *Brick and Clay Record* 41, no. 12 (Dec. 15, 1912): 466–68. Designed by the architects Huehl and Schmid, the Medinah Temple was dedicated on October 30 and completed in December 1912. The order for Medinah's terra cotta was placed in October 1911 and was Midland's ninetieth contract. Although still standing, the building is threatened with demolition or major alterations.

24. Order (no. 1137), listed in Gilfillen, *Index*, 317–18.

25. I compiled the total number of orders for Midland and the American company and compared them; however, the counts for American are only approximate as order counts per year were not precise. The number of orders does not equal the number of buildings that used terra cotta; some orders were additions for the same building, some were for gateways for streets, pylons, garden decorations, and other uses. Gilfillen, *Index*.

26. Midland advertisement, *American Carpenter and Builder* (Dec. 1915): 117.

27. I determined this by reviews of three different Midland catalog portfolios, undated (c. 1917, c. 1922, c. 1924).

28. Schmitt, "Sullivanesque Architecture and Terra Cotta," 172–73.

29. *Midland Terra Cotta Company: Plates* (Chicago: Midland Terra Cotta Co., c. 1917), plate 45.

30. "Special Offer to Introduce High Grade Terra Cotta," *American Carpenter and Builder* (Feb. 1915): 102.

31. *Sweet's Catalogue of Building Construction* (New York: F. W. Dodge, 1914), 138–39.

32. I looked at many journals from a period of many years, with emphasis on 1911–20. I checked the "List of Advertisers," when available. Midland advertisements seem to have appeared most often in the *American Architect* during 1915 and in the *Western Architect* during the 1920s.

33. Illinois Society of Architects, *Handbook for Architects and Builders* (1911–20), various pages. Northwestern always had a

prominent advertisement of text on a half page inside the front cover until 1916, when it went to full-page ads (always on page 10), sometimes with illustrations. American consistently had a quarter-page notice. Another manufacturer, the Advance Terra Cotta Company, ran quarter-page advertisements in the 1913 through 1916 editions and half-page ones for 1917 and 1918. For the 1911 through 1913 editions, Midland had quarter-page advertisements that were positioned immediately below the American ones. In 1914, Midland included a drawing from a design plate in its half-page advertisement. This conspicuously contrasted with the adjacent American notice, which now appeared below the Midland ad. This seemed to illustrate Midland's claim of superiority.

34. Study of various volumes of these trade journals over a span of years. I checked the "List of Advertisers," when available.

35. "Statement of Ownership Required by the Act of August 24, 1912," *American Carpenter and Builder* (Nov. 1914): 85. Offices were at 5341 East End Avenue and, later, at 1827 South Prairie Avenue.

36. Determined by review of all issues of *American Carpenter and Builder* (renamed *American Builder* in 1917) for 1913–23. The first article was entitled "We Discover the Great Advantage." The April "Terra Cotta Talks" was subtitled "Building Boom Strikes Main Street" and was followed by "Modern Store Fronts of Terra Cotta" in May 1914.

37. *American Builder* (Apr. 1920): 200. Mendius concluded the letter by writing: "The co-operation and service which you have extended enabled us to make our advertising in the *American Builder* most profitable and the benefits derived have far exceeded our expectations. We hope to be with you for a good many years to come, thereby availing ourselves of a sure medium to a still greater success."

38. *American Builder* (Feb. 1915): 86, 87, 102; *American Builder* (Mar. 1915): 104–5.

39. I determined this by reviewing plates that appeared in dated issues of *American Carpenter and Builder*. A Midland advertisement featuring a reduced version of plate 44 appeared on page 99 of the April 1915 issue, where it was noted: "A plate from our 1915 Portfolio—Now ready for distribution—Write for it."

40. I determined this by reviewing "Catalog Portfolios," *Midland Terra Cotta Company*, n.d. (c. 1917, c. 1922, c. 1924).

41. I studied hundreds of shop drawings at NWAA and identified the draftsmen responsible. I compared freehand printing to that on plates. Other clues also suggested Nejdl and Johnson. Important "Key Elevations" for shop drawings were consistently drawn by Nejdl and Johnson. In addition, both men did most, if not all, of the shop drawings for building designs credited to the Midland company when it acted as architect. Of the two, George J. Nejdl appears to have done more of the key elevations and shop drawings for "Midland designed" buildings.

42. I compiled a list of buildings from identification notes

on order records using Gilfillen, *Index*. I cross-referenced most to available shop drawings at NWAA.

43. Determined by author's field surveys and study of shop drawings, NWAA.

44. Order ledger listings in Gilfillen, *Index*, 347 (order no. 594).

45. Midland advertisements, *American Carpenter and Builder* (Feb. 1915): 86, 87; (Mar. 1915): 104, 105.

46. Midland advertisements, *American Carpenter and Builder* (Feb. 1916): 183; (Mar. 1916): 115.

47. Midland's first constructed architectural commission was the First National Bank in Coon Rapids, Iowa. Built in 1913, the building was designed in the classical revival style. A large arched entrance was flanked by Ionic columns. Additional eclectic designs followed from Midland. Study of Midland shop drawings (order no. 3114), NWAA.

48. Author's field survey and Gilfillen, *Index*, 345 (order no. 551).

49. Author's field surveys and Gilfillen, *Index*, 360 (Peoria, order no. 6149) and 361 (Rockford, order no. 6183).

50. Author's field survey and Gilfillen, *Index*, 366 (order no. 7129).

51. Author's field survey and study of Midland shop drawing, courtesy of NWAA.

52. Author's field survey and Gilfillen, *Index*, 384 (order no. 21090).

53. Author's field survey and Midland shop drawing (order no. 21041), courtesy of NWAA.

54. Midland shop drawing (order no. 21087), courtesy of NWAA.

55. Author's field surveys and Gilfillen, *Index*, 386 (order no. 21157).

56. Author's field surveys and Midland shop drawings (order no. 23066), courtesy of NWAA.

57. Author's field surveys and Midland shop drawings (order no. 21071), courtesy of NWAA.

58. Author's field surveys and Midland shop drawings (order no. 21004), courtesy of NWAA.

59. I studied hundreds of Midland shop drawings, NWAA, and, when draftsmen were identified, compiled a list and made comparisons.

60. Author's review of Midland shop drawings, NWAA. Other draftsmen's initials and names also appeared on some of the sheets of shop drawings. However, for the "Key Elevations" and most important drawings directly related to design decisions, Nejdl's name or, occasionally, Johnson's name appeared. Furthermore, Nejdl's drawings of partial detail elevations often showed the actual ornamental features; i.e., entwined floral motifs and designs. These were drawn in pencil as if to study connections and associations. These studies usually depicted corners where two different stock pieces abutted, seemingly so the draftsman might learn how the ornamental features related.

61. Many of the Midland Terra Cotta Company shop drawings were in the possession of the American Terra Cotta Corporation and were part of the collection of American documents acquired by NWAA. After the Midland company was dissolved, American may have acquired its shop drawings in anticipation of providing replacement terra cotta. Replacement orders for damaged or broken terra cotta were frequent with all of the terra-cotta companies. Another possibility is that after Midland ceased operation, a former Midland employee took the drawings with him to a new position with American. A number of Midland shop drawings, like other company records, were lost and probably destroyed. Information from Alan Lathrop, director, NWAA, personal interview by author, July 1990.

62. Author's field surveys and Gilfillen, *Index*, 394, 399 (Midland order nos. 22227, 22382). The building was also cited in *The Economist* (Jan. 6, 1923): 68.

63. John T. Hetherington practiced architecture before Illinois enacted registration laws and he received his license (A 284) under the "grandfather" provision. Murray D. Hetherington was a 1915 graduate of the Chicago School of Architecture, where he was considered an outstanding pupil. The firm also did city planning work and Krieg planned the town of Indrio, Florida, in 1924. In 1925, Krieg engaged in appraisal work connected with street widening projects for the Board of Local Improvements, City of Chicago. Illinois Society of Architects, *Handbook for Architects and Builders* (1922), 73; *Illinois Board of Examiners of Architects First Biennial Report* (Chicago: Board of Examiners of Architects, 1899), 34; *The Chicago School of Architecture Yearbook for 1914–15* (Chicago: Armour Institute of Technology and Art Institute of Chicago, 1914), n.p (one page was devoted to a student project, "A Suburban Railroad Station," by M. D. Hetherington); Marquis, *Who's Who in Chicago*, 502.

64. Study of Midland Shop Drawing (order no. 24130), NWAA.

65. Author's field surveys and review of orders for Krieg, Hetherington, and Hetherington, Gilfillen, *Index*, 56.

66. Author's field surveys and inventory of buildings prepared from Gilfillen, *Index*.

67. Marquis, *Who's Who in Chicago and Vicinity, 1936*, 556.

68. *Illinois Society of Architects Monthly Bulletin* 28 and 29, nos. 1 and 2 (June–July 1944): 8. Walter Krieg had retired in 1963 and he and his wife, Mildred (Van Duzer), moved to Eugene, Oregon, where his two sisters lived. The family home at 180 Maplewood Road in Riverside was sold. William G. Krieg had moved his family from Chicago into the Riverside house around 1920 and Walter took possession of the house after William left for California in 1931. Alumni Records, Archives, UIUC. Walter's wife and sisters were also University of Illinois graduates. William G. Krieg, in addition to being an architect, businessman, parent, and politician, was an avid sportsman and listed his interests as "hunting, fishing, motoring, golf, and marksmanship." Earlier in his life, he had been active in a number of gun clubs. Sources:

Marquis, *Book of Chicagoans, 1917*, 394; idem, *Who's Who in Chicago*, 502; idem, *Book of Chicagoans, 1911*, 399.

69. *Illinois Society of Architects Monthly Bulletin* 28 and 29, nos. 1 and 2 (June–July 1944): 8.

70. The "Listing of Architects" in 1911–24 editions of the Illinois Society of Architects' *Handbooks for Architects and Builders* verifies this; William G. Krieg's name doesn't appear between 1915 and 1919.

71. *Illinois Society of Architects Monthly Bulletin* 6, no. 10 (Apr. 1922): 4.

72. Determined by review of orders listed in Gilfillen, *Index*, and my tabulation by year.

73. Comparison of Sullivanesque buildings by year, from an inventory of Sullivanesque designs I prepared using numerous sources including my field surveys, publications, order listings from Gilfillen's *Index*, and Midland shop drawings, NWAA.

74. Determined from author's field surveys and Midland shop drawings, NWAA. There were probably more than ten but only that number has been verified. In 1927, the orders for Midland terra cotta totaled 234; therefore, the overwhelming majority of orders was for historically derived ornament and utilitarian pieces such as bulkheads and simple windowsills.

75. Darling, *Chicago Ceramics and Glass*, 199.

76. What enticed Schneider to join Midland is not entirely known although American was in financial difficulty at the time. In 1930, American had about 50 orders for terra cotta whereas Midland had 116. At that time, it appeared that Midland was more secure than American. During the lean Depression years of 1931–33, Midland orders totaled 129 for the three years, but at American only about 50 orders were secured for the same period. Determined orders listed by year, Gilfillen, *Index*.

77. Schmitt, "George G. Elmslie's Culminating Designs," 18.

78. Order listings, Gilfillen, *Index*, 465.

79. Determined by tabulating orders by year listed in Gilfillen, *Index*.

CHAPTER 7:
SULLIVANESQUE ARCHITECTS IN CHICAGO

1. *Inland Architect and News Record* 19 (Mar. 1892): 27. Listings of C. M. Almquist commissions appeared frequently. For example, three apartment houses were listed in the *Inland Architect and News Record* 18 (Aug. 1891): 14, and several issues of *The Economist*. A total of fifteen C. M. Almquist projects were listed in ten bi-weekly editions of *The Economist* from July 15, 1916, to December 23, 1916. Thirteen commissions were listed in the first six months of 1913, January 11 to June 28; all were for "flats," except for two identified as "store and flats."

2. Author's inventory of C. M. Almquist buildings prepared from orders listed in Gilfillen, *Index*, 346, 353, 385–87, 393,

402. Additional determinations were made from building permit records, CCL; field surveys; study of available shop drawings, NWAA.

3. "A Moving Picture Theater," *The Brickbuilder* 22, no. 10 (Oct. 1913): 233–36.

4. Samuelson, untitled, unpublished list of Northwestern terra-cotta orders.

5. "A White Faced Laundry," *Brick and Clay Record* (June 16, 1914): 1382, 1384.

6. Orders listed in Gilfillen, *Index*, 344.

7. *The Economist*, various issues; Gilfillen, *Index*, listing of Midland orders; Illinois Society of Architects, *Handbook for Architects and Builders* (1914, 1915, 1916).

8. Elbert S. Somers's architectural registration lapsed in 1921, which suggests that he either retired or died. "Registration Lapses," *Illinois Society of Architects Monthly Bulletin* 9, no. 2 (Oct. 1924): 3.

9. Aroner's designs (none Sullivanesque) included a three-story apartment hotel (1915) at Sunnyside Avenue and Sheridan Road; a social center (1915) for Congregation Anshe Emeth on Gary Place; and the classically inspired Palace Theater (1921), South Bend, Indiana. *The Economist* (Oct. 9, 1915): 660; Gilfillen, *Index*; author's field surveys and study of shop drawings for the Palace Theater, NWAA.

10. Study of shop drawings, NWAA.

11. David Carnegie, a son of William G. Carnegie, personal interview by author, Oct. 15, 1991.

12. "He claimed he was the youngest person ever registered in architecture in the State of Illinois. His first job was the Knights of Pythias Hall, just north of 111th Street on Michigan Avenue," recalled his son. Letter dated July 20, 1991, William G. Carnegie Jr. to the author. Carnegie lived at 834 East 90th Street in Chicago. He opened an office in Chicago's Loop at 117 North Dearborn Street. In 1912, he listed offices at 5 South Wabash and 11100 South Michigan Avenue. But, by the end of 1912, his office was relocated to 59 East Madison Street, where it remained for many years. *State of Illinois Biennial Report of the Board of Examiners of Architects* (1909, 1911, 1913); Illinois Society of Architects, *Handbook for Architects and Builders* (1911, 1912, 1913); Reuben H. Donnelley, comp., *Lakeside Classified Directory for Chicago* (Chicago: E. Chicago Directory Co., 1912), 1552.

13. These commissions included several small apartment buildings of simplified Tudor Gothic style on South Park (now Dr. Martin Luther King Drive), some bungalows, and several two-story commercial buildings. He also designed, in 1912, an automobile salesroom and garage for R. J. Tou, which was his only use of terra cotta from the American Terra Cotta and Ceramic Company. David Carnegie interview; field surveys; author's inventory prepared from Gilfillen, *Index*, 25.

14. The working drawings were labeled: "Alterations and Additions to Bank, Store and Office Building" and dated April 23, 1914. The order (no. 4182) for terra cotta was

placed with the Midland Company on June 8, 1914. Review of drawings, access provided courtesy David Carnegie; Gilfillen, *Index*, 340.

15. Review of working drawings prepared by William G. Carnegie (Apr. 23, 1914), access provided courtesy of David Carnegie.

16. Author's inventory of Carnegie's buildings and projects compiled from his records retained by his son, David Carnegie; "Building Permit Listings for the City of Chicago," *The Economist* (1911–23); field surveys.

17. Midland Terra Cotta Company advertisements, *American Carpenter and Builder* (Oct. 1915): 107; (Sept. 1916): 94; (Apr. 1918): 92, respectively.

18. "All Sorts of Building Plans," *American Builder* (Dec. 1919): 87.

19. National Terra Cotta Society, *Architectural Terra Cotta: The Store*, 3d ed. (New York: National Terra Cotta Society, n.d.), 25.

20. Carnegie must have been considered a rising star within the professional circle in Chicago. He became a member of the Illinois Society of Architects and soon was among the leaders of the organization. In 1915, Carnegie chaired the Committee on Public Action and served on a subcommittee for Illinois registration law. In 1916, he filled one of the six officer positions as second vice president of the society; he also continued to serve on the Committee on Public Action. He later became an allied member of the Chicago Architecture Club. At a meeting of the Illinois Society of Architects held at the Art Institute of Chicago on September 24, 1918, there was a panel discussion on "Problems of Reconstruction after the World War." Carnegie served on the panel with George Maher, James Dibelka, Henry Holsman, and George Knapp. Illinois Society of Architects, *Handbook for Architects and Builders* (1915), 5; ibid. (1916), 5, 83; *Western Architect* (June 1915): 49; *Illinois Society of Architects* (newsletter) 3, no. 4 (Oct. 1918): 1.

21. David Carnegie interview.

22. Review of photographs of renderings, access courtesy of David Carnegie.

23. Scott, *Semi-Centennial Alumni Record of the University of Illinois*. 530. Dubin graduated from Crane Technical High School, Chicago. A good athlete, he was a member of the famed 1910 basketball team of Hull-House and also played for the University of Illinois's varsity team. Obituary, *Chicago Sun-Times*, Jan. 28, 1958.

24. Shop drawing, Midland Terra Cotta Co. (order no. 6174), NWAA.

25. Author's inventory of Dubin and Eisenberg buildings prepared from Gilfillen, *Index*; field surveys; and/or review of shop drawings, NWAA.

26. Shop drawing, Midland Terra Cotta Co. (order no. 22391), courtesy NWAA.

27. Alumni Records, Archives, UIUC. Henry Dubin won the School of Architecture's Francis J. Plym Fellowship in

1917 for travel and study in Europe. Upon his return, he joined his brother's firm. In 1932, Dubin and Eisenberg was reorganized as Dubin and Dubin. Two other brothers, Eugene A. Dubin (1908–98) and Robert Dubin, were not architects. Eugene was a structural engineer who had graduated from the University of Illinois (1930) and had his own consulting practice, and Robert was a sociologist who taught at the University of Oregon. In addition, there was a half-brother, Allen Schwalb, who also was an engineer in Chicago and a 1933 graduate of the University of Illinois. George H. Dubin was married in March 1922 to Rhea Gordon. They had one child, a daughter named Gloria (b. 1927). Henry Dubin was married in 1919. He and his wife, Anne, had two children, both sons, and both became architects. Arthur Delmers Dubin (b. Chicago, March 14, 1923) was a 1949 graduate of the University of Michigan, and Martin David Dubin (b. Chicago, November 22, 1927) graduated from the University of Illinois in 1950. Both joined their father and uncle in the firm and became partners. George H. Dubin, died on January 26, 1958, in Chicago's Columbus Hospital. Henry Dubin died on April 22, 1963, in Highland Park Hospital and his wife died on January 18 of the following year.

28. Henry Dubin's own residence (1931) in Highland Park, Illinois, was a steel-framed modern design that gained honors, including the 1931 House Beautiful Award. Obituary, *Chicago Tribune*, Apr. 23, 1963.

29. One panel from the Gage Building was the gift of Henry Dubin to the Department of Architecture, UIUC, in 1956. The other cast-iron panel was the gift of Marvin Probst of the firm Graham, Anderson, Probst, and White. Records of School of Architecture, UIUC.

30. Author's inventory of buildings prepared from listing of terra-cotta orders, Gilfillen, *Index*. Author's field surveys determined appearance and condition.

31. Review of available shop drawings for terra cotta, NWAA; author's inventory prepared from orders listed in Gilfillen, *Index*.

32. For example, from July to December 1916, Himelblau was responsible for 30 two-story flats, 148 three-story flats, 33 apartment buildings, 13 stores with flats, 5 one-story stores, 3 garages, and a dairy. The largest apartment building had 18 dwelling units. Listings of building permits in *The Economist* (July 1, 8, 15, 22, 29; Aug. 5, 12, 19, 26; Sept. 2, 9, 16, 23, 30; Oct. 7, 14, 21, 28; Nov. 4, 11, 18, 25, 1916).

33. His parents were Louis and Fannie Himelblau. He had two brothers, Meyer and Harry, and a sister, Clara. His uncle retained the usual spelling of Himmelblau, but his father had dropped one letter "m" in the family surname. Obituary, *Chicago Tribune*, Dec. 19, 1944, 12.

34. Telephone conversation and a letter from A. L. Himelblau's son, Alan, to the author, Nov. 1987.

35. With overall plan dimensions of 100´ × 175´, the building was constructed by C. E. Swerberg for $86,000. *The Economist* (Nov. 13, 1915): 895. Author's field survey.

36. Author's inventory prepared from terra-cotta orders listed in Gilfillen, *Index*.

37. Ibid.

38. Author's field surveys and inventory prepared from orders listed in Gilfillen, *Index*.

39. Ibid.

40. Ibid.

41. Himelblau's office was at 30 North Dearborn Street, Suite 904, after his initial (1915) office location at 179 West Washington Avenue. Both locations were in the Loop. Although Abraham was his first name, he was known as "Abe" socially. In listings of architects and for identification on his drawings, however, only "A. L. Himelblau" was given. In 1921, Himelblau moved his family to Chicago's North Side. He and his wife, Yenta (Smith), had three children: Lucile, Myria, and Alan, who became a civil engineer. Telephone conversation and a letter from Alan Himelblau to the author, Nov. 1987.

42. Obituaries, *Chicago Times*, Dec. 19, 1944, 24; *Chicago Daily News*, Dec. 18, 1944, 23; *Chicago Sun*, Dec. 19, 1944, 18. Himelblau was buried in the Mizpah section of Memorial Park Cemetery, Skokie.

43. Grotz received his Illinois architect's license (A 671) through the "grandfather" provision. Grotz seems to have been on the periphery of the architectural profession in Chicago as he didn't participate in mainstream professional activities. He didn't hold memberships in the Illinois Society of Architects, the Chicago chapter of the American Institute of Architects, or the Chicago Architectural Club. *State of Illinois First Biennial Report of the Board of Examiners of Architects*, 4–7 and Form A; confirmed by a check of membership rolls from lists in Illinois Society of Architects, *Handbook for Architects and Builders* (1911–26); *Annual of the Chicago Architectural Club/Catalog of the Annual Exhibition*, 1900–28; Chicago city directories, 1912–16. In twenty-five years of architectural listings, Grotz's address changed more than eleven times. He maintained an office in the Loop for only two years (1916–17), at 54–58 West Randolph. Other locations were in western and northwestern Chicago neighborhoods.

44. Author's inventory prepared from orders listed in Gilfillen, *Index*. All eleven orders were for Midland terra cotta. Records of Northwestern orders are not available, but it is highly unlikely Northwestern would have been a supplier, given the nature of Grotz's work.

45. Shop drawing, Midland Terra Cotta Company (order no. 21094), NWAA. The address was omitted from drawings and listings of orders; the only notation was "City." The location or existence of the structure in Chicago is unknown.

46. Building permit files, CCL; Gilfillen, *Index*, 389. Building permit information was handwritten and frequently misspelled. Although nearly illegible, the owner's name appears to be given as George Wlahackis. The Midland order ledger, also handwritten and reproduced in Gilfillen's *Index*, is clearer; therefore "Valhakis," the spelling given there, is assumed to be correct.

47. Author's field surveys and review of available shop drawings from the Midland Terra Cotta Company, NWAA.

48. Review of shop drawings, Midland Terra Cotta Company (order nos. 22394, 24008), NWAA.

49. Roseberry, *University of Illinois Directory for 1929*, 63. Bein attended the university for the 1918–19 academic year. Bein's first name was misspelled as "Morris" in the university directory. This error appeared frequently; terra-cotta shop drawings (at NWAA) sometimes identified the architect's name as "Morris" L. Bein while other sheets by different draftsmen for the same job labeled Maurice L. Bein. Apparently he didn't use the French pronunciation but pronounced his name as "Morris." "New Architects," *Illinois Society of Architects Monthly Bulletin* 5, no. 1 (July 1920): 11.

50. Author's inventory of Bein designs incorporating terra cotta was prepared from Gilfillen, *Index*, review of shop drawings at NWAA, and field surveys.

51. Ibid.

52. However, Harris's student records were in the name Mandel Herbert Hymowitz. Roseberry, *University of Illinois Directory for 1929*, 396. Both names were given for clarification in his entries.

53. In 1924, Harris's office was located at 118 North La-Salle Street in the Loop. By 1929, he resided on the North Side at 4940 Monticello Avenue. Illinois Society of Architects, *Handbooks for Architects and Builders* (1915–24).

54. Author's inventory of Harris buildings prepared from orders listed in Gilfillen, *Index*; field surveys; and shop drawings of Midland Terra Cotta Co., NWAA.

55. Carl W. Condit, *Chicago, 1910–29* (Chicago: University of Chicago Press, 1973), 21.

56. Jens J. Jensen also is sometimes confused with Elmer C. Jensen, a partner (1907) in the architectural firm of Jenney, Mundie, and Jensen, later (1913), Mundie and Jensen. Marquis, *Who's Who in Chicago and Vicinity*, 1941, 425.

57. Kathleen Roy Cummings, *Architectural Records in Chicago* (Chicago: Art Institute of Chicago, 1981), 35, 37.

58. Author's inventory of buildings prepared from orders listed in Gilfillen, *Index*; field surveys; and, for demolished buildings, shop drawings, NWAA. *The Economist* (July 21, 1923): 175, featured an article and drawing of a five-story Venetian Gothic building by Jensen for Frolich, McCabe, and Chadwick at 173–75 North Michigan Avenue.

59. Author's inventory of buildings prepared from orders listed in Gilfillen, *Index*; shop drawings at NWAA; and field surveys.

60. In 1924, at age fifty, Kuehne changed careers. He became an executive with both the Chicago Mutual Plate Glass Insurance Company and the Lessing Building and Loan Association. He held positions of manager and secretary for both companies. For a time, he was also treasurer of the Chicago Fraternal Life Association. Throughout these associations, his offices remained in the same Halsted Street building. Carl Osker Kuehne was born August 16, 1874, in Germany; his father

and mother, Karl Oscar and Anna (Doerfel) Kuehne, came to America while he was still a boy. Carl O. Kuehne met Amelia Centmer while attending the University of Illinois and they were married on July 12, 1899, in Champaign. They had three children: Carl W., Gertrude, and Esther. Kuehne's son attended the University of Illinois. In 1950, two days after his birthday, Carl O. Kuehne died. He was buried in Memorial Park Cemetery. *State of Illinois Biennial Report of the Board of Examiners of Architects* (1899–1915). Chicago City Directories, 1911, 1912, 1914–15, 1923, 1925, listings of architects. According to university alumni records, Kuehne reported that he became an executive with two different companies in 1924. Alumni Records, Archives, UIUC.

61. A review of various issues of *The Economist*, listing of building permits, Jan.–Feb. 1911, Jan.–Feb. and June 1913, Oct.–Dec. 1915, July–Dec. 1916, and July 1921 revealed no listing for Carl O. Kuehne.

62. Author's inventory prepared from orders listed in Gilfillen, *Index;* author's field surveys; and shop drawings, NWAA.

63. Review of shop drawings, NWAA.

64. David Naylor, *American Picture Palaces: The Architecture of Fantasy* (New York: Van Nostrand Reinhold, 1981), 61.

65. The son of Marcus and Minna Levy, Alexander Louis Levy was born on February 1, 1872, in Brookfield, Missouri. Married on April 28, 1898, Alexander Levy and his wife, Eliza (Westerfield), had two sons, Alexander L. Levy Jr. and Marcus W. Levy. Klein was born on March 12, 1889 in Cincinnati, Ohio; he graduated from high school in Madison, Indiana. Klein married Hortense Cahn on June 24, 1914. The Levy and Klein office was in a suite (1658–60) in the Conway Building, Washington and LaSalle Streets in the Loop. Alumni Records, Archives, UIUC.

66. Review of shop drawings (Midland order no. 6192), NWAA.

67. Author's inventory of Levy and Klein designs prepared from orders listed in Gilfillen, *Index;* field surveys; and shop drawings, NWAA.

68. Ibid.

69. Author's inventory prepared from field surveys. Levy and Klein designs were determined by building permit records, CCL. Terra-cotta manufacturer was confirmed from the untitled, unpublished list of Northwestern terra-cotta orders compiled by Timothy Samuelson.

70. Author's field surveys and inventory prepared from orders listed in Gilfillen, *Index*.

71. Isadore Hirsch Braun was born February 16, 1894, in Lipto, Hungary. His university degree (1916) was from the Armour Institute of Technology. Upon graduation, Braun worked for Chicago architectural firms Childs and Smith (1916–17) and Graham, Anderson, Probst, and White (1918) before entering the navy. After military service, Braun became chief draftsman for Berlin, Swern, and Randall. AIA, *American Architects Directory* (1955), 60.

72. *The Year Book for 1914–15* (Chicago: Chicago School of Architecture, 1915), n.p.

73. Midland Terra Cotta Company orders record Halperin and Braun as architects in November 1921. Gilfillen, *Index*, 387. *Donnelley's Directory: A Catalog of Chicago Manufacturers and Distributors* (Chicago: Reuben H. Donnelley, 1922), 29, lists Halperin and Braun under the heading of architectural firms and with an address of 19 South LaSalle Street. Biographical information supplied by Braun says that the Halperin and Braun firm began in 1923. AIA, *American Architects Directory* (1955), 60.

74. Review of shop drawings, NWAA.

75. Ibid.

76. Born on February 12, 1891, in Carson, Iowa, M. O. Nathan was the son of Abe and Mollie (Siegel) Nathan. Myer Oscar Nathan graduated from high school in Boone, Iowa. He attended the University of Iowa for two years (1908–10) before transferring to the University of Illinois architectural engineering program. He was a member of Zeta Beta Tau fraternity and active in campus organizations at Illinois. Nathan had a long career. He was with Proudfoot, Bird, and Rawson in Des Moines. He moved to Chicago and worked for the City of Chicago Bridge Department for one year (1915) before joining the architect Alexander L. Levy. Subsequently he was with Smith, Hinchman, and Grylls, Architects, in Detroit, but he soon returned to Chicago. In 1924, he married. His family included two children. His work in the 1950s included conventional designs for shopping centers in St. Louis Park and Rochester, Minnesota, and Milwaukee, Wisconsin. Scott, *Semi-Centennial Alumni Record of the University of Illinois*, 545–46; AIA, *American Architects Directory* (1955), 401.

77. Author's inventory prepared from orders listed in Gilfillen, *Index;* field surveys; and shop drawings, NWAA.

78. Author's inventory prepared from orders listed in Gilfillen, *Index;* shop drawings, NWAA; building permit records, CCL; and field surveys.

79. Timothy Samuelson, personal interview by author, Aug. 24, 1992.

CHAPTER 8: CHICAGO STREETS

1. This assessment is based on extensive review of many publications and built structures to determine broad and differing influences of the time on architectural design. Professional journals, especially *Western Architect*, were important in disseminating the Sullivanesque, but the Midland and Radford companies were especially effective in reaching builders and their architects

2. Marquis, *Book of Chicagoans*, 1917, 556; statement of ownership, *American Carpenter and Builder* (Nov. 1914): 85. In 1917, the owners were William Radford, H. M. Radford, Roland D. Radford, E. L. Hatfield, and George W. Ashby. *American Builder* (June 1917): 92.

3. This assumption is based on the fact that George W.

Ashby was vice president and one of the founders of the Radford Architectural Company. A review of lists of architects, Illinois Society of Architects, *Handbook for Architects and Builders* (1914–21, various editions), indicates he was the only officer of the Radford company who was a registered architect. He was a partner in the architecture firm of Ashby, Ashby, and Schulze. The other partners were Wilbert B. Ashby and Carl Elliot Schulze. Many articles and advertisements in various issues of *American Carpenter and Builder* cite George W. Ashby as a designer of school buildings.

4. Illinois Society of Architects, *Handbook for Architects and Builders* (1915–25).

5. Gilfillen, *Index*, 354.

6. Ibid., 359.

7. After 1916, city directories no longer listed Ermeling among the city's architectural firms although his name continued to appear on the annual roster of Illinois registered architects. City directories, Lakeside and Donnelley's, and Illinois Society of Architects, *Handbook for Architects and Builders* (1915–25).

8. Ermeling's published design plates included the following from *American Carpenter and Builder:* "Dining Room Detail Sheet," 20, no. 1 (Oct. 1915): 68–69; "Details of Open Stairway in Living Room," 20, no. 2 (Nov. 1915): 64–65; "Details of a Sun Porch," 20, no. 3 (Dec. 1915): 62–63; "Details of Unique Fireplace Nook," 20, no. 4 (Jan. 1916): 68–69; "In the Modern Straight Line Style," 21, no. 2 (Nov. 1916): 67.

9. "A Fireplace Alcove," *American Carpenter and Builder* 22, no. 4 (Jan. 1917): 53.

10. *American Carpenter and Builder* 21, no. 1 (Apr. 1916): 57.

11. The first Midland advertisement and the first article about Midland terra cotta appeared in February 1914. By 1919, buildings in Midland advertisements were mostly eclectic designs. Review of all issues of *American Carpenter and Builder,* 1913–17, and *American Builder,* 1917–25.

12. "Architects and Engineers," *Industrial Chicago,* 1:629. Because of his lengthy practice in Chicago, Linderoth was granted an Illinois architect's license (A 567) under the grandfather provision. *State of Illinois First Biennial Report of the Board of Examiners of Architects,* 36.

13. In the first six months of 1913, Linderoth had thirty-seven commissions, all located on the South Side. Of this number, all but five were for two- or three-story flats; the exceptions were three stores, a two-story wagon shop, and a one-story garage. Author's list of Linderoth's works was compiled from lists of building permits published in weekly issues of *The Economist* (Jan. 11–June 28, 1913) and compared to inventory prepared from terra-cotta orders listed in Gilfillen, *Index,* field surveys, and shop drawings, NWAA. Of the nine buildings, eight had terra cotta supplied by the Midland Terra Cotta Company; one was from the American Terra Cotta and Ceramic Company.

14. Author's field surveys; review of shop drawings, NWAA.

15. Advertisement, *American Carpenter and Builder* (Feb. 1915): 86–87, and (Mar. 1915): 104–5.

16. Sanborn Map Company, *Chicago,* vol. 16 (Chicago: Sanborn Map Co., 1976), map 97.

17. *Industrial Chicago,* 1:560–63.

18. Evans, *Art Pottery,* 347.

19. The first order (1910) was placed with the American Terra Cotta and Ceramic Company. Gilfillen, *Index,* 21.

20. William Gibson Barfield was born on September 19, 1857, in Lincolnshire, England. His parents were Benjamin H. and Henrietta (Gibson) Barfield. William G. Barfield was a graduate of Owen's College, Manchester, immigrated to the United States in 1882, and became a U.S. citizen in 1884. His architectural career in Chicago began in 1882. For more than twenty-five years, Barfield commuted from his Hinsdale residence to his Loop office at 58 West Washington. Married in 1895 to Mary E. Peck of Chicago, Barfield had two children, Wilhelmina and Norman Douglas. His son became an architect and practiced in Hinsdale. Marquis, *Who's Who in Chicago* (1926), 59; idem, *Who's Who in Chicago and Vicinity* (1931), 59, and (1936), 59. Barfield was listed in Marquis, *Book of Chicagoans* (1911), 36, and (1917), 36.

21. Author's inventory prepared from orders listed in Gilfillen, *Index,* 35–36, and field surveys.

22. A photo showing Curtiss Street, with the theater visible, appears in Montrew Dunham and Pauline Wandschneider, *Downers Grove, 1832–1982* (Downers Grove, Ill.: Heritage Festival Task Force, 1982), 116.

23. Bouchard's Sullivanesque design and most of his apartment buildings were done after dissolution of his partnership (1910–14) with Roy L. France. Author's inventories for buildings by Bouchard, the partnership of Bouchard and France, and, separately, Roy L. France. These inventories were prepared by review of issues of *The Economist* and compared to terra-cotta orders in Gilfillen, *Index,* and Midland catalog plates (c. 1922). Inventories were checked by author's field surveys. Roy L. France (b. 1888) subsequently designed some progressive buildings loosely based on Sullivanesque compositional principles but without definitive Sullivanesque ornament. Bouchard was still listed on State of Illinois Architects Registration rosters as late as 1956. *Architects and Contractors Register* (1956): 34.

24. Obituary, *Illinois Society of Architects Monthly Bulletin* 28, nos. 4–5 (Oct.–Nov. 1943): 8.

25. National Terra Cotta Society, *Architectural Terra Cotta: The Store,* 31.

26. A review of building permit listings in *The Economist,* various issues (1914–24), confirms this.

27. Author's inventory prepared from orders listed in Gilfillen, *Index;* author's field surveys; and shop drawings, NWAA.

28. Walter went by his middle name, Mead; his first name

was Wayne, and various editions of city directories and architect's rosters sometimes identified him as W. Mead Walter. Walter's submission to the 1922 international design competition for the Chicago Tribune Tower was identified as by Mead Walter. It was an atrocious design. Highly eclectic, historical forms were piled upon historical forms, and multiple domes, inspired by Wren's St. Paul's Cathedral, were perched atop an ill-proportioned office block. Stanley Tigerman and Stuart E. Cohen, *Chicago Tribune Competition and Late Entries*, vol. 1 (New York: Rizzoli, 1980), plate 47.

29. Condit, *Chicago School of Architecture*, 186.

30. "Individual Resource Form" (survey) by LSB, CCL, Jan. 25, 1989.

31. Building permit information, CCL, and author's field survey.

32. Kingsley graduated from high school in Cleveland; his architectural training was through apprenticeship. Married in 1897, he and his wife had two children. AIA, *American Architects Directory* (1955), 301.

33. Sanborn Map Company, *Chicago*, vol. 9 (Chicago: Sanborn Map Co., 1923), map 133.

34. Author's inventory prepared from orders listed in Gilfillen, *Index*, 317.

35. "Efficient Planning in Mercantile Structures," *The Brickbuilder* 23 (1914): 293–94.

36. Kingsley's eclectic designs ranged from the 1915 Roberts Fireproof Storage Company at 836–38 Custer Avenue, Evanston, Illinois, to a 1923 design for a three-story building for the Iredale Fireproof Storage Warehouse Company in Highland Park, Illinois. *The Economist* (Oct. 30, 1915): 798, (Dec. 15, 1923): 1386. The Reebie terra cotta was modeled by Fritz Albert and supplied by the Northwestern Terra Cotta Company. Kingsley's expertise as a warehouse architect was in such demand that he opened an office in New York City and in May 1923 relocated there, although he continued to maintain a branch office in Chicago. Darling, *Chicago Ceramics and Glass*, 194–96; *The Economist* (Apr. 28, 1923): 1018.

37. *Western Architect* 22 (June 1915).

38. Author's inventory prepared from field surveys and from orders listed in Gilfillen, *Index*, 124, 133, 149, 340, 371.

39. In 1915, John Ahlschlager and Son designed a $100,000 three-story building, one hundred feet wide by two hundred feet long, for the Nugent Baking Company in Savannah, Georgia. The architectural style employed is not known. *The Economist* (Sept. 18, 1915): 518.

40. *National Builder* 63 (July 1920): 50.

41. Author's inventory prepared from orders listed in Gilfillen, *Index;* shop drawings, NWAA; and field surveys.

42. Ibid.

43. Author's inventory prepared from Gilfillen, *Index*. It appears that Minchin's Sullivanesque design for the Glass Novelty Company was an aberration as his prior designs, while he was in partnership (1920–24) with Alexander H. Spitz, were eclectic. The firm submitted an eclectic design to the Chicago Tribune Competition (1922). Sidney Henry Minchin was born October 7, 1891, in Berlin, Germany. He came to this country at the age of eight with his parents, Henry and Sonnia Minchin. He studied architecture at the Lewis Institute in Chicago, attended the University of Illinois for the 1911–12 school year, and then studied at the Chicago School of Architecture, with classes at the Art Institute of Chicago and the Armour Institute. In 1915, he received his bachelor of science degree from the Armour Institute of Technology and married in November. He and his wife, Nina (Nesirow), had two children, Jarvis and Gloria. Around 1920, Minchin formed a partnership with Alexander H. Spitz as the firm Minchin-Spitz and Company, with offices at 19 West Jackson Street. Marquis, *Who's Who in Chicago*, 61.

44. Author's inventories of designs were prepared for each architect. Principal sources include Gilfillen, *Index;* available shop drawings, NWAA; and field surveys to determined appearance, style, and status. In many cases, building permit records, CCL, were consulted to determine facts such as dates, architect of record, and owner.

45. Ibid.

46. Ibid.

47. Ibid.

48. This was determined by extensive field surveys to identify an inventory of Sullivanesque buildings and cross-referenced to author's research for construction dates of these buildings.

49. Louis Sullivan, *Louis H. Sullivan: A System of Architectural Ornament*, foreword by John Zukowsky and Susan Glover Godlewski (New York: Rizzoli, 1990), 7.

50. Rissman was born November 1, 1893; his parents were Ike and Ida (Bearst) Rissman. Rissman graduated from Crane Technical High School in 1911. After graduating from the Armour Institute, Rissman worked in Chicago and then served in construction for the navy during World War I. He started his practice with Hirschfield in 1919 and that same year married Ruby Grossman of Chicago. They had a son, Marshall William Rissman. Maurice B. Rissman died June 2, 1942. Marquis, *Who's Who in Chicago*, 733; idem, *Who's Who in Chicago and Vicinity* (1931), 820, (1936), 849, and (1941), 700; Withey, *Biographical Dictionary of American Architects (Deceased)*, 513.

51. Hirschfield was married in 1922 and had two children. In World War I, he was in governmental service with the Bureau of Yards and Docks (1918–19). Around 1926, Hirschfield dropped the second letter "i" in his last name and began spelling it Hirschfeld. After Rissman died, Hirschfeld practiced alone until 1953 when the partnership of Hirschfeld and Pawlin was organized. AIA, *American Architects Directory* (1955), 250.

52. Samuelson, untitled, unpublished list of Northwestern terra-cotta orders.

53. Review of shop drawings (Midland 22069), NWAA.

54. Decorative features based on historical styles were incorporated in Rissman and Hirschfeld designs such as those for the Sheridan-Brompton Apartment Building (1924), the Hotel Surfridge (1924), the Knickerbocker Hotel (1929), the Millinery Building (1928), and multi-unit residential towers at 2440 Lake View Avenue (1929), 3330 Lake Shore Drive.

55. Author's inventory prepared from orders listed in Gilfillen, *Index*, 56, 417, 423, 428, and field surveys. Another terra-cotta order was for a bulkhead on a storefront remodeling. Historically based terra cotta from the American company was used on the earlier (1924), more prestigious commission for the Argyle Arms Apartment Building, Sheridan Road at Argyle. Review of shop drawings, NWAA.

56. An elaborate Hollywood, California, residence for A. L. Gore was published in *Architectural Digest* 7, no. 4 (1931): 135–37.

57. In April 1921, Ablamowicz passed his examination to practice architecture in Illinois, and in 1923 he formed a partnership with M. F. Winiarski. Their offices were at 1859 West Chicago Avenue. *American Contractor* (Apr. 21, 1923): 36.

58. Author's field surveys and inventory prepared from orders (Midland nos. 25171, 26014) listed in Gilfillen, *Index*, 423, 428; shop drawings, Midland Terra Cotta Company, NWAA.

59. Roseberry, *University of Illinois Directory for 1929*, 79. In the 1920s, Bjork moved to the North Shore suburb of Wilmette and resided at 216 Linden Avenue. In the mid-1930s, he moved to Evanston, Illinois, first to 624 Asbury and later to 1106 Seward Street, which was his last residence. Bjork was born on March 17, 1883, and died on May 10, 1967. Alumni Records, Archives, UIUC.

60. Mae Felts Herringshaw, ed., *Herringshaw's City Blue Book of Current Biography, 1913* (Chicago: American Publisher's Association, 1913), 58.

61. Bjork seems to have designed only four structures that included terra cotta among construction materials. These were a factory on the South Side, two small stores, and a store building with apartments. Inventory prepared from orders listed in Gilfillen, *Index*.

62. *American Contractor* (Apr. 12, 1924): 35.

63. Perkins, *Evanstoniana*, 154–55. Cauley's house designs included one for Mary Anderson (1925), 2915 Colfax Street; one for Lyons (1926), 1101 Colfax; and two for John Penny, 1313 Chancellor (1940) and 1317 Chancellor (1961). The Orrington Hotel, developed by Victor C. Carlson in Evanston, was designed by Cauley. Another Evanston commission was an apartment building (1928) at 1519 Hinman Avenue. A graduate of the Armour Institute of Technology in 1922, Cauley returned to college during the Depression to study law and became a lawyer. However, he resumed an architectural practice after World War II and combined his architectural and legal training by becoming active in historic preservation. He received his L.L.D. in 1938 from Kent College of

Law and received a J.D. in April 1969 from Illinois Institute of Technology. AIA, *American Architects Directory* (1955), 87.

64. Kenan Heise and Mark Frazel, *Hands on Chicago* (Chicago: Bonus Books, 1987), 231.

65. Frederick William Fischer was a civil engineer for construction with a number of railroads before he went to Chicago in March 1889. Fischer, an architect licensed under Illinois's "grandfather" provision, joined Julius Floto in 1893 to form the architecture firm of Fischer and Floto. After five years, the partnership was dissolved and Fischer practiced alone. Fischer's office was located on Commercial Avenue. Born December 30, 1861, in Cincinnati, F. William Fischer was the son of Julius and Julie Floto Fischer. He married Laura E. Rathfon of Medaryville, Indiana, in 1890 and they had three children: Athena, Walter R., and Harold R. Fischer. F. William Fischer's mother must have been related to Julius Floto (1864–1950), an architect (registration A 71) in Chicago. Marquis, *Book of Chicagoans*, 1917, 231; idem, *Who's Who in Chicago and Vicinity*, 1941, 270; *State of Illinois Biennial Report of the Board of Examiners of Architects* (1899–1915).

66. Building permit files, CCL.

67. After moving to Chicago from Cincinnati, Fisher joined in partnership with Herman Joseph Gaul. After 1899 he practiced alone until 1916 when his oldest son, Joseph G. Fisher, joined him in partnership. In 1916, Fisher's office was at 4011 North Robey (now Damen) Avenue. Albert J. Fisher was born in 1863 in Cincinnati, Ohio. He married Rose Leider and they had five children: Joseph G., Alfred J., Marpuller E., Arthur M., and Francis. Fisher died on October 21, 1938. *Chicago Tribune*, Oct. 22, 1938; "List of Architects," *State of Illinois Biennial Report of the Board of Examiners of Architects* (1899–1917); *Illinois Society of Architects Monthly Bulletin* 23, nos. 6–7 (Dec. 1938–Jan. 1939): 8.

68. Author's field surveys and inventory from orders listed in Gilfillen, *Index*, 358.

69. Arthur Jacobs married Hortense Fround and they had two sons, Lawrence V. and Howard A. Jacobs. In 1912, Jacobs received his architect's license (B 624) after passing the Illinois registration examination and he opened his own office at 128 North LaSalle Street. His commissions included apartment buildings and some commercial structures. Many of these were remodelings. Later, his practice concentrated on industrial work and, during World War II, federal housing projects. Obituary, *Illinois Society of Architects Monthly Bulletin* 31, nos. 11–12 (May–June 1947): 8; obituary, *Chicago Daily News*, Mar. 19, 1947, 39; Withey, *Biographical Dictionary of American Architects (Deceased)*, 319.

70. Author's inventory prepared from orders listed in Gilfillen, *Index*, and field surveys.

71. Nathan Koenigsberg was born April 7, 1889. After coming to Chicago, he studied architecture at the Armour Institute of Technology. He married in 1924 and had two children. Koenigsberg was chief draftsman for the architect Leon E. Stanhope from 1914 to 1919 and was with Frank D.

Chase, Architect, for a short time before moving on to A. G. Zimmerman's firm. Leo H. (Harold) Weisfeld was born on January 24, 1889, in Chicago. He was educated in city schools and graduated from Crane Technical High School. In 1918, he married Thelma Silverburg. He worked as a draftsman for various architectural firms before teaming with Nathan Koenigsberg in 1920. The Koenigsberg and Weisfeld partnership lasted for twenty years. After 1940, Koenigsberg practiced alone under the firm name of Nathaniel Koenigsberg, Architect. Lists of registered architects, Illinois Society of Architects, *Handbook for Architects and Builders* (1915–24); AIA, *American Architects Directory* (1956), 308; Scott, *Semi-Centennial Alumni Record of the University of Illinois*, 516.

72. Author's inventory prepared from orders listed in Gilfillen, *Index;* field surveys; and shop drawings of Midland Terra Cotta Company, NWAA.

73. Author's inventory prepared from Gilfillen, *Index*, and field surveys.

74. Shop drawings, Midland Terra Cotta Company (order no. 22348), NWAA.

75. Author's inventory prepared from orders listed in Gilfillen, *Index;* field surveys; and building permit information from CCL.

76. Author's inventory prepared from orders listed in Gilfillen, *Index*, and field surveys.

77. Information plaque next to terra-cotta piece at the Art Institute of Chicago (c. 1988): "Gift of Commission on Chicago Historical and Architectural Landmarks, 1987.3."

78. Author's inventory prepared from orders listed in Gilfillen, *Index;* field surveys; and shop drawings of Midland Terra Cotta Company, NWAA.

79. Shop drawings of Midland Terra Cotta Company, NWAA.

80. Ibid.

81. Author's inventory prepared from orders listed in Gilfillen, *Index;* field surveys; building permit information from CCL; and *Chicago Historic Resources Survey* (Chicago: Commission on Chicago Landmarks and the Chicago Department of Planning and Development, 1996), 111–355.

82. Author's inventories prepared from orders listed in Gilfillen, *Index;* field surveys; and shop drawings, NWAA.

83. Ibid.

EPILOGUE

1. Rastorfer, "Terra Cotta: Past to Present," 110.

2. Bennett used this phrase on more than one occasion in conversations with the author while the author was employed in Bennett's firm, Loebl Schlossman Bennett and Dart, Architects, of Chicago, during 1968–71.

3. See Robert Venturi, *Learning from Las Vegas* (1972; Cambridge, Mass.: MIT Press, 1977), 87–107.

4. Sinkevitch, *AIA Guide to Chicago*, 318.

5. *New Chicago Architecture*, exh. cat. (Chicago: Rizzoli, 1981), 194.

6. Richard Haas, *Richard Haas: An Architecture of Illusion* (New York: Rizzoli, 1981), 99–105.

7. Louis J. Millet of Healy and Millet collaborated with Louis Sullivan for the original decorative designs of the Trading Room. *The Prairie School: Design Vision for the Midwest*, Museum Studies/Art Institute of Chicago, vol. 21, no. 2 (Chicago: Art Institute of Chicago, 1995), 96–97.

8. Chapman is a principal in the Louisville, Kentucky, architectural firm of Grossman, Chapman, Kingsley, Architects. *Architectural Record* (Jan. 1987): 116.

INDEX

Page numbers in *italic* refer to black-and-white illustrations. First color-plate section follows page 70; second color-plate section follows page 150.

Aarens, Harry B., 252, 286, 290
—*buildings by:*
   one-story commercial buildings, Chicago, 252, 290
   service garage, Belmont Avenue, Chicago, 252, 286
Aberdeen, South Dakota, 278
Ablamowicz, Sigmond V., 252, 253, 286
Ablamowicz and Winiarski, Architects, 252
—*buildings by:*
   commercial buildings, Chicago, 252, 253
Adams, Minnesota, 274. *See also second color-plate section*
Adler, Dankmar, 4, 16, 23, 27, 101, 146. *See also* Adler and Sullivan, Architects
Adler and Sullivan, Architects, 15–17, 20, 23, 27, 34, 46, 81, 92, 93, 98,

100, 101, 112, 119, 128, 130, 139, 143, 145–47, 152, 153, 155, 157, 160, 176, 237, 260, 268, 270, 273, 274, 276, 280, 281, 283, 285–98. *See also* Sullivan, Louis H.
—*buildings by:*
   Auditorium Building, Chicago, 17, 18, 41, 93, 146, 153, 160, 283
   Bayard/Condict Building, New York, New York. *See* Sullivan, Louis H., buildings by
   Charnley House, Chicago, 22, 93, 94, 95, 130, 286
   Getty Tomb, Chicago, 18, 19, 19, 64
   Grand Opera House/Das Deutsche Haus (remodeling), Milwaukee, Wisconsin, 81, 281
   Guaranty/Prudential Building, Buffalo, New York. *See* Sullivan, Louis H., buildings by
   Kehilath Anshe Ma'ariv Synagogue, Chicago, 153, 293
   McVicker's Theatre (remodeling), Chicago, 143, 153, 283
   Meyer Wholesale Store Building, Chicago, 6, 23, 25, 176, 285

Ryerson Tomb, Chicago, 19
St. Nicholas Hotel, St. Louis, Missouri, 22, 112, 276
Schiller/Garrick Theater Building, Chicago, 22, 95, 146, 147, 153, 237, 263, 285
Stock Exchange Building, Chicago, 22, 97, 263, 283
Sullivan (Albert W.) Townhouse, Chicago, 22, 94, 293
Sullivan (Louis) Cottage, Ocean Springs, Mississippi, 93, 153, 276
Transportation Building, World's Columbian Exposition, Chicago, 22, 153, 263
Union Trust Building, St. Louis, Missouri, 22, 42, 48, 276. *See also first color-plate section*
Victoria Hotel, Chicago Heights, Illinois, 22, 24, 94, 95, 130, 298
Wainwright Building, St. Louis, Missouri, 4, 5, 6, 16, 17, 19, 20, 21, 22, 29, 33, 276
Wainwright Tomb, St. Louis, Missouri, 19, 276
Walker Warehouse, Chicago, 17, 283

Advance Terra Cotta Company, 109, 152, 178

Ahlgrin, F. F., 271

Ahlschlager, John. *See* Ahlschlager and Son

Ahlschlager and Son, 69, 243, 245, 273, 293

—*buildings by:*

Schulze Baking Company, Chicago, 245, *246*, 293

Wagner Baking Company, Detroit, Michigan, 69, 245, 273

Aitkin, Minnesota, 274

Alban, William L., 70, 72, 161, 274

—*building by:*

Skinner and Chamberlain Company Building, Albert Lea, Minnesota, 70, *71*, 72, 161, *162*, 274. *See also first color-plate section*

Albany, Illinois, 90, 269

Albert, Fritz, 116, 153, 154, 166, 197

Albert Lea, Minnesota, 70, 72, 161, 274

Alden, John M., 73, 276

—*building by:*

garage for W. A. Tilden, St. Paul, Minnesota, 72, 276

Aldrich, Harry Glen, 87, 309 n. 94. *See also* Aldrich and Aldrich, Architects

Aldrich, Norman Kellogg, 87. *See also* Aldrich and Aldrich, Architects

Aldrich and Aldrich, Architects, 87, 88, 90, 269, 270

—*buildings by:*

Folley Mortuary, Galesburg, Illinois, 88, 269

McCollum Brothers Candy Company factory building, Galesburg, Illinois, *9*, 87, *89*, 269

Moose Lodge Hall, Farmington, Illinois, 88, 269

Princeton Hotel, Princeton, Illinois, 87, 270

Tate Hardware store building, Knoxville, Illinois, 87, 270

Algona, Iowa, 56, 57, 120, 272

Alhambra Ceramic Works, 236

Alice, Texas, 62, 278

Allen, Glenn, 268

Allison, Lyman J., 291

Almenraeder, Frederick, 153

Almquist, Carl M., 200, 287, 289–91

—*buildings by:*

Keats Building, Chicago, 200, 287

Louis Erickson Building, Chicago, 200, 291

store building, Chicago, 289. *See also second color-plate section*

Swanson and Erickson Buildings, Chicago, 200, *201*, 290, 291

Alton, Illinois, 91, 269

Alton, Kansas, 64

American Architecture of Today, The, 47

American Builder, 68, 73, 155, 179, 188, 206, 231, 233

American Carpenter and Builder, 78, 155, 176, 178, 179, 187, 206, 231–35

American Ceramic Society, 172

American Contractor, 155, 178

American Institute of Architects (AIA), 7, 42, 119, 125, 146, 187, 250

American Milk Company, Construction Department, 280

American Terra Cotta and Ceramic Company, The, 30, 53, 55, 70, 75, 85, 104, 106, 109, 112, 121, 135, 136, 138, 151–54, 157, 158, 160–62, 164, 166, 167, 170, 173, 174, 176, 178, 188, 195, 197, 212, 220, 236, 245

American Terra Cotta Manufacturers Association, 166

Amsterdam School, 112

Anderson Contracting, 242

Anderson, David E., 69, 274

—*building by:*

commercial building for Ben Harris, Stambaugh, Michigan, 69, 274

Anderson, Indiana, 271

Andretta, Italy, 147

Anis, Albert, 294, 295

Anna, Illinois, 87

Antioch, Illinois, 298

Arabesque style, 4

Archer, Charles, 296

Architectural Decorating Company, 131, 142, 143

Architectural Record, 37, 56, 154, 178

Architectural Terra Cotta: The Store, 207, 238

Arlington Heights, Illinois, 264

Armour Institute of Technology, 47, 199, 227, 250, 255

Aroner, Jacob S., 202, 286. *See also* Aroner and Somers, Architects

—*building by:*

Edelmann Building, Chicago, 202, 286

Aroner and Somers, Architects, 200, 202, 286, 287, 296

—*buildings by:*

Jewel Laundry, Chicago, 202, 287

Orpheus Theater, Chicago, 200, 202, 296

Penner Building, Chicago, 202, *203*, *204*, 286

art deco style, 12, 40, 45, 90, 113, 116, 118, 147, 148, 154, 258

art glass/leaded glass, 98, 142, 146

Art Institute of Chicago, 22, 27, 47, 82, 148, 161, 199, 203, 227, 250, 257, 263, 264

art nouveau, 4

art pottery, 156, 157, 160, 161, 174, 188, 189, 236

arts and crafts movement, 80, 85, 100, 106, 126, 130, 139, 142, 156, 160, 175, 189, 190, 233, 236, 262

Ashby, George W., 178, 230, 231, 291, 327 n. 3

Ashby, Ashby, and Schulze, Architects, 299. *See also* Ashby, George W.

Ashelman and Gage, Architects, 277

Ashland, Ohio, 160

Atchison, John D., 34, 51, 298. *See also* Atchison and Edbrooke, Architects; Rugh and Atchison, Architects

—*buildings by:*

Evanston Apartments, Evanston, Illinois, 34, 298

Fairchild Block, Winnipeg, Manitoba, Canada, 34, 282

Atchison and Edbrooke, Architects, 34, 64

Athens, Texas, 278

Atkin, Minnesota, 74

Atlantic City, New Jersey, 61, 277

Aurora, Illinois, 108, 109, 111, 298

Austin, Shambleau, and Wiser, Architects, 86, 271

—*building by:*

South Bend Tribune Building, South Bend, Indiana, 86, 271

Automobile Sales Building, 2522 S. Michigan, Chicago, 157, *159*, 293

Ayres, Atlee B., 62, 278, 280

—*buildings by:*

Cameron County Courthouse, Brownsville, Texas, 62, 278

Jim Wells County Courthouse, Alice, Texas, 62, 278

Kleberg County Courthouse, Kingsville, Texas, 62, 279

Refugio County Courthouse, Refugio, Texas, 62, 280

Babcock, Ida M., 166

Bachman, George F., 69, 274

—*building by:*

Smith Building, Flint, Michigan, 69, 274

Baileys Harbor, Wisconsin, 113, 280

Baird, John, 263

Baltimore, Maryland, 29
Baltimore and Ohio Chicago Terminal Railroad, 170
Baraboo, Wisconsin, 128, 130, 135, 136, 280
Barber, Edgar L., 81, 272
—building by:
   Farmers Store, Charter Oak, Iowa, 81, 272
Barfield, William G., 236, 292, 298, 328 n. 20
—buildings by:
   Roser Store and Apartment Building, Chicago, 236, 237, 292
   theater for E. A. Baxter, Downers Grove, Illinois, 236, 237, 298
Barglebaugh, Charles Erwin, 50, 61, 62
Barglebaugh and Whitson, Architects, 68, 279
—building by:
   Armor/Hogg Building, Houston, Texas, 62, 63, 279
   Barnheisel Building, Chicago, 178
Baroque style, 226
Baton Rouge, Louisiana, 273
Baty and Halloran, Architects, 61
—building by:
   Mason County Bank, New Haven, West Virginia, 61, 280
Bauhaus, 113, 261
Baumann and Huehl, Architects, 170
Baxter, O'Dell, and Halprin, Architects, 273
Beaux-Arts classicism, 22, 49, 62, 68
Bebb and Mendel, Architects, 51, 280
—building by:
   Oriental Block/Corona Hotel, Seattle, Washington, 51, 280. See also first color-plate section
Beech, Wilfred W., 125
Bein, Maurice Lewis, 217, 219, 286, 287, 291, 297
—buildings by:
   automobile sales and service building/Capital Garage, Chicago, 219, 287
   Robins Building, Chicago, 217, 218, 291
   store for M. A. Bender, Chicago, 217, 286
   three-story buildings, Chicago, 217, 291
Beloit, Wisconsin, 194, 196, 280
Beman, S. S., 202
Bemidji, Minnesota, 274
Bennett, Richard, 262
Benson, Edward, 291

Bentley, Percy Dwight, 84, 281
—building by:
   Oyen Building, La Crosse, Wisconsin, 84, 281
Benton Harbor, Michigan, 273
Bergen, Norway, 158
Berger and Kelly, Architects, 269
Berlage, H. P., 106, 112
Berlin Academy, 147
Bernard, L. C., 271
Berry, George A., Jr., 167
Berry, Parker N., 90, 120–24, 158, 270, 292, 313 n. 77
—buildings by:
   Adeline Prouty Old Ladies Home, Princeton, Illinois, 123, 270
   apartment building for Dr. Frank C. Titzell, Iowa City, Iowa, 124
   Farmers National Bank, Princeton, Illinois, 122, 270
   First State Bank, Manlius, Illinois, 120, 121, 270
   Interstate National Bank, Chicago, 123, 292
   Princeton Dry Goods, Princeton, Illinois, 121, 124, 270
—unbuilt projects by:
   Henry C. Adams Land and Loan Office Building addition and alteration, Algona, Iowa, 120, 121, 122, 123
   Lincoln State Bank, Chicago, 124
Berwin, Illinois, 298
Billingham, M. C. J., 69, 274
—building by:
   Kalamazoo Gazette-Telegraph Building, Kalamazoo, Michigan, 69, 274
Bishop, Thomas R., 295, 296, 299
Bishop's College School, Lennoxville, Quebec, Canada, 35
Bismarck, North Dakota, 277
Bjork, David Theodore, 253, 287, 330 n. 59
—building by:
   store and apartment building for A. Frazier, Chicago, 253, 254, 287
Bjork Brothers Construction Company, 253
Blake, Edgar O., 299
Blooming Prairie, Minnesota, 72, 274
Blue Island, Illinois, 238, 298
Boberg, Ferdinand, 119
Bock, Richard W., 97, 146, 147, 166, 317 n. 28
Boise, Idaho, 268

Bohlen, D. A. See Bohlen and Son, Architects
Bohlen and Son, Architects, 271
Boone and Corner, Architects, 280
Bouchard, Louis C., 237, 287
—building by:
   Nesbit Apartment Building, Chicago, 237, 238, 287. See also second color-plate section
Bowly, Devereux, 263
Boyle, H. E. See Boyle and Son, Architects
Boyle and Son, Architects, 269
Braucher, Ernest N., 291, 296
Braun, Isadore H., 227, 327 n. 71
Bray and Nystrom, Architects, 73, 74, 275, 276
—buildings by:
   Horace Mann School, Virginia, Minnesota, 73, 276
   Manuel Training School, Eveleth, Minnesota, 73, 275
Breckenridge, Michigan, 69, 273
Breese, Illinois, 44
Brenner, Daniel, 35
Breuer, Marcel, 261
Brick and Clay Record, 155, 200
Brickbuilder, The, 162, 200
Brighton, Illinois, 269
Brinkmann, William, 285
Bronzeville, Chicago, 256
Brostrom, Ernest Olaf, 66
—buildings by:
   Peacock Apartments/Newbern Hotel, Kansas City, Missouri, 67, 68, 276
   Rushton/Holsum Bakery, Kansas City, Missouri, 67
Brown, W. J., 272
Brownsville, Texas, 62, 278
Brunkhorst, Alfred, 169, 170, 172
Brunkhorst, John, 169
Bruns, Benedict J., 256, 287, 291
—buildings by:
   Burtonian Building, Chicago, 256, 291
   Charel Building, Chicago, 256, 291
   Fred Hein/one-story store, Chicago, 3, 256, 257, 287. See also second color-plate section
   Lawfrank Building, Chicago, 256, 291
Bucyrus, Ohio, 69, 277
Budina, Adolph O., 120
Buechner and Orth, Architects, 72, 274
—building by:
   store for F. Werwerka, Blooming Prairie, Minnesota, 72, 274

Buffalo, New York, 23, 35, 44, 67, 277
Buffington, LeRoy, 29
bungalow movement, 231
Burfiend, William F., 84, 281
—building by:
    Zahn's Department Store, Racine,
        Wisconsin, 84, 281
Burke, Edmund, 282
Burlington, Iowa, 81, 272
Burnham, Daniel, 27. See also D. H.
    Burnham and Company
Burnham and Company. See D. H.
    Burnham and Company
Burnham Library, 250
Burns, James, 288
Burt, Iowa, 81, 272
Butter Building, Milwaukee, Wiscon-
    sin, 84, 281
Byzantine style, 4

Cable, Max Lowel, 299
Caldwell, Idaho, 269
Calumet City, Illinois, 116, 197, 298
Cameron, Texas, 278
Canton, South Dakota, 278
Carbondale, Illinois, 269
Carlson, W. C., 299
Carnegie Institute of Technology, 139
Carnegie, John L., 203
Carnegie, William G., 199, 202–7,
    209, 293, 294, 324 nn. 12, 20
—buildings by:
    Carnegie Flats, Chicago, 207
    Dekker Brothers Market, Chicago,
        207, 208, 293
    Foote Real Estate Office Building,
        Chicago, 205, 206, 207, 294
    Jurgensen Tea Company, Chicago,
        205, 206, 208, 293
    Roseland Safety Deposit Bank, Chi-
        cago, 10, 203–6, 205, 206, 293
—unbuilt projects by:
    apartment buildings, Chicago, 209
    Redd Cab Company, Chicago, 209,
        210
Carpenter, Frank A., 270
Catalogue of the Fourteenth Annual Exhi-
    bition of the Chicago Architectural Club,
    48
Cauley, Frank William, 253, 286, 330
    n. 62
—building by:
    Abrams Store Building, Chicago,
        253, 286
Cedar Rapids, Iowa, 56, 272
Celtic Christian art, 4
Cerny, Jerry J., 288, 298

Chamber of Commerce Building, Chi-
    cago, 170
Champaign, Illinois, 90, 269
Chapman, H. Stow, 266, 331 n. 8
Charleston, Illinois, 269
Charter Oak, Iowa, 272
Charvat, Anton, 256, 297
—building by:
    L. Klein Store, Chicago, 256, 297
Chase, Frank D., 281
Chassaing, Edouard, 154
Cheyenne, Wyoming, 282
Chicago, Illinois, 1, 2, 4, 7–9, 16–19,
    22, 27, 29, 34, 35, 46, 47, 51, 53, 79,
    82, 87, 94, 95, 97, 101–4, 112, 113,
    119, 120, 123, 124, 131, 138, 139,
    142, 143, 145, 147, 151–58, 161,
    164, 166, 168–70, 173, 176, 178,
    194, 195, 197, 200, 202, 207, 209–
    12, 215, 217, 219, 220, 222, 223,
    225, 228, 229–31, 233–38, 243, 245,
    247–50, 252–59, 261–64, 283–97
Chicago Architectural Annual, The, 48
Chicago Architectural Club, 47, 48,
    153, 161, 166
Chicago Arts and Crafts Society, 100,
    166
Chicago Coliseum, 155
Chicago College of Law, 160
Chicago Crucible Company, 154
Chicago fire (1871), 8, 143
Chicago Heights, Illinois, 22, 94, 130,
    152, 298
Chicago Historical Society, 146, 220
Chicago School (movement), 1, 2, 12,
    139, 175, 248, 263, 264, 301 n. 13
Chicago School of Architecture (insti-
    tution), 47, 199, 203, 227
Chicago Terra Cotta Company, 143,
    151
Chicago window (type), 103, 235
Cicero, Illinois, 169, 170, 195, 197,
    225, 245, 255, 298
Cincinnati, Ohio, 69, 277
classical revival style, 178, 243
Claude, Louis W., 119, 120, 128, 130.
    See also Claude and Starck, Archi-
    tects
Claude and Starck, Architects, 74, 82,
    90, 130–36, 142, 270, 274, 280–82,
    315 n. 124
—buildings by:
    Detroit Lakes Public Library, De-
        troit Lakes, Minnesota, 131, 143,
        274, 314 n. 117
    Eager Free Library, Evansville, Wis-
        consin, 131, 132, 280

Flagg Township Library, Rochelle,
    Illinois, 131, 133, 143, 270, 314 n.
    116
High School, Baraboo, Wisconsin,
    135 136, 137, 280
Hoquiam Public Library, Hoquiam,
    Washington, 132, 280
Lancaster Municipal Building, Lan-
    caster, Wisconsin, 133, 281
Lincoln School, Madison, Wiscon-
    sin, 134, 134, 135, 281. See also
    first color-plate section
Lincoln School, Monroe, Wisconsin,
    sin, 134, 135, 136, 281
Scott Free Library, Merrill, Wiscon-
    sin, 131, 132, 132, 143, 145, 281,
    314 n. 115
Tomah Public Library, Tomah, Wis-
    consin, 132, 315 n. 118
Wilmette Free Library, Wilmette,
    Illinois, 131
Clay Products Exposition, 155
Cleburne, Texas, 50, 278
Cleveland, Ohio, 68, 243, 277
Clifford Shopbell and Company, Ar-
    chitects, 84, 85, 271
—buildings by:
    Bozeman-Waters National Bank,
        Poseyville, Indiana, 85, 86, 271.
        See also second color-plate section
    Fellwock Automobile Company,
        Evansville, Indiana, 85, 271
Clinton, Iowa, 56, 77–80, 187, 272,
    307 n. 63
Clutier, Iowa, 272
Cohen, Joseph, 295
Colburn, Serenus Milo, 29
Colcord, Albert E., 249, 293
—buildings by:
    Sekema Building, Chicago, 249, 293
    Wagner Building, Chicago, 249, 293
Colcord, Charles F., 48
Coleman, John N., 256
—building by:
    Jordan Building, Chicago, 256
collegiate Gothic style, 209, 219
Collins, James Edward, 299
Colton, Charles E., 277
Columbus, Wisconsin, 57, 58, 81, 280
commercial style, 12. See also Chicago
    School
Common Clay, 161, 162, 163, 164–66,
    165, 170
Commonwealth Power Company, 274
composition plaster, 142, 143
Conkling-Armstrong Terra Cotta
    Company, 45, 152

Conover and Porter, Engineers, 128, 130

Contemporary Terra Cotta Competition, 266

Cook, Harold Jewett, 277

Cornell University, 101

Corsicana, Texas, 49

Corwin, Cecil S., 95, 119

Cowan, H. R., 81, 272

—building by:
Smith Brothers Building, Burt, Iowa, 81, 272

Cowles and Mutscheller, Architects, 69. See also Rosatti, Joseph

Cox Brothers, 170

Craftsman, The, 85, 106, 139

Crane Elevator Company, 23

Crookston, Minnesota, 274

Crowe, John, 166

Crowen, Samuel N., 286, 289, 295

cubism, 147

Crystal Lake, Illinois, 160, 164, 167

Dallas, Texas, 48–50, 61, 279

Darien, Wisconsin, 280

Darling, Sharon, 154

Darwin, Charles, 4

Davis, Brinton D., 66. See also Henry, J. Earl

Davis, H. C., 61, 280

De Camp, Ben, 69, 277

—building by:
Queen City Livery, Cincinnati, Ohio, 69, 277

Decatur, Illinois, 87

Decorator's Supply Company, 142, 143, 316 nn. 7–9

Del Gardo Museum, New Orleans, Louisiana, 155

Denison, Iowa, 81

Denver, Colorado, 64, 157, 209, 268

Depression/Great Depression, 166, 197, 215, 261

Des Moines, Iowa, 228, 272

Des Plaines, Illinois, 189, 249, 298

De Stijl, 112

Detroit, Michigan, 69, 79, 228, 273

Detroit Lakes, Minnesota, 131, 274

D. H. Burnham and Company, 27, 37

Dickman and Nieman, Architects, 64, 277

—building by:
Graham Building, Muskogee, Oklahoma, 64, 277

Dielmann, Leo M. J., 280

Dobbins, Seward G., 61, 276

Dodd, William J., 42, 161

Dodge Construction News, 148

Douglas, Arizona, 268

Downers Grove, Illinois, 236, 298

Downes and Eads, Architects, 74, 275

—building by:
Telephone Exchange Building, Minneapolis, Minnesota, 74, 275

Drake Realty Company, 64, 276

—building by:
apartment complex, Omaha, Nebraska, 64, 276

Dresser, Christopher, 4

Drotts, Phillip T., 66

Dubin, George Harold, 209, 296, 325 n. 23

—building by:
store building for J. Weiss and P. Javshitz, Chicago, 209, 296

Dubin, Henry, 210, 325 n. 27

Dubin and Dubin, Architects, 209, 325 n. 17

Dubin and Eisenberg, Architects, 209, 210, 289, 291, 297, 298

—buildings by:
store for B. Schuhter, Chicago, 209, 297

store buildings, Chicago, 209, 289

Dubin Dubin Black and Montoussamy, Architects, 209

Dubuque, Iowa, 81, 272

Duluth, Minnesota, 33, 274

Dunning, Max, 161

Dutch architecture, 106, 111, 112

Dwight, Illinois, 87

Eager, Almeron, 131

Eames and Young, Architects, 22

Eau Claire, Wisconsin, 82

Eckstrom, Christian A., 285

Ecole des Beaux-Arts, Paris, France, 41, 147

Economist, The, 155

Edbrooke, Harry W. J., 34, 64, 268, 306 n. 22. See also Atchison and Edbrooke, Architects

—building by:
Lewis and Son Department Store, Denver, Colorado, 64, 65, 268

Edgell, G. H., 47

Edison Park, Chicago, 257

Edwardsville, Illinois, 87, 91

Egyptian revival style, 243

Eichberg, S. Milton, 256, 286

Eisenberg, Abraham J., 209. See also Dubin and Eisenberg, Architects

Eisendrath, Simeon B., 119, 139, 283, 288

—buildings by:
Apartment Building, Chicago, 139, 288

Plymouth Building, Chicago, 139, 283

Eisentraut-Colby-Pottenger, Architects, 66. See also Brostrom, Ernest Olaf

Eldorado, Illinois, 90, 269

Elgin, Minnesota, 274

Ellerbe and Round, Architects, 72, 275

—building by:
First National Bank, Mankato, Minnesota, 72, 74, 275. See also first color-plate section

Elmslie, George G., 2, 12, 14, 44, 87, 92, 101–4, 106, 108, 109, 111–14, 116, 118–20, 124–26, 128, 141, 142, 148, 151, 152, 154, 170, 171, 197, 230, 273, 274, 288, 290, 293, 298, 299. See also Purcell and Elmslie, Architects; Purcell, Feick, and Elmslie, Architects

—buildings by:
American National Bank, Aurora, Illinois, 108, 109, 298

Capitol Building and Loan Association, Topeka, Kansas, 111, 125, 147, 148, 273

Congregational Church, Western Springs, Illinois, 114

Dormitory for Yankton College, Yankton, South Dakota, 112, 278

Edison School, Hammond, Indiana, 116, 118, 148, 271. See also second color-plate section

First National Bank, Adams, Minnesota, 274. See also second color-plate section

Forbes Hall/Science Building for Yankton College, Yankton, South Dakota, 112, 278

Graham Building, Aurora, Illinois, 108, 298

Healy Chapel, Aurora, Illinois, 111, 298

Keystone Building/Joseph George and Newhall Building, Aurora, Illinois, 108, 110, 298

Maxwelton Braes Resort and Golf Club, Baileys Harbor, Wisconsin (with Hermann V. von Holst), 113, 280

Morton School, Hammond, Indiana (with William S. Hutton), 116, 118, 119, 147, 271. See also second color-plate section

Old Second National Bank, Aurora, Illinois, 109, 147, 152, 298

Peoples Gas Light and Coke Company Office, Irving Park Road, Chicago, 113, 290

Peoples Gas Light and Coke Company Office, Larrabee Street, Chicago, 113, *115*, 288

Peoples Gas Light and Coke Company Office, South Chicago, Chicago, 113, *114*, 293

Redfield-Peterson House, Glenview, Illinois, 114

State of Indiana Boy's School, Plainfield, Indiana, 118

Thornton Township High School, Calumet City, Illinois, 116, *117*, 148, 197, 298

Washington Irving School, Hammond, Indiana, 116, 118, 271

—ornamentation of, 112

El Paso, Texas, 46, 279

Erby, Henry F., 160

Ermeling, Ralph W., 231–34, 290, 292

—*buildings by:*

Crawford Building, Chicago, 231, 292

Kutten Store and Flat, Chicago, 231, *232*, 290

—*unbuilt projects by:*

"A Fireplace Alcove," 232

buildings in "Modern Straight Line style," 232

design plates for *American Carpenter and Builder/American Builder*, 232, *233*, *234*

Evanston, Illinois, 34, 40, 240, 253, 298

Evansville, Indiana, 85, 271

Evansville, Wisconsin, 131, 280

Evansville and Terre Haute Railroad, 85

Eveleth, Minnesota, 73, 275

Fairbury, Illinois, 269

Fallon, Katherine, 166

Fanning and Howey, Architects, 118

Fargo, North Dakota, 64, 277

Farmington, Illinois, 269

Federal Terra Cotta Company, 152

Feick, George, 101, 102. *See also* Purcell, Feick, and Elmslie, Architects

Fellows, W. K., 161

Ferris, Hugh, 259

fibrous plastic, 142, 143

Filas and Vittner, Architects, 298

Fischer, F. William, 253, 293, 330 n. 65

—*building by:*

Frazer Brothers' Henryetta Block, Chicago, 253, 293

Fisher, Albert J., 254, 255, 288, 330 n. 67

—*buildings by:*

Hoellin Building, Chicago, 255, 288

retail building, Lincoln Avenue, Chicago, 254, 255, 288

Fitzpatrick, F. W., 11

Flanders, James E., 48, 49, 279, 280

—*buildings by:*

First Methodist Church, Pittsburg, Texas, 49, 279

Navarro County Courthouse, Corsicana, Texas, 49

St. John's Methodist Church, Stamford, Texas, 49, 280

Trinity Methodist Church, Dallas, Texas, 49, 279

Fleury, Albert, 146

Flint, Michigan, 69, 274

Flossmoor, Illinois, 104

Floto, Julian, 256, 257, 292

—*building by:*

Stasch Building, Chicago, 257, 292

Fond du Lac, Wisconsin, 84, 281

Fortin, Joseph T., 285, 296

Fort Wayne, Indiana, 86, 271

Fort Worth, Texas, 50, 279

Fossum, George, 278

Fountain of the Pioneers, Kalamazoo, Michigan, 148

Franklin Grove, Illinois, 269

Freeport, Illinois, 90, 269

Freise, A. H., 173

Friedman, Raphael N., 295

Fry, Frank L., 256, 257, 296

—*building by:*

one-story store, Roosevelt Road, Chicago, 257, 296

Fry Gillan Malinaro, Architects, 314 n. 116

Fuedel, Arthur, 146

Funston, Edmund B., 82, 281, 308 n. 77

—*building by:*

Badger Building, Racine, Wisconsin, 82, *83*, 281

Furness, Frank, 4, 16, 44, 302 n. 2

Gainesville, Texas, 50, 279

Galena, Illinois, 269

Galesburg, Illinois, 34, 87, 88, 189, 269

Galleria, Louisville, Kentucky, 42

Garden, Hugh M. G., 35, 157, 161, 304 n. 56. *See also* Schmidt, Richard E.; Schmidt, Garden, and Martin, Architects

Gary, Indiana, 271

Gates, William D., 53, 160–62, 164, 166, 167, 197

Gatterdam, Frederick E., 169, 321 n. 2

Gatterdam and Krieg, Architects, 169

Gaudí, Antoni, 4

Gebhard, David, 101

Genoa, Illinois, 189, 269

Georgian style, 219

Gerhardt, Paul, 296

Gerlach, Henry G., 72, 275, 307 n. 45

—*building by:*

Zimmerman and Bangerter Building, Mankato, Minnesota, 72, 275

Gill, Irving, 119, 139

—*building by:*

Pickwick Theatre, San Diego, California, 139

Gladding, McBean, and Company, 50, 261

Glenview, Illinois, 114

Goff, Bruce, 62, 64, 278

—*buildings by:*

mausoleum for Grant McCullough, Tulsa, Oklahoma, 64, 278

Tulsa Chamber of Commerce Building, Tulsa, Oklahoma, 64, 278

Gothic or Gothic revival style, 86, 95, 125, 176, 194, 227, 245

Graf, William, 215

Graham, John, 277

Graham Foundation, 35

Grand Meadow, Minnesota, 102, 275

Grand Rapids, Michigan, 70, 274

Grand Rapids, Minnesota, 275

Grant, William, 109

Grant Locomotive Company, 170

Granville, Minnesota, 275

Green Bay, Wisconsin, 281

Green, W. E. E., 73, 275, 307 n. 47

—*building by:*

First National Bank, Luverne, Minnesota, 73, 275

Greene, Herbert M., 50

Greenville, Tennessee, 278

Griffin, Walter Burley, 50, 87, 106

Griffith and Barglebaugh, Architects, 61, 279

—*building by:*

First National Bank Building, Paris, Texas, 61, 279

Grinnell, Iowa, 56, 272

Gropius, Walter, 261

Gross, Oskar, 146, 317 n. 22

Grossman and Proskauer, Architects, 288

Grotz, Charles J., 215, 216, 295–97, 326 n. 43
—buildings by:
 building for James Svejda, Chicago, 216, 297
 building for J. Drew, Chicago, 215
 building for J. Slader, Chicago, 216, 295
 one-story building, W. 51st St., Chicago, 216, 297
 two-story building, W. 47th St., Chicago, 216, 297
 Valhakis Store Building, Chicago, 215, 216, 296

Grubey Faience and Tile Company, 80

Guske, James, 291

Haas, Richard, 263
—mural by:
 Homage to the Chicago School, 263, 265

Hallberg, L. G., 286

Halperin, Casriel, 227. See also Halperin and Braun, Architects

Halperin and Braun, Architects, 227, 228, 287, 295, 296, 327 n. 73
—buildings by:
 Behrstock Store, Chicago, 228, 296
 commercial building for J. F. Dooley, Chicago, 227, 296
 store building for Goldberg, Fried, and Cantor, Chicago, 228, 287
 storefront, Chicago, 228

Hamilton, James, 253

Hammond, Indiana, 116, 147, 271

Handbook for Architects and Builders, 155, 178

Hanifen, John Walker, 88, 89, 233, 270, 309 nn. 96, 97
—buildings by:
 Cummings store, LaSalle, Illinois, 88, 270
 Erlenborn Mortuary, LaSalle, Illinois, 88, 270
 Fitch Laundry, LaSalle, Illinois, 89, 270. See also second color-plate section
 Jordan Hardware, Ottawa, Illinois, 88, 270
 McLellan Company store building, LaSalle, Illinois, 88, 270
 Skelly store and gas station, LaSalle, Illinois, 88, 270

Hansen, Paul, 257, 286
—building by:
 garage building, Broadway, Chicago, 257, 286

Hansen and Waggoner, Architects. See Waggoner, Karl M.

Harbeck, Jervis (Harry) R., 79, 272
—building by:
 Iowa State Bank, Clinton, Iowa, 79, 80, 80, 272. See also first color-plate section

Harris, Fred A., 272

Harris (Hymowitz), Mandel H., 219, 287, 291, 298
—buildings by:
 one-story stores, Chicago, 219
 sales/service garages, Chicago, 219

Harris, Ralph C., 289

Harris, Will J., 85, 308 n. 84

Hastings, Nebraska, 120

Hastings and Chivetta, 22

Hatfield, E. L., 178

Hatzfeld, Clarence, 258, 287, 293
—buildings by:
 commercial building, Chicago, 13, 258, 258, 293. See also second color-plate section
 store building for E. Dichs, Chicago, 257, 258, 287

Hattabaugh, Mary Azona, 53

Healy, George Louis, 146

Healy and Millet, 145, 146

Hecht, Albert S., 238, 298
—building by:
 Woolworth's Five and Ten Store, Blue Island, Illinois, 238, 239, 240, 298

Hector, Minnesota, 102, 275

Heidel, W. C., 166

Henry, C. D., 269

Henry, J. Earl, 66, 273, 306 n. 29
—building by:
 Belkamp School, Louisville, Kentucky, 66, 273

Hetherington, John T., 194

Hetherington, Murray D., 194

Hewitt, Edwin H., 33, 275, 303 n. 33
—building by:
 Brooks Residence, 33, 275

Hewitt and Emerson, Architects, 270

Hewson, S. J., and Company, 30

Highland Park, Illinois, 151

Hilgers, George, 126. See also Steele and Hilgers, Architects

Hill, Vernon I., 274

Himelblau, A. L., 199, 211, 212, 214, 215, 229, 283, 286–92, 294–99, 325 nn. 32, 33, 326 n. 41
—buildings by:
 commercial and garage building on Montrose, Chicago, 212, 213, 291

commercial building, Oak Park, Illinois, 212, 213, 299
commercial building for S. Dlott, Chicago, 212, 288
Emmermann Apartment Building, Chicago, 211, 286
Kaplan and Schachter Store Building, Chicago, 212, 297
store building on South State Street, Chicago, 211, 294
three-story building, Chicago, 214
two-story buildings, Chicago, 212, 214

Himelblau, Abraham L. See Himelblau, A. L.

Hinsdale, Illinois, 104

Hirschfeld, R. A., 161

Hirschfield, Leo Saul, 250, 329 n. 51. See also Rissman and Hirschfield, Architects

Hoffman, William L., Jr., 294

Hogenson, Edward A., 245, 298
—buildings by:
 factory, Cicero, Illinois, 245
 Lusterite Enamels Factory, Cicero, Illinois, 245, 298

Holabird and Roche, Architects, 27, 77, 139, 283

Holabird and Root, 27

Holland, Michigan, 69, 274

Holstead and Sullivan, Architects, 275

Honaker, Virginia, 61, 280

Hoopeston, Illinois, 90, 269

Hoquiam, Washington, 132, 280

Hosmer, Claire C., 82, 281
—building by:
 Gebhardt and Company Building, Milwaukee, Wisconsin, 82, 281

Hotpoint Corporation, 170

Hottinger, Gustav, 152, 153, 318 n. 55

Houston, Texas, 62, 279

Hubbell, J. P., 50

Hubbell and Greene, Architects, 50, 279
—building by:
 John Deere Plow Company/Texas Implement Building, Dallas, Texas, 50, 279

Huehl and Schmid, Architects, 173

Hunt, Jarvis, 139

Hunter, Bonnie Marie, 102

Huron, South Dakota, 278

Hutton and Hutton, Architects, 118. See also Hutton, William S.

Hutton, William S., 114, 118, 197, 271. See also Hutton and Hutton, Architects

—buildings by:
Edison School, Hammond, Indiana
(with George G. Elmslie), 116,
118, 119, 148, 271. See also second
color-plate section
Morton School, Hammond, Indiana
(with George G. Elmslie), 116,
118, 119, 119, 147, 271. See also
second color-plate section
State of Indiana Boy's School,
Plainfield, Indiana (with George
G. Elmslie), 118
Thornton Township High School,
Calumet City, Illinois (with
George G. Elmslie), 116, 117,
148, 197, 298
Washington Irving School, Ham-
mond, Indiana (with George G.
Elmslie), 116, 118, 271
Hymowitz, Mandel H. See Harris,
Mandel H.

Iannelli, Alfonso, 106, 116, 146–48
Illinois Society of Architects, 118, 154,
155, 178, 195
Illinois Society of Architects Monthly Bul-
letin, 118
Independent Order of Odd Fellows
Lodge Hall and Commercial Build-
ing, Rochester, Minnesota, 72, 73,
276. See also first color-plate section
Indianapolis, Indiana, 85, 86, 166, 271
Indianapolis Terra Cotta Company, 75,
85, 166, 320 n. 112
Industrial Chicago, 17, 142
International Modernism, 261
International Style, 27, 113, 157
Interstate Architect and Builder, 33
Iowa City, Iowa, 124

Jacksonville, Florida, 44, 45, 61, 268
Jacobs, Arthur, 255, 288, 291, 298, 330
n. 69
—buildings by:
commercial building, Cicero, Illinois, 255, 298
commercial building for A. Guthman, Chicago, 255, 288
Jacobs, Fred D., 62, 279
—building by:
New Palace Theater, McAllen, Texas, 62, 279
Jacobson (first name unknown), 263,
289
Jacobson and Jacobson, Architects, 75,
76, 166, 275
—building by:

Minnesota Mutual Fire Insurance
Company Building, Owatonna,
Minnesota, 75, 76, 166, 275
Jamestown, North Dakota, 277
Jefferson, Iowa, 81, 272
Jeffery, H. T., 68, 277
—building by:
St. Clair Market, Cleveland, Ohio,
68, 277
Jenney, William Le Baron, 42, 139, 161
Jensen, Jens, 220
Jensen, Jens J., 220, 287, 290, 291, 297,
299
—buildings by:
commercial building for Charles
Andrews, Chicago, 220, 222, 290
Masonic Hall and stores, Oak Park,
220, 221, 299
Miller Building, Chicago, 220, 287
Silverman Building, Cicero Ave.,
Chicago, 222, 290
store building, Chicago, 220
three-story building, Chicago, 220
Johnson, George, 173, 186, 191, 193
Johnson, Gilbert A., 91. See also Peter-
son and Johnson, Architects
Johnson and Son, Architects. See Oscar
Johnson and Son, Architects
Johnstone, Percy T., 289
Joliet, Illinois, 299
Jordan, Joseph J., 257
Julian Academy, Paris, France, 148
Jump River, Wisconsin, 82
Juul, E. A., 85, 281, 282
—buildings by:
Curtis Hotel, Plymouth, Wisconsin,
85, 281
store building, Sheboygan, Wiscon-
sin, 85, 282
William F. Christen commercial
building, Valders, Wisconsin, 85,
282
Juul and Smith, Architects. See Juul,
E. A.

Kahn, Albert, 273
Kahn, Louis I., 135
Kalamazoo, Michigan, 69, 148, 274
Kane, Michael B., 91, 271
—building by:
Wordon Elementary School, Wor-
don, Illinois, 91, 271
Kankakee, Illinois, 90, 269
Kansas City, Missouri, 41, 42, 66, 67,
276
Kansas University, 47
Karlsruhe, Germany, 148

Kaufmann, Edgar, Jr., 4
Kawneer Company, 69, 274
—building by:
retail building, Niles, Michigan, 69,
274
Keck, Bert, 274
Kees, Frederick, 29, 303 n. 24
Kees and Colburn, Architects, 29, 30,
33, 50, 69, 275
—buildings by:
Advance Thresher Building, Minneapolis, Minnesota, 30, 50, 275. See
also first color-plate section
Chamber of Commerce Building,
Minneapolis, Minnesota, 29, 30,
31, 32, 275. See also first color-plate
section
Deere and Webber Company Build-
ing, Minneapolis, Minnesota, 33,
275
Donaldson Company Building, Min-
neapolis, Minnesota, 30, 275
Emerson-Newton Implement Com-
pany Building, Minneapolis, Min-
nesota, 30, 275
Great Northern Implement Compa-
ny Building, Minneapolis, Minne-
sota, 30, 33, 275
Keith's Magazine, 85
Kelmscott Gallery, 138
Kendrick, C. E., 271
Kenosha, Wisconsin, 84, 281
Kevy, L. A., 62, 279
—building by:
White Seed Company, Plainview,
Texas, 62, 279
Kimball, Thomas R., 128
Kimball, Steele, and Sandham, Archi-
tects, 128. See also Steele, William L.
Kingsley, George S., 173, 243, 289,
329 nn. 32, 36
—buildings by:
Hebard Storage/Union Van, Chica-
go, 173, 243, 244, 289
Reebie and Brother Warehouse,
Chicago, 243
Wenter and Drechaler Storage
Warehouse, Oak Park, Illinois,
243
Kingsville, Texas, 62, 279
Klafter, Joseph H., 289–91, 294
Klawiter, F. C., 84, 281
—building by:
Community Building, Green Bay,
Wisconsin, 84, 281
Klein, William Julius, 223. See also
Levy and Klein, Architects

Kleinpell, W. F., 120
Klutho, Henry J., 44–46, 51, 152, 268
—buildings by:
Burbridge Hotel, Jacksonville, Florida, 44, 268
Criminal Court Building, Jacksonville, Florida, 45, 268
East Jacksonville Elementary School Number Three, E. Jacksonville, Florida, 45, 268
Florida Life Building, Jacksonville, Florida, 45, 268
James Hotel, Palotka, Florida, 45, 268
Klutho Residence, Jacksonville, Florida, 44
Lynch Building, Jacksonville, Florida, 45
Napier/Wilkie Apartments, Jacksonville, Florida, 45, 268
Nolan Garage, Jacksonville, Florida, 45, 268
St. James Building, Jacksonville, Florida, 44, 45, 268
Seminole Hotel, Jacksonville, Florida, 44
Knox and Elliot, Architects, 277
Knoxville, Illinois, 270
Kocher, Jacques J., 249, 294–96
—buildings by:
Holmes Building, Chicago, 250, 295
Pearlman Service Garage, Chicago, 250, 294
Kocher and Larson, Architects. See Kocher, Jacques J.
Koedel, C. H., 209
Koenigsberg, Nathan, 256, 330 n. 71. See also Koenigsberg and Weisfeld, Architects
Koenigsberg and Weisfeld, Architects, 256, 287, 290, 291, 330 n. 71
—buildings by:
commercial building for A. Nelson, Chicago, 255, 256, 287
commercial building for Dr. Harry Sered, Chicago, 256, 291
one-story commercial building, Chicago, 256, 290
Kopf, J. Edwin, 86, 271
—building by:
Williams Building, Indianapolis, Indiana, 86, 271
Koster, John L., 292
Krause, William P., 136, 138
Krieg, Arthur Walter, 195, 323 n. 68. See also Krieg Associates, Architects
Krieg, Frederick Gustav, 169

Krieg, William G., 168–70, 172, 173, 175, 185, 186, 193–95, 197, 295. See also Krieg Associates, Architects; Krieg, Hetherington, and Hetherington, Architects
—building by:
apartment complex, Chicago, 194, 194, 195, 295
Krieg Associates, Architects, 195. See also Krieg, William G.
—building by:
industrial building with office and shelter, W. 47th St., Chicago, 195
Krieg, Hetherington, and Hetherington, Architects, 194, 280, 323 n. 63. See also Krieg, William G.
—buildings by:
Beloit Water, Gas, and Electric Light Company, Beloit, Wisconsin, 194, 196, 280
store and apartment for Ludwig Prohofer, Cicero, Illinois, 195
Kuehn, F. C. W., 278
Kuehne, Carl Osker, 222, 287–89, 292, 326 n. 60
—buildings by:
North American Business Exchange, Chicago, 223, 289
one-story commercial buildings, Chicago, 222, 224, 287, 288
Kurke, William F., 64, 277
—building by:
hotel for T. F. Powers, Fargo, North Dakota, 64, 277

La Crosse, Wisconsin, 281
Ladehoff, John H., 77, 78, 187, 270, 272, 307 n. 62
—buildings by:
Pahl Building, Clinton, Iowa, 77, 79, 187, 272
Snow White Drug Store, Clinton, Iowa, 78, 79, 272
Sullivan Building, Savanna, Illinois, 78, 270
Ladehoff and Sohn, Architects. See Ladehoff, John H.
La Grange, Illinois, 166
Lake Andes, South Dakota, 278
Lampe, Clarence J., 295
Lancaster, Wisconsin, 133, 281
Lang, Albert, 286
Lang, John T., 120
Lang, Otto H. See Lang and Witchell, Architects
Lang and Witchell, Architects, 49, 50, 278, 279, 280

—buildings by:
Central Fire Station Building, Dallas, Texas, 49, 279
Cooke County Courthouse, Gainesville, Texas, 49, 279
Cotton Exchange Building, Dallas, Texas, 49, 279
Johnson County Courthouse, Cleburne, Texas, 50, 278
Raleigh Hotel, Waco, Texas, 49, 280
Sears Roebuck and Company Warehouse, Dallas, Texas, 49, 279
Southwestern Life Building, Dallas, Texas, 49, 279
Laredo, Texas, 279
LaSalle, Illinois, 88, 89, 233, 270
Laurel Building, Muscatine, Iowa, 81, 272
Lautz, William H., 294, 296, 297
Legel, J. G. See Legel and Company, Architects
Legel and Company, Architects, 90, 269
—building by:
First Trust and Savings Bank, Albany, Illinois, 90, 269
Legge, James, 143, 153, 158
Leitha, J. F., 81, 272
—building by:
Fuhrman Building, Dubuque, Iowa, 81, 272
LeRoy, Minnesota, 102, 275
Levy, Alexander Louis, 223, 297. See also Levy and Klein, Architects
—building by:
three-story building, Chicago, 223
Levy and Klein, Architects, 157, 199, 223, 225–27, 229, 287–89, 291, 292, 295–98, 327 n. 65
—buildings by:
buildings for M. Astrahan, Chicago, 157, 158, 226
Blumenthal Building, Cicero, Illinois, 225, 226, 298
Cracko Building, Chicago, 225, 227, 291
Levinson (Spaulding) Building, Chicago, 225, 291
mixed-use buildings, Chicago, 226
store buildings, Chicago, 225
Lietha, J. F., 272
Linden, Frank Louis, 145
Linden Glass Company/Linden Company, 145
Linderoth Ceramic Company, 236. See also Linderoth, Swen
Linderoth, Swen, 235, 236, 295–97

—*buildings by:*
  Anderson Building, Chicago, 235, *236*, 296
  Bunde Store Building, Chicago, 235, 297
Lindquist, Fred, 296
Link, Theodore C., 41, 276, 304 n. 60
—*buildings by:*
  Roberts, Johnson, and Rand Shoe Company, St. Louis, Missouri, 41, 276
  Union Station, St. Louis, Missouri, 41, 276
Link and Cameron, Architects. *See* Link, Theodore C.
Lippincott's Magazine, 29
Liska, Charles, 286
Lockhart, G. L., 275
Lonek, Adolph, 298
Los Angeles, California, 42, 268
Louisville, Kentucky, 42, 64, 66, 273
Ludgin and Leviton, Architects, 290
Ludowici Celander Company, 261
Luna, Iowa, 272
Lund, Anders G., 238–40, 292, 293, 296, 297
—*buildings by:*
  apartment buildings, Chicago, 238, *241*, 292
  store buildings, Chicago, 239
Luverne, Minnesota, 275
Luxfer prism glass, 78, 90, 205
Lynch, E. P., 64, 273
—*building by:*
  Olympic Building, Louisville, Kentucky, 64, *67*, 273

Mackintosh, Charles Rennie, 4
Madison, Minnesota, 102, 275
Madison, Wisconsin, 56, 81, 102, 128, 130, 134, 135, 281
Magney and Tusler, Architects, 75
Maher, George Washington, 40, 41, 276, 287, 299
—*buildings by:*
  Farson House, Oak Park, Illinois, 40, 299
  Patten House, Evanston, Illinois, 40, 299
  Schneidenhelm House, Evanston, Illinois, 40
  Swift Hall of Engineering, Northwestern University, Evanston, Illinois, 41, 299
  University Building, Evanston, Illinois, 40, 299

Watkins Medical Products, Winona, Minnesota, 41, 276
Mahler, H. H., 286
Manhattan Building, Chicago, 139
Mankato, Minnesota, 275
Manlius, Illinois, 120, 121, 270
Marceline, Kansas, 276
Marengo, Illinois, 270
Mark and Sheftall, Architects, 268
Marsh and Russell, Architects, 268
Martin, Edgar, 35. *See also* Schmidt, Garden, and Martin
Martinsville, Indiana, 86, 187, 271
Mason City, Iowa, 81, 272
Masonic Temple, Prairie du Sac, Wisconsin, 82, 281
Massachusetts Institute of Technology (MIT), 34, 85, 139
Matteson, Victor Andre, 270
Maury, Mason, 42, 273
—*buildings by:*
  Kaufman-Straus Building, Louisville, Kentucky, 42, *43*, 273
  Women's Club, Louisville, Kentucky, 42
Maury and Dodd, Architects, 42. *See also* Maury, Mason
McAllen, Texas, 62, 279
McCauley, Willis J., 283
McClellan, Edward G., 249, 250, 295
—*buildings by:*
  commercial and apartment buildings, Chicago, 250
  Jensen Store Building, 75th St., Chicago, 250, 295
  Olson buildings, South Ashland, Chicago, 250, 295
McClure, Holmes, and Nechodoma, Architects. *See* Nechodoma, Antonín
McCoy, J. F., 269
McGee, W. A., 269
Measom, A., 173
Mechanicsburg, Indiana, 271
Medinah Temple, Chicago, 173
Mediterranean style, 130
Meldahl, Jens J., 245, 294
—*building by:*
  American Tag Company, Chicago, 245, 294
Mendius, Hans M., 171, 172, 175, 179, 321 n. 14
Meredith, D. D., 259, 287
—*buildings by:*
  one-story commercial building, Chicago, 259, *260*, 287
  three-story commercial building, Chicago, 259

Merrill, Wisconsin, 131, 281
Meyer, Scherer, and Rockcastle, Architects, 314 n. 117
Michael Reese Hospital, 215
Michigan City, Indiana, 118, 271
Midland Terra Cotta Company, 9, 23, 53, 61, 62, 64, 68, 69, 72, 73, 77–79, 81, 82, 84–91, 116, 122, 123, 138, 152, 154, 167–98, 200, 202, 203, 205, 206, 209, 210, 212, 214–17, 219, 220, 225–31, 234, 235, 237, 238, 243, 245, 247, 250, 252–59, 262, 263, 269–75, 278, 279, 281, 282, 289, 292, 298, 299
—advertising, 176, 178, 179, *180–82*, 183, 187, 197, 234, 256
—*buildings by (as architect):*
  Bosert and Cohlgraff Store, Chicago, 289. *See also second color-plate section*
  Carlson and Hasslen Building, Ortonville, Minnesota, 189, 275
  Genoa Lumber Company, Genoa, Illinois, 189, 269
  Graham Building, Kenosha, Wisconsin, 84, 281
  Gunther Garage, Galesburg, Illinois, 189, 269
  Hilgerman Building, Rhinelander, Wisconsin, 84, 189, 281
  Judd Garage, St. Charles, Illinois, 189, *190*, 299
  Masonic Temple, St. Joseph, Illinois, 187, 270. *See also second color-plate section*
  Milligan Company Building, Jefferson, Iowa, 81, 272
  Overland Automobile Company, Buildings for, Peoria, Illinois, 187–89, 191, 270; Rockford, Illinois, 187, 270
  Post Office and Store Building, Wilmette, Illinois, 190, 191, *192*, 299
  Quilici Store, Des Plaines, Illinois, 189, 191, 247, *248*, 298
  Toner Store, Martinsville, Indiana, 86, 187, *188*, 271. *See also second color-plate section*
  Winkleman Store Building, Des Plaines, Illinois, 190, 191, 298
—catalog plates/portfolios, *169, 171,* 174, 176, *177,* 178, 179, *180–82,* 183, *184–86,* 193, *193,* 198
Mies van der Rohe, Ludwig, 261
Miller, August W., 172
Miller, William C., 289, 291
Millet, Louis J., 145, 146, 317 n. 16

Milwaukee, Wisconsin, 72, 81, 82, 84, 281

Minchin, Sidney, 245, 297, 329 n. 43
—*building by:*
Glass Novelty, Chicago, 245, 247, 297

Minneapolis, Minnesota, 29, 30, 33, 74, 102, 120, 171, 275

Mishawaka, Indiana, 87, 271

Mission Revival Style, 47

Mitchell, L. M., 286

Mitchell, South Dakota, 102, 278

Mitchell/Giurgola, Architects, 22

Modernism/Modern Architecture, 262, 264

Moline, Illinois, 270

Monroe, Wisconsin, 134, 135, 281

Moreau, Fernand, 154, 166

Morey's and People's Hotel, Sioux City, Iowa, 76, 78, 272

Morris, William, 100

Morry, Minnesota, 275

Mount Vernon, Indiana, 271

Mundie, W. B., 161

Muscatine, Iowa, 81, 272

Muskogee, Oklahoma, 64, 277

Nagle, James, 264. *See also* Nagle, Hartray, and Associates, Architects

Nagle, Hartray, and Associates, Architects, 264
—*buildings by:*
First Bank of Oak Park, Oak Park, Illinois, 264
Housing for the Elderly, Taylorville, Illinois, 264
Ramada Renaissance Hotel, Springfield, Illinois, 264
Rudich Townhouse, Chicago, 264

Nampa, Idaho, 269

Nathan, M. O., 223, 228, 286, 291, 296, 327 n. 76
—*buildings by:*
automobile service garage, Chicago, 228, 286
Manor Garage and Auto Sales, Chicago, 228, 291
store building for Isaac Frank, Chicago, 228, 296
store buildings, Chicago, 228

National Builder, 178, 245

National Building Museum, 266

National Register of Historic Places, 29, 30, 34, 35, 72, 108, 132

National Terra Cotta Society, 153, 166, 207, 238

Nechodoma, Antonín, 61, 282

—*building by:*
Bank of Nova Scotia, San Juan, Puerto Rico, 61, 282

Neenah, Wisconsin, 85, 281

Nejdl, George J., 173, 186, 191, 193

Nelson, B., 166

Nevcks, A. E., 271

Newark, Ohio, 9, 277

New Castle, Indiana, 271

New Haven, West Virginia, 61, 280

Newhouse, Henry L., 294

Newhouse and Bernham, Architects, 294

New Orleans, Louisiana, 273

new urbanism, 262

New York, New York, 27, 139, 143, 172, 250, 259, 277

Nicol and Dietz, Architects, 271

Nicholson, William A., 259, 293
—*building by:*
Spiker Building, Chicago, 259, 293

Niedecken, George M., 103

Nielsen, N. P., 64, 272
—*building by:*
McClintock Building, Topeka, Kansas, 64, 272

Niles, Michigan, 274

Nimmons, George C., 283

Ninneman, Robert P., 189, 247, 249, 298
—*building by:*
Quilici Store, Des Plaines, Illinois, 247, *248*, 298

North Platte, Nebraska, 276

Northwest Architectural Archives (NWAA), 193

Northwestern Terra Cotta Company, 23, 51, 55, 109, 147, 151–57, 160, 166, 169, 173, 174, 176, 178, 197, 202, 225, 251, 252
—*publication of:*
Northwestern Terra Cotta (periodical), 157

Norton, John W., 106, 146, 147

Norweta (pottery), 154. *See also* Northwestern Terra Cotta Company

Nuremberg University, Nuremberg, Germany, 153

Oak Park, Illinois, 40, 82, 93, 95, 101, 194, 212, 220, 243, 263, 264, 299

Ocean Springs, Mississippi, 53, 276

Ohio State University, 166

Oklahoma City, Oklahoma, 47, 48, 277

Oklahoma City Chamber of Commerce, 48

Old Colony Building, Chicago, 139

Olson and Berg, Architects, 295

Omaha, Nebraska, 64, 128, 276

Orchestra Hall, Chicago, 39

Oregon, Illinois, 270

Orion, Illinois, 270

Ortonville, Minnesota, 189, 275

Oscar Johnson and Son, Architects, 287, 288

Ottawa, Illinois, 88, 270

Ottumwa, Iowa, 272

Ottenheimer, Henry L., 120, 138. *See also* Ottenheimer, Stern, and Reichert, Architects

Ottenheimer, Stern, and Reichert, Architects, 138

Overbeck, H. A., 279

Owatonna, Minnesota, 55, 75, 77, 91, 145, 146, 148, 160, 164, 166, 275

Owen, W., 297

Packard, A. A., 299

Pagels, William F., 296, 299

Palatka, Florida, 45, 268

Palmer, Hall, and Hunt, Architects, 33, 274
—*building by:*
Patrick Wholesale Building, Duluth, Minnesota, 33, 274

Pappageorge and Haymes, Architects, 264
—*building by:*
Greenview Passage, Chicago, 264

Paris Exhibition (1900), 19

Paris, Illinois, 90, 270

Paris, Texas, 61, 279

Patelski, Erich, 228, 297
—*buildings by:*
Margolis Apartments, Chicago, 229
Telechanski Building, Chicago, 229, 297

Peagram, George H., 41

Peck, Ferdinand, 17

Pentecost, Douglas S., 259, 289
—*building by:*
Dr. Stewart Three-Flat, Chicago, 259, 289

Peoria, Illinois, 87, 90, 187–89, 270

Perkins, Dwight H., 293

Perkins and McWayne, 278

Perth Amboy Terra Cotta Company, 152

Peterson, Edward A., 90. *See also* Peterson and Johnson, Architects

Peterson, William C., 164

Peterson and Johnson, Architects, 90, 270, 310 n. 106
—*buildings by:*

Comstock Building, Rochelle, Illinois, 90, 270

Floberg Building, Rockford, Illinois, 90, 270. See also second color-plate section

Philbrick, Allen, 146, 317 n. 24

Phoenix, Arizona, 46, 268

Pittsburg, Kansas, 273

Pittsburg, Texas, 49, 279

Pittsburgh, Pennsylvania, 125, 139

Plainfield, Indiana, 118

Plainview, Texas, 62, 279

plaster ornamentation, 141–43, 145, 146, 148

Platz, Clara J., 169

Plymouth, Wisconsin, 85, 281

Pompeiian style, 155

Portland, Oregon, 278. See also first color-plate section

Poseyville, Indiana, 85, 271

Portfolio of Plans, 231

postmodernism, 262, 264

Potter, Lawson, and Pawlowsky, Architects, 315 n. 118

Prairie du Sac, Wisconsin, 82, 281

Prairie School, 1, 12, 22, 23, 40, 44, 50, 81, 84, 85, 90, 95, 97, 98, 104, 125, 130, 139, 142, 175, 227, 231, 248, 264, 301 n. 13

Presto, William C., 59, 77, 120, 136, 138, 288, 291, 315 n. 125
—buildings by:
   bowling alley for A. D. Schuller, Chicago, 138, 291
   building at Montrose and Artesian, Chicago, 138, 291
   Krause Music Store, Chicago, 59, 60, 136, 138, 288

Primley, Walter S., 170, 172, 321 n. 16

Princeton, Illinois, 120–23, 270

Princeton, Indiana, 85

Principles of Architectural Composition, The, 56

Pueblo, Colorado, 268

Pullman, Illinois, 202

Purcell, William Gray, 2, 101, 102, 104, 108, 119, 147, 311 n. 30. See also Purcell and Elmslie, Architects; Purcell, Feick, and Elmslie, Architects

Purcell and Elmslie, Architects, 52, 60, 69, 70, 72–74, 81, 82, 101, 102, 104, 106, 108, 111, 112, 119, 134, 141, 142, 147, 148, 158, 167, 168, 272, 275, 278, 282, 296, 299. See also Purcell, Feick, and Elmslie, Architects
—buildings by:

apartment building for Newman, Baskerville, and Marsh, Chicago, 104, 296

Bradley House, Madison, Wisconsin, 102, 281

Branson and Company, Bankers, Mitchell, South Dakota, 102, 278

Community House, Eau Claire, Wisconsin, 82

Farmers and Merchants State Bank, Hector, Minnesota, 102, 275

First State Bank, LeRoy, Minnesota, 102, 275

Land Office, Stanley, Wisconsin, 82, 282

Madison State Bank, Madison, Minnesota, 101, 275

Municipal Building, Kasson, Minnesota, 111

Purcell House, Minneapolis, Minnesota, 102, 275

service buildings for Henry Babson, Riverside, Illinois, 104, 299

Town Hall, Jump River, Wisconsin, 82

Woodbury County Courthouse, Sioux City, Iowa (with William Steele), 106, 107, 108, 147, 148, 272. See also second color-plate section

Purcell and Feick, Architects, 101, 102

Purcell, Feick, and Elmslie, Architects, 102, 103, 120, 135, 143, 148, 157, 176, 189, 204, 251, 264, 275–76, 281, 285
—buildings of:
   Edison Shop, Chicago, 69, 74, 82, 103, 105, 285
   Exchange State Bank, Grand Meadow, Minnesota, 101, 275
   First National Bank, Rhinelander, Wisconsin, 82, 102, 103, 143, 157, 176, 189, 204, 251, 264, 281
   Merchants Bank of Winona, Winona, Minnesota, 41, 102, 104, 135, 148, 176, 276. See also second color-plate section
—unbuilt project by:
   bank design, Mankato, Minnesota, 111

Queen Anne Style, 4, 87, 93

Racine, Wisconsin, 82, 84, 281

Radcliffe, Barney S., 172

Radford, Roland D., 230

Radford, William A., 178, 230

Radford Architectural Company, 230, 234

Raeuber, William J., 281, 282

Ramsey, Charles K., 20
—building by:
   Houser Building, St. Louis, Missouri, 20

Ravenswood, Chicago, 236

Rawson and Eisenberg, Architects, 294

Raymond's Clothing and Hill Hotel Building, Sioux City, Iowa, 76, 272

Refugio, Texas, 62, 280

Renaissance revival style, 227

Rezney, James B., 120, 139, 297

Rezny and Krippner, Architects, 139, 298

Rhinelander, Wisconsin, 82, 84, 102, 143, 157, 176, 189, 251, 281

Richardson, H. H., 16–18, 41
—building by:
   Marshall Field Warehouse, Chicago, 16, 17

Richland Center, Wisconsin, 82

Richmond, California, 268

Richmond, Indiana, 271

Riedel, John M. E., 86, 271
—building by:
   store building for G. Rizos, Fort Wayne, Indiana, 86, 271

Ricker, Nathan C., 124

Rinaker, J. L, 269

Risch, 173

Rissman, Maurice Barney, 250, 329 n. 50. See also Rissman and Hirschfield, Architects

Rissman and Hirschfield, Architects, 157, 250, 288, 291
—buildings by:
   Schoenberg Building, Chicago, 157, 252, 288
   Shooman Building, Chicago, 157, 250, 251, 291
   1344 Devon Building, Chicago, 252

River Forest, Illinois, 95, 97, 104, 130, 147, 299

Riverside, Illinois, 55, 104, 195, 299

Robertson, Howard, 56

Rochelle, Illinois, 90, 131, 270

Rochester, Minnesota, 72, 276

Rockford, Illinois, 87, 90, 187, 195, 270

rococo revival style, 223, 226

Romanesque/Romanesque revival style, 4, 16, 17, 20, 29, 30, 41, 42

Rookwood Pottery, 80, 156

Root, John W., 42

Root, Walter C., 42, 304 n. 62. See also Root and Siemens, Architects

Root and Siemens, Architects, 41, 42, 276

—building by:
    Scarritt Building and Arcade, Kansas City, Missouri, 42, 276
Rosatti, Joseph, 69, 273
—building by:
    First State Savings Bank/Farmers State Bank, Breckenridge, Michigan, 69, 273
Roseland, Chicago, 202, 258
Roy, Franz, 293
Royal Academy, Berlin, Germany, 148, 153
Rudolph, Christopher, 264
—building by:
    Mitchell's Jewelry, Arlington Heights, Illinois, 264
Rugh, Herbert, 34
Rugh and Atchison, Architects, 282. See also Atchison, John D.
Rush, Endacott, and Rush, Architects, 64, 278. See also Goff, Bruce
Russell, Lewis E., 287
Russia, 256
Rusy, Anthony F., 296
Ruttenberg, Albert M., 291, 295
Ryan, F. S., 172

Saginaw, Michigan, 39, 69, 274
Sailor, Homer, 120
St. Charles, Illinois, 189, 299
St. Joseph, Illinois, 187, 270
St. Louis, Missouri, 4, 16, 19, 20, 22, 41, 68, 91, 136, 276
St. Louis Terra Cotta Company, 68, 91
St. Louis World's Fair, 154
St. Paul, Minnesota, 29, 39, 70, 72, 276
Salina, Kansas, 64, 273
Salt Lake City, Utah, 280
San Diego, California, 139
San Francisco, California, 268
San Juan, Puerto Rico, 61, 282
Sand, John, 154
Sandegren, Andrew, 289
Sandham, J. Dow, 128
Sanguinet and Staats, Architects, 50, 279
—building by:
    Flat Iron Building, Fort Worth, Texas, 50, 279
Saulk City, Wisconsin, 282
Sault Saint Marie, Minnesota, 274
Savanna, Illinois, 78, 90, 270
Saxe, Ira C., 298
Schaffner, Daniel J., 292
Schall's Candy Company Building, Clinton, Iowa, 80, 272. See also first color-plate section

Scheller, Jesse E., 297
Schindler, R. M., 143
Schlacks, Henry J., 120, 138, 315 n. 132. See also Schlacks and Ottenheimer, Architects
Schlacks and Ottenheimer, Architects, 138
Schmidt, Garden, and Martin, Architects, 35, 49, 274, 276, 283. See also Schmidt, Richard E.
Schmidt, Hugo, 288
Schmidt, Richard E., 35–40, 119, 120, 157, 283, 286, 290, 304 nn. 42, 43
—buildings by:
    Bunte Brothers Candy Factory, Chicago, 39, 40, 290
    Chapin and Gore Building, Chicago, 35, 37, 38, 39, 157, 283
    factory building, St. Paul, Minnesota, 39, 40, 276
    hotel, Saginaw, Michigan, 39, 274
    Madlener House, Chicago, 35, 36, 37, 286
    Michael Reese Hospital, Chicago, 39, 40, 293
    Montgomery Ward Warehouse, Chicago, 39, 49, 283
Schmitt, William T., 64, 273
—buildings by:
    Besse Hotel, Pittsburg, Kansas, 273
    Lincoln School, Salina, Kansas, 64, 273
Schneider, Kristian, 55, 106, 109, 112, 116, 153, 154, 158, 164, 166, 167, 197
Schnetzler, C. H., 269
Schultz, A. L., and Son, 170
Schultz, William, 259, 295
—building by:
    store and flat, 4939 S. Ashland, Chicago, 259, 295
Schulze, William, 272
Schwartz, Albert A., 248, 249, 295
—building by:
    Kelly Building/New Sanctuary Church, Chicago, 248, 249, 249, 295
Scott-Larson Company, 297
Scott, Milton W., 62, 280
—building by:
    automobile sales and garage, Waco, Texas, 62, 280
Seattle, Washington, 51, 280. See also first color-plate section
Seeman, Emil Henry, 120
Seguin, Texas, 280
Sevic, William, 259, 295

—building by:
    Fuhrman and Foster Company, Chicago, 259, 295
Shavie and Murray, Architects, 314 n. 115
Sheboygan, Wisconsin, 85, 282
Sherry, E. J., 291
Shopbell, Clifford, 85. See also Clifford Shopbell and Company, Architects
Shopbell, Fowler, and Thole, Architects, 86, 309 n. 90
Sidney, Ohio, 57, 61, 277
Silsbee, Joseph Lyman, 93, 94, 101, 310 n. 3
Sindahl-Matheson, Architects, 84, 281
—building by:
    Jandrey Grove Company Building, Neenah, Wisconsin, 11, 84, 281
Sioux City, Iowa, 66, 76, 77, 106, 111, 112, 124–28, 147, 272
Sioux Falls, South Dakota, 278
Skidmore, Owings, and Merrill (SOM), 37, 264
Smith, Lyndon P., 27
Smith, Myrle E., 87, 271
—building by:
    theater for Roy Robleder, Mishawaka, Indiana, 87, 271
Smith, Robert S., 297, 298
Somers, Elbert S., 202. See also Aroner and Somers, Architects
Soule, R. Spencer, 273
South Bend, Indiana, 86, 271
Sovereign Hotel, Chicago, 215
Spanish Colonial/Spanish revival style, 47, 252
Spencer, Robert C., 40. See also Spencer and Powers, Architects
Spencer and Powers, Architects, 40, 106, 299
—building by:
    McCready House, Oak Park, Illinois, 40, 299
Spencer and Son, Architects, 269
Spier and Rohns, Architects, 274
Spierling, Ernest John, 145, 316 n. 14
Spierling and Linden, 145, 146
Spindler, Oscar, 143, 316 n. 8
Spitzer, Maurice, 259, 287
—building by:
    commercial building for Bender and Luckman, Chicago, 259, 287
Springfield, Illinois, 87, 90, 124, 166, 264, 270
Spring Valley Tile Works, 160
stained glass, 145
Stambaugh, Michigan, 69, 274

Stamford, Texas, 49, 280
Stanley, Wisconsin, 82, 282
Starck, Edward F., 130. *See also* Claude and Starck, Architects
Steele, William L., 12, 52, 76, 106, 108, 111, 112, 119, 120, 124–28, 142, 158, 272, 273, 278, 313 nn. 89–90, 313 nn. 92–94, 314 nn. 95, 98, 107. *See also* Steele and Hilgers, Architects
—*buildings by:*
Charles Mix County Courthouse, Lake Andes, South Dakota, 125, 278
Everist House, Sioux City, Iowa, 111, 273
Exchange Building, Sioux City, Iowa, 126, 128, 273
Kresge Building, Sioux City, Iowa, 125, 126, *126*, 273
Sioux City Journal, Sioux City, Iowa, 126, 127, *127*, 142, *144*, 272
Williges Building, Sioux City, Iowa, 128, *129*, 273
Woodbury County Courthouse, Sioux City, Iowa, 106, *107*, 125, 272. *See also second color-plate section*
—ornamentation of, 126
Steele and Hilgers, Architects, 112, 126, 128, 278
—*buildings by:*
Forbes Hall/Science Building, Yankton College, Yankton, South Dakota, 112, 128, 278
Yankton College dormitory, Yankton, South Dakota, 112, 128, 278
Steinborn, Ed, 291, 293, 296
Stern, Isaac S., 291
Stickley, Gustav, 85, 106, 139
stock terra cotta, 2, 9, 14, 61, 62, 68, 81, 84, 85, 90, 91, 152, 155–57, 161, 168, 172–76, 178, 179, 187, 190, 200, 203, 205, 209, 212, 217, 219, 223, 225, 228–31, 235, 238, 243, 245, 247, 252, 255–57, 259, 260, 262
Strandel, Charles A., 296
Stratton and Baldwin, Architects, 273
Strause, A. M., 86, 271
—*building by:*
Kaplan Building, Fort Wayne, Indiana, 86, 271
Stuebe, Leonard F. W., 90, 269
—*building by:*
Babst Building, Kankakee, Illinois, 90, 269
Stueben, Theodore, 288
Sullivan, Andrienne, 93

Sullivan, Louis H., 1, 2, 4, 6–9, 11–14, 33, 44–48, 52–60, 66–68, 73–77, 84, 85, 90–95, 97, 98, 100, 101, 108, 111, 112, 118–21, 124–26, 130, 135, 136, 138, 139, 141–43, 145, 148, 151–53, 155, 157, 158, 160, 162–64, 167, 168, 170–72, 175, 176, 183, 185, 188, 197, 198, 210, 211, 227, 230, 233, 250, 260, 262, 263, 266, 271, 272, 275, 277, 278, 280, 281, 285, 288, 294, 299. *See also* Adler and Sullivan, Architects
—*buildings by:*
Adams and Company Land and Loan Office Building, Algona, Iowa, 56, 120, 121, *122*, 272
Babson Residence, Riverside, Illinois, 55, 153, 299
Bayard/Condict Building, New York, New York, 27, 48, 97, 152, 277
Bradley Residence, Madison, Wisconsin, 56, 81, 281
Farmers' and Merchants' Union Bank, Columbus, Wisconsin, 40, 57, 58, 81, 164, 280
Felsenthal Store Building, Chicago, 54, *55*, 294
Gage Building, Chicago, 27, 42, 48, 57, 211, 283
Guaranty/Prudential Building, Buffalo, New York, 2, 8, *26*, 35, 48, 152, 277
Home Building Association, Newark, Ohio, 9, 57, 136, 143, 162, *164*, 277
Krause Music Store, Chicago, 9, 57, 59, *60*, 136, 138, 288. *See also first color-plate section*
Merchants National Bank, Grinnell, Iowa, 56, *58*, 263, 272
National Farmers' Bank, Owatonna, Minnesota, 55, 56, 69, 77, 91, 145, 146, 148, 160, 164, 175, 275, 306 n. 5. *See also first color-plate section*
People's Savings and Loan Association Bank, Sidney, Ohio, 2, *3*, 57, 58, 61, 136, 145, 146, 276. *See also first color-plate section*
People's Savings Bank, Cedar Rapids, Iowa, 40, 56, 84, 146, 272
Purdue State Bank, West Lafayette, Indiana, 57, 58, *59*, 271
St. Paul's Methodist Church, Cedar Rapids, Iowa, 56, 272
Schlesinger and Mayer/Carson Pirie Scott Building, Chicago, 8, 9, 27,

28, 47, 53, 57, 68, 125, 139, 146, 152, 153, 285, 303 n. 21. *See also first color-plate section*
Van Allen and Son Dry-Goods Store, Clinton, Iowa, 56, 57, 77, 272
—drawing plates, 157
—ornamentation, 1, 4, 6–9, 11–14, 97, 98, 100, 141, 151, 152, 162, 175, 176, 185, 210, 250
—*projects by:*
Adams Building expansion, Algona, Iowa, 57, 120
Odd Fellows Temple, Chicago, 100
—teacher at Chicago School of Architecture, 227
—Teco design(s), 161
—*writings of:*
Autobiography of an Idea, 59
Democracy: A Man-Search, 59
Kindergarten Chats, 7, 59
A System of Architectural Ornament, 7, 59, 250
"The Tall Office Building Artistically Considered," 29
Sweets Catalogue of Building Construction, 154, 176
Syracuse, New York, 139, 277

Taylorville, Illinois, 264
Teco (pottery), 154, 156, 160, 161, 167, 188, 236. *See also* American Terra Cotta and Ceramic Company
Tegtmeyer, William O., 151
Teich, Frederick J., 298
Tenbusch and Hill, Architects, 33
—*building by:*
Cathedral of the Sacred Heart, Duluth, Minnesota, 33
terra cotta, 8, 9, 14, 22, 50, 51, 84, 97, 98, 106, 108, 109, 116, 141, 148–58, 160–62, 164, 166–76, 178, 179, 183, 185–91, 193–95, 196–98, 200–207, 209–12, 214–17, 219, 220, 222, 223, 225–29, 233, 235–40, 242, 243, 245, 250, 252–64, 266
—firing of, 150, 151
—glazing of, 150, 174
—modelers of, 149, 153, 154, 166, 174, 197
—molds for, 149, 153, 173, 174
—preparation for, 149
—pressing, 150
—shop drawings for, 149, 151, 172, 173, 190, 191, 193, 221
—slips, 150
Terra Cotta, Illinois, 160, 167

Terra Cotta Tile Works, 160. *See also* American Terra Cotta and Ceramic Company
Teutonic Building, Chicago, 170
Thole, Edward J., 85. *See also* Shopbell, Fowler, and Thole, Architects
Tidyman, M., 82
Tocha, Anton A., 287
Tomah, Wisconsin, 132, 282
Tomlinson, Henry W., 79
Topeka, Kansas, 64, 111, 273
Toronto, Ontario, Canada, 282
Trost, Henry C., 46, 51, 305 n. 75. *See also* Trost and Trost, Architects
Trost and Trost, Architects, 46, 47, 268, 279. *See also* Trost, Henry C.
—buildings by:
  Caples Building, El Paso, Texas, 47, 279
  Hotel Gadsden, Douglas, Arizona, 47, 268
  Mills Building, El Paso, Texas, 47, 279
  Posener Building, El Paso, Texas, 47, 279
  Rio Grande Valley Bank Building, El Paso, Texas, 47, 279
  Roberts-Banner Building, El Paso, Texas, 47, 279
  YMCA, El Paso, Texas, 46, 279
  YMCA, Phoenix, Arizona, 46, 268
True, Brunkhorst, and Company, 152
True, Hottinger, and Company, 152
Tucson, Arizona, 268
Tudor style, 130, 194
Tulsa, Oklahoma, 64, 278
Two Rivers, Wisconsin, 282

Unger, William, 69, 277
—building by:
  building for L. D. Pickering, Bucyrus, Ohio, 69, 277
United Cigar Company, 292
University of Illinois (Urbana-Champaign), 27, 66, 87, 88, 118, 120, 124, 199, 209, 210, 217, 222, 223, 228, 253, 256
University of Michigan, 34, 253
University of Minnesota, 33
University of Wisconsin, 92, 128
Urbana, Illinois, 66, 271

Valders, Wisconsin, 85, 282
van der Rohe, Mies. *See* Mies van der Rohe, Ludwig
Vedra, Charles, 297
Venturi, Robert, 262

Verplank, J. J., 271
Victorian Gothic/Gothic revival style, 4, 11, 16, 29
Vienna, Austria, 152
Viennese movement, 139
Vinci, John, 27, 264
Viollet-le-Duc, 4
Virginia, Minnesota, 73, 276
von Holst, Hermann V., 113, 116, 280, 288, 290, 293, 312 n. 60
—buildings by:
  Maxwelton Braes Resort and Golf Club, Baileys Harbor, Wisconsin (with George G. Elmslie), 113, 280
  Peoples Gas Light and Coke Company Office, Irving Park Road, Chicago (with George G. Elmslie), 113, 290
  Peoples Gas Light and Coke Company Office, Larrabee Street, Chicago (with George G. Elmslie), 113, 115, 288
  Peoples Gas Light and Coke Company Office, South Chicago (with George G. Elmslie), 113, 114, 293

Waco, Texas, 49, 62, 280
Waggoner, Karl M., 81, 272, 308 n. 69
—building by:
  Bagley and Beck Building/J. C. Penney, Mason City, Iowa, 81, 272
Wagner, Fritz, 152, 153
Wagner, Fritz, Jr., 167
Walker, W. G., 269
Walkerton, Indiana, 271
Wallace, H. E., 271
Waller, Silber, and Company, Architects, 278
Walter, Mead, 240, 242, 287–89, 299, 328 n. 28
—buildings by:
  apartment hotel for Dr. B. Hotchkin, Chicago, 242, 288
  Henderson Building, Chicago, 240, 242, 287
  Lord's Department Store, Evanston, Illinois, 240, 242, 299
  McKee Building, Chicago, 240, 289
Washburn, George W., 81, 272
—building by:
  Bock's Florist, Burlington, Iowa, 81, 272
Watkins, E. R., 271
Waukegan, Illinois, 104, 299
Waukon, Iowa, 273
Weakley and Hawes, Architects, 64, 273, 306 n. 26

—building by:
  store and flat, Louisville, Kentucky, 64, 66, 273
Webster, Charles Woods, 299
Weese, Ben, 262, 263
—buildings by:
  Community Bank of Lawndale, Chicago, 262
  Francisco Terrace, Oak Park, Illinois, 263
  LaSalle Tower/Hotel Renovation, Chicago, 263, 265, 288
Weese, Harry. *See* Weese and Associates, Architects; *see also* Weese, Ben
Weese and Associates, Architects, 97, 263, 299.
Weese Seegers and Weese, 288. *See also* Weese, Ben
Weisfeld, Leo H., 256. *See also* Koenigsberg and Weisfeld, Architects
Welch, Wilmarth Company, Architects, 90, 270
—building by:
  store building for M. Pearman, Paris, Illinois, 90, 270
Wells, William, 47, 48, 51. *See also* Williams and Wells, Architects
Wellesley College, 102
Wesley, Iowa, 273
Westerlind, Carl W., 287
Western Architect, 11, 29, 30, 33, 40, 45, 50, 56, 64, 68–70, 74, 84, 106, 112, 123, 125, 154, 178, 211, 237, 245
Western Springs, Illinois, 114
West Lafayette, Indiana, 57, 58, 271
West Park District, Chicago, Illinois, 220
Wheaton College, 160
Wheelock, Harry B., 34, 153, 157, 285, 304 n. 37
—building by:
  Western Methodist Book Concern, Chicago, 34, 153, 157, 285
White, F. Manson, 278
—building by:
  Auditorium Building, Portland, Oregon, 278. *See also first color plate section*
White, Melville P., 161
Whitson, Lloyd R., 62
Whittlesey, Charles F., 120, 268
Wickersham, A., 280
Williams, Arthur J., 47. *See also* Williams and Wells, Architects
Williams and Wells, Architects, 47, 48, 277

—*buildings by:*
   Colcord Building, Oklahoma City,
     Oklahoma, 48, 277
   Pioneer Telephone and Telegraph
     Company Building, Oklahoma
     City, Oklahoma, 48, 277
Willis, George, 62
Wilmette, Illinois, 131, 190, 299
Wilson, W. R., 74, 276
—*building by:*
   Burg and Sons Warehouse, St. Paul,
     Minnesota, 74, 75, 276
Winiarski, M. F., 252
Winkle Terra Cotta Company, 22, 152,
   317 n. 47
Winnetka, Illinois, 299
Winona, Minnesota, 41, 102, 135, 148,
   176, 276
Winslow Brothers Iron Works, 139,
   152, 153, 211, 310 n. 15
Winnipeg, Manitoba, Canada, 34, 282
Wisconsin Library Bulletin, 130
Witchell, Frank O., 50. *See also* Lang
   and Witchell, Architects
Woodlawn Hospital, 119
Wordon, Illinois, 91, 271
World's Columbian Exposition (1893
   World's Fair), Chicago, 22, 153, 166
World War I, 164, 166, 173, 199, 228,
   250, 253

World War II, 261
Wright, Frank Lloyd, 2, 12, 22, 23, 44,
   60–62, 66, 67, 73, 74, 79, 81, 82, 87,
   92–95, 97, 98, 100, 101, 108, 113,
   119, 120, 128, 130, 131, 134, 139,
   141–43, 147, 156, 166, 175, 234,
   235, 257, 263, 289, 290, 292–94, 299
—*buildings by:*
   City National Bank and Park Inn,
     Mason City, Iowa, 81, 147
   Dana House, Springfield, Illinois,
     143, 147, 166
   Ennis House, Los Angeles, Califor-
     nia, 235
   Francis Apartments, Chicago, 97, 293
   Francisco Terrace Apartments, Chi-
     cago, 95, 263, 290
   German Warehouse, Richland Cen-
     ter, Wisconsin, 82
   Harlan House, Chicago, 94, 95, 293
   Heller House, Chicago, 97, 99, 147,
     294
   Husser House, Chicago, 97, 289
   Larkin Building, Buffalo, New York,
     67, 135, 147
   Martin House, Buffalo, New York,
     147
   Midway Gardens, Chicago, 147
   Roloson Townhouses, Chicago, 95,
     96, 292

   Williams Residence, River Forest,
     Illinois, 97, 299
   Winslow House, River Forest, Illi-
     nois, 23, 95, 130, 299
—ornamentation of, 98, 100
—Teco design(s), 161
—*unbuilt projects by:*
   Broadacre City, 100
   Cheltenham Beach, 35
—*writings by:*
   Genius and the Mobocracy, 98, 101
   Wasmuth Folio, 61

Yankton College, 112, 128, 278
Yankton, South Dakota, 112, 128, 278
*Year Book for 1914–15, The Chicago
   School of Architecture*, 227
Young Hoffman Gallery, 263

Zaldokas, Mathew E., 299
Zettler, Emil R., 109, 112, 116, 146,
   148, 317 n. 30
Zeunert, Robert, 153
Zimmerman, W. Carbys, 178, 289
Zook, R. Harold, 294

RONALD E. SCHMITT is an architect and a professor in the School of Architecture at the University of Illinois at Urbana-Champaign. His writings include architectural guidebooks, papers for national meetings of the Society of Architectural Historians, and "Sullivanesque Architecture and Terra Cotta," in *The Midwest in American Architecture*, edited by John Garner (University of Illinois Press, 1991). He is the coauthor, with Paul Kruty, of *George G. Elmslie: Architectural Ornament from the Edison and Morton Schools, Hammond, Indiana*.

The University of Illinois Press
is a founding member of the
Association of American University Presses.

———————————————————————

Text type is 10/16 Janson, derived
from types of 1690 by Miklós Kis
with Meta display, designed by
Erik Spiekerman in 1993;
composed by Jim Proefrock
at the University of Illinois Press.
Designed by Copenhaver Cumpston
Manufactured by Thomson-Shore, Inc.

UNIVERSITY OF ILLINOIS PRESS
1325 South Oak Street, Champaign, IL 61820–6903
www.press.uillinois.edu